OSWAAL BOOKS®
LEARNING MADE SIMPLE

OBJECTIVE LOGICAL REASONING

For All Competitive Examinations

SSC/Defence/Banking/LIC/RRB/CAT & other Important Examinations

Get the #OswaalEdge

100% Updated	Chapter-wise Segregation	Crisp Revision	Extensive Practice	Valuable Exam Insights
with latest questions of different examinations	with concise thoery & learning objectives	with smart mind maps	with fully solved 1500+ practice questions with 3 levels of difficulty	with chapter-wise weightage analysis

OSWAAL BOOKS®
LEARNING MADE SIMPLE

This Edition: 2026

ISBN: 9789359581330

Disclaimer

This publication has been prepared by qualified subject matter experts with rigorous editorial review. Despite our best efforts, errors may exist. Readers are encouraged to report any by scanning the QR code on the Table of Contents page so corrections can reach all users.

This book is a study aid. Examination results depend on multiple factors including individual preparation and the specific examination conducted. No particular outcome is guaranteed.

Links in this book provide access to supplementary content. Accessibility depends on internet connectivity and device compatibility. Third-party content linked herein was verified at the time of printing; however, the Publisher does not guarantee that such content will remain accurate, available, or appropriate over time.

Views expressed by individual contributors are their own and do not represent the Publisher's position. The Publisher does not endorse personal opinions or political statements contained herein.

All maps, boundaries, and diagrams are artistic representations for educational reference only and are not geographically or politically authoritative.

For details on personal data processing, see our Privacy Policy at www.oswaalbooks.com/privacy. This publication is governed by the laws of India. Disputes shall be subject to the exclusive jurisdiction of courts in Agra, Uttar Pradesh.

Published by: Oswaal Books and Learning Private Limited, Oswaal House, 1/11, Sahitya Kunj, M.G. Road, Agra-282002 (U.P.), India

contact@oswaalbooks.com

+91-562-2857671

Printed at: Maqsood Printers, Agra

Contents

Preface

Welcome to the world of logical reasoning, a vital component of various competitive examinations. This book *'Objective Logical Reasoning'* has been meticulously crafted to help you master the art of logical & Analytical reasoning and ace your exams with confidence.

In today's dynamic and competitive world, the ability to reason effectively stands as a fundamental skill. Whether you're preparing for competitive exams, aiming to enhance your cognitive abilities, or simply seeking to sharpen your logical thinking, this book is designed to be your trusted companion.

The Logical reasoning sections delve into the intricacies of language, testing your ability to decipher complex information, draw inferences, and discern patterns within the context of words and sentences. On the other hand, the non-verbal reasoning sections challenge your visual acumen, spatial awareness, and logical thinking through an assortment of figures, diagrams, and patterns.

Some unique features of this book are:

- **Crisp Revision:** Concepts Review & Mind Maps offer bite-sized and just-in-time revision tools.
- **Extensive Practice:** With More than 700 Previous year questions from various competitive exams segregated based on difficulty level.
- **Concept Clarity:** Easy to Grasp theory complemented by Solved examples.
- **Expert Tips:** Helps you get expert knowledge to master the Reasoning & Analytical Ability on your first attempt.
- **Learning Objectives:** Outlines what aspirant should understand or be able to achieve after the course
- **To-the-point theory:** The book provides concise and clear explanations of Logical & Analytical Reasoning concepts without overwhelming readers with too much information.
- **Quick and easy techniques:** The book offers shortcuts and easy-to-follow techniques to help readers solve typical exam questions quickly and efficiently.

In conclusion, this book aims to provide a one-stop solution for all the aspirants who are preparing for competitive exams.

Our books have always been well received by our readers and this is a testament to our research-oriented approach. Our learning pedagogy supplements our editorial research and makes our book current and relevant. We hope our resources will help students to supplement their examination preparation strategy and help them secure high scores.

We wish our readers great success ahead!

Happy learning!

Team Oswaal

Deciphering Logical Reasoning

In competitive examinations, a balanced proficiency in Logical reasoning is essential. These tests aim to gauge an individual's overall cognitive aptitude, including analytical skills, logical reasoning, problem-solving abilities, and adaptability to various question formats.

1. **Logical Reasoning:**
   - **Reading Comprehension:** Understand and analyze passages, extracting key information, and inferring implied meanings.
   - **Critical Reasoning:** Evaluate arguments, identify assumptions, draw conclusions, and assess the validity of statements.
   - **Syllogisms and Logical Deductions:** Apply logical rules to assess the validity of conclusions drawn from given statements.
   - **Analogies and Relationships:** Recognize patterns, similarities, and relationships between words or concepts.
   - **Coding-Decoding:** Decipher coded language or symbols based on given patterns or rules.
   - **Word Problems:** Solve problems involving verbal statements, equations, and logical deductions.
2. **Strategies for Preparation:**
   - **Practice Regularly:** Solve a variety of problems regularly to improve speed and accuracy.
   - **Understand Concepts:** Grasp the underlying principles and rules governing different types of reasoning problems.
   - **Time Management:** Practice time-bound solving to manage the limited time available in exams effectively.
   - **Review Mistakes:** Learn from errors to understand the reasoning behind correct solutions.
   - **Mock Tests:** Take simulated exams to simulate real test conditions and assess your readiness.
3. **Effective Techniques:**
   - **Elimination Method:** Eliminate improbable choices to increase the probability of selecting the correct answer.
   - **Backtracking:** Revisit questions if time permits, but avoid excessive dwelling on a single problem.
   - **Visualization:** Develop visual methods or mental imagery to tackle non-verbal reasoning problems effectively.
   - **Keyword Analysis:** Pay attention to keywords or cues in verbal reasoning questions to derive accurate answers.
   - **Relate to Real Life:** Relate problems to real-life scenarios to understand and solve them efficiently.
   - Understanding and practicing both verbal and non-verbal reasoning concepts extensively can significantly enhance performance in competitive examinations.

Importance of Logical Reasoning

Logical & Analytical reasoning play crucial roles in various competitive examinations by assessing different cognitive abilities:

- **Critical Thinking:** Verbal reasoning assesses your ability to comprehend and evaluate written information, draw conclusions, and think critically about the presented material.
- **Language Skills:** It evaluates vocabulary, grammar, and reading comprehension, which are fundamental in most competitive exams.
- **Logical Deduction:** Tests often include questions related to syllogisms, logical reasoning, and argument analysis, checking your ability to follow and draw logical conclusions from written information.
- **Visual-Spatial Skills:** This section assesses your ability to understand and analyze visual information, such as patterns, sequences, and relationships between shapes or objects.
- **Abstract Thinking:** Non-verbal reasoning evaluates your capability to recognize and manipulate abstract concepts and patterns.
- **Problem-Solving:** Questions may involve series completion, analogies, classifications, and spatial reasoning, which are crucial for problem-solving skills.

In competitive examinations, Logical & Analytical reasoning sections aim to gauge different aspects of intelligence and cognitive abilities. They help examiners assess candidates' logical thinking, problem-solving capabilities, and ability to interpret information accurately, making them significant parts of such assessments. Strong performances in these sections often indicate a candidate's adaptability, quick thinking, and overall intellectual aptitude, which are valued across various professions and academic pursuits.

Tips to Crack Logical Reasoning in the First Attempt

The Reasoning Ability is a crucial section in many competitive exams in India, such as bank exams, UPSC, SSC, CAT, and other MBA entrance exams. Reasoning Ability has a major role in competitive exams in India as it tests essential knowledge and skills required for various fields & evaluates analytical and logical thinking skills. Cracking the Reasoning Ability section of a competitive exam in the first attempt requires hard work, dedication, and a strategic approach. Here are some tips that can help you achieve success in your first attempt:

1 Think Right

Calming yourself and thinking positive is the first and the best course of action that one is required to take. Think and believe that the exam goal is achievable if worked upon smartly.

2 Start studying from the beginning

All the aspirants are aware of how vast, comprehensive and detailed the syllabus of the Reasoning Ability Section is. To crack the exam in the first attempt you have to start preparing for the exam from the beginning of your 12th class. It is only then that you will be able to complete the entire syllabus. Following this approach will also allow you plenty of time to revise.

3 Respect the syllabus and arrange the materials accordingly

While preparing for the Reasoning Ability nothing can be labelled as less important. Questions can come from the most unexpected topics too. Laying down your whole syllabus in front of you will help you to decide on the study material you require.

4 Get the right tools and study material

Gathering and preparing from the appropriate study material is something you cannot be ignorant towards. You can refer to Oswaal 'Objective Logical Reasoning to enhance your preparation. the is on the lines of the current syllabus and can be entrusted upon before the examination.

5 Schedule total time for each subject

Creating a schedule which gives due time to all the subjects is a must. Giving proper time to all the subjects daily will help you cover the syllabus on time, giving you enough time for revision.

6 Understand the concepts

No one can crack the Reasoning Ability exam just by mugging up all the concepts and topics. The syllabus of the exam is in-depth such that you need to understand every concept.

7 Practice a lot of Sample Papers

Oswaal 'Objective Logical Reasoning' will not only help you in understanding the examination pattern, but they will also help you in figuring out the questons that come up every year and this might give you an edge over other students. The includes all the typologies of Questons asked in the Examination, Previous Years Papers with solutions, Mind Maps, etc. Referring to various sample papers might also help you in comprehending the areas which require more work.

8 Revise whenever you get me

Make sure you revise as much as possible. The revision will help you in keeping the concepts fresh in your mind.

9 Analysing your performance

While you are solving papers, make sure you keep a track of time i.e. how much time does it take to solve one section or one question? Make a report of the sections and type of questions which take minimum and maximum time.

Exam-wise Weightage Analysis

Chapters	SSC-CHSL	SSC-CGL	IBPO PO	IBPS Clerk	CAT	LIC AAO	RRB	Airforce Group X & Y
Logical Deduction	2-4	2-3				3-5	4-6	6-8
Statements and Arguments	2-4	2-3	3-5	2-4	1-2		3-5	4-6
Statements and Assumptions	1-3	1-2					2-4	4-6
Courses of Action	2-4	2-3	3-5	3-5		2-3	3-5	4-6
Statements and Conclusions	1-3	1-2	3-5	2-4		2-4	2-4	2-4
Deriving Conclusions and Passages	2-3		5-10	5-10		5-7		
Theme Detection								
Cause and Effect Reasoning	1-2	1-2	3-5	1-3		2-3	1-3	2-4
Assertion and Reason	1-2	1-2						2-4
Syllogism		1						
Decision Making								
Critical Reasoning		1-2						

Statements and Arguments

Definitions

- **Statement:** A claim, assertion or proposition made about a topic or an issue
- **Argument:** Reasons or justifications given in support of or against a statement
- **Assumption**

Type of Questions

- Identify assumptions
- Assess arguments
- Draw conclusions
- Evaluate inferences

Concepts used

- **Logical Flaw:** A central loophole in the reasoning to arrive at the argument
- **Scope of an argument:** The logical validity of an argument depends on the scope of the given statements.
- **Conclusions:** Inferences or interpretations drawn from the statements
- **Inferences:** Deductions made based on the statements and assumptions

Strategies

- Read statements carefully
- Analyze logical connections
- Consider alternative perspectives
- Identify gaps in reasoning
- Avoid stereotypes and biases

Common Errors

- Jumping to conclusions
- Missing key assumptions
- Illogical inferences

Example

Statement : The new phone is the best in the market.

Argument : It has the most advanced features.

This illustrates analyzing a statement and a related argument.

Statements and Assumptions

Definitions

- **Statement:** A proposition or claim that provides a fact, idea, or opinion
- **Assumption:** Unstated premise or assertion, essential for an argument's logical validity

Strategies

- Read statements carefully
- Break down arguments clearly
- Assess relationship between statements and assumptions
- Eliminate irrelevant or contradictory assumptions

Common Errors

- Accepting unsupported assumptions
- Using prior knowledge or bias
- Missing key implicit assumptions

Identifying Assumptions

- Understand the statements
- Look for unstated information or logical gaps
- Evaluate logical connections
- Identify unsupported claims
- Test potential assumptions
- Use elimination strategies

Types of Questions

- Statement followed by assumptions
- Identify implicit assumptions
- Evaluate if assumptions are correct/incorrect

Concepts Used

- Logical connections
- Missing information
- Real world knowledge
- Unsupported claims
- Alternative assumptions
- Elimination strategies

Example

Statement: Going to the new restaurant will be an enjoyable experience.

Assumption: New restaurants are enjoyable.

This illustrates identifying a key assumption underlying a statement.

Courses of Action

Definitions
- **Situation:** The problem or context presented in the question.
- **Action:** A potential step to address the situation.
- **Outcome:** The expected result of taking the action.

Type of Questions
- Evaluate suggested actions
- Determine appropriate action

Concepts used
- Situation Analysis
- Action Evaluation
- Outcome Assessment
- Feasibility check

Strategies
- Read and understand situation carefully
- Consider feasibility and impact of actions
- Analyze reasoning behind actions
- Eliminate Illogical or unethical actions

Common Errors
- Misinterpreting situation
- Not considering the practicality of an action
- Failure to analyze actions critically
- Selecting inappropriate or extreme actions

Additional Tips
- Consider alternative actions
- Focus on end goal/objective

Example
Situation: A company's sales declined last quarter.
Action : Lower prices to attract more customers add a period at the end.
This illustrates evaluating an action in relation to a situation

Causes and Effect Reasoning

Definitions
- **Cause:** Action or condition that precedes and leads to an effect
- **Effect:** Event or outcome that occurs as a result of a cause

Type of Questions
- Identify cause and effect
- Determine causal relationship
- Analyze chain of causes and effects.

Concepts Used
- **Cause** - Event or factor that leads to an effect
- **Effect** - Outcome or result of a cause
- **Casual Relationship** - Connection between cause and effect

Strategies
- Understand timeline of events
- Analyze relationship between events
- Consider alternative causes
- Identify missing links

Common Errors
- Reversing cause and effect
- Confusing correlation with causation
- Overlooking secondary or alternate causal relations

Additional Tips
- Causes can lead to multiple effects
- Effects can have multiple causes
- Causal relationships can be layered and multi-factored.

Example
Cause: Heavy rain
Effect: Flooding
Heavy rain causes flooding by rapidly accumulating water faster than drainage systems can handle.

Assertion and Reason

Definitions

- **Assertion:** Primary statement or claim put forward
- **Reason:** Supporting evidence or explanation for the assertion

Type of Questions

- Evaluate the connection between assertion and reason
- Determine if reason justifies assertion
- Identify if assertion and/or reason are true or false.

Concepts Used

- **Assertion** - Main statement or claim made
- **Reason** - Justification given for the assertion
- **Logical connection** - Relationship between assertion and reason.

Strategies

- Analyze assertion and reason critically.
- Assess if reason logically supports assertion
- Check if reason is relevant and sufficient
- Identify gaps in reasoning or fallacies

Common Errors

- Accepting unsupported assertions
- Missing flaws in logical connection
- Assuming assertion is true based on true reason
- Basing judgement on unrelated reason.

Additional Tips

- Assertion can be true even if reason is false
- Reason can be true even if assertion is false
- Multiple reasons may support one assertion.

Example

Major Premises: Going to the beach will be fun.
Minor Premise: The weather forecast shows sun.
Conclusion: This asserts going to the beach will be fun because the weather forecast predicts sun. However, the reason does not sufficiently support the assertion Good weather alone is not a sufficient reason to support the idea that the beach will be fun.

Syllogism

Definitions
- **Syllogism:** A deductive reasoning form consisting of two premises and a conclusion, with a specific logical structure.

Type of Questions
- **Statement followed by conclusions -** Identify the logical validity of the conclusions.
- **Identify valid conclusions:** Find logical flaws or missing connections in the reasoning process.
- **Evaluate logical relationships:** Check if the given order of argument follows a logically acceptable structure or not.

Concepts Used
- **Logical connections:** Understand relationships between premises.
- **Missing information:** Recognize gaps in the given
- **Not using prior knowledge:** The questions many times make it clear that the premises have to be taken to be true irrespective of one's common beliefs or prior knowledge.
- **Unsupported claims:** Be critical of conclusions lacking strong premises.
- **The power of tentative or speculative conclusions:** These kind of conclusions have a logical buffer which adds to their logical strength.
- **Elimination strategies:** Remove irrelevant or contradictory information.

Strategies
- **Read statements carefully:** Understand the given premises.
- **Break down arguments:** Analyze major and minor premises separately.
- **Draw conclusions logically:** Infer the most valid conclusion.
- **Assess relationship:** Evaluate the connection between premises and conclusion.
- **Eliminate irrelevant or contradictory assumptions:** Discard unnecessary information.

Common Errors
- **Using assumption to evaluate a conclusion:** Be careful to not assume premises which are not explicitly mentioned.
- **Going for the extreme choice:** Remember that tentative or speculative conclusions are generally logically stronger.
- **Missing key terms in the premises:** Words like some, always, many etc affect the validity of a conclusion.
- **Failing to simplify premises:** Try to understand the premises in simpler or clearer terms.

Components of Syllogism
- **Major Premise:** General statement or proposition.
- **Minor Premise:** Specific statement related to the major premise.
- **Conclusion:** Inference drawn from the major and minor premises.

Example
Major Premises: All men are mortal.
Minor Premise: Socrates is a man.
Conclusion: Therefore, Socrates is mortal.

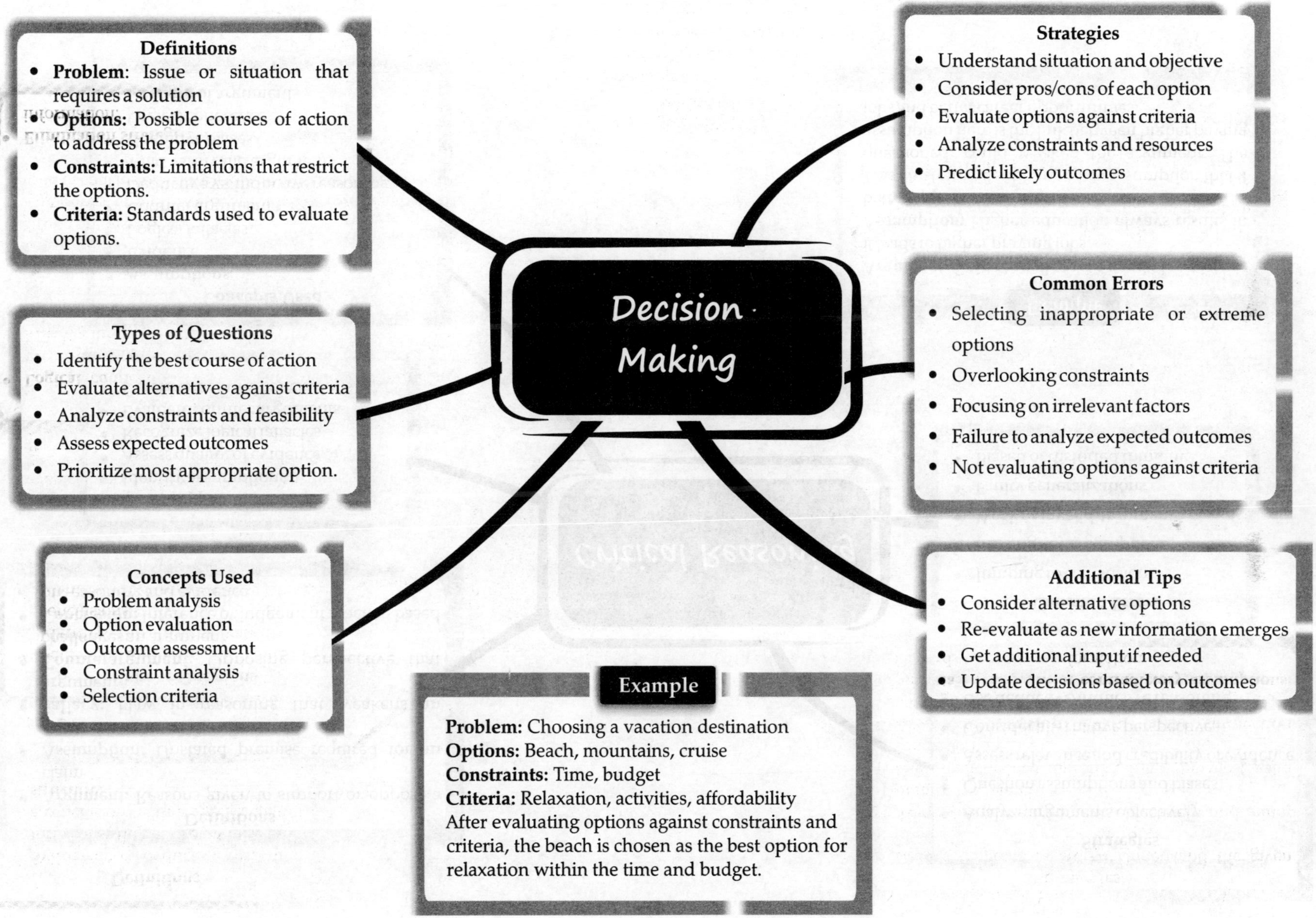
Decision Making
Definitions
• Problem: Issue or situation that requires a solution
• Options: Possible courses of action to address the problem
• Constraints: Limitations that restrict the options.
• Criteria: Standards used to evaluate options.
Types of Questions
• Identify the best course of action
• Evaluate alternatives against criteria
• Analyze constraints and feasibility
• Assess expected outcomes
• Prioritize most appropriate option.
Concepts Used
• Problem analysis
• Option evaluation
• Outcome assessment
• Constraint analysis
• Selection criteria
Strategies
• Understand situation and objective
• Consider pros/cons of each option
• Evaluate options against criteria
• Analyze constraints and resources
• Predict likely outcomes
Common Errors
• Selecting inappropriate or extreme options
• Overlooking constraints
• Focusing on irrelevant factors
• Failure to analyze expected outcomes
• Not evaluating options against criteria
Additional Tips
• Consider alternative options
• Re-evaluate as new information emerges
• Get additional input if needed
• Update decisions based on outcomes
Example
Problem: Choosing a vacation destination
Options: Beach, mountains, cruise
Constraints: Time, budget
Criteria: Relaxation, activities, affordability
After evaluating options against constraints and criteria, the beach is chosen as the best option for relaxation within the time and budget.

Critical Reasoning

Definitions

- **Argument:** Reasons given to support or oppose a claim
- **Assumption:** Unstated premise required for an argument to be valid
- **Fallacy:** Flaw in reasoning that weakens an argument
- **Counterargument:** Opposing perspective that challenges an argument
- **Conclusion:** Inference or judgement reached based on reasoning and evidence.

Type of Questions

- Identify assumptions
- Assess quality of evidence
- Recognize logical fallacies
- Evaluate counter arguments
- Determine sound conclusions

Concepts Used

- Assumptions
- Evidence
- Logical fallacies
- Counter arguments
- Deductive vs. inductive reasoning
- Valid vs. invalid arguments
- Cognitive biases
- Logical coherence
- Strength of arguments

Strategies

- Analyze arguments objectively
- Question assumptions and biases
- Assess relevance and credibility of evidence
- Consider alternative perspectives
- Use deductive/inductive reasoning

Common Errors

- Jumping to conclusions
- Missing key assumptions
- Weak or invalid arguments
- Faulty generalizations
- Biased or distorted thinking

Example

Argument: Going to college is a good idea because it leads to higher praying jobs.

Assumption: Higher education always results in better opportunities

This illustrates identifying a key assumption that if questioned, could weaken the argument. The assumption here is the link between higher paying jobs and better career opportunities.

Chapter 1

Logical Deduction

LEARNING OBJECTIVES:

- To understand the Concept of Logical Deduction
- The Categorization of Deductive Arguments
- Types of Standard forms of Propositions and its parts
- The Four-Fold Classification of Propositions
- Two inferential process of deductions
- Rules for deriving the conclusion from given two premises

Logical Deduction is a type of reasoning which constructs or evaluates deductive arguments. Deductive Arguments are attempts to show that a conclusion necessarily follows from a set of premises or hypotheses. A deductive argument is valid if the conclusion necessarily follows from them; in other words, the conclusion must be true if the premises are true. A deductive argument is sound if it is valid and its premises are true. Deductive arguments can be categorised as valid or invalid, sound or unsound. Deductive reasoning is a method of gaining knowledge. An example of a deductive argument:

Premise 1: All men are mortal.

Premise 2: Socrates is a man.

Conclusion: Therefore, Socrates is mortal.

The first premise states that all objects classified as "men" have the attribute of being "mortal". The second premise states that "Socrates" is classified, belonging to the set of "men". The conclusion states that "Socrates" must be mortal because he inherits this attribute from his classification as a man.

One way to solve logical deduction is the Venn-diagram method. But the problem is that it is tedious, lengthy and complicated too.

A proposition is a statement that asserts that either a part of, or the whole of, one set of objects – the set identified by the subject term in the sentence expressing that statement – either is included in, or is excluded from, another set – the set identified by the predicate term in that sentence.

The standard form of a proposition is:

Quantifier + Subject + Copula + Predicate

Thus, the proposition consists of four parts:

- **Quantifier:** The words 'all', 'no' and 'some' are called quantifiers because they specify a quantity 'All' and 'no' are universal quantifiers because they refer to every object in a certain set, while the quantifier 'some' is a particular quantifier because it refers to at least one existing object in a certain set.

1. **Quantifier:** All, No, Some, Atleast, Atmost, etc.
2. **All/No:** Universal quantifiers (as it refers to every object in a certain set).
3. **Some/Atleast/Atmost:** Particular quantifiers (as it refers to atleast one existing object in a certain set).
4. **Subject (denoted by 'S'):** The subject is that about which something is said.
5. **Predicate (denoted by 'P'):** The predicate is the part of the proposition that denotes what is affirmed or denied about the subject.
6. **Copula:** The copula is that part of the proposition that denotes the relation between the subject and the predicate.

Example

All/Some etc. – Quantifier
Men – Subject
Are – Copula
Animals – Predicate

FOUR-FOLD CLASSIFICATION OF PROPOSITIONS:

A proposition is said to have a universal quantity if it begins with a universal quantifier, and a particular quantity if it begins with a particular quantifier. Besides, propositions which assert something about the inclusion of the whole or a part of one set in the other are said to have affirmative quality, while those which deny the inclusion of the whole or a part of one set in the other are said to have a negative quality. Also, a term is distributed in a proposition if it refers to all members of the set of objects denoted by that term. Otherwise, it is said to be undistributed. Based on the above facts, propositions can be classified into four types :

1. **Universal Affirmative Proposition (denoted by A):** It distributes only the subject, i.e., the predicate is not interchangeable with the subject while maintaining the validity of the proposition.
For example: All snakes are reptiles. This is proposition A since we cannot say 'All reptiles are snakes'.
2. **Universal Negative Proposition (denoted by E):** It distributes both the subject and the predicate, i.e., an entire class of predicate term is denied to the entire class of the subject term, as in the proposition.
For example: No boy is intelligent.
3. **Particular Affirmative Proposition (denoted by I):** It distributes neither the subject nor the predicate.
For example: Some men are foolish. Here, the subject term 'men' is used not for all but only for some men and similarly the predicate term 'foolish' is affirmed for a part of subject class. So, both are undistributed.
4. **Particular Negative Proposition (denoted by O):** It distributes only the predicate.
For example: Some animals are not wild. Here, the subject term 'animals' is used only for a part of its class and hence is undistributed while the predicate term 'wild' is denied in entirety to the subject term and hence is distributed.

These facts can be summarised as follows:

Statement Form	Quantity	Quality	Distributed
(A): All S is P.	Universal	Affirmative	S only
(E): No S is P.	Universal	Negative	Both S and P
(I): Some S is P.	Particular	Affirmative	Neither S nor P
(O): Some S is not P	Particular	Negative	P only

The phenomenon of deriving a conclusion from a single proposition or a set of given propositions, is known as logical deduction. The given propositions are also referred to as the premises.

TWO INFERENTIAL PROCESSES OF DEDUCTION:

I. **Immediate Deductive Inference:** Here, the conclusion is deduced from one of the given propositions, by any of the three ways– conversion, obversion and contraposition.

1. **Conversion:** The conversion proceeds by interchanging the subject term and the predicate term, i.e., the subject term of the premise becomes the predicate term of the conclusion and the predicate term of the premise becomes the subject of the conclusion. The given proposition is called convertend, whereas the conclusion drawn from it is called its converse.

Table of Valid Conversions

Convertend	Converse
A: All S is P Ex: All pins are tops.	I: Some P is S Ex: Some tops are pins.
E: No S is P. Ex: No fish is whale.	E: No P is S. Ex: No whale is fish.
I: Some S is P. Ex: Some boys are poets.	I: Some P is S. Ex: Some poets are boys.
O: Some S is not P.	No valid conversion

Note: In a conversion, the quality remains the same and the quantity may change.

2. **Obversion:** In obversion, we change the quality of the proposition and replace the predicate term by its complement.

Table of Valid Obversions

Obvertend	Obverse
A: All birds are mammals.	E: No birds are non-mammals.
E: No poets are singers.	A: All poets are non-singers.
I: Some nurses are doctors.	O: Some nurses are not non-doctors.
O: Some politicians are not statesmen.	I: Some politicians are non-statesmen.

3. **Contraposition:** To obtain the contrapositive of a statement, we first replace the subject and predicate terms in the proposition and then exchange both these terms with their complements.

Proposition	Contrapositive
A: All birds are mammals.	A: All non-mammals are non-birds.
I: Some birds are mammals.	I: Some non-mammals are non-birds.

Note: The valid converse, obverse or contrapositive of a given proposition always logically follows from the proposition.

II. **Mediate Deductive Inference (SYLLOGISM):** Syllogism is a deductive argument in which conclusion has to be drawn from two propositions referred to as the premises. It was introduced by Aristotle.

Example:
1. All lotus are flowers.
2. All flowers are beautiful.
3. All lotus are beautiful.

Clearly, the propositions 1 and 2 are the premises and the proposition 3, which follows from the first two propositions, is called the conclusion.

Term: In logic, a term is a word or a combination of words, which by itself can be used as a subject or predicate of a proposition.

Syllogism is concerned with three terms:
1. **Major Term :** It is the predicate of the conclusion and is denoted by P (first letter of 'Predicate').
2. **Minor Term:** It is the subject of the conclusion and is denoted by S (first letter of 'Subject').
3. **Middle Term:** It is the term common to both the premises and is denoted by M (first letter of 'Middle').

Example:
Premises:
1. All dogs are animals.
2. All tigers are dogs.

Conclusion :
All tigers are animals.
Here 'animals' is the predicate of the conclusion and so, it is the major term, P.
'Tigers' is the subject of the conclusion and so, it is the minor term, S.
'Dogs' is the term common to both the premises and so, it is the middle term, M.
Major and Minor Premises: Of the two premises, the major premise is the one in which the middle term serves as the subject, while the minor premise is the one in which the middle term serves as the predicate.

RULES FOR DERIVING THE CONCLUSION FROM TWO GIVEN PREMISES

Example 1: The conclusion should not contain the middle term.
Statements:
1. All men are girls.
2. Some girls are students.

Conclusion:
1. Some girls are men.
2. All girls are men.

Explanation: In the above example neither of the conclusion is valid, as the middle term, i.e., "girls" is present in both the conclusions.

Example 2: No term can be distributed in the conclusion unless it is distributed in the premises.
Statements:
1. Some dogs are goats.
2. All goats are cows.

Conclusions:
1. All cows are dogs.
2. Some dogs are cows.

Explanation: Here, in conclusion 1, the term "cows" is distributed but it is not distributed in the premise, i.e., premise-2. Since it is a A-type proposition and the term "cows" to be distributed must be the "subject" of the proposition.
So, conclusion 1 cannot follow whereas only conclusion 2 follows.

Example 3: The middle term (M) should be distributed at least once in the premises, otherwise no conclusion follows:

Statement Type	Distribution Condition
A	"M" must be Subject
E	"M" must be Subject/Predicate
O	"M" must be Predicate
I	Cannot be distributed/ Not distributed

Statements:
1. All fans are watches.
2. Some watches are black.

Conclusions:
1. All watches are fans.
2. Some fans are black.

Explanation: In the above premises, the middle term is "watches". Since it is not distributed in both premises, no conclusion can be drawn except the conversions of the premises.

Example 4: No conclusion follows:
(a) If both premises are particular, i.e., I type.
Statements:
1. Some books are pens.
2. Some pens are erasers.

Conclusions:
1. All books are erasers.
2. Some erasers are books.

Since both premises are particular, so no definite conclusion follows.
(b) If both premises are negative, i.e., E-type.
Statements:
1. No flower is mango.
2. No mango is cherry.

Conclusions:
1. No flower is cherry.
2. Some cherries are mangoes.

Since both premises are negative, neither conclusion follows.

Example 5: If the middle term is distributed twice, the conclusion cannot be universal.
Statements:
1. All fans are chairs.
2. No tables are fans.

Conclusions:
1. No tables are chairs.
2. Some tables are chairs.

Here, the first premise is an A proposition and so, the middle term 'fans' forming the subject is distributed. The second premise is an E proposition and so, the middle term 'fans' forming the predicate is distributed. Since the middle term is distributed twice, so the conclusion cannot be universal.

Example 6: If one premise is negative, the conclusion must be negative.
Statements:
1. All grasses are trees.
2. No tree is shrub.

Conclusions:
1. No grasses are shrubs.
2. Some shrubs are grasses.

Since one premise is negative, the conclusion must be negative. So, conclusion 2 cannot follow.

Example 7: If one premise is particular, the conclusion must be particular.
Statements:
1. Some boys are thieves.
2. All thieves are dacoits.

Conclusions:
1. Some boys are dacoits.
2. All dacoits are boys.

Since one premise is particular, the conclusion must be particular. So, conclusion 2 cannot follow.

Example 8: If both premises are affirmative, the conclusion must be affirmative.
Statements:
1. All women are mothers.
2. All mothers are sisters.

Conclusions:
1. All women are sisters.
2. Some women are not sisters.

Since both premises are affirmative, the conclusion must be affirmative. So, conclusion 2 cannot follow.

9. If both premises are universal, the conclusion must be universal.

➤ **Complementary pair:** A pair of contradictory statements, i.e., a pair of statements such that if one is true, the other is false and when no definite conclusion can be drawn, either of them is bound to follow, is called a complementary pair. E and I-type propositions together form a complementary pair and usually either of them follows, in a case where we cannot arrive at a definite conclusion, using the rules of syllogism.

Let us study the various possible cases and draw all possible inferences in each case, along with verification through Venn diagrams.

Case 1: All men are boys. All boys are students.

➤ **Immediate Deductive Inferences:** The converse of first premise, i.e., 'Some boys are men' and the converse of second premise, i.e., 'Some students are boys' both hold.

➤ **Mediate Deductive Inferences:** Since both the premises are universal and affirmative, the conclusion must be universal affirmative. Also, the conclusion should not contain the middle term. So, it follows that 'All men are students'. The converse of this conclusion, i.e., 'Some students are men' also holds.

Venn diagram	Inferences
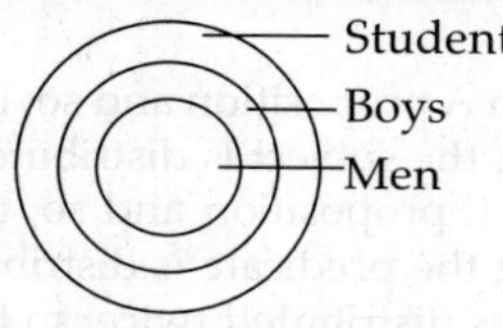	1. Some boys are men. 2. Some students are boys. 3. All men are students. 4. Some students are men.

Case 2: All birds are animals. All fishes are animals.

➤ **Immediate Deductive Inferences:** The converse of first premise, i.e., 'Some animals are birds' and the converse of second premise, i.e., 'Some animals are fishes' both hold.

➤ **Mediate Deductive Inferences:** Both, being A-type propositions, distribute subject only. Thus, the middle term 'animals' is not distributed even once in the premises. So, no definite conclusion follows.

Venn diagram	Inferences
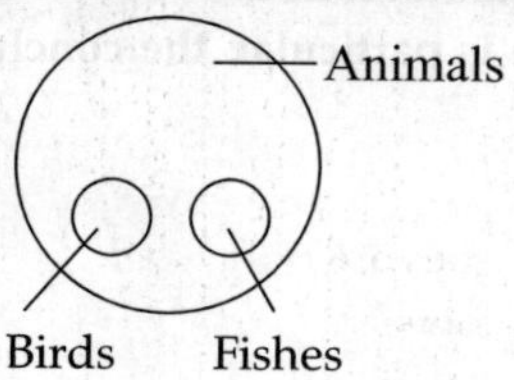 or 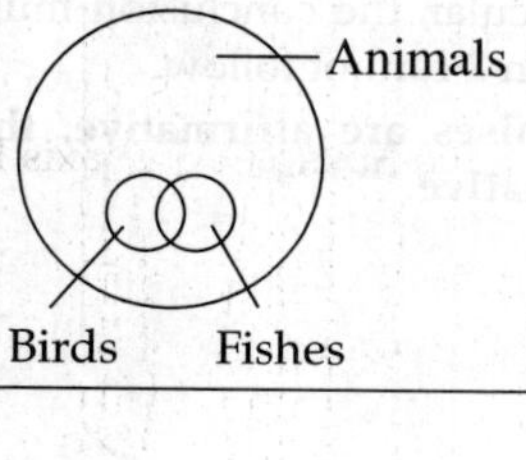	1. Some animals are birds. 2. Some animals are fishes. 3. Either 'No bird is fish' or 'Some bird are fishes' as E and I-type propositions form a complementary pair.

Case 3: All puppets are dolls. Some dolls are rattles.

➤ **Immediate Deductive Inferences:** The converse of the first premise, i.e., 'Some dolls are puppets' and the converse of the second premise, i.e., 'Some rattles are dolls', both hold.

➤ **Mediate Deductive Inferences:** First premise, being an A-type proposition, distributes the subject only while the second premise, being an I-type proposition, distributes neither subject nor predicate. Since the middle term 'dolls' is not distributed even once in the premises, so no definite conclusion can be drawn.

Venn diagram	Inferences
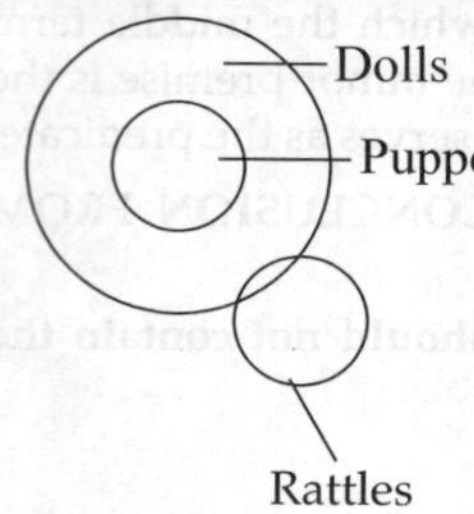 or 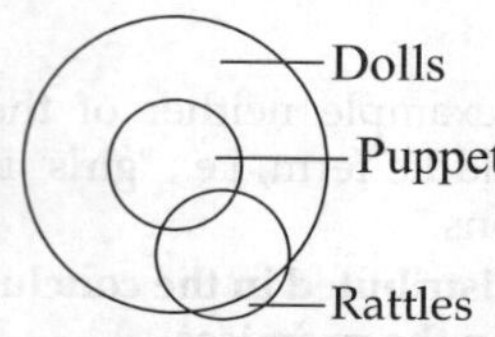	1. Some dolls are puppets. 2. Some rattles are dolls. 3. Either 'No puppet is rattle' or 'Some puppets are rattles' as E and I-type propositions form a complementary type.

Case 4: Some writers are players. All players are musicians.

➤ **Immediate Deductive Inferences:** The converse of the first premise, i.e., 'Some players are writers' and the converse of the second premise, i.e., 'Some musicians are players', both hold.

➤ **Mediate Deductive Inferences:** Since one premise is particular, the conclusion must be particular and should not contain the middle term. So, it follows that 'Some writers are musicians'. The converse of this conclusion, i.e., 'Some musicians are writers' also holds.

Venn diagram	Inferences
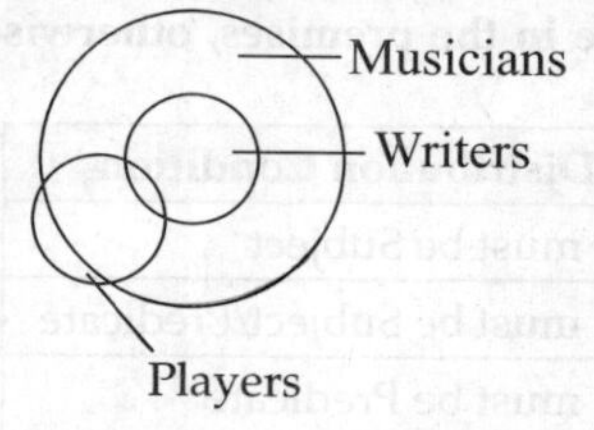	1. Some players are writers. 2. Some musicians are players. 3. Some writers are musicians. 4. Some musicians are writers.

While deriving logical conclusions, always remember that the following conclusions hold:

1. The converse of each of the given premises;
2. The conclusion that directly follows from the given premises in accordance with the rules of syllogism;
3. The converse of the derived conclusions.

1 Level Beginner

Directions (Qs. 1 to 25): In each question below, two statements are given, followed by two or more conclusions numbered I, II, III, etc., Mark the correct option based on the given conclusions.

1. Statements: All roads are waters. Some waters are boats.

Conclusions:

I. Some boats are roads.
II. All waters are boats.

(A) Only conclusion I follows.
(B) Only conclusion II follows.
(C) Either I or II follows.
(D) Neither I nor II follows.
(E) Both I and II follow.

2. Statements: All roads are poles. No pole is a house.

Conclusions:

I. Some roads are houses.
II. Some houses are poles.

(A) Only conclusion I follows.
(B) Only conclusion II follows.
(C) Either I or II follows.
(D) Neither I nor II follows.
(E) Both I and II follow.

3. Statements: Every minister is a student. Every student is inexperienced.

Conclusions:

I. Every minister is inexperienced.
II. Some inexperienced are students.

(A) Only conclusion I follows.
(B) Only conclusion II follows.
(C) Either I or II follows.
(D) Neither I nor II follows.
(E) Both I and II follow.

4. Statements: All flowers are trees. No fruit is tree.

Conclusions:

I. No fruit is flower.
II. Some trees are flowers.

(A) Only conclusion I follows.
(B) Only conclusion II follows.
(C) Either I or II follows.
(D) Neither I nor II follows.
(E) Both I and II follow.

5. Statements: No bat is ball. No ball is wicket.

Conclusions:

I. No bat is wicket.
II. All wickets are bats.

(A) Only conclusion I follows.
(B) Only conclusion II follows.
(C) Either I or II follows.
(D) Neither I nor II follows.
(E) Both I and II follow.

6. Statements: Some doctors are fools. Some fools are rich.

Conclusions:

I. Some doctors are rich.
II. Some rich are doctors.

(A) Only conclusion I follows.
(B) Only conclusion II follows.
(C) Either I or II follows.
(D) Neither I nor II follows.
(E) Both I and II follow.

7. Statements: Some kings are queens. All queens are beautiful.

Conclusions:

I. All kings are beautiful.
II. All queens are kings.

(A) Only conclusion I follows.
(B) Only conclusion II follows.
(C) Either I or II follows.
(D) Neither I nor II follows.
(E) Both I and II follow.

8. Statements: No women teacher can play. Some women teachers are athletes.

Conclusions:

I. Male athletes can play.
II. Some athletes can play.

(A) Only conclusion I follows.
(B) Only conclusion II follows.
(C) Either I or II follows.
(D) Neither I nor II follows.
(E) Both I and II follow.

9. Statements: All bags are cakes. All lamps are cakes.

Conclusions:

I. Some lamps are bags.
II. No lamp is bag.

(A) Only conclusion I follows.
(B) Only conclusion II follows.
(C) Either I or II follows.
(D) Neither I nor II follows.
(E) Both I and II follow.

10. Statements: All mangoes are golden in colour. No golden-coloured things are cheap.

Conclusions:

I. All mangoes are cheap.
II. Golden-coloured mangoes are not cheap.

(A) Only conclusion I follows.
(B) Only conclusion II follows.
(C) Either I or II follows.
(D) Neither I nor II follows.
(E) Both I and II follow.

11. Statements: Some taxis have horns. Some taxis have lights.

Conclusions:

I. Every taxi has either horn or light.

II. Some taxis have neither light nor horn.
III. Some taxis have horns as well as lights.
IV. No taxi has horn as well as light.
(A) Only I and II follow.
(B) Only II and III follow.
(C) Only II and IV follow.
(D) Either III or IV follows.
(E) All follow.

12. Statements: Some houses are offices. Some offices are schools.
Conclusions:
I. Some schools are houses.
II. Some offices are houses.
III. No house is school.
IV. Some schools are offices.
(A) Only II and III follow.
(B) Only I and IV follow.
(C) Only either III or IV, and I follow.
(D) Only II and IV and either I or III follow.

13. Statements: Some books are pens. No pen is pencil.
Conclusions:
I. Some pens are books.
II. Some pencils are books.
III. Some books are not pencils.
IV. All pencils are books.
(A) Only I follows.
(B) Only II and III follow.
(C) Only I and III follow.
(D) Only I and II follow.

14. Statements: All terrorists are guilty. All terrorists are criminals.
Conclusions:
I. Either all criminals are guilty or all guilty are criminals.
II. Some guilty persons are criminals.
III. Generally criminals are guilty.
IV. Crime and guilt go together.
(A) Only I follows.
(B) Only I and III follow.
(C) Only II follows.
(D) Only II and IV follow.

15. Statements: Some tables are TVs. Some TVs are radios.
Conclusions:
I. Some tables are radios.
II. Some radios are tables.
III. All radios are TVs.
IV. All TVs are tables.
(A) None follows.
(B) All follow.
(C) Only I and III follow.
(D) Only II and IV follow.

16. Statements: Some bottles are drinks. All drinks are cups.
Conclusions:
I. Some bottles are cups.
II. Some cups are drinks.
III. All drinks are bottles.
IV. All cups are drinks.
(A) Only I and II follow.
(B) Only II and III follow.
(C) Only II and IV follow.
(D) Only III and IV follow.
(E) Only I and IV follow.

17. Statements: All branches are flowers. All flowers are leaves.
Conclusions:
I. All branches are leaves.
II. All leaves are branches.
III. All flowers are branches.
IV. Some leaves are branches.
(A) None follows.
(B) Only I and IV follow.
(C) Only II and III follow.
(D) All follow.

18. Statements: Some bags are pockets. No pocket is a pouch.
Conclusions:
I. No bag is a pouch.
II. Some bags are not pouches.
III. Some pockets are bags.
IV. No pocket is a bag.
(A) None follows.
(B) Only I and III follow.
(C) Only II and III follow.
(D) Only either I or IV follows.
(E) All follow.

19. Statements: All aeroplanes are trains. Some trains are chairs.
Conclusions:
I. Some aeroplanes are chairs.
II. Some chairs are aeroplanes.
III. Some chairs are trains.
IV. Some trains are aeroplanes.
(A) None follows.
(B) Only I and II follow.
(C) Only II and III follow.
(D) Only III and IV follow.

20. Statements: All politicians are honest. All honest are fair.
Conclusions:
I. Some honest are politicians.
II. No honest is politician.
III. Some fair are politicians.
IV. All fair are politicians.
(A) None follows.
(B) Only I follows.
(C) Only I and II follow.
(D) Only I and III follow.

21. Statement: Some swords are sharp. All swords are rusty.

Conclusions:

I. Some rusty things are sharp.

II. Some rusty things are not sharp.

(A) If only conclusion I follows.

(B) If only conclusion II follows.

(C) If either conclusion I or II follows.

(D) If neither conclusion I nor II follows.

(E) If both conclusions I and II follow.

22. Statement:

All men are married. Some men are educated.

Conclusions:

I. Some married are educated.

II. Some educated are married.

(A) If only conclusion I follows.

(B) If only conclusion II follows.

(C) If either conclusion I or II follows.

(D) If neither conclusion I nor II follows.

(E) If both conclusions I and II follow.

23. Statements:

Some adults are boys. Some boys are old.

Conclusions:

I. Some adults are not old.

II. Some boys are not old.

(A) If only conclusion I follows.

(B) If only conclusion II follows.

(C) If either conclusion I or II follows.

(D) If neither conclusion I nor II follows.

(E) If both conclusions I and II follow.

24. Statements :

Some books are tables. Some tables are mirrors.

Conclusions :

I. Some mirrors are books.

II. No book is mirror.

(A) If only conclusion I follows.

(B) If only conclusion II follows.

(C) If either conclusion I or II follows.

(D) If neither conclusion I nor II follows.

(E) If both conclusions I and II follow.

25. Statement:

Raman is always successful. No fool is always successful.

Conclusions:

I. Raman is a fool.

II. Raman is not a fool.

(A) If only conclusion I follows.

(B) If only conclusion II follows.

(C) If either conclusion I or II follows.

(D) If neither conclusion I nor II follows.

(E) If both conclusions I and II follow.

Level 2 Intermediate

Directions (Qs. 1 to 25): In each question below, two statements are given and followed by two or more conclusions numbered I, II, III, etc.,

Mark the correct option based on the given conclusions.

1. Statements: All tigers are jungles. No jungle is bird. Some birds are rains.

Conclusions:

I. No rain is jungle.

II. Some rains are jungles.

III. No bird is tiger.

(A) Only I and II follow.

(B) Only III follows.

(C) Only either I or II, and III follow.

(D) All follow.

(E) None of the above.

2. Statements: No rabbit is lion. Some horses are lions. All rabbits are tables.

Conclusions:

I. Some tables are lions.

II. Some horses are rabbits.

III. No lion is table.

(A) None follows.

(B) Only either I or III follows.

(C) Only II and III follow.

(D) Only III follows.

(E) None of the above.

3. Statements: All snakes are trees. Some trees are roads. All roads are mountains.

Conclusions:

I. Some mountains are snakes.

II. Some roads are snakes.

III. Some mountains are trees

(A) Only I follows. **(B)** Only II follows.

(C) Only III follows. **(D)** Both I and II follow.

(E) None follows.

4. Statements: All trees are flowers. No flower is fruit. All branches are fruits.

Conclusions:

I. Some branches are trees.

II. No fruit is tree.

III. No tree is branch.

(A) None follows.

(B) Only either I or III follows.

(C) Only II follows.

(D) Only either I or III, and II follow.

(E) None of the above.

5. Statements: Some uniforms are covers. All covers are papers. All papers are bags.

Conclusions:

I. All covers are bags.

II. Some bags are covers, papers and uniforms.
III. Some uniforms are not papers.
(A) Only I follows.
(B) Only I and II follow.
(C) Only III follows.
(D) All I, II and III follow.
(E) None of the above.

6. **Statements:** Some pictures are frames. Some frames are idols. All idols are curtains.
Conclusions:
I. Some curtains are pictures.
II. Some curtains are frames.
III. Some idols are frames.
(A) Only I and II follow.
(B) Only II and III follow.
(C) Only I and III follow.
(D) All follow.
(E) None of the above.

7. **Statements:** Some towels are brushes. No brush is soap. All soaps are rats.
Conclusions:
I. Some rats are brushes.
II. No rat is brush.
III. Some towels are soaps.
(A) None follows.
(B) Only either I or II follows.
(C) Only II follows.
(D) Only I and III follow.
(E) None of the above.

8. **Statements:** All fruits are vegetables. All pens are vegetables. All vegetables are rains.
Conclusions:
I. All fruits are rains.
II. All pens are rains.
III. Some rains are vegetables.
(A) None follows.
(B) Only I and II follow.
(C) Only II and III follow.
(D) Only II and III follow.
(E) All follow.

9. **Statements:** Some hills are rivers. Some rivers are deserts. All deserts are roads.
Conclusions:
I. Some roads are rivers.
II. Some roads are hills.
III. Some deserts are hills.
(A) None follows.
(B) Only I follows.
(C) Only I and II follow.
(D) Only II and III follow.
(E) All follow.

10. **Statements:** Some saints are balls. All balls are bats. Some tigers are balls.
Conclusions:
I. Some bats are tigers.
II. Some saints are bats.
III. All bats are balls.
(A) Only I and II follow.
(B) Only II follows.
(C) Only I and III follow.
(D) Only III follows.
(E) None of the above.

11. **Statements:** All jungles are buses. All books are buses. All fruits are books.
Conclusions:
I. Some fruits are jungles.
II. Some buses are books.
III. Some buses are jungles.
IV. All fruits are buses.
(A) Only I, II and III follow.
(B) Only I, II and IV follow.
(C) Only II, III and IV follow.
(D) All follow.
(E) None of the above

12. **Statements:** All buildings are windows. No toys is building. Some tigers are toys.
Conclusions:
I. Some tigers are buildings.
II. Some windows are tigers.
III. All toys are tigers.
IV. Some windows are toys.
(A) None follows.
(B) Only I and II follow.
(C) Only III and IV follow.
(D) Only I and III follow.
(E) All follow.

13. **Statements:** No table is fruit. No fruit is window. All windows are chairs.
Conclusions:
I. No window is table.
II. No chair is fruit.
III. No chair is table.
IV. All chairs are windows.
(A) None follows.
(B) Only I and II follow.
(C) Only III and IV follow.
(D) All follow.
(E) None of the above.

14. **Statements:** Some papers are cats. All cats are bats. No bat is horse.
Conclusions:
I. Some papers are horses.
II. No horse is cat.
III. Some bats are papers.
IV. All papers are bats.
(A) Only I and II follow.
(B) Only II and III follow.
(C) Only III and IV follow.
(D) Only I and IV follow.
(E) All follow.

15. Statements: Some tapes are discs. Some discs are cassettes. Some cassettes are songs.

Conclusions:

I. Some songs are discs.
II. Some cassettes are tapes.
III. Some songs are tapes.
IV. No song is a disc.

(A) Only either I or IV follows.
(B) Only either II or IV follows.
(C) Only III and IV follow.
(D) Only III and either II or IV follows.
(E) None of the above.

16. Statement :

Many scooters are trucks. All trucks are trains.

Conclusions :

I. Some scooters are trains.
II. No truck is a scooter.

(A) If only conclusion I follows.
(B) If only conclusion II follows.
(C) If either conclusion I or II follows.
(D) If neither conclusion I nor II follows.
(E) If both conclusions I and II follow.

17. Statement :

All cars are cats. All fans are cats.

Conclusions :

I. All cars are fans.
II. Some fans are cars.

(A) If only conclusion I follows.
(B) If only conclusion II follows.
(C) If either conclusion I or II follows.
(D) If neither conclusion I nor II follows.
(E) If both conclusions I and II follow.

18. Statement :

Some dedicated souls are angels. All social workers are angles.

Conclusions :

I. Some dedicated souls are social workers.
II. Some social workers are dedicated souls.

(A) If only conclusion I follows.
(B) If only conclusion II follows.
(C) If either conclusion I or II follows.
(D) If neither conclusion I nor II follows.
(E) If both conclusions I and II follow.

19. Statement :

All birds are tall. Some tall are hens.

Conclusions :

I. Some birds are hens.
II. Some hens are tall.

(A) If only conclusion I follows.
(B) If only conclusion II follows.
(C) If either conclusion I or II follows.
(D) If neither conclusion I nor II follows.
(E) If both conclusions I and II follow.

20. Statement :

Some desks are caps. All caps are cameras.

Conclusions :

I. Some caps are desks.
II. No desk is red.

(A) If only conclusion I follows.
(B) If only conclusion II follows.
(C) If either conclusion I or II follows.
(D) If neither conclusion I nor II follows.
(E) If both conclusions I and II follow.

21. Statement :

All fish are tortoise. No tortoise is a crocodile.

Conclusions :

I. No crocodile is a fish.
II. No fish is a crocodile.

(A) If only conclusion I follows.
(B) If only conclusion II follows.
(C) If either conclusion I or II follows.
(D) If neither conclusion I nor II follows.
(E) If both conclusions I and II follow.

22. Statement :

Some dreams are nights. Some nights are days.

Conclusions :

I. All days are either nights or dreams.
II. Some days are nights.

(A) If only conclusion I follows.
(B) If only conclusion II follows.
(C) If either I and II follows.
(D) If neither I nor II follows.
(E) If both I and II follow.

23. Statement :

All flowers are trees. No fruit is tree.

Conclusions :

I. No fruit is flower.
II. Some trees are flowers.

(A) If only conclusion I follows.
(B) If only conclusion II follows.
(C) If either I and II follows.
(D) If neither I nor II follows.
(E) If both I and II follow.

24. Statement :

No women teacher can play. Some women teachers are athletes.

Conclusions :

I. Male athletes can play.
II. Some athletes can play.

(A) If only conclusion I follows.
(B) If only conclusion II follows.
(C) If either I and II follows.
(D) If neither I nor II follows.
(E) If both I and II follow.

25. Statement :

Bureaucrats marry only intelligent girls. Tanya is very intelligent.

Conclusions :

I. Tanya will marry a bureaucrat.
II. Tanya will not marry a bureaucrat.

(A) If only conclusion I follows.
(B) If only conclusion II follows.
(C) If either I and II follows.
(D) If neither I nor II follows.
(E) If both I and II follow.

3 Level Expert

Directions (Qs. 1 to 15): In each question below, two statements are given and followed by two or more conclusions numbered I, II, III, etc., Mark the correct option based on the given conclusions.

1. **Statements:** All benches are desks. Some desks are roads. All roads are pillars.

   Conclusions:

   I. Some pillars are benches.
   II. Some pillars are desks.
   III. Some roads are benches.
   IV. No pillar is bench.

   (A) None follows.
   (B) Only either I or IV, and III follow.
   (C) Only either I or IV follows.
   (D) Only either I or IV, and II follow.
   (E) All follow.

2. **Statements:** Some trains are roads. No road is jungle. All flowers are jungles.

   Conclusions:

   I. Some trains are flowers.
   II. Some trains are jungles.
   III. Some flowers are trains.
   IV. No road is flower.

   (A) None follows. **(B)** Only II follows.
   (C) Only III follows. **(D)** Only IV follows.
   (E) All follow.

3. **Statements:** Some bricks are trees. All trees are pens. All pens are boats.

   Conclusions:

   I. Some boats are bricks.
   II. Some pens are bricks.
   III. Some trees are bricks.
   IV. Some bricks are boats.

   (A) Only I and II follow.
   (B) Only III and IV follow.
   (C) None follows.
   (D) All follow.
   (E) None of the above.

4. **Statements:** All cups are glasses. Some glasses are bowls. No bowl is a plate.

   Conclusions:

   I. No cup is a plate.
   II. No glass is a plate.
   III. Some plates are bowls.
   IV. Some cups are not glasses.

   (A) None follows.
   (B) Only either I or III follows.
   (C) Only II and III follow.
   (D) Only III and IV follow.
   (E) None of the above.

5. **Statements:** Some dogs are rats. All rats are trees. Some trees are not dogs.

   Conclusions:

   I. Some trees are dogs.
   II. All dogs are trees.
   III. All rats are dogs.
   IV. No tree is dog.

   (A) None follows.
   (B) Only I follows.
   (C) Only I and II follow.
   (D) Only II and III follow.
   (E) All follow.

6. **Statements:** Some pearls are stones. Some stones are diamonds. No diamond is a gem.

   Conclusions:

   I. Some gems are pearls.
   II. Some gems are diamonds.
   III. No gem is a diamond.
   IV. No gem is a pearl.

   (A) Only I and II follow.
   (B) Only III and IV follow.
   (C) Only either I or IV and either II or III follow.
   (D) Only III and either I or IV follow.
   (E) None of these.

7. **Statements:** No man is sky. No sky is road. Some men are roads.

   Conclusions:

   I. No road is man.
   II. No road is sky.
   III. Some skies are men.
   IV. All roads are men.

   (A) None follows.
   (B) Only I follows.
   (C) Only II and III follow.
   (D) Only I and III follow.
   (E) None of the above.

8. **Statements:** All myths are fictions. No fiction is novel. All novels are stories.

   Conclusions:

   I. No myth is novel.
   II. Some fictions are novels.
   III. Some fictions are myths.
   IV. Some myths are novels.

   (A) Only either I or II and both III and IV follow.
   (B) Only either I or IV and II follow.
   (C) Only either I or IV and both II and III follow.
   (D) All follow.
   (E) None of the above.

9. **Statements:** All rods are bricks. Some bricks are ropes. All ropes are doors.

   Conclusions:

   I. Some rods are doors.
   II. Some doors are bricks.
   III. Some rods are not doors.
   IV. All doors are ropes.

   (A) Only I and II follow.

(B) Only I, II and III follow.
(C) Only either I or III, and II follow.
(D) Only either I or III, and IV follow.
(E) None of the above.

10. Statements: No paper is pen. No pen is pencil. All erasers are papers.

Conclusions:

I. Some papers are erasers.
II. No pencil is eraser.
III. No pen is eraser.
IV. All papers are erasers.

(A) Only I and II follow.
(B) Only II and III follow.
(C) Only I, II and III follow.
(D) All follow.
(E) None of the above.

11. Statements: All doors are buses. All buses are leaves. No leaf is a flower.

Conclusions:

I. No flower is a door.
II. No flower is a bus.
III. Some leaves are doors.
IV. Some leaves are buses.

(A) None follows.
(B) Only I and II follow.
(C) Only II and III follow.
(D) Only II, III and IV follow.
(E) All follow.

12. Statements: All pencils are birds. All birds are skies. All skies are hills.

Conclusions:

I. All pencils are hills.
II. All hills are birds
III. All skies are pencils.
IV. All birds are hills.

(A) Only I and II follow.
(B) Only I and III follow.
(C) Only III and IV follow.
(D) All follow.
(E) None of the above.

13. Statements: Some tigers are lions. Some lions are rabbits. Some rabbits are horses.

Conclusions:

I. Some tigers are horses.
II. Some rabbits are tigers.
III. Some horses are lions.
IV. All horses are rabbits.

(A) All follow.
(B) None follows.
(C) Only I and II follow.
(D) Only II and IV follow.
(E) Only IV follows.

14. Statements: All oceans are rivers. Some springs are rivers. All wells are springs.

Conclusions:

I. Some springs are oceans.
II. Some wells are rivers.
III. Some rivers are oceans.
IV. No well is river.

(A) None follows.
(B) Only either I or III, and IV follow.
(C) Only either II or IV, and III follow.
(D) All follow.
(E) Only either II or IV, and I follow.

15. Statements: Some spoons are bowls. All bowls are knives. All knives are forks.

Conclusions:

I. All spoons are forks.
II. All bowls are forks.
III. Some knives are bowls.
IV. Some forks are spoons

(A) Only II and III follow.
(B) Only II and IV follow.
(C) Only III and IV follow.
(D) All follow.
(E) None of the above.

ANSWER KEY

Level-1: Beginner

1.	(D)	2.	(D)	3.	(E)	4.	(E)	5.	(D)	6.	(D)	7.	(D)	8.	(D)	9.	(C)	10.	(B)
11.	(D)	12.	(D)	13.	(C)	14.	(C)	15.	(A)	16.	(A)	17.	(B)	18.	(C)	19.	(D)	20.	(D)
21.	(A)	22.	(E)	23.	(D)	24.	(C)	25.	(B)										

Level-2: Intermediate

1.	(C)	2.	(B)	3.	(C)	4.	(E)	5.	(B)	6.	(B)	7.	(B)	8.	(E)	9.	(B)	10.	(A)
11.	(C)	12.	(A)	13.	(A)	14.	(B)	15.	(A)	16.	(A)	17.	(D)	18.	(D)	19.	(B)	20.	(A)
21.	(E)	22.	(B)	23.	(E)	24.	(D)	25.	(C)										

Level-3: Expert

1.	(D)	2.	(D)	3.	(D)	4.	(A)	5.	(B)	6.	(D)	7.	(E)	8.	(E)	9.	(E)	10.	(E)
11.	(E)	12.	(E)	13.	(B)	14.	(C)	15.	(E)										

Solutions with Detailed Explanations

Level-1: BEGINNER

1. **Option (D) is correct.**
Explanation: The initial premise is classified as an A-type proposition and distributes solely the subject. Consequently, the middle term 'waters', functioning as its predicate, remains undistributed. The subsequent premise, an I-type proposition, fails to distribute either subject or predicate. Hence, the middle term 'waters', functioning as its subject, remains undistributed. Given that the middle term lacks distribution in both premises, no conclusive inference can be drawn.

2. **Option (D) is correct.**
Explanation: Since both the premises are universal and one premise is negative, the conclusion must be universal negative. So, neither I nor II follows.

3. **Option (E) is correct.**
Explanation: The term 'Every' is synonymous with 'All'. Consequently, as both premises are universal and affirmative, the conclusion must also be universal and affirmative, and it should not include the middle term. Therefore, the inference in statement I is valid. Statement II represents the converse of the second premise, and therefore, it is also valid.

4. **Option (E) is correct.**
Explanation: Building on the previous discussion, given that the conclusion should be universal negative and exclude the middle term, the inference 'No flower is fruit' follows. Statement I represents the converse of this conclusion, thus it is valid. Statement II corresponds to the converse of the first premise, thereby holding true as well.

5. **Option (D) is correct.**
Explanation: Since both premises are negative, no definite conclusion follows.

6. **Option (D) is correct.**
Explanation: Since both premises are particular, no definite conclusion follows.

7. **Option (D) is correct.**
Explanation: Since one premise is particular, the conclusion must be particular. So, neither I nor II follows.

8. **Option (D) is correct.**
Explanation: Since one premise is negative, the conclusion must be negative. Therefore, neither conclusion follows.

9. **Option (C) is correct.**
Explanation: As the middle term 'cakes' remains undistributed in the premises, no definitive conclusion can be drawn. However, I and II exclusively involve the extreme terms and complement each other. Hence, either I or II could logically follow.

10. **Option (B) is correct.**
Explanation: The conclusion must be a universal negative statement and should not include the middle term. Therefore, the logical inference 'No mango is cheap' follows. Additionally, considering that all mangoes are golden in color, we can substitute 'mangoes' with 'golden-colored mangoes'. Consequently, statement II is valid.

11. **Option (D) is correct.**
Explanation: Since both premises are particular, no definite conclusion follows. However, III and IV form a complementary pair. Thus, either III or IV follows.

12. **Option (D) is correct.**
Explanation: Given that both premises are particular, no conclusive inference can be made. However, I and III exclusively involve the extreme terms and complement each other, forming a complementary pair. Thus, either I or III could logically follow. Statement II represents the converse of the first premise, and statement IV is the converse of the second premise; both of these hold true.

13. **Option (C) is correct.**
Explanation: Considering that one premise is particular and the other negative, the conclusion must be a particular negative statement that does not include the middle term. Hence, the logical inference 'Some books are not novels' follows (statement III). Additionally, statement I, being the converse of the first premise, is also valid.

14. **Option (C) is correct.**
Explanation: Since the middle term 'terrorists' is distributed twice in the premises, the conclusion cannot be universal. So, it follows that 'Some guilty persons are criminals'. Thus, II holds.

15. **Option (A) is correct.**
Explanation: Since both premises are particular, no definite conclusion follows.

16. **Option (A) is correct.**
Explanation: Given that one premise is particular, the conclusion must also be particular and should not include the middle term. Therefore, the logical inference 'Some bottles are cups' follows (statement I). Additionally, statement II, representing the converse of the second premise, is also valid.

17. **Option (B) is correct.**
Explanation: Since both premises are universal and affirmative, the conclusion must be universal affirmative and should not contain the middle term. So, it follows that 'All branches are leaves'. Thus, I follows. IV is the converse of this conclusion and so it also holds.

18. **Option (C) is correct.**
Explanation: Since one premise is particular and the other negative, the conclusion must be a particular negative and should not contain the middle term. So, II follows. Also, III is the converse of the first premise and thus it also holds

19. **Option (D) is correct.**
Explanation: Since the middle term 'trains' is not distributed even once in the premises, no definite conclusion follows. However, III is the converse of the second premise while IV is the converse of the first premise. So, both of them hold.

20. **Option (D) is correct.**
Explanation: Clearly, it follows that 'All politicians are fair'. I is the converse of the first premise, while III is the converse of the above conclusion. So, both I and III hold.

21. **Option (A) is correct.**
Explanation: Since one premise is particular, the conclusion must be particular and should not contain the middle term. So, I follows. Since both premises are affirmative, the conclusion cannot be negative. Thus, II does not follow.

22. **Option (E) is correct.**
Explanation: Since one premise is particular, the conclusion must be particular and should not contain the middle term. So, I follows . II is the converse of I and thus it also holds.

23. **Option (D) is correct.**
Explanation: Both premises are I-type propositions and as such, the middle term "boys" is not distributed even once in the premises. So, no definite conclusions follows.

24. **Option (C) is correct.**
Explanation: Since both premises are particular no definite conclusion follows. However, I and II involve only the extreme terms and form a complementary pair. Thus, either I or II follows.

25. **Option (B) is correct.**
Explanation: Since both premises are universal and one premise is negative, the conclusion must be universal negative and should not contain the middle term. So, only II follows.

Level-2: INTERMEDIATE

1. **Option (C) is correct.**
Explanation: In the first set of premises:
1. "All tigers are jungles."
2. "No jungle is bird."
Given that both premises are universal and one is negative, the conclusion must be universal negative (E-type) and should not contain the middle term. Thus, the logical inference 'No tiger is bird' follows (statement III), and its converse is valid.
In the second set of premises:
1. "No jungle is bird."
2. "Some birds are rains."
Since one premise is particular and the other negative, the conclusion must be a particular negative (O-type) and should not contain the middle term. Therefore, the logical inference 'Some jungles are not rains' follows.
Also, since statements I and II involve the same terms and form a complementary pair, either I or II could logically follow.

2. **Option (B) is correct.**
Explanation: In the first set of premises:
1. "Some horses are lions."
2. "No rabbit is lion."
Given that one premise is particular and the other negative, the conclusion must be a particular negative (O-type) and should not contain the middle term. Thus, the logical inference 'Some horses are not rabbits' follows.
In the second set of premises:
1. "All rabbits are tables."
2. "No rabbit is lion."
Since the middle term 'rabbits' is distributed twice, the conclusion must be particular. Also, as one premise is negative, the conclusion must also be negative. Therefore, the logical inference 'Some tables are not lions' follows.
Since statements I and III involve the same terms and form a complementary pair, either I or III could logically follow.

3. **Option (C) is correct.**
Explanation: In the first set of premises:
1. "All snakes are trees."
2. "Some trees are roads."
Since the middle term 'trees' is not distributed in the premises, no definite conclusion can be drawn.
In the second set of premises:
1. "Some trees are roads."
2. "All roads are mountains."
Given that one premise is particular, the conclusion must be particular and should not contain the middle term. Thus, the logical inference 'Some trees are mountains' follows (statement III), and its converse is valid.
In the third set of premises:
1. "All snakes are trees."
2. "Some trees are mountains."
Since the middle term 'trees' is not distributed in the premises, no definite conclusion can be drawn.

4. **Option (E) is correct.**
Explanation: In the first set of premises:
1."All trees are flowers."
2."No flower is fruit."
Since both premises are universal and one is negative, the conclusion must be a universal negative (E-type) statement that does not contain the middle term. Thus, the logical inference 'No tree is fruit' follows. Statement II, being the converse of this conclusion, also holds.
In the second set of premises:
1. "All branches are fruits."
2. "No flower is fruit."
Similarly, given that both premises are universal and one is negative, the conclusion must be a universal negative (E-type) statement that does not contain the middle term. Thus, the logical inference 'No branch is flower' follows.
In the third set of premises:
1. "All trees are flowers."
2. "No branch is flower."
As stated, it follows that 'No tree is branch'. Therefore, statement III is valid.
Hence, both statements II and III follow.

5. **Option (B) is correct.**
Explanation: In the first set of premises:
1. "Some uniforms are covers."
2. "All covers are papers."
Given that one premise is particular, the conclusion must be particular and should not contain the middle term. Thus, the logical inference 'Some uniforms are papers' follows.
In the second set of premises:
1. "All covers are papers."
2. "All papers are bags."
Since both premises are universal and affirmative,

the conclusion must be universal affirmative (A-type) and should not contain the middle term. Thus, the logical inference 'All covers are bags' follows. Also, the converse of this conclusion, 'Some bags are covers', is also valid.

In the third set of premises:
1. "Some uniforms are covers."
2. "All covers are bags."

Given that one premise is particular, the conclusion must be particular and should not contain the middle term. So, the logical inference 'Some uniforms are bags' follows. Similarly, the converse of this conclusion, 'Some bags are uniforms', also holds.

Thus, the converse of the third premise, 'Some bags are papers', also holds.

Now, statement II represents the cumulative result of the conclusions 'Some bags are covers', 'Some bags are papers', and 'Some bags are uniforms'. Thus, statement II follows.

6. **Option (B) is correct.**

Explanation: In the first set of premises:
1. "Some pictures are frames."
2. "Some frames are idols."

Since both premises are particular, no definite conclusion follows.

In the second set of premises:
1. "Some frames are idols."
2. "All idols are curtains."

Given that one premise is particular, the conclusion must be particular and should not contain the middle term. Thus, the logical inference 'Some frames are curtains' follows. Statement III, being the converse of this conclusion, also holds.

In the third set of premises:
1. "Some pictures are frames."
2. "Some frames are curtains."

Since both premises are particular, no definite conclusion can be drawn.

7. **Option (B) is correct.**

Explanation: In the first set of premises:
1. "Some towels are brushes."
2. "No brush is soap."

Given that one premise is particular and the other negative, the conclusion must be a particular negative (O-type) statement that does not contain the middle term. Thus, the logical inference 'Some towels are not soaps' follows (statement I).

In the second set of premises:
1. "No brush is soap."
2. "All soaps are rats."

Since the middle term 'soap' is distributed twice and one premise is negative, the conclusion must be particular and negative. Therefore, the logical inference 'Some brushes are not rats' follows (statement II).

Since statements I and II involve the same terms and form a complementary pair, either statement I or II could logically follow.

8. **Option (E) is correct.**

Explanation: In the first set of premises:
1. "All fruits are vegetables."
2. "All vegetables are rains."

Given that both premises are universal affirmative and the conclusion must not contain the middle term, the logical inference 'All fruits are rains' follows (statement I).

In the second set of premises:
1. "All pens are vegetables."
2. "All vegetables are rains."

Since both premises are universal affirmative and the conclusion must not contain the middle term, the logical inference 'All pens are rains' follows (statement II).

Regarding statement III, it seems there might be a misunderstanding. The converse of the third premise, "All vegetables are rains," would be "All rains are vegetables," not "All fruits are rains." Thus, statement III does not hold in this context.

9. **Option (B) is correct.**

Explanation: In the first set of premises:
1. "Some hills are rivers."
2. "Some rivers are deserts."

Since both premises are particular, no definite conclusion follows.

In the second set of premises:
1. "Some rivers are deserts."
2. "All deserts are roads."

Since one premise is particular, the conclusion must be particular and should not contain the middle term. Thus, the logical inference 'Some rivers are roads' follows (statement I), and its converse is valid.

In the third set of premises:
1. "Some hills are rivers."
2. "Some rivers are roads."

Also, since both premises are particular, no definite conclusion can be drawn.

10. **Option (A) is correct.**

Explanation: In the first set of premises:
1. "Some saints are balls."
2. "All balls are bats."

Given that one premise is particular, the conclusion must be particular and should not contain the middle term. Thus, the logical inference 'Some saints are bats' follows (statement II).

In the second set of premises:
1. "Some tigers are balls."
2. "All balls are bats."

Similarly, since one premise is particular, the conclusion must be particular and should not contain the middle term. Thus, the logical inference 'Some tigers are bats' follows (statement I), and its converse is valid.

Therefore, both statements I and II follow.

11. **Option (C) is correct.**

Explanation: In the first set of premises:
1. "All fruits are books."
2. "All books are buses."

Given that III is the converse of the first premise and II is the converse of the second premise, both statements hold.

In the second set of premises:
1. "All fruits are books."
2. "All books are buses."

Since both premises are universal and affirmative, the conclusion must be universal affirmative and should not contain the middle term. Thus, the logical inference 'All fruits are buses' follows (statement IV).

In the third set of premises:

1. "All jungles are buses."
2. "All books are buses."

Since the middle term 'buses' is not distributed in the premises, no definite conclusion can be drawn.

In the fourth set of premises:

1. "All fruits are buses."
2. "All books are buses."

As stated above, no definite conclusion can be drawn.

In the fifth set of premises:

1. "All jungles are buses."
2. "All fruits are buses."

Thus, no definite conclusion follows.

12. Option (A) is correct.

Explanation: No toy is building. All buildings are windows.

Since the middle term 'buildings' is distributed twice and one premise is negative, the conclusion must be particular negative and should not contain the middle term.

So, it follows that 'Some windows are not toys'.

Some tigers are toys. No toy is building.

Since one premise is particular and the other premise is negative, the conclusion must be particular negative and should not contain the middle term. So, it follows that 'Some tigers are not buildings'.

13. Option (A) is correct.

Explanation: No table is fruit. No fruit is window.

Since both premises are negative, no definite conclusion follows.

No fruit is window. All windows are chairs.

Since the middle term 'windows' is distributed twice and one premise is negative, the conclusion must be particular negative. So, it follows that 'Some chairs are not fruits'.

14. Option (B) is correct.

Explanation: Several documents are associated with cats, and all cats fall under the category of bats. Given the this premise, the conclusion must also be particular and devoid of the middle term. Thus, it can be inferred that 'Some papers belong to the category of bats'. The converse, 'Some bats are papers', also holds true. Every cat belongs to the category of bats, and no bat belongs to the category of horses. Since both premises are universal and one is negative, the conclusion must be a universal negative without including the middle term. Thus, it logically follows that 'No cat belongs to the category of horses'. The converse, 'No horse belongs to the category of cats', is also valid.

Several papers are associated with bats, and no bat belongs to the category of horses. With one premise being particular and the other negative, the conclusion must be a particular negative without the middle term. Therefore, it can be concluded that 'Some papers do not belong to the category of horses'.

15. Option (A) is correct.

Explanation: Since each combination of premises shall contain two particular premises, no definite conclusion can be drawn. However, I and IV involve the extreme terms of the second and third premises and form a complementary pair. Thus, either I or IV follows.

16. Option (A) is correct.

Explanation: Since the first premise is particular, the conclusion must be particular and should not contain the middle term. Thus, only I follows.

17. Option (D) is correct.

Explanation: Since the middle term "cats" is not distributed even once in the premises, no definite conclusion follows.

18. Option (D) is correct.

Explanation: The first premise is an I type proposition. So, the middle term "angels" forming the predicate is not distributed. The second premise is an A type preposition. So, the middle term "angels" forming the predicate is not distributed. Since the middle term is not distributed even once in the premises, no definite conclusion follows.

19. Option (B) is correct.

Explanation: Since the middle term is not distributed even once in the premises, no definite conclusion follows. However, II is the converse of the second premise and so it holds.

20. Option (A) is correct.

Explanation: Since one premise is particular and the other premise is negative, the conclusion must be a particular negative and should not contain the middle term. So, it follows that "Some desks are not red." However, I is the converse of the first premise and thus it holds.

21. Option (E) is correct.

Explanation: Since both premises are universal and one premise is negative, the conclusion must be universal negative. Also, the conclusion should not contain the middle term. So, II follows. I is the converse of II and thus it also holds.

22. Option (B) is correct.

Explanation: Since both premises are particular, no definite conclusion follows. However, II is the converse of the second premise and thus it holds.

23. Option (E) is correct.

Explanation: As discussed above, the conclusion must be universal negative and should not contain the middle term. So, it follows that "No flower is fruit." I is the converse of this conclusion and thus it follows. II is the converse of the first premise and so it also holds.

24. Option (D) is correct.

Explanation: Since one premise is negative, the conclusion must be negative. So, neither conclusion follows.

25. Option (C) is correct.

Explanation: The data does not mention whether all intelligent girls are married to bureaucrats. So, either I or II may follow.

Level-3: EXPERT

1. Option (D) is correct.

Explanation: In the first set of premises:

1. "All benches are desks."

2. "Some desks are roads."
Since the middle term 'desks' is not distributed in the premises, no definite conclusion can be drawn.
In the second set of premises:
1. "Some desks are roads."
2. "All roads are pillars."
Given that one premise is particular, the conclusion must be particular and should not contain the middle term. Thus, the logical inference 'Some desks are pillars' follows (statement II), and its converse is valid.
In the third set of premises:
1. "All benches are desks."
2. "Some desks are pillars."
Since the middle term 'desks' is not distributed in the premises, no definite conclusion can be drawn. Since statements I and IV involve the extreme terms and form a complementary pair, either statement I or IV could logically follow.

2. **Option (D) is correct.**
Explanation: In the first set of premises:
1. "Some trains are roads."
2. "No road is jungle."
Given that one premise is particular and the other negative, the conclusion must be a particular negative statement that does not contain the middle term. Thus, the logical inference 'Some trains are not jungles' follows.
In the second set of premises:
1. "No road is jungle."
2. "All flowers are jungles."
Since both premises are universal and one is negative, the conclusion must be a universal negative statement that does not contain the middle term. Therefore, the logical inference 'No flower is road' follows (statement IV), and its converse is valid.
In the third set of premises:
1. "Some trains are roads."
2. "No flower is road."
Hence, it follows that 'Some trains are not flowers'. Thus, statement III is valid.

3. **Option (D) is correct.**
Explanation: In the first set of premises:
1. "Some bricks are trees."
2. "All trees are pens."
Given that III is the converse of the first premise, it holds.
In the second set of premises:
1. "Some bricks are trees."
2. "All trees are pens."
Since one premise is particular, the conclusion must be particular and should not contain the middle term. Thus, the logical inference 'Some bricks are pens' follows (statement II), and its converse is valid.
In the third set of premises:
1. "All trees are pens."
2. "All pens are boats."
Since both premises are universal and affirmative, the conclusion must be universal affirmative and should not contain the middle term. Thus, the logical inference 'All trees are boats' follows.
In the fourth set of premises:
1. "Some bricks are trees."
2. "All trees are boats."
Since one premise is particular, the conclusion must be particular and should not contain the middle term. Thus, the logical inference 'Some bricks are boats' follows (statement IV), and its converse (statement I) also holds.
Thus, all statements (I, II, III, and IV) follow.

4. **Option (A) is correct.**
Explanation: In the first set of premises:
1. "All cups are glasses."
2. "Some glasses are bowls."
Since the middle term 'glasses' is not distributed in the premises, no definite conclusion can be drawn.
In the second set of premises:
1. "Some glasses are bowls."
2. "No bowl is a plate."
Given that one premise is particular and the other negative, the conclusion must be a particular negative statement that does not contain the middle term. Thus, the logical inference 'Some glasses are not plates' follows.

5. **Option (B) is correct.**
Explanation: In the first set of premises:
1. "Some dogs are rats."
2. "All rats are trees."
Here, one premise is particular, the conclusion must be particular and should not contain the middle term. Thus, the logical inference 'Some dogs are trees' follows (statement I), and its converse is valid.
In the second set of premises:
1. "All rats are trees."
2. "Some trees are not dogs."
Since the middle term 'trees' is not distributed in the premises, no definite conclusion can be drawn.

6. **Option (D) is correct.**
Explanation: In the first set of premises:
1. "Some pearls are stones."
2. "Some stones are diamonds."
Since both premises are particular, no definite conclusion follows.
In the second set of premises:
1. "Some stones are diamonds."
2. "No diamond is a gem."
Given that one premise is particular and the other negative, the conclusion must be a particular negative and should not contain the middle term. Thus, the logical inference 'Some stones are not gems' follows. However, these statements I and IV involve the extreme terms of the three premises and form a complementary pair, either statement I or IV could logically follow.

7. **Option (E) is correct.**
Explanation: In the first set of premises:
1. "No man is sky."
2. "No sky is road."
Since both premises are negative, no definite conclusion follows.
In the second set of premises:
1. "No man is sky."
2. "Some men are roads."
Here, one premise is particular and the other negative, the conclusion must be a particular negative and should not contain the middle term. Thus, the logical

inference 'Some roads are not skies' follows.
In the third set of premises:
1. "No sky is road."
2. "Some men are roads."
As stated, it follows that 'Some men are not skies'.
Therefore, only statement II follows.

8. **Option (E) is correct.**
Explanation: III represents the converse of the initial premise, thus it remains valid. It is established that all myths fall under the category of fictions, and no fiction can be classified as a novel. Given the universality of both premises and the negativity of one premise, the conclusion must also be universally negative, without containing the middle term. Thus, the logical deduction 'No myth is novel' is warranted, affirming the validity of statement I.
Also, when analyzing the statements 'No fiction is novel' and 'All novels are stories,' it is evident that the middle term 'novels' is distributed twice within the premises. Even, the conclusion must be particular. Also, as one premise is negative, the conclusion must also be negative. Hence, it logically follows that 'Some stories are not fictions.' Thus, only statements I and III hold true.

9. **Option (E) is correct.**
Explanation: Every rod is a brick. Certain bricks are ropes.
The term 'bricks' is not distributed at all in the premises, no conclusive inference can be drawn.
Some bricks are ropes. All ropes are doors.
Given one premise is particular, the conclusion must also be particular and should not include the middle term. Therefore, the logical conclusion is 'Some bricks are doors'. Statement II, which represents the converse of this conclusion, remains valid.
All rods are bricks. Certain bricks are doors.
Once more, as the middle term 'bricks' is not distributed in the premises, no definite conclusion can be reached. But, both statements I and III involve the extreme terms. Despite not being contradictory, they fail to form a complementary pair.
Thus, only statement II holds true in this context.

10. **Option (E) is correct.**
Explanation: I is the converse of the third premise and thus remains valid.
No paper is a pen. No pen is a pencil.
As both premises are negative, no definitive conclusion can be drawn.
All erasers are papers. No paper is a pen.
Since both premises are universal and one premise is negative, the conclusion must be universally negative and should not include the middle term. Thus, it can be inferred that 'No eraser is a pen'. III represents the converse of this conclusion and therefore holds true.
Hence, only statements I and III are applicable.

11. **Option (E) is correct.**
Explanation: IV represents the converse of the second premise and thus remains valid.
All doors are buses. All buses are leaves.
Given both premises are universal and affirmative, the conclusion must be universally affirmative and should not include the middle term. Therefore, it can be inferred that 'All doors are leaves'. III represents the converse of this conclusion and therefore holds true.
All buses are leaves. No leaf is a flower.
Since both premises are universal and one premise is negative, the conclusion must be universally negative and should not include the middle term. Therefore, the logical inference is 'No bus is a flower'. II represents the converse of this conclusion and thus holds true.
All doors are buses. No bus is a flower.
Following the same logic, it can be deduced that 'No door is a flower'. I represents the converse of this conclusion and therefore also holds true.

12. **Option (E) is correct.**
Explanation: All pencils are birds. All birds are skies.
Given both premises are universal and affirmative, the conclusion must be universally affirmative (A-type) and should not include the middle term. Thus, it can be inferred that 'All pencils are skies'.
All birds are skies. All skies are hills.
Following the same logic, it can be deduced that 'All birds are hills'. Therefore, IV follows.
All pencils are skies. All skies are hills.
It is evident that 'All pencils are hills'. Thus, I follows.
Hence, I and IV are applicable.

13. **Option (B) is correct.**
Explanation: Since each combination of premises shall contain two particular premises, no definite conclusion can be drawn.

14. **Option (C) is correct.**
Explanation: III represents the converse of the first premise and thus remains valid.
All oceans are rivers. Some springs are rivers.
As the middle term 'rivers' is not distributed even once in the premises, no definite conclusion can be drawn.
All wells are springs. Some springs are rivers.
Similarly, as the middle term 'springs' is not distributed even once in the premises, no definite conclusion can be derived.
However, II and IV involve the extreme terms and form a complementary pair. Hence, either II or IV follows.

15. **Option (E) is correct.**
Explanation: III represents the converse of the second premise and therefore remains valid.
Some spoons are bowls. All bowls are knives.
As one premise is particular, the conclusion must also be particular and should not include the middle term. Thus, it logically follows that 'Some spoons are knives'.
All bowls are knives. All knives are forks.
Since both premises are universal and affirmative, the conclusion must be universally affirmative and should not include the middle term. Therefore, it follows that 'All bowls are forks'. Thus, II follows.
Some spoons are knives. All knives are forks.
As one premise is particular, the conclusion must also be particular and should not include the middle term. Thus, it logically follows that 'Some spoons are forks'. IV represents the converse of this conclusion and thus also holds true.
Hence, II, III, and IV are applicable.

■ ■ ■

Chapter 2

Statements and Arguments

LEARNING OBJECTIVES:

- Identify the valid and invalid arguments.
- Understand the strengthening and weakening arguments.

A statement is a proposition or assertion put forward for consideration in analytical reasoning. It is a declarative sentence that conveys a specific piece of information or makes a claim. Statements can be factual, opinionated, or hypothetical.

Arguments in analytical reasoning, on the other hand, refer to the reasoning or justification provided to support or challenge a given statement. An argument is a set of statements intended to establish the validity or soundness of a claim. It uses evidence, logical reasoning, examples, or other forms of support to persuade others of the truth or plausibility of a statement.

In analytical reasoning tasks, one may encounter a statement followed by a set of arguments related to that statement. The task of an individual is to assess the arguments based on their strength, relevance and logical consistency with the given statement. This entails analysing the evidence or reasoning presented in the arguments and determining whether they effectively support or weaken the statement. The goal is to evaluate the logical coherence and persuasive strength of the arguments in relation to the given statement.

IDENTIFYING THE VALID AND INVALID ARGUMENTS:

➢ A valid argument is one in which the conclusion logically follows from the premises. It means that if the premises of an argument are true, then the conclusion must also be true. The validity of an argument is determined solely by its logical structure, regardless of whether the premises or conclusion are factually true or false. Here's an example of a valid argument:

Premise 1: All cats have fur.

Premise 2: Fluffy is a cat.

Conclusion: Therefore, Fluffy has fur.

In this example, if both premises are true, then the conclusion must also be true. The conclusion logically follows from the premises, making it a valid argument.

An argument is considered invalid if the conclusion does not logically follow from the premises, even if the premises are true. In other words, the truth of the premises does not ensure the truth of the conclusion. The invalidity of an argument is determined by a flaw in its logical structure, regardless of the truth or falsity of the premises or conclusion. Here's an example of a flawed argument:

Example:

Premise 1: All cats have tails.

Premise 2: Dogs have tails.

Conclusion: Therefore, dogs are cats.

In this case, the conclusion does not logically follow from the premises. Even if one accepts that all cats have tails (Premise 1) and that all dogs have tails (Premise 2), this does not logically lead to the conclusion that dogs are cats. The argument is invalid because the conclusion is not a logical consequence of the premises.

Invalid arguments can take various forms, such as logical fallacies, flawed reasoning, or the absence of critical information. To ensure sound reasoning and critical thinking, it is critical to identify invalid arguments. In analytical reasoning, evaluating the logical structure and coherence of arguments is essential for distinguishing between valid and invalid arguments.

STRENGTHENING AND WEAKENING ARGUMENTS:

➢ When making important decisions, it is useful to distinguish between "strengthening" and "weakening" arguments. "Strengthening" arguments are important and directly related to the issue at hand. They provide substantial support or evidence in favour of a specific position or decision. "Weakening" arguments, on the other hand, are of minor importance and may not be directly related to the main question, or they may address trivial aspects of the question.

Example:

1. Should the government invest in renewable energy sources?

Strengthening argument: Investing in renewable energy sources would significantly reduce reliance on fossil fuels, resulting in lower pollution and greenhouse gas emissions. This would contribute to a cleaner and more sustainable environment for future generations.

In this case, the strengthening argument directly addresses the question and provides compelling reasons to support investment in renewable energy sources. It emphasises the benefits of reducing pollution and promoting sustainability, which are in line with the overall goal.

Weakening argument: Instead of focusing on renewable energy, the government should invest in other sectors such as healthcare and education. These sectors are more critical to the population's well-being and development.

The weakening argument, on the other hand, diverts attention away from the main question by suggesting alternate priorities. While healthcare and education are undoubtedly important, this argument does not directly address the issue of renewable energy investment and instead focuses on unrelated issues.

Decision-makers can critically assess the relevance and significance of different arguments in the context of the question or decision at hand by understanding the distinction between strengthening and weakening arguments. This enables them to make more informed and reasoned decisions based on the most important and significant factors.

Example 1: Statement: Should education be brought under the control of the central government like defence?

Argument I: No, education is a state subject and it should remain with the state.

Argument II: Yes, this is the only way to establish uniformity in growth of education across the states.

Sol. As we can understand from the statement that the benefits of education can reach better to the masses if looked after by the state government rather than the central body, so, Argument 1 holds strong, and second is weak.

Example 2: Should India immediately stop digging coal from its mine?

Argument I: Yes, India has a limited reserve of coal.

Argument II: No, India is a country dependent on carbon-based fuels—especially coal.

Argument III: No, coal is a vital source of jobs and economic growth for India.

Sol. We know the reserve of coal is limited. But we have not discovered an alternate source of energy till date. So, Argument 1 is not strong. It is true that we haven't till date found a renewable source of energy, which is available in plenty and can substitute coal. So, Argument 2 holds strong. Further, stopping coal mining would surely throw the engaged workers out of employment. So, Argument 3 also holds strong.

Level 1 Beginner

Directions (Qs. 1 to 20): Each of the following questions begins with a statement and is followed by two or more arguments. You must decide which of the arguments is a strong one and which is a weak one. Mark the answer:

(A) If only argument I is strong.
(B) If only argument II is strong.
(C) If either I or II is strong.
(D) If neither I nor II is strong
(E) If both I and II are strong.

1. **Statement:** Should agriculture in rural India be mechanised?

   Argument I: Yes, it would lead to higher production.

   Argument II: No, many villagers would be left unemployed.

2. **Statement:** Should the educated unemployed youth be paid "unemployment allowance" by the government?

   Argument I: Yes, it will provide them some monetary help to either seek employment or to kick start some self-employment venture.

   Argument II: No, it will depend on their urge to do something to earn their livelihood and thus promote idleness among the unemployed youth. **[Bank PO 2011]**

3. **Statement:** Should all the practicing doctors be brought under government control so that they get a salary from the government and treat patients free of cost?

   Argument:

   I. No, how can any country do such an undemocratic thing?

   II. Yes, despite many problems, it will certainly help minimise, if not eradicate, unethical medical practices. **[RBI 2009]**

4. **Statement:** Should there be more than one high courts in each state in India?

   Argument:

   I. No, this will be a sheer wastage of taxpayer's money.

   II. Yes, this will help reduce the backlog of cases pending for a very long time **[IBPS 2012]**

5. **Statement:** Should there be concentration of foreign investment in only a few states?

   Argument:

   I. No, it is against the policy of overall development of the country.

   II. Yes, many states lack infrastructure to attract foreign investment. **[SBI PO 2015]**

6. **Statement:** Should India engage into a dialogue with neighbouring countries to stop cross border tension?

   Argument:

I. Yes, this is the only way to reduce cross-border terrorism and stop the loss of innocent lives.

II. No, neighbouring countries cannot be relied upon in such matters, they may still engage in subversive activities. **[SBI PO 2013]**

7. **Statement:** Should system of offering jobs only to the wards of government employees be introduced in all government offices in India?

Argument:

I. No, it denies opportunity to many deserving individuals and the government may stand to lose in the long run.

II. No, it is against the principle of equality. Does not government owe its responsibility to all its citizens? **[SBI PO 2014]**

8. **Statement:** Should the sex determination test during pregnancy be completely banned?

Arguments:

I. Yes, this leads to indiscriminate female feticide and eventually will lead to social imbalance.

II. No, people have a right to know about their unborn child. **[Bank PO]**

9. **Statement:** Should there be only one rate of interest for term deposit of verifying durations in banks?

Arguments:

I. No, people will refrain from keeping money for long duration resulting in the reduction in the liquidity level of banks.

II. Yes, this will be much simpler for common people, and they may be encouraged to keep more money in banks **[Bank PO]**

10. **Statement:** Should the oil companies be allowed to fix the price of petroleum products depending on market conditions?

Arguments:

I. Yes, this is the only way to make the oil companies commercially viable.

II. No, this will put additional burden on the retail price of essential commodities and will cause a lot of hardship to the masses. **[Bank PO]**

11. **Statement:** Should there be a maximum limit for the number of ministers in Central Governments?

Arguments:

I. No, the political party in power should have the freedom to decide the number of ministers to be appointed.

II. Yes, the number of ministers should be restricted to a certain percentage of the total number of seats in parliament to avoid unnecessary expenditure. **[Bank PO]**

12. **Statement:** Should India become a permanent member of 'UN's Security Council?

Arguments:

I. Yes, India has emerged as a country which loves peace and amity.

II. No, let us first solve problems of our own people like poverty and malnutrition. **[IBPS]**

13. **Statement:** Should people below the age of 18 years be allowed to join armed forces?

Arguments:

I. No, persons below the age of 18 do not attain both physical and mental maturity to shoulder such a burden.

II. Yes, this will help the country develop its armed forces which will serve the country for a longer time **[Bank PO]**

14. **Statement:** Should there be a ban on product advertising?

Arguments:

I. No, it is an age of advertising. Unless your advertisement is better than your other competitors, the product will not be sold.

II. Yes, the money spent on advertising is really huge and it inflates the cost of the product. **[Bank PO]**

15. **Statement:** Should all the infrastructural development projects in India be handed over to the private sector?

Arguments:

I. No, the private sector entities are not equipped to handle such projects.

II. Yes, such projects are handled by the private sector in the developed countries. **[Bank PO]**

16. **Statement:** Should our country extend generous behaviour and goodwill to our erring and nagging neighbours?

Arguments:

I. Yes, goodwill always pays dividends.

II. No, our generous behaviour and goodwill be onsidered as our weakness. **[Bank PO]**

17. **Statement:** Should judiciary be independent of the executive?

Arguments:

I. Yes. This would help curb the unlawful activities of the executive.

II. No. The executive would not be able to take bold measures. **[RBI]**

18. **Statement:** Should Indian scientists working abroad be called back to India?

Arguments:

I. Yes. They must serve the motherland first and forget about discoveries, honours, facilities and all.

II. No. We have enough talent, let them stay where they want. **[SBI]**

19. **Statement:** Should the tuition fees in all post-graduate courses be hiked considerably?

Arguments:

I. Yes. This will bring in some sense of seriousness among the students and will improve the quality.

II. No. This will force the meritorious poor students to stay away from post-graduate courses. **[SBI PO]**

20. **Statement:** Should all correspondence courses at graduate level be stopped?

Argument:

I. No, correspondence courses help needy students to pursue studies and earn at the same time.

II. Yes, quality education is not possible without teachers and classrooms.

21. **Statement:** Should all the students graduating in any discipline desirous of pursuing post-graduation of the subjects of their choice be allowed to enroll in the post-graduate courses?

Arguments:

I. Yes. The students are the best judge of their capabilities and there should not be restrictions on taking post-graduate courses.

II. No. The students need to study relevant subjects in graduate courses to enroll in a postgraduate course and the students must fulfill such conditions.

III. No. There are not enough institutes offering post-graduate courses which can accommodate all the graduates desirous of seeking post-graduate education of their own choice.

(A) None is strong.
(B) Only I and II are strong.
(C) All are strong.
(D) Only I and III are strong.
(E) Only II is strong.

22. **Statement:** Should there be only few banks in place of numerous smaller banks in India?

Arguments:

I. Yes. This will help secure the investor's money as these big banks will be able to withstand intermittent market-related shocks.

II. No. Many people will loose their jobs as after the merger many employees will be redundant.

III. Yes. This will help consolidate the entire banking industry and will lead to healthy competition.

(A) None is strong.
(B) Only I and II are strong.
(C) Only II and III are strong.
(D) Only I and III are strong.
(E) All are strong. **[SBI PO]**

23. **Statement:** Should the income generated out of agricultural activities be taxed?

Arguments:

I. No. Farmers are otherwise suffering from natural calamities and low yield coupled with low procurement price and their income should not be taxed.

II. Yes. Much of the population is dependent on agriculture and hence their income should be taxed to augment the resources.

III. Yes. Many big farmers earn much more than many of the service earners and they should be taxed to remove the disparity.

(A) Only I am strong.
(B) Only I and II are strong.
(C) Only II and III are strong.
(D) All are strong.
(E) None of these **[SBI PO]**

24. **Statement:** Should all the indirect taxes in India can be combined into a single tax on all commodities?

Arguments:

I. Yes. This will considerably simplify the tax collection mechanism and the cost of collecting tax will also reduce.

II. Yes. The manufacturers and traders will be benefited by this which in turn will boost tax collection.

III. No. Other country has adopted such system.

(A) None is strong.
(B) Only I and III are strong.
(C) Only II is strong.
(D) Only II and III are strong.
(E) None of these **[SBI PO]**

25. **Statement:** Should India immediately stop digging coal from its mines?

Arguments:

I. Yes. The present stock of coal will not last long if we continue mining at the present rate.

II. No. We do not have alternate energy source of sufficient quantity.

III. No. This will put millions of people at a disadvantage and their lives will get adversely affected and also the industry.

(A) None is strong.
(B) Only I and III are strong.
(C) Only II is strong.
(D) Only II and III are strong.
(E) None of these

Level 2 Intermediate

Directions (Qs. 1 to 23): Each of following questions consists of a statement and is followed by two arguments (I and II). You must decide which of the arguments is a strong one and which is weak one. Mark the answer:

(A) If only argument I is strong.
(B) If only argument II is strong.
(C) If either I or II is strong.
(D) If neither I nor II is strong.
(E) If both I and II are strong.

1. **Statement:** Should the parents in India in future be forced to opt for only one child as against the two or many at present?

Arguments:

I. Yes. This is the only way to check the ever-increasing population of India.

II. No. This type of pressure tactic is not adopted by any other country in the world. **[Bank PO 2005]**

2. **Statement:** Should military service be made compulsory in our country?

Arguments:

I. No. It is against the policy of non- violence.

II. Yes. Every citizen should protect his country **[MAT 2004]**

3. **Statement:** Should only one company be allowed to run the transport system in any one big city?

Arguments:

I. Yes. This will put an end to unhealthy competitions among different companies.

II. No. The commuter should be given a wider choice of transport system. **[Bank PO 2003]**

4. **Statement:** Should all the foreign banks be asked to close down their operations in India?

Arguments:

I. No. This will have an adverse effect on Indian economy.

II. Yes. This is the only way to make the Indian banks survive and prosper. **[Bank PO 2003]**

5. **Statement:** Should the government open more medical colleges in the country?

Arguments:

I. Yes. There is urgent need of qualified doctors and the ratio between doctors and the citizens is the lowest in India.

II. No. The Government should ensure quality education in the existing Medical Colleges as majority of the colleges lack necessary infrastructure. **[IBPS 2002]**

6. **Statement:** Should India change its course from the economic reform process and look inward for all round economic development?

Arguments:

I. No. There is no way to look backward after having started the process.

II. Yes. This will benefit India in the long run as the reform process borrowed from western countries will adversely affect our economy.**[SBI PO 2005]**

7. **Statement:** Should the admission to professional courses in India be given only on merit without any concession to any particular group of students?

Arguments:

I. Yes. This will improve the quality of the professionals as they will be able to complete the courses successfully.

II. No. This will keep a large number of socially and economically backward students out of the reach of the professional courses. **[Bank PO 2004]**

8. **Statement:** Should there be concentration of foreign investment in only few states?

Arguments:

I. No. It is against the policy of overall development of the country.

II. Yes. A large number of states lack infrastructure to attract foreign investment. **[SBI PO 2002]**

9. **Statement:** Should luxury hotels be banned in India?

Arguments:

I. Yes. These are places from where international criminals operate.

II. No. Affluent foreign tourists will have no place to stay.

10. **Statement:** Should India engage into a dialogue with neighbouring countries to stop cross border tension?

Arguments:

I. Yes. This is the only way to reduce the cross-border terrorism and stop loss of innocent lives.

II. No. Neighbouring countries cannot be relied upon in such matters, they may still engage in subversive activities. **[SBI PO 2001]**

11. **Statement:** Should there be uniforms for students in the colleges in India as in the schools?

Arguments:

I. Yes, this will improve the ambience of the colleges as all the students will be decently dressed.

II. No. The college students should not be regimented and they should be left to choose their clothes for coming to the college.

12. **Statement:** Should small states be formed out of bigger states in India?

Arguments:

I. Yes, there will be greater administrative convenience.

II. No, it will jeopardize the national integration.

13. **Statement:** Should new big industries be started in Mumbai?

Arguments:

I. Yes. It will create job opportunities.

II. No. It will further add to the pollution of the city. **[MAT 2004]**

14. **Statement:** Should the private schools be allowed to decide the schools fees depending on the market condition?

Arguments:

I. Yes. This is the only way to make the schools commercially viable.

II. No. This will put additional burden to the masses in the education of children.

15. **Statement:** Should there be only a uniform rate of income tax irre..pective of the level of income?

Arguments:

I. Yes, this will substantially reduce the work of the officials of the income tax department.

II. No, this will reduce government tax collection to a large extent.

16. **Statement:** Should non-vegetarian food be totally banned in our country?

Arguments:

I. Yes. It is expensive and therefore it is beyond the means of most people in our country.

II. No. Nothing should be banned in a democratic country like ours. **[MBA 2002]**

17. **Statement:** Should a less populated country like South - Africa become a permanent member of UN's Security Council?

Arguments:

I. Yes. South - Africa has emerged as a country which loves peace and amity.

II. No. Let us first solve problems of their own people like poverty, apartheid.

18. **Statement:** Should person convicted of criminal offenses in the past be allowed to contest elections in India?

Arguments:

I. No, such person cannot serve the cause of the people and country.

II. Yes, it is democracy -Let people decide whom to vote.

19. Statement: Should income tax be abolished in India?

Arguments:

I. Yes. It is an unnecessary burden on the wage earners.

II. No. It is a good source of revenue.

[Bank PO 2004]

20. Statement: Should all professional colleges in India be encouraged to run their own courses without affiliations to any university?

Arguments:

I. Yes, it is the only way to create more opportunities for those who seek professional training.

II. No, this will dilute the quality of professional training as all such colleges may not be equipped to conduct such courses.

21. Statement: Should there be differential rate of income tax for different income levels?

Arguments:

I. Yes, this is justified and those who earn less will be required to pay less tax in comparison to those who earn more.

II. No, this goes against the basic principle of equality among all the tax payers and the rate of income tax should be same for all those who earn more than the stipulated.

22. Statement: Should all the small savings schemes run by postal department be immediately withdrawn?

Arguments:

I. No, people belonging to lower economic class are more comfortable with postoffices and they canget higher return from their meager savings.

II. Yes, the postal department need not be burdened with additional work and the public sector banks can take up this responsibility.

[Vijaya Bank PO Exam 2004]

23. Statement: Should all those convicted criminals sentenced for life and have spent at least ten years in jail be freed immediately?

Arguments:

I. No, they are hardcore criminals, and they should be made to complete their full term in jail.

II. Yes, they have already been punished enough and now are ready to lead normal life.

[Vijaya Bank PO Exam 2004]

Level 3 Expert

Directions (Qs. 1 to 7): Each of the questions consists of a statement and is followed by two arguments. You have to decide which one is strong and which one is weak. Mark the answer:

(A) If argument I is strong.

(B) If argument II is strong.

(C) If neither I nor II is strong.

(D) If both I and II are strong.

1. Statement: Should the practice of transfers of clerical cadre employees from government offices of one city to those of another be stopped?

Arguments:

I. No. Transfer of employees is a routine administrative matter and we must continue it.

II. Yes. It involves lot of governmental expenditure and inconvenience too many compared to the benefits it yields.

2. Statement: Should India go in for computerization in all possible sectors?

Arguments:

I. Yes. It will bring efficiency and accuracy in the work.

II. Yes. When advanced countries are introducing computers in every field, how can India afford to lag behind?

3. Statement: Should all the elected legislative members be put through compulsory training for running the government? **[TANCET MCA Exam 2005]**

Arguments:

I. Yes, it will certainly be helpful.

II. No, people elect only mature individuals who are able to hold the office.

4. Statement: Should primary education be made free in India? **[TANCET MCA Exam 2005]**

Arguments:

I. Yes, in a welfare state it is duty of the government to impart primary education.

II. No, India does not have adequate number of primary schools to accommodate all.

5. Statement: Should the degree be delinked from job? **[TANCET MCA Exam 2005]**

Arguments:

I. Yes, because such step would discourage the students from joining universities.

II. No, because educators are the backbone of democracy.

6. Statement: Is a coalition government suitable for democracy? **[TANCET MCA Exam 2005]**

Arguments:

I. Yes, because such governments cannot become dictatorial.

II. No, because such governments cannot be stable.

7. Statement: Should rural banks be abolished? **[TANCET MCA Exam 2005]**

Arguments:

I. Yes, because they are not running properly.

II. No, because they will develop villages.

Directions (Qs. 8-12): Each of the questions consists of a statement and is followed by two arguments (I and II). Numbered I and II. You have to decide which of the arguments is a 'strong' argument and which is a 'weak' argument. Mark the answer:

(A) if only argument I is strong.
(B) if only argument II is strong.
(C) if either I or II is strong.
(D) if neither I nor II is strong.
(E) if both I and II are strong.

8. Statement: Should the state governments be allowed to retain major shares of the central taxes collected in the respective states? **[Syndicate Bank PO Exam 2004]**

Arguments:

I. No, the central government should receive the major share as most of the developmental programmes are funded by the central government.

II. Yes, most of the state governments are sort of funded and they badly need more fundings.

9. Statements: Should the in–charge of all the police stations in the country be transferred every two years? **[Syndicate Bank PO Exam 2004]**

Arguments:

I. No, this will create lot of administrative hassles and also will create lot of inconvenience to the police officers.

II. Yes, this is the only way to eradicate the nexus, between police officers and anti-social elements.

10. Statement: Should the major part of school examinations be made objective type?

Arguments:

I. No, objective type examination does not test students ability to express.

II. Yes, this is the best method of assessing one's ability and knowledge.

11. Statement: Should all the private sector banks be immediately merged with the public sector banks? **[Syndicate Bank PO Exam 2004]**

Arguments:

I. No, the private sector banks are profit making entities and hence they should not be merged.

II. Yes, this will be safeguard the hard entered money of the customers and their interested will be secured

12. Statement: Should all the factories in the cities be shifted to the outskirts, far away from the main city? **[Syndicate Bank PO Exam 2004]**

Arguments:

I. Yes, this is an essential Step for controlling pollution in the city.

II. No, such a Step will lead to lot of inconvenience to the employees of the factories and their families as well.

Directions (Qs 13 to 15): Each of the questions consists of a statement and is followed by four arguments (I, II, III and IV). You have to decide which of the given arguments is a 'strong' arguments and which is a 'weak' argument.

13. Statement: Should the rule of wearing helmet for both driver and pillion rider while driving a motor bike be enforced strictly? **[Bank PO 2004]**

Arguments:

I. Yes. It is a rule and rules should be followed strictly by all.

II. No. Each individual knows how to protect his own life and it should be left to his discretion.

III. No, it does not ensure safety as only the head is protected and rest of the body is not.

IV. Yes. It is a necessity as head, being the most sensitive organ, is protected by the helmet.

Mark the answer based on the above arguments:

(A) None is strong.
(B) Only I and III are strong.
(C) Only I and IV are strong.
(D) Only II and IV are strong.
(E) All are strong.

14. Statement: Should all those who are convicted for heinous crimes like murder or rape, beyond all reasonable doubts be given capital punishment or death penalty?

Arguments:

I. No. The death penalty should be given only in very rare and exceptional cases.

II. Yes. This is the only way to punish such people who take others' lives or indulge in inhuman activities.

III. Yes. Such severe punishments only will make people refrain from such heinous acts and the society will be safer.

IV. No. Those who are repentant for the crime they committed should be given a chance to improve and lead a normal life.

Mark the answer based on the above arguments:

(A) Only II and IV are strong.
(B) All are strong.
(C) Only III is strong.
(D) Only II and III are strong.
(E) Only I, II and III are strong.

15. Statement: Should the rule of driving for minors vehicles be enforced strictly?

Arguments:

I. Yes. It is a rule and rules should be followed strictly by all.

II. No. Each individual knows how to protect his own life and it should be left to his discretion.

III. No. It does not ensure safety as many of them can drive properly.

IV. Yes. It is a necessity as young kids do more mistakes in driving which causes accidents .

Mark the answer based on the above arguments:

(A) None is strong.

(B) Only I and III are strong.

(C) Only I and IV are strong.

(D) Only II and IV are strong.

(E) All are strong.

ANSWER KEY

Level-1: Beginner

1.	(A)	2.	(E)	3.	(B)	4.	(B)	5.	(A)	6.	(A)	7.	(E)	8.	(A)	9.	(A)	10.	(B)
11.	(B)	12.	(A)	13.	(A)	14.	(D)	15.	(D)	16.	(E)	17.	(A)	18.	(D)	19.	(B)	20.	(E)
21.	(E)	22.	(A)	23.	(C)	24.	(E)	25.	(D)										

Level-2: Intermediate

1.	(A)	2.	(B)	3.	(B)	4.	(D)	5.	(B)	6.	(D)	7.	(E)	8.	(A)	9.	(B)	10.	(A)
11.	(B)	12.	(E)	13.	(C)	14.	(B)	15.	(B)	16.	(B)	17.	(A)	18.	(A)	19.	(B)	20.	(B)
21.	(C)	22.	(E)	23.	(B)														

Level-3: Expert

1.	(C)	2.	(A)	3.	(A)	4.	(C)	5.	(A)	6.	(A)	7.	(B)	8.	(C)	9.	(A)	10.	(A)
11.	(D)	12.	(A)	13.	(C)	14.	(C)	15.	(C)										

Solutions with Detailed Explanations

Level-1: BEGINNER

1. **Option (A) is correct.**

   Explanation: It must be noted that with mechanisation, the productivity will increase, leading to economic development of the country. While II is vague as mechanization will only eliminate wasteful employment.

2. **Option (E) is correct.**

   Explanation: With some monetary help to the educated unemployed youth, their 'self-employment' venture will come to reality. With unearned money in hand, it will kill their desire to work and hence promote idleness among the unemployed youth. So argument II also holds.

3. **Option (B) is correct.**

   Explanation: The langauge is changed : Labeling a policy as 'undemocratic' due to its beneficial impact on the general populace is unjustified. Were all practicing doctors to be placed under government control, it could effectively suppress any malpractices, if they indeed exist.

4. **Option (B) is correct.**

   Explanation: An increase in the number of High Courts will surely speed up the work and help to do away with the pending cases. So, argument II holds strong. In light of this, the expenditure incurred would be 'utilisation', not wastage of money. So, argument I does not hold.

5. **Option (A) is correct.**

   Explanation: To ensure an overall development of the country, an equitable distribution of foreign investment is mandated. So I is a strong argument. Ruling out foreign investment on the pretext of a few states lacking infrastructure to attract foreign investment works against the overall development of the country. So, II does not hold.

6. **Option (A) is correct.**

   Explanation: Irrespective of the matter at hand, opting for a peaceful resolution through mutual agreement is evidently the preferred choice. So, argument I holds up. Moreover, the problem mentioned in II can be avoided through constant monitoring and vigilance. As a result, II appears to be ambiguous.

7. **Option (E) is correct.**

   Explanation: The notion of offering jobs only to the wards of government employees will only support nepotism. If the government stand to lose in the long run with this practice, then is a strong argument. Equal opportunities is what is guaranteed in a democratic country, so anything that is against the principle of equality is unfeasible. Thus, both arguments hold strong.

8. **Option (A) is correct.**
Explanation: Sex determination reveals the gender of the unborn child. Few families have favouritism for male child, thus leading to indiscriminate female foeticide. II lacks a rationale. So, argument II does not hold strong.

9. **Option (A) is correct.**
Explanation: Clearly, the proposed scheme would discourage people from keeping deposits for longer durations (the rate of interest being the same for short durations) and not draw in more funds. So, only argument I holds.

10. **Option (B) is correct.**
Explanation: Since the price of oil governs the prices of other essential commodities, so this will adversely impact the prices of essential commodities too. This will increase hardships of the commoners. So, only argument II holds, strong.

11. **Option (B) is correct.**
Explanation: The more the number of ministers in the Central Government , the more the expenditure. So, the number of ministers should be restricted. Also, giving liberty to the party in power could promote extension of unreasonable favour to some people at the cost of government funds. So, argument I does not hold.

12. **Option (A) is correct.**
Explanation: An international forum like UN's Security Council, which seeks to bring different nations on friendly terms will definitely be overwhelmed to have India (proclaimed to be a country which loves peace and amity). Hence, statement II diverts from the main argument. As a result, argument II is ambiguous.

13. **Option (A) is correct.**
Explanation: Since armed forces demand a strong person both physically and mentally who can endure hardships, so (I) is s strong argument . On the basis of this, II argument is not strong. Clearly, argument II is vague. So, argument I holds strong. Clearly, argument II is vague.

14. **Option (D) is correct.**
Explanation: It is an advertisement through which a brand can reach its consumers and make them aware of their products and their utility. So I is a strong argument. But it is also true that advertisement a costly affair and the expenses on it add to the price of the product. So, argument II is also valid. So, argument II is also valid.

15. **Option (D) is correct.**
Explanation: Argument I does not give a reason behind the assertion that private sector entities are not equipped to handle such projects. The same principle applies for the second argument also. As a result, argument II fails as well.

16. **Option (E) is correct.**
Explanation: There is truth in the assertion that Goodwill always pays dividend, because with goodwill many important and controversial issues can be solved peacefully with mutual assent. Likewise, an excess of goodwill may be misinterpreted as a vulnerability of the nation, allowing the opposition to gain dominance on every occasion.

17. **Option (A) is correct.**
Explanation: It is true that independent judiciary is necessary for impartial judgement, so that the Executive does not take wrong measures. So, argument I holds clarity. While II argument is vague and without a strong reason.

18. **Option (D) is correct.**
Explanation: Every person must be free to move wherever he wants to go. No compulsion should be made to confine him to one's own country. So, argument I is authoritative without any solid reason. However, talented can be of great benefit to the nation and some alternatives as special incentives or better pay may be made available to them to retain them within their motherland. So, argument II does not hold.

19. **Option (B) is correct.**
Explanation: A fee increase will not make students more serious. As a result, argument I is hazy. However, driving away the meritorious poor students to stay away from post-graduate courses is a grave sin. As a result, argument II is correct.

20. **Option (E) is correct.**
Explanation: The primary benefit of correspondence courses cater to those needy students who pursue studies and earn at the same time. So I is a strong argument. On the other hand, the drawback is that quality education is not possible without teachers and classrooms. So II is also a strong argument.

21. **Option (E) is correct.**
Explanation: While students may have the best understanding of their capabilities, their interests alone cannot compel them to select a course that does not align with their strengths. Furthermore, the absence of institutes cannot deprive students of post-graduate opportunities. Therefore, argument III lacks validity. The primary criterion remains studying pertinent subjects during graduate courses to qualify for post-graduate programs. Argument II presents a valid rationale and therefore stands firm.

22. **Option (A) is correct.**
Explanation: The security of the investor's money is not related to the size of the bank. Besides, even after consolidation, the number of investors their amounts, hence the duties, shall remain the same and so, no employees will be redundant. Reducing the number of smaller banks will also not affect the mutual competition among the banks. Thus, none of the arguments holds strong.

23. **Option (C) is correct.**
Explanation: It is not advisable to tax the income be generated out of agricultural activities, especially

when the income of farmers is not adequate. Agriculture, being the predominant occupation in India, if tax is implemented on the income from it, it would draw in huge funds into the government coffers. On the other hand, certain big farmers earn substantial incomes from agriculture but do not pay tax. So, both arguments II and III hold strong.

24. Option (E) is correct.
Explanation: Both I and II arguments are valid, since they present compelling arguments for why a single tax system would aid in the elimination of multiple taxes on a product. Furthermore, the concept of imitating other countries in the implementation of a certain policy is irrelevant. As a result, argument III fails.

25. Option (D) is correct.
Explanation: Argument I states that India should stop coal mining because the present stock of coal will not last long if the current rate of mining continues. This argument is strong as it raises a valid concern about the depletion of coal resources, which could have significant consequences for energy supply and environmental sustainability.
Argument II opposes the immediate cessation of coal mining, highlighting the lack of a sufficient quantity of alternative energy sources. This argument is also strong because it underscores the practical challenges associated with abruptly stopping coal mining without adequate alternative energy sources in place.
Argument III argues against stopping coal mining, emphasizing the potential adverse effects on millions of people and industries that rely on coal. This argument is strong as it highlights the socio-economic impacts of such a decision, including job losses and disruptions to various sectors.
Overall, arguments II and III present valid reasons both in terms of practical energy considerations and socio-economic impacts, supporting the conclusion that India should not immediately stop digging coal from its mines.

Level-2: INTERMEDIATE

1. Option (A) is correct.
Explanation: The adoption of such a policy will definitely help to regulate the population growth, which in turn facilitate proper growth of the economy. So I is a strong argument. While comparing this policy to that of the policy of any other country in the world is baseless. So, argument II does not hold.

2. Option (B) is correct.
Explanation: Deploying military force isn't solely about aggression; rather, it serves to safeguard the nation from both internal and external threats. So both the arguments do not hold strong.

3. Option (B) is correct.
Explanation: Monopolization of the transport system will eliminate all competition in the field, which may result in high fares and poor services. This will worsen the problems of the commuters. In fact, the commuter should be given a wider choice of transport system. So only II argument is strong.

4. Option (D) is correct.
Explanation: India has its own nationalised banks to handle the financial activity. As a result, argument I is vague. Furthermore, Indian banks can compete successfully with foreign banks by providing better facilities and services to their customers. As a result, argument II fails as well. So, none of the arguments hold up.

5. Option (B) is correct.
Explanation: Instead of expanding medical colleges, prioritize improving the quality of education in existing ones, especially considering the inadequate infrastructure. Thus, only argument II holds weight, while argument I does not.

6. Option (D) is correct.
Explanation: The claim that the reform process borrowed from western countries will adversely affect our economy is absurd and baseless. Any economic reform process, whenever implemented will benefit the development of the country. So I is also weak as an argument. As a result, neither argument I nor II are valid.

7. Option (E) is correct.
Explanation: Professional occupations require quality and merit, and students with the necessary talent may turn out to be better professionals than those who enrol on a subsidy. As a result, argument I holds up. Supporting the economically backward classes for their overall growth and development is one of the tenets of our Constitution. So, argument II also holds.

8. Option (A) is correct.
Explanation: Foreign investment in only few states imply concentration of wealth and progress there, thus depriving other states of the provision. This leads to inequitable economic distribution which is against the policy of overall development of the country. Also, no backward state ought to be neglected. So, argument II is invalid.

9. Option (B) is correct.
Explanation: Since luxury hotels are a place for staying for the affluent foreign tourists, it will devoid the country of this trademark. Drawing a correlation between the prohibition of luxury hotels and their association with international criminals is unfounded and lacks merit.

10. Option (A) is correct.
Explanation: Any problem needs to be approached through a mutual talk, so a dialogue with neighbouring countries to stop cross border tension is the first option instead of engaging in violence. This will also amount to saving the loss of innocent lives. Subversive activities of a nation can be curbed through constant check and vigilance. So, argument II seems to be vague.

11. Option (B) is correct.
Explanation: Imposing a dress code on college students restricts their freedom in college, following the regimentation experienced during their school years.

College is where students develop a sense of responsibility, making argument II compelling. Additionally, the college environment is shaped by students' dedication and behavior, not their attire, rendering argument I ambiguous.

12. **Option (E) is correct.**
Explanation: Forming small states out of bigger states in India, will smoothen the administrative process. But, on the other hand, the national integration will be bothered. So both I and II are strong.

13. **Option (C) is correct.**
Explanation: Opening up of new industry is advantageous in opening more employment avenues, and disadvantageous in that it adds to the pollution. So, either of the arguments holds strong.

14. **Option (B) is correct.**
Explanation: Education is a backbone of a country and it's fee must be in limits . As such, the interest of the common people must be taken care of, rather than the profitability of some schools. So, only argument II holds strong.

15. **Option (B) is correct.**
Explanation: Reduction of work load of IT officials cannot be the driving force behind the uniform rate of income tax irrespective of the level of income. A low-income bracketed person cannot be taxed at par with a high-income bracketed person. So I is weak. II is strong because with reduced government tax collection, the citizens will suffer.

16. **Option (B) is correct.**
Explanation: It is seen that restriction on the diet of people will be denying them their basic human right. So, only argument II holds.

17. **Option (A) is correct.**
Explanation: A peace-loving country like South-Africa might easily join a worldwide forum aimed at bringing different nations on amicable terms with one another. So, argument I is still valid. Argument II focuses on a different aspect. The domestic challenges should not prevent it from building international ties. So, argument II is vague.

18. **Option (A) is correct.**
Explanation: Any person having criminal background cannot be eligible to serve a nation as he will set a bad example to the countrymen. So argument I is strong. While argument II is vague, as in a democracy, any random opinion is not acceptable in the name of democracy.

19. **Option (B) is correct.**
Explanation: Income tax is levied as it is a source of revenue for the government. Since, this is the earning of the government, it is the duty of the citizens to pay tax so that the former can ensure the country can function and have the needed infrastructure. So, only argument II holds strong.

20. **Option (B) is correct.**
Explanation: The emphasis on the word 'only ' makes I a void argument. Since colleges work on the directives issued by a university, so the colleges might find it difficult to attain uniformity. This will dilute the quality of professional training. So, only argument II is strong.

21. **Option (C) is correct.**
Explanation: The correct answer is: if either I or II is strong.
Argument I advocates for a differential rate of income tax based on income levels, justifying that those with lower incomes should pay less tax compared to those with higher incomes. This argument is strong as it aligns with the principle of progressive taxation, where individuals contribute to the tax system according to their ability to pay.
Argument II opposes the idea of a differential rate of income tax, arguing that it violates the principle of equality among taxpayers, suggesting that the tax rate should be the same for all individuals earning above the stipulated threshold. This argument is also strong as it emphasizes the importance of treating all taxpayers equally under the law.
Both arguments present valid perspectives on the issue of differential income tax rates, with Argument I emphasizing fairness and social justice, while Argument II stresses equality and uniformity in taxation. Hence, the correct answer is if either I or II is strong.

22. **Option (E) is correct.**
Explanation: Since postoffices are readily accessible in small towns and villages; additionally, they also offer low interest rate. Hence, they definitely benefit low-income group. It is to be noted that there are many small savings schemes being offered by other banks too; so this scheme acts as an additional work for postoffices. Thus, both I and II are strong.

23. **Option (B) is correct.**
Explanation: Yes, the criminals have already been punished and now they should be made to lead a normal life. So, argument II is strong.

Level-3: EXPERT

1. **Option (C) is correct.**
Explanation: It is absurd to conclude that any convention that has been followed since years, must be followed. So, argument I is not strong. Just because a process entails governmental expenditure and inconvenience does not call for its termination. The transfer of cadres is done to do away with corruption. So, argument II also does not hold.

2. **Option (A) is correct.**
Explanation: Computers are speed- efficient and more accurate. So, argument I holds, while II does not. This is because a development in one country might not be the priority for another country.

3. **Option (A) is correct.**
Explanation: Putting the elected legislative members on compulsory training will be helpful. So, only argument I is strong.

4. **Option (C) is correct.**
Explanation: Argument I does not answer the question - if primary education be made free in India. Same goes for II. So neither is correct.

5. **Option (A) is correct.**

Explanation: If the degree is delinked from job, then students will get discouraged to join colleges because jobs are connected to degrees and if degree be delinked from job, boys will not join colleges. Only I is strong.

6. **Option (A) is correct.**

Explanation: A coalition government is more democratic than one-party governments as it eliminates the fear of dictatorship. II lacks a valid reason, so it is weak. Only I is strong.

7. **Option (B) is correct.**

Explanation: Rural banks are involved in the development of the villages. So, argument II is strong.

8. **Option (C) is correct.**

Explanation: It is true that , the Central Government should receive the major share because most of the development programmers are funded by Central Government and whenever the situation arises when State Governments are short of funds the Central Government comes to the rescue. So both I and II are true.

9. **Option (A) is correct.**

Explanation: If all the police officers are transferred after every two years, then it will create a lot of administrative hassles and it will also create lot of inconvenience to the police officers. The emphasis on 'only' eliminates II as a strong argument.

10. **Option (A) is correct.**

Explanation: The main purpose of examination is to assess quality and merit of a candidate. If objective type examination does not test students ability to express, then it is a strong argument. Argument II lacks justification.

11. **Option (D) is correct.**

Explanation: Neither of the arguments offers a valid point or logic to prove the statement correct.

12. **Option (A) is correct.**

Explanation: In terms of controlling pollution in the city, I is a strong argument supporting the concept that factories in the cities be shifted to the outskirts. Argument II lacks a logic.

13. **Option (C) is correct.**

Explanation: If the rule ensures the safety of two-wheeler riders, so if it fails to deliver this purpose and does not ensure safety as only the head is protected and rest of the body , then I and IV are strong arguments. Besides, it is the basic duty of the Government to look after the safety of the citizens and it ought not leave it to the discretion of the individuals.

14. **Option (C) is correct.**

Explanation: Persons convicted for heinous crimes like murder or rape need the harshest of punishment so that their crimes do not set examples to other criminals. Argument I is vague while the use of the word 'only' in argument II makes it weak. It is difficult to gauge whether the repentance is fake or actual. So Argument IV is not strong. Only III is a strong argument.

15. **Option (C) is correct.**

Explanation: The rule was designed to reduce the accidents, as the majority of accidents result due to carelessness of drivers, resulting in injuries and, eventually, death. And the goal of a regulation cannot be met unless it is obeyed by everybody, which necessitated severe enforcement. As a result, is arguments I and IV are strong, while arguments III is not. Furthermore, it is the fundamental responsibility of the government to ensure citizens' safety, and it should not be left to individuals' discretion. As a result, argument II fails.

■ ■ ■

Chapter 3

Statements and Assumptions

LEARNING OBJECTIVES:

- ❖ Identify the correct and incorrect assumptions.
- ❖ To understand the Concepts of Statement and Assumptions

Statements and assumptions are critical components used to analyse arguments or draw conclusions based on information provided. Let us define each one:

Statement: A proposition or a claim that offers a fact, idea, or opinion is referred to as a statement. It serves as the foundation for an argument or conversation. In verbal reasoning, one is frequently given a group of sentences to analyse in order to find their logical implications or relationships.

Consider the following statement: "All mammals are warm-blooded animals." This statement asserts a general fact regarding mammals, namely that all mammals are warm-blooded.

Assumption: An assumption is a fundamental premise or inference that underpins an argument or conclusion. It is a statement that is taken for granted or assumed to be true in the absence of explicit evidence. Assumptions are frequently unsaid or implicit, and identifying them requires thorough examination.

One may be given a collection of statements and asked to evaluate the assumptions associated with those statements via verbal reasoning. The idea is to determine which assumptions must be true for the statements to be valid or logical.

IDENTIFYING THE CORRECT AND INCORRECT ASSUMPTIONS:

➢ Identifying correct or incorrect assumptions in statement and assumption questions needs thorough examination and logical reasoning. Here are few things we can do to assist ourselves in this process:

- **Understand the following statements:** Read the statements carefully and make sure one understands what they imply. Take note of any relevant terms, linkages, or links between the assertions.
- **Identify unstated information:** Look for missing or implied information that is not expressly expressed in the assertions. Assumptions frequently include filling in these gaps or drawing logical conclusions based on the information provided.
- **Compare statements with real-world knowledge:** Assess the assertions using your general knowledge or common sense. Consider whether the assertions correspond to your understanding of the subject or whether they contradict well established facts.
- **Evaluate the logical connection:** Examine the assertions' relationships and identify what assumptions are required for them to be logically valid. Consider what further facts or beliefs are required for the claims to be true.
- **Look for unsupported claims:** Identify any claim in the statements that lack proof or justification. Assumptions frequently include accepting the reality of these unproven claims.
- **Test the assumption:** Once an individual found potential assumptions, assess them all separately. Consider whether the assumption is required for the claims to be true. If removing or negating an assumption weakens or invalidates the statements, it is most likely correct.
- **Consider alternative assumption:** Consider other assumptions that could be made and how they would affect the assertions. If a different assumption invalidates the assertions or contradicts the presented facts, it implies that the initial assumption was right.
- **Use elimination strategies:** If you are given several possibilities for assumptions, you can utilise elimination procedures to rule out wrong ones. Look for options that are irrelevant, contradict the claims, or offer additional information that is not supported by the given statements.

Directions: Each question below has a statement followed by two assumptions labelled I and II. Consider the statement and determine which of the above assumptions is implicit.

(a) If only assumption I is implicit.
(b) If only assumption II is implicit.

(c) If either I or II is implicit.
(d) If neither I nor II is implicit.
(e) If both I and II are implicit.

Example 1: Railway officials have started many new trains for general category people and introduced non-AC coaches in the existing ones.

Assumption:

I. Overcrowding in trains is a common problem faced by commuters, especially the general category people.

II. Low-income passengers face long waitlisted ticket periods.

Sol. (e) Such decisions are always made with the public's needs and the department's financial soundness in mind. As a result, both I and II are implied.

Example 2: Detergents should be used to clean clothes.

Assumption:

I. Detergents form lather.

II. Detergents contain enzymes that break up stains so they can be washed away.

Sol. (b) There is no mention of the detergent producing lather. As a result, argument I is not implied. Furthermore, the sentence states that detergent will fix difficulties. As a result, argument II is implied.

Level 1 Beginner

Directions (Qs. 1 to 25): Each of the following questions begins with a statement and is followed by two assumptions. Determine which of the given assumption is valid and which is erroneous.

(A) If only assumption I is implicit.
(B) If only assumption II is implicit.
(C) If either I or II is implicit.
(D) If neither I nor II is implicit.
(E) If both I and II are implicit.

1. **Statement:** The government has decided to pay compensation to the tune of ₹1 lakh to the family members of those who are killed in railway accidents.

   Assumption:

   I. The government has enough funds to meet the expenses due to compensation.

   II. There may be reduction in incidents of railway accidents in near future. **[Bank PO]**

2. **Statement:** "I have not received telephone bills for nine months in spite of several complaints" telephone customer's letter to the editor of a daily.

   Assumption:

   I. Every customer has a right to get bills regularly from the telephone company.

   II. The customer's complaints point to defect in the services which is expected to be corrected. **[Bank PO]**

3. **Statement:** The management of XYZ Pvt. Ltd. asked the union of the workers to call off strike immediately otherwise the management would be forced to close down the factory.

   Assumption:

   I. No alternative other than closing down the factory is left for the management of XYZ Pvt. Ltd.

   II. Such threat may have some effect on the workers' union. **[Bank PO]**

4. **Statement:** Nobody can predict as to how long our country would take to contain the unfortunate and disastrous terrorist activities.

   Assumption:

   I. It is impossible to put an end to terrorist activities.

   II. Efforts to control the terrorist activities are on. **[SBI PO]**

5. **Statement:** His recent investment in the shares of Company A is only a gamble.

   Assumption:

   I. He may incur loss on his investment.

   II. He may gain from his investment. **[RBI]**

6. **Statement:** Provide mid-day meals to the children in primary schools to increase the number of students attending schools.

   Assumption:

   I. Mid-day meals will attract the children to the schools.

   II. Those children who are otherwise deprived of good food will attend the schools. **[SIDBI]**

7. **Statement:** "Private property, trespassers will be prosecuted" – A notice on a plot of land.

   Assumption:

   I. The passerby may read the notice and may not trespass.

   II. The people are scared of prosecution. **[SBI PO]**

8. **Statement:** If he is intelligent, he will pass the examination.

   Assumption:

   I. To pass, he must be intelligent.

   II. He will pass the examination. **[SSC]**

9. **Statement:** Kartik left for Delhi on Tuesday by train to attend a function to be held on Friday at his uncle's house in Delhi.

   Assumption:

   I. Kartik may reach Delhi on Wednesday.

   II. Kartik may reach Delhi before Friday. **[Bank PO]**

10. **Statement:** The civic authority has advised the residents in the area to use mosquito repellents or sleep inside nets as large number of people are suffering from malaria.

    Assumption:

I. Local residents have enough money to arrange for the repellents or nets.

II. People may ignore and continue to get mosquito bites as they have other pressing needs. **[Bank PO]**

11. Statement: The 'M' Cooperative Housing Society has put up a notice at its gate that sales persons are not allowed inside the society.

Assumption:

I. All the sales persons will stay away from the 'M' Cooperative Housing Society.

II. The security guard posted at the gate may be able to stop the sales persons entering the society. **[Bank PO]**

12. Statement: "To keep myself up to date, I always listen to 9:00 p.m. news on radio." A candidate tells the interview board.

Assumption:

I. The candidate does not read newspaper.

II. Recent news is broadcasted only on radio. **[RRB]**

13. Statement: There has been a remarkable increase in the air traffic in India during the past few years.

Assumption:

I. Travelling by air has become a status symbol now.

II. Large number of people are able to afford air travel now. **[RBI]**

14. Statement: A renowned coaching institute has decided to make batches of 40 students instead of 25 students in each classroom the next academic session to bridge the gap between the income and the expenditure to a large extent.

Assumption:

I. The income generated by way of fees of the additional students will be sufficient enough to bridge the gap.

II. The institute will get all the additional students in each class from the next academic session. **[Bank PO]**

15. Statement: The head of the organisation congratulated the entire staff in his speech for their sincere effort to bring down the deficit and urged them to give their best for attaining a more profitable position in future.

Assumption:

I. The employees may get motivated and maintain and if possible enhance their present level of work.

II. The employees may now relax and slowdown in their day to day work as there is no immediate threat of huge deficit. **[SBI PO]**

16. Statement: Please send an official letter rather than semiofficial on this subject this time.

Assumption:

I. The format and emphasis of different type of letter is different.

II. We can send different type of letter on the same subject. **[Central Bank of India PO]**

17. Statement: Please check the availability of two tickets from Delhi to Lucknow.

Assumption:

I. The person checking knows the desired mode of travel.

II. The person checking knows the details of the person travelling. **[Central Bank of India PO]**

18. Statement: If you want to increase your writing speeds use 0.7 pen.

Assumption:

I. These are different types of pen available.

II. The person being told understands what is 0.7 pen. **[Central Bank of India PO]**

19. Statement: Bank should always check financial status before lending money to a client.

Assumption:

I. Checking before lending would give a true picture of the client financial status.

II. Client sometimes may not present the correct picture of their ability to repay loan amount to the bank. **[Syndicate Bank PO]**

20. Statement: The government has decided to run all commercial vehicles on bio-fuels in order to save the depleting fossil fuel reserves.

Assumption:

I. It is possible to switch over from fossil fuels to bio-fuels for vehicles.

II. Sufficient amount of bio-fuels can be produced in the country to run all commercial vehicles. **[Syndicate Bank PO]**

21. Statement: In order to build more space, extra FSI needs to be brought.

Assumption:

I. The person being told does not know the meaning of FSI.

II. More space will reduce the construction cost. **[Central Bank of India]**

22. Statement: Give adequate job-related training to the employees before assigning them full-fledged work.

Assumption:

I. Training helps in boosting the performance of employees.

II. Employees have no skill sets before training is provided to them. **[Syndicate Bank PO]**

23. Statement: Let there be a Signboard also indicating the directions and instruction.

Assumption:

I. Signboard can be prepared without using any language.

II. Signboard is the only effective tool to indicate directions. **[Central Bank of India PO]**

24. Statement: Gambling through lotteries is banned by the Central Government in all the states with immediate effect.

Assumption:

I. This may save innocent citizens from getting cheated of their hard-earned money.

II. The citizens may not gamble in any other way if the lotteries are banned. **[Indian Overseas Bank PO]**

25. **Statement:** The school authority has decided to increase the number of students in each classroom to seventy from the next academic session to bridge the gap between income and expenditure to largest extent.

Assumption:

I. The income generated by way of fees of the additional students will be sufficient enough to bridge the gap.

II. The school will get all the additional students in each class from the next academic session.

[Canara Bank PO]

2 Level Intermediate

Directions (Qs. 1 to 22): Each of the following questions begins with a statement and is followed by two assumptions. Determine which of the given assumption is valid and which is erroneous.

(A) If only assumption I is implicit.
(B) If only assumption II is implicit.
(C) If either I or II is implicit.
(D) If neither I nor II is implicit.
(E) If both I and II are implicit.

1. **Statement:** It is faster to travel by air to Delhi from Bengaluru.

Assumption:

I. Bengaluru and Delhi are connected by air.

II. There are no other means of transport available to Delhi from Bengaluru. **[SSC 2002]**

2. **Statement:** Bank 'A' has announced reduction of half percentage on the interest rate on retail lending with immediate effect.

Assumption:

I. Other banks may also reduce the retail lending rates to be in competition.

II. Bank 'A' may be able to attract more customers for availing retail loans. **[Bank PO 2003]**

3. **Statement:** Who rises from the prayer a better man, his prayer is answered.

Assumption:

I. Prayers make man more human.

II. Prayer atones all of our misdeeds. **[MAT 2005]**

4. **Statement:** "Use of cell phone and pager not allowed inside the auditorium. Please switch off such devices while you are inside the auditorium" — A notice.

Assumption:

I. All those who have such devices will switch them off before they take their seat in the auditorium.

II. Generally, people do not bring such devices when they come to attend functions in the auditorium. **[Bank PO 2004]**

5. **Statement:** The government has made an appeal to all the citizens to honestly pay income tax and file returns reflecting the true income level to help the government to carry out developmental activities.

Assumption:

I. People may now start paying more taxes in response to the appeal.

II. The total income tax may considerably increase in the near future. **[Bank PO 2005]**

6. **Statement:** Railway officials have started ten new trains and increased the frequency of fourteen running trains.

Assumption:

I. The existing trains are not sufficient to provide accommodation to all passengers.

II. The new and additional trains would have sufficient passenger so that they will be economically viable. **[IBPS 2002]**

7. **Statement:** Why don't you go to the court if the employer does not pay you the Provident Fund contribution?

Assumption:

I. Courts can intervene in matters of dispute between employer and employees.

II. It is obligatory for the employer to pay the Provident Fund contribution to the employees.

[Bank PO 2003]

8. **Statement:** Unable to manage with the present salary, Tarun joined another company.

Assumption:

I. The new company has better work environment and offers higher salary to the all its employees.

II. The present company offers moderate pay packet.

9. **Statement:** The company has recently announced series of incentives to the employees who are punctual and sincere.

Assumption:

I. Those who are not punctual at present many get motivated by the announcement.

II. The productivity of the company may increase.

10. **Statement:** The principal instructed all the teachers to be careful in class because some students may disturb others student.

Assumption:

I. The teachers will handle the situation properly and they will point out the naughty students.

II. The student will welcome the decision of the principal. **[SBI PO 2002]**

11. **Statement:** An advertisement by Easy Airline, a private airliner: 'Travel to Meerut by our air line and get a chance to win an all-expenses paid holiday to Bangkok'.

Assumption:

I. Easy air flights are available for Bangkok.

II. The city of Meerut has an airport.

[RBI Grade B Exam 2011]

12. Statement: The government has decided to disinvest large chunk of its equity in select public sector undertakings for a better fiscal man.

Assumption:

I. The amount generated out of the disinvestment process may reduce substantially the mounting fiscal deficits.

II. There will be enough demand in the market for the shares of these undertakings. **[RBI 2004]**

13. Statement: Raman will pass the SSC exam, if he is talented.

Assumption:

I. To pass the SSC exam, he must be talented.

II. Raman will qualify the SSC examination.

14. Statement: Apart from the entertainment value of television, its educational value cannot be ignored.

Assumption:

I. People take television to be a means of entertainment only.

II. The educational value of television is not realised properly. **[MAT 2004]**

15. Statement: Pawan started his journey on Tuesday from his town to attend a marriage party of his friend in Mumbai by train which will be held on Friday.

Assumption:

I. Pawan may reach Mumbai on Wednesday.

II. Pawan may reach Mumbai before Friday.

16. Statement: Considering the substantial number of dengue cases in the area, medical authorities have urged the locals to sleep under nets or apply Mosquito repellents.

Assumption:

I. For buying the repellents and nets, the local residents are capable enough.

II. Local residents may ignore and continue to get mosquito bites as they have other pressing needs.

17. Statement: The district administration has issued a circular to all the farmers under its jurisdiction advising them for not using pesticides indiscriminately as it may pollute the ground water.

Assumption:

I. People may stop using ground water if the farmers continue to use pesticides indiscriminately.

II. Farmers may refrain from using pesticides indiscriminately. **[RBI 2004]**

18. Statement: An advertisement for Bank X: 'Want to open a bank account? Just dial our home service, and we will come to your doorstep.'

Assumption:

I. People may choose Bank X for their financial transaction.

II. Now a days banking has become very competitive.

19. Statement: The government has decided to levy 2 per cent on the tax amount payable for funding drought and relief programmers.

Assumption:

I. The government has not sufficient money to fund drought relief programmes.

II. The amount collected by way of surcharge may be adequate to fund drought relief.

[Bank PO 2003]

20. Statement: The Product X that you have asked for is not with us but can be made available against firm order from you.

Assumption:

I. The product X is not in great demand.

II. Product X is out of stock as new model is coming up. **[MBA 2002]**

21. Statement: An announcement passengers own interest are advised to fasten their seat belts while seated in the trolley of the ropeway.

Assumption:

I. People are always careful about own safety.

II. Unless advised, passengers might not use the seat belt. **[RBI 2003]**

22. Statement: The government has decided its subsidy on LPG, however the subsidy on kerosene remains unchanged.

Assumption:

I. Those people who buy LPG can afford to purchase it for a higher price.

II. Many people may stop buying LPG and instead use kerosene. **[RBI 2004]**

23. Statement: The General Administration Department has issued a circular to all the employees informing them that henceforth the employees can avail their lunch break at any of the half-hour slots between 1.00 p.m. and 2.30 p.m.

Assumption:

I. The employees may welcome the decision and avail lunch break at different time slots.

II. There may not be any break in the work of the organisation as the employees will have their lunch break at different time slots.

[Bank PO 2005]

Level 3 Expert

Directions (Qs. 1 to 6): Each of the following questions begins with a statement and is followed by two assumptions. Determine which of the given assumption is valid and which is erroneous.

(A) Only II is implicit
(B) Only I is implicit
(C) Only I and II are implicit
(D) None of these
(E) Only I and III are implicit

1. **Statement:** In advertisement, Riya used cold cream for fair complexation.

Assumption:

I. People like to use cold cream for fair complexion.

II. People are easily fooled.

III. People respond to advertisements.

[Indian Bank Exam 2020]

2. **Statement:** "Slogans against smoking in office should be put on the notice board" – an employee in an office suggests.

Assumption:

I. The employee felt that his suggestion will be considered.

II. People smoke in the office.

III. Some people will stop smoking after reading the slogans.

3. **Statement:** Television X, the neighbour's envy, the owner's pride – a TV advertisement.

Assumption:

I. Catchy slogans appeal to people.

II. People are envious of their neighbours' superior possessions.

III. People want to be envied by their neighbours.

4. **Statement:** "We have the distinction of being the only company in India as well as the second in the world to have won an ISO:9002 certification in our line of business" – Statement of Company X's Chairman.

Assumption:

I. There were not many companies in the line of business of Company X.

II. Getting ISO:9002 in the line of business of Company X is not easy.

III. The Company X desires to expand its business.

[SBI PO 2000]

(A) Only I is implicit

(B) Only II is implicit

(C) Only III is implicit

(D) Only II and III are implicit

(E) None of these

5. **Statement:** Unable to manage with the present salary, Arron has decided to join another company.

Assumption:

I. The new company has better work environment.

II. The present company offers moderate pay packets.

III. The new company offers higher salary to all its employees. **[MBA 2002]**

(A) Only I is implicit

(B) Only II is implicit

(C) Only III is implicit

(D) Only II and III are implicit

(E) None of these

6. **Statement:** The X passenger car manufacturing company announced a sharp reduction in the prices of its luxury cars.

Assumption:

I. There may be an increase in the sale of luxury cars of Company X.

II. The other such car manufacturers may also reduce their prices.

III. The competitor companies may not reduce their prices.

(A) Only I is implicit

(B) Only II is implicit

(C) Only III is implicit

(D) Only II and III are implicit

(E) None of these

Directions (Qs. 7 to 14): Each of the following questions begins with a statement and is followed by two assumptions. Determine which of the given assumptions is valid and which is erroneous.

(A) If only assumption I is implicit.

(B) If only assumption II is implicit.

(C) If either I or II is implicit.

(D) If neither I nor II is implicit.

(E) If both I and II are implicit.

7. **Statement:** 'Due to inadequate rainfall this year, the harvest obtained by farmers of village C is less than expected. As a result, this year we will be buying the crop from village Z as it is more convenient and cheaper for us to buy the crop from the farmers of one village rather than buying it from the farmers of different villages – statement by a distributor.

Assumption:

I. At least some farmers in village Z produce the same crop as farmers in village C.

II. The harvest in village Z was much more than expected. **[Andhra Bank PO Exam, 2015]**

8. **Statement:** Only good singers are invited for the conference. No one without sweet voice is a good singer.

Assumption:

I. All invited singers in the conference have sweet voice.

II. Those singers who do not have sweet voice are not invited in the conference.

[SSC CGL Tier 1 Exam, 2016]

9. **Statement:** Using calculator for simpler calculations adversely affects the mathematical abilities of children.

Assumption:

I. Using calculator complex calculations may not affect mathematical abilities.

II. Complex calculation may not be done manually without the help of a calculation.

[RBI Grade B Exam 2011]

10. **Statement:** For underwater battles only weaponry X should be used.

Assumption:

I. Not all weaponry can function well under water battles.

II. There are different kinds of weapoary available for battles on ground and under water.

[RBI Grade B Exam 2011]

11. Statement: As the prices of petrol and diesel shoot up more and more people are resorting to the use of electric cars.

Assumption:

I. Using electricity for powering cars is less expensive than using petrol or diesel.

II. Many people cannot afford the raised prices of petrol and diesel.

12. Statement: Book your railway tickets at least three months in advance to ensure a confirmed reservation.

Assumption:

I. No booking is taken by the railways before three months from the date of journey.

II. Air tickets need to be booked as much in advance as train tickets. **[RBI Grade B Exam 2011]**

13. Statement: The government has decided to earmark separate lane in the metropolis for passenger vehicle with more than one occupant.

Assumption:

I. The move may help decongest the roads of the metropolis.

II. Many people may resort to car pool system to avoid traffic snarls. **[SBI PO Exam 2010]**

14. Statement: The railway authority has announced that it will carry out major repair work for two days beginning Saturday on the main line connecting the two big cities in the state bringing the rail service to a halt.

Assumption:

I. People may reschedule their journey in view of the railway authority's decision.

II. People may still plan their travel by train between the two cities even on these two days.

[SBI (PO) Exam, 2011]

15. Statement: The US President has down sized his country's nuclear arsenal, helped to negotiate a deal to halt Iran's nuclear-weapons programmed and led a global initiative to secure radioactive materials. But his legacy on nuclear issues remains uncertain, as the progress in securing nuclear materials has been slow. Which of the following is an assumption of the speaker?

Assumption:

(A) There could be a break in the President's initiative at securing radioactive materials.

(B) One's lasting fame depends on the velocity with which one's initiatives are carried out.

(C) The deteriorating progress will eventually lead to the failure of the initiative.

(D) The US can never convince a country to give up its nuclear initiatives.

(E) None of the above **[IBPS PO Mains, 2018]**

ANSWER KEY

Level-1: Beginner

1.	(A)	2.	(E)	3.	(B)	4.	(B)	5.	(C)	6.	(A)	7.	(E)	8.	(A)	9.	(B)	10.	(A)
11.	(E)	12.	(D)	13.	(B)	14.	(A)	15.	(A)	16.	(E)	17.	(A)	18.	(E)	19.	(A)	20.	(A)
21.	(D)	22.	(A)	23.	(D)	24.	(A)	25.	(E)										

Level-2: Intermediate

1.	(A)	2.	(B)	3.	(D)	4.	(A)	5.	(E)	6.	(E)	7.	(E)	8.	(B)	9.	(E)	10.	(E)
11.	(E)	12.	(A)	13.	(A)	14.	(E)	15.	(B)	16.	(A)	17.	(B)	18.	(E)	19.	(E)	20.	(A)
21.	(E)	22.	(B)	23.	(B)														

Level-3: Expert

1.	(E)	2.	(E)	3.	(E)	4.	(D)	5.	(B)	6.	(A)	7.	(A)	8.	(E)	9.	(D)	10.	(E)
11.	(A)	12.	(D)	13.	(E)	14.	(A)	15.	(B)										

Solutions with Detailed Explanations

Level-1: BEGINNER

1. Option (A) is correct.

Explanation: Since government has decided to pay compensation to the tune of lakh to the family members of the victim, it is obvious that the government has enough funds to meet the expenses due to compensation. But, it is difficult to infer is this move will affect the reduction in incidents of railway accidents in near future. So, (I) is implicit and (II) is not.

2. Option (E) is correct.

Explanation: The insistence of the customer on getting the bills and bringing it to the notice in the public forum (editorial section of newspaper) makes it evident that every customer has a right to get bills regularly from the telephone company. An editorial section draws attention to negligence or complaints. Thus, both argument I and II are implicit.

3. **Option (B) is correct.**
Explanation: Argument I is an extreme option; while argument II is evident in the warning of the management of XYZ Pvt. Ltd. Moreover, a warning is usually given to the workers to threaten them about losing their jobs.

4. **Option (B) is correct.**
Explanation: The assertion that our country is taking time to contain the unfortunate and disastrous terrorist activities underlines that efforts to control the terrorist activities are on. While I is an extreme assumption, without logicality. So, only assumption II is implicit.

5. **Option (C) is correct.**
Explanation: The statement categorizes the recent investment in shares of Company A as a gamble, implying inherent uncertainty. Assumption I, the possibility of incurring a loss, is implicit as it aligns with the notion of risk associated with gambling. Likewise, Assumption II, the potential for gaining from the investment, is also implicit, acknowledging the inherent dual nature of gambling, which involves both risks and rewards. Since the statement characterizes the investment as a gamble, it implies the likelihood of both positive and negative outcomes, making it reasonable to infer either possibility. Therefore, the correct answer is "If either I or II is implicit."

6. **Option (A) is correct.**
Explanation: Attracting the children in primary schools by offering mid-day meals to increase the number of students attending schools, evince that Mid-day meals will attract the children to the schools. Assumption II is a narrow option owing to the use of 'good food'.

7. **Option (E) is correct.**
Explanation: A notice is given with the intent of people reading them and abiding by the contents. So, argument I is implicit. The message that trespassers will be prosecuted convey that people are scared of prosecution. So both I and II are implicit.

8. **Option (A) is correct.**
Explanation: The statement mentions that he will pass if he is intelligent. So, argument I is implicit. It cannot be ascertained from the statement that he will pass the examination. So only I is implicit.

9. **Option (B) is correct.**
Explanation: Clearly, it is impossible to predict when Kartik will arrive in Delhi. Kartik, on the other hand, has departed for Delhi to attend an event on Friday. As a result, he must have scheduled his journey to arrive in Delhi before Friday.

10. **Option (A) is correct.**
Explanation: The suggestion to use mosquito repellents or nets implies that people can afford to buy the same. So, I is implicit. In fact, people may not ignore the advice as the problem of malaria is serious; henceforth, they will comply with. So, argument II is not implicit.

11. **Option (E) is correct.**
Explanation: The purpose of any notice is to attract attention and enforce compliance. Therefore, the notice prohibiting salespersons from entering the society suggests that they are expected to adhere to it. Consequently, the presence of a security guard stationed at the gate implies that they may indeed prevent salespersons from entering the society premises. Both assumptions I and II are implicit in this scenario, indicating that the notice is expected to be followed by the salespersons and that the security guard is capable of enforcing it.

12. **Option (D) is correct.**
Explanation: The statement made by the candidate, expressing their habit of listening to the 9:00 p.m. news on the radio to stay updated, does not inherently imply either assumption I or II. Assumption I, regarding the candidate not reading newspapers, is not implicit because the candidate's preference for radio news does not necessarily preclude their engagement with other sources of information such as newspapers. Assumption II, suggesting that recent news is exclusively broadcast on radio, is also not implicit as it oversimplifies the sources of news available to individuals. In the absence of evidence supporting either assumption, the correct answer is "If neither I nor II is implicit," indicating that the statement does not inherently imply either assumption.

13. **Option (B) is correct.**
Explanation: The increase in the air traffic in India evince that huge numbers of peoples are travelling by air and are able to afford air travel now. So, only argument II implicits.

14. **Option (A) is correct.**
Explanation: The correct answer, "If only assumption I is implicit," is justified because the statement primarily focuses on the decision of a renowned coaching institute to increase the size of its classroom batches from 25 to 40 students as a strategy to bridge the gap between income and expenditure. Assumption I, which suggests that the income generated from the additional students' fees will be adequate to bridge this financial gap, aligns directly with the institute's decision to expand class sizes. However, assumption II, regarding the certainty of enrolling all additional students in each class from the next academic session, is not explicitly addressed in the statement. The statement does not provide assurance or evidence that the institute will indeed attract all the additional students as assumed in assumption II. Therefore, only assumption I is implicit as it directly supports the rationale behind the institute's decision to increase class sizes.

15. **Option (A) is correct.**
Explanation: The congratulatory message by the head of the organization is meant to motivate employees and enhance their present level of work (urged them to give their best for attaining a more profitable position in future.)

16. Option (E) is correct.

Explanation: The mention of sending official letter 'this time' proves that the format and emphasis of different type of letter is different depending on occasions. The use of "official" and "semi - official" implies II.

17. Option (A) is correct.

Explanation: It is only by knowing the desired mode of travel that the person can check the availability of two tickets from Delhi to Lucknow. So, Argument I is implicit. The details of the person travelling are not required to check the availability .

18. Option (E) is correct.

Explanation: The correct answer, "If both I and II are implicit," is justified as both assumptions are integral to the statement's coherence. Assumption I, suggesting the existence of different types of pens, is implicit because the statement implies a choice among various pen options. Assumption II, assuming that the person being told understands what a 0.7 pen is, is also implicit because the statement recommends using this specific pen size, indicating an expectation that the individual comprehends the reference. Therefore, both assumptions are necessary for the statement's logic, assuming the availability of different pen types and the understanding of the recommended pen size by the recipient of the advice.

19. Option (A) is correct.

Explanation: The sentence's norm contains an implicit I. This is why it is recommended to check. What would the banks look for? Obviously, what the clients disclose. Banks would take the disclosure at face value. As a result, argument II is not implicit. However, argument II is ambiguous. If the speaker is referring to cross-checking, argument II becomes implied.

20. Option (A) is correct.

Explanation: If the decision has been made by the government. It must have assumed that its implementation would be practicable. Argument II would not be implied because of "produced in the country". It is probable that the government had import in mind for the aforementioned pulses.

21. Option (D) is correct.

Explanation: The correct answer, "If neither I nor II is implicit," is appropriate because the statement does not inherently suggest either assumption I or II. Assumption I, regarding the person being told not knowing the meaning of FSI (Floor Space Index), is not implicit because the statement does not provide any indication of the person's knowledge or lack thereof regarding FSI. Assumption II, suggesting that more space will reduce construction costs, is also not implicit because the statement focuses on the necessity of acquiring extra FSI to build more space but does not directly address the impact on construction costs. Therefore, since neither assumption is inherently implied by the statement, the correct answer is that neither I nor II is implicit.

22. Option (A) is correct.

Explanation: Argument I is implicit in the need for training. But argument II takes things to an extreme with the phrase "skill sets".

23. Option (D) is correct.

Explanation: If a Signboard can be prepared without using any language cannot be inferred from the statement. The use of 'only' makes II an ineffective assumption. So, neither assumption I nor II is implicit.

24. Option (A) is correct.

Explanation: The imposition of ban on gambling by lotteries by the Central Government manifests the risks associated with gambling by lotteries. Moreover, government mostly takes steps in the interests of the citizens. So, argument I is implicit. The emphasis on 'any other way' negates II as a valid assumption.

25. Option (E) is correct.

Explanation: When a move a made, it is assumed to be effective. Hence, argument I is implicit. It is also assumed that the stipulated target will be met. Hence, argument II is implicit.

Level-2: INTERMEDIATE

1. Option (A) is correct.

Explanation: The statement advises to travel by air between the two cities. So, argument I is implicit. Besides, it talks of air transport being a faster means of travel. This means that other means of transport, slower than air transport, are available. So, argument II is not implicit.

2. Option (B) is correct.

Explanation: While reducing interest rates on loans may indeed be a strategy to attract more customers, it cannot be automatically assumed that this approach would universally appeal to other banks. The statement acknowledges that interest rates are just one factor among many that influence customer decisions. Therefore, it implies that other banks might have different priorities or strategies for customer acquisition and retention, which may not necessarily align with simply lowering interest rates. Thus, the argument suggests that while interest rate reduction can be a viable tactic for some banks, it's not the sole determinant of attractiveness, and other banks may prioritize different aspects in their customer engagement strategies.

3. Option (D) is correct.

Explanation: The statement states that with prayers, a person comes out as an improved being, and for such a person God always answers him. This does not imply that the person becomes more human or that his misdeeds have been atoned for. So, argument I and II are not implicit.

4. Option (A) is correct.

Explanation: The warning clearly states that cell phones and pagers will cause disruption in the auditorium. As a result, argument I is implicit. Furthermore, such a notification has been issued in light of the fact that many people arrive at the theatre with such gadgets. As a result, argument II is not implied.

5. Option (E) is correct.

Explanation: The appeal will stir the citizens to contribute to the development of the country by paying taxes, and thus proving to be a responsible citizen.

This appeal will go further to considerably increase the total income tax collection in near future. So, both assumptions I and II are implicit.

6. **Option (E) is correct.**
Explanation: Such decisions are always made keeping in mind the public requirements and their economic viability for the concerned department. So, both arguments I and II are implicit.

7. **Option (E) is correct.**
Explanation: The insistence on approaching the court if the employer does not pay you the Provident Fund contribution, demonstrates that courts can intervene in matters of dispute between employer and employees. This aspect of letting the court intervene proves that an employer is obligated to pay the Provident Fund to the employee. So, both assumptions I and II are implicit.

8. **Option (B) is correct.**
Explanation: The fact that Tarun joined a new company clarifies that the present company offers moderate pay packet. But, nothing can be deduced about work environment or salary of all other employees. So, only assumption II is implicit.

9. **Option (E) is correct.**
Explanation: The reason behind the announcement of a series of incentives, is done to instigate motivation among employees. If punctuality and sincerity increase, since they have a direct co-relation to the productivity of the company, the latter will also increase. So, both I and II are implicit.

10. **Option (E) is correct.**
Explanation: Teachers have clearly been urged to preserve classroom protocol and to call out misbehaving students who interfere with other students' studies. As a result, assumption I is implicit. Furthermore, following the directions would undoubtedly assist good pupils focus on their academics and maintain a positive working environment in the classroom. As a result, assumption II is likewise implicit.

11. **Option (E) is correct.**
Explanation: Both assumptions I and II directly follow from the statement. The advertisement by the TV company proves that slogans that are unique and catchy definitely catch the attention of consumers. The content of the slogan- 'the neighbour's envy, the owner's pride' shows that people are envious of their neighbours superior possessions. There is nothing indicative of the want of people. So, III is not implicit.

12. **Option (A) is correct.**
Explanation: The drastic decision to disinvest large chunk of its equity in select public sector undertakings for a better fiscal management clearly proves that the amount generated out of the disinvestment process may reduce substantially the mounting fiscal deficits. However, the public response to the new policy cannot be ascertained. So, II is not implicit.

13. **Option (A) is correct.**
Explanation: The statement mentions that Raman will pass if he is talented. So, assumption I is implicit. Further, this means that it is not necessary that he will pass. So, assumption II is not implicit.

14. **Option (E) is correct.**
Explanation: The focus on the part 'educational value cannot be ignored' testifies that people take television to be a means of entertainment only. This also justifies the assumption that the educational value of television is not realised properly. So, assumption II is also implicit.

15. **Option (B) is correct.**
Explanation: It is impossible to predict when Pawan will arrive in Mumbai. Pawan, on the other hand, has departed for Mumbai to attend an event on Friday. As a result, he must have scheduled his journey to arrive in Mumbai before Friday. As a result, just assumption II is implied.

16. **Option (A) is correct.**
Explanation: To avoid malaria, the municipal government has recommended citizens to stay away from mosquitos. People would undoubtedly follow such advice. As a result, assumption II is not implied. In addition, mosquito repellents or netting have been recommended. This means that everyone can afford to buy the same. As a result, assumption I is implicit.

17. **Option (B) is correct.**
Explanation: The grave warning issued in the circular advising farmers to not use pesticides indiscriminately as it may pollute the ground water, will probably make them refrain from using them indiscriminately, as this will endanger the lives of them and their families. But refraining from using ground water is less viable, and not apparent in the statement. However, assumption I cannot be assumed from the given statement and so it is not implicit.

18. **Option (E) is correct.**
Explanation: The advertising attempts to get individuals to create accounts with Bank X by guaranteeing them assistance at their convenience. Assumption I is implied since 'home service' has been utilised as a method for garnering clientage. Furthermore, the advertising attempts to emphasise upon consumers the easy and simple process to open an account in bank X. This may entice more account holders to open accounts with Bank X. As a result, assumption II is implied. Furthermore, providing banking services at home implies that banking has become so competitive that the bank is giving door-to-door service to attract customers. As a result, assumption III is also implied.

19. **Option (E) is correct.**
Explanation: Any surcharge implemented , is intended to collect money from people ; so the surcharge levied to fund drought relief programmes clarify that the Government does not have sufficient money to fund drought relief programmes. So, I is implicit. Besides, the percentage of surcharge must have been decided after studying the expected inflow in relation to amount of funds required. So, II is also implicit.

20. **Option (A) is correct.**
Explanation: The statement affirms that the seller barely keeps the stock of product X; it is only upon a confirmed order from the customer that the seller can provide it. So I is definitely implicit. However, assumption II is to be vague in this context.

21. **Option (E) is correct.**
Explanation: The emphasis on 'in their own interest' in the statement indicates that people are cautious about their safety. So, assumption I is implicit. Moreover, the cautionary note in the announcement testifies that unless advised, passengers might not use the seat belts. So, assumption II is also implicit.

22. **Option (B) is correct.**
Explanation: The choice was made with the understanding that those who use LPG can afford to pay a slightly higher price. The administration does not want to harm the most vulnerable people who still use paraffin. As a result, only assumption I is implicit, II is incorrect as government has decided to reduce its subsidy on LPG , so people will be tempted to buy LPG, not stop buying LPG assumption II is not.

23. **Option (B) is correct.**
Explanation: The reaction of the employees to the new decision cannot be deduced from the statement. So, assumption I is not implicit. However, the change in lunch break to any of the half-hour slots between 1.00 and 2.30 p.m. justifies that there may not be any break in the work of the organization as the employees will have their lunch break at different time slots. So, assumption II is implicit.

Level-3: EXPERT

1. **Option (E) is correct.**
Explanation: The phenomenon of individuals seeking cold cream for achieving a fair complexion, as depicted in advertisements, underscores the influential role of marketing in consumer behavior. Advertisements, while primarily aimed at raising awareness of products, often leverage societal beauty standards and aspirations to persuade consumers. While their intention is not necessarily deceitful, advertisements can subtly shape perceptions and desires, potentially fostering unrealistic expectations. Nevertheless, they serve as conduits for product information dissemination, albeit with the responsibility to maintain transparency and ethical standards to ensure consumer trust and well-being. Thus, only I and III are implicit.

2. **Option (E) is correct.**
Explanation: The suggestion to post a notice about smoking in the office arises from the observed presence of individuals smoking on the premises. By placing such a notice on the office bulletin board, it aims to raise awareness among employees about the harmful effects of smoking. Those who encounter the notice may reconsider their smoking habits upon reading the slogans or messages displayed, potentially leading to a decision to quit smoking altogether. This proactive measure not only addresses health concerns associated with smoking in the workplace but also promotes a healthier environment conducive to the well-being of all employees. Nothing can be said about the effects. Thus, only I and II are implicit.

3. **Option (E) is correct.**
Explanation: Both assumptions I and II directly follow from the statement. The advertisement by the TV company proves that slogans that are unique and catchy definitely catch the attention of consumers. The content of the slogan- 'the neighbour's envy, the owner's pride' shows that people are envious of their neighbours superior possessions. There is nothing indicative of the want of people. So, III is not implicit.

4. **Option (D) is correct.**
Explanation: According to the statement, there are just two companies in this industry that are ISO 9002 certified. Since, there is no information regarding the total number of enterprises in this industry can be derived. As a result, assumption I is not implied. Furthermore, if obtaining ISO 9002 certification had been simple, there would have been a huge number of ISO:9002 organisations, implying that assumption II is implicit. Also,the company must have met such high worldwide standards in order to build a name for itself in its field. As a result, assumption III is also implied.

5. **Option (B) is correct.**
Explanation: The statement makes no mention of the atmosphere of the new company.. As a result, assumption I is not implied. It is because Arun is dissatisfied with his current income, it is clear that the current employer provides fair pay. As a result, assumption II is implied. The statement simply mentions Arun, not all of the new company's employees. As a result, assumption III is not implied.

6. **Option (A) is correct.**
Explanation: Company X reduces the prices.
This can only be justified if the company believes this will increase its own sales.
Hence, Assumption I is implicit.
Nothing in the statement suggests anything about what competitors will or will not do.
Hence, Assumptions II and III are not implicit.

7. **Option (A) is correct.**
Explanation: Both assumptions I and II are implicit. The distributor will buy crops from village Z proves that at least some farmers in village Z produce the same crop as farmers in village C. Given the low harvest in village C, and the decision to procure crops from village Z, the harvest in village Z was much more than expected.

8. **Option (E) is correct.**
Explanation: If all good singers have sweet voice, and only they are invited in the conference, it implies that all invited singers in the conference have sweet voice and those singers who do not have sweet voice are not invited in the conference. Both the assumptions I and II follows.

9. **Option (D) is correct.**
Explanation: Using calculator for complex calculation cannot be deduced from the statement. So, assumption I is not implicit. Moreover, it should be noted that assumption II is not implicit.

10. **Option (E) is correct.**
Explanation: The statement asserts that only weaponry X should be utilized for underwater battles. The implicit assumptions supporting this assertion are twofold: firstly, not all weaponry functions ef-

fectively in underwater environments, emphasizing the necessity for specialized equipment designed for such conditions; secondly, the existence of distinct categories of weaponry tailored for battles on ground versus underwater suggests the importance of utilizing weaponry X exclusively for underwater combat scenarios. These implicit assumptions reinforce the argument for the exclusive use of weaponry X in underwater battles, highlighting the need for specialized tools optimized for the challenges posed by underwater warfare.

11. **Option (A) is correct.**
Explanation: The statement discusses the rising prices of petrol and diesel, prompting a transition towards electric cars, justified by the affordability of electricity as a fuel source. Implicit in this argument is assumption I, which posits that electricity is indeed a cheaper alternative compared to petrol and diesel. This assumption is grounded in the understanding that electric vehicles offer cost savings over time due to lower fueling costs and potentially reduced maintenance expenses. Additionally, it acknowledges broader trends such as advancements in renewable energy technology, which can further drive down electricity prices and enhance the economic viability of electric vehicles. Therefore, the assertion that electricity is a cheaper source implicitly relies on the underlying belief in its cost-effectiveness relative to traditional fossil fuels like petrol and diesel.

12. **Option (D) is correct.**
Explanation: The statement does not imply that reservations are made before three months before the date of travel. As a result, assumption I is not implied. The statement makes no mention of airline tickets. As a result, assumption II is not implied.

13. **Option (E) is correct.**
Explanation: The move will reduce the traffic on roads and people will buy cars in the metropolis.

14. **Option (A) is correct.**
Explanation: People will undoubtedly rearrange their trips between the two cities after the statement of railway authorities. If major repair work continue for two days on the main line connecting the two big cities bringing rail service to a halt; then, people will never plan their travel by train between the two cities even on these two days.

15. **Option (B) is correct.**
Explanation: The argument in the text is that the US President's legacy would be destroyed owing to the delayed progress of his initiative, namely "securing radioactive materials," which implies that he will be able to gain glory if he can speed up his initiative. So, the basic idea is that one's potential to reach permanent glory is decided by the speed with which one's projects proceed.

■ ■ ■

Chapter 4

Course of Action

LEARNING OBJECTIVES:

- ❖ Identify the appropriate and inappropriate actions.
- ❖ Address the Course of Actions
- ❖ Develop problem-solving & decision making skills
- ❖ Evaluate different options & select the most effective Action.

Individuals are presented with situations or problems and must identify the appropriate steps or actions to address them effectively in the "Course of Action" chapter of verbal reasoning. This entails analysing the given circumstances and deciding on a course of action that either completely solves the problem or reduces its complexity, thereby improving the overall situation. The questions in this chapter frequently involve considering two or three different courses of action and determining the best one based on the given context. This chapter assists individuals in developing problem-solving and decision-making skills by evaluating various options and selecting the most appropriate action.

APPROPRIATE AND INAPPROPRIATE ACTION:

We can distinguish between appropriate and inappropriate actions as follows:

- **Understand the given situation:** Begin by carefully reading and understanding the situation or problem presented in the question. Pay attention to the context, key details, and any constraints or limitations mentioned.
- **Analyse the actions:** Evaluate each course of action provided and consider its potential consequences and effectiveness in addressing the given situation. Make an attempt to assess whether the actions are feasible, practical, and logical given in the context.
- **Consider the outcome:** Assess the potential outcome or result of each action. Determine if the action is likely to solve the problem, improve the situation, or mitigate the issue at hand. Evaluate the expected impact of the action on all relevant stakeholders.
- **Evaluate the reasoning:** Examine the reasoning or justification provided for each action. Assess whether the reasoning is sound, logical, and supported by the information given in the question. Look for any gaps or assumptions in the reasoning that may render the action inappropriate.
- **Assess feasibility and practicality:** Consider the practicality and feasibility of each action. Evaluate whether the action can be realistically implemented, considering any constraints, resources or potential obstacles as mentioned in the question.
- **Consider ethical and legal aspects:** Take into account any ethical or legal considerations associated with each action. Determine if the action aligns with ethical standards, laws and regulations. Assess whether the action respects the rights and well-being of individuals involved.
- **Eliminate inappropriate actions:** Identify actions that are impractical, ineffective or have undesirable consequences. Eliminate actions that are illogical, unsupported or based on flawed reasoning. Actions that are infeasible, unethical, or illegal should also be ruled out.
- **Select the appropriate action:** Choose the course of action that is most likely to effectively address the situation or problem, considering all the factors mentioned above. The appropriate action should be feasible, logical, supported by sound reasoning, and have a positive impact on the situation or problem.

Example 1: Cases of road accidents are increasing constantly, particularly in the urban areas.

Courses of action:

I. Reduce the number of vehicles on road.

II. Organize campaigns and awareness programmes on road safety.

(a) If only (I) follows.

(b) If only (II) follows.

(c) If either (I) or (II) follows.
(d) If neither (I) nor (II) follows.
(e) If both (I) and (II) follow.

Sol. (b) (I) does not follow because reducing the number of vehicles on road cannot be materialized and is an illogical step. (II) follows because with the spread of road safety campaigns, people will be more aware about the importance of driving safely by following traffic rules.

Example 2: The dolphin population in India has been decreasing sharply over the past few years.

Courses of Action:

I. Dolphins should be declared an endangered species and bred in aquariums or protected areas.

II. Locals should be enlisted to protect dolphins.

Sol. (e) Both courses of action protect dolphins, and the dolphin population will undoubtedly increase.

Level 1 Beginner

Directions (Qs. 1–18): Each of the questions below contains a statement followed by two or more options for course of action. A course of action is a step for an administrative decision to be made for improvement, follow-up, or additional action in relation to a problem, policy, or other issue. Based on the information in the statement, you must assume that everything in the statement is true, and then decide which of the suggested courses of action is/are logically worth pursuing.

Give answer:

(A) If only course of action I is follows.
(B) If only course of action II is follows.
(C) If either course of action I or II is follows.
(D) If neither course of action I nor II is follows.
(E) If both course of action I and II are follows.

1. **Statement:** The ground water in the locality has been found to contain high level of arsenic making it dangerous to drink.

Course of Action:

I. The people living in the area should be shifted to another area to avoid a catastrophic situation.

II. The government should make arrangements for supply of safe drinking water. **[Bank PO]**

2. **Statement:** A large number of employees have gone on a mass casual leave in protest against the company's new recruitment policy.

Course of Action:

I. The company should immediately withdraw the requirement policy.

II. All these employees should immediately be suspended from their service. **[Agriculture Officers]**

3. **Statement:** A large cache of live ammunition has been found in the scrap yard of a local steel factory.

Course of Action:

I. The steel factory should immediately be closed down till all these ammunitions are located and shifted to safe places.

II. The government should immediately set up an enquiry to unearth the details and take corrective measures to avoid such incidence in future. **[Bank PO]**

4. **Statement:** A group of school students was reported to be enjoying at a picnic spot during school hours.

Course of Action:

I. The Principal of the school should contact the parents of those students and inform them with a real warning for future.

II. Some disciplinary action must be taken against those students for the awareness of all the other students. **[RRB]**

5. **Statement:** As many as ten coaches of a passenger train have derailed and blocked both pairs of the railway tracks.

Course of Action:

I. The railway authorities should immediately send men and equipments to the spot to clear the railway tracks.

II. All the trains running in both the directions should be diverted to other routes. **[Bank PO]**

6. **Statement:** India has been continuously experiencing military threats from its neighboring countries.

Course of Action:

I. India should engage into an all-out war to stop the nagging threats.

II. India should get the neighbours into a serious dialogue to reduce the tension at its borders. **[SBI PO]**

7. **Statement:** There has been less than forty percent voter turn out in the recent assembly elections.

Course of Action:

I. The election commission should cancel the entire election process as the votes cast are not adequate to represent people.

II. The election commission should take away the voting rights of those who did not exercise their rights. **[SBI PO]**

8. **Statement:** Many medical and engineering graduates are taking up jobs in administrative service and in banks.

Course of Action:

I. All the professionals should be advised to refrain from taking up such jobs.

II. The government should appoint a committee to find out the reasons for these professionals taking up such jobs and to suggest remedial measures. **[Bank PO]**

9. **Statement:** Drinking water supply to many parts of town has been disputed due to loss of water because of leakage in pipes supplying water.

Course of Action:

I. The government should order an enquiry into matter.

II. The Civic body should set up a fact finding team to analyze the damages and take effective steps.

10. **Statement:** Many people have encroached into the government property and built their houses and business establishments.

Course of Action:

I. The government should take immediate steps to remove all unauthorised constructions on government land.

II. All the encroached should immediately be put behind bars and also be slapped with a heavy fine.

11. **Statement:** The number of dropouts in govt. schools have significantly increased in the urban area over the past years.

Course of Action:

I. The govt. should immediately close down all such schools in the urban area where the dropout goes beyond 20 percent.

II. The parents of all the students who dropped out of govt. schools in urban areas should be punished.

12. **Statement:** Two local passengers train collided while running in opposites directions on the same track as the signaling system failed for a brief period.

Course of Action:

I. The services of the motorman of the train should immediately be terminated.

II. The Govt. should immediately constitute a task force to review the functioning of the signaling system.

13. **Statement:** A major part of the local market in the city was gutted due to a short circuit causing extensive damage to goods and property.

Course of Action:

I. The Govt. should issue strict guidelines for all establishments regarding installation and maintenance of electrical fittings.

II. The Government should relocate all the markets to the outskirts of the city.

14. **Statement:** A university librarian reported increase cases of theft of books from the library.

Course of Action:

I. Stricter security arrangements should be put in place in order to prevent such incidents.

II. All the students in the university should be made to pay a heavy fine in order to replace the lost books.

15. **Statement:** A major river in the city was reduced to a polluted and dirty canal after tonnes of sewage made way into it over the years.

Course of Action:

I. All those who dumped garbage and sewage into the river should be penalized.

II. The Government should modify the sewage system and find an alternate way to dump the city's waste.

16. **Statement:** The Officer in charge of a company had a hunch that some money was missing from the safe.

Course of Action:

I. He should get it recounted with the help of the staff and check it with the balance sheet.

II. He should inform the police.

17. **Statement:** There has been a significant drop in the water level of all the lakes supplying water to the city.

Course of Action:

I. The water supply authority should impose a partial cut in supply to tackle the situation.

II. The government should appeal to all the residents through mass media for minimal use of water.

18. **Statement:** There is an alarming increase in the number of people suffering from malaria in many part of the city.

Course of Action:

I. The Municipal Corporation has advised all the govt. hospitals to store adequate supply of malaria drugs.

II. The Municipal Corporation has urged people to use mosquito repellants and keep their premises clean.

Directions (Qs. 19-25): Each of the questions below contains a statement followed by three options for action. A course of action is a step for an administrative decision to be made for improvement, follow-up, or additional action in relation to a problem, policy, or other issue. Based on the information in the statement, you must assume that everything in the statement is true, and then decide which of the suggested courses of action is/are logically worth pursuing.

Give answer:

(A) Only I follow
(B) Only II follow
(C) Only III follow
(D) Only II and III follow
(E) None of these

19. **Statement:** The member belonging to two local club occasionally fight with each other on the main road and block traffic movement.

Course of Action:

I. The local police station should immediately deploy police personnel round the clock on the main road.

II. Those involved in fighting should be identified and put behind bars.

III. The local administration should disband the management of the clubs with immediate effect.

[RBI Grade B Officer]

20. **Statement:** Many school's buses have CNG kit fitted without observing the safety guidelines properly. This resulted into some instances of these buses catching fire due to short circuit and endangering the lives of the school children.

Course of Action:

I. The regional transport authority should immediately carry out checks of all the school's buses fitted with CNG kit.

II. The management of all the schools should stop hiring buses fitted with CNG kit.

III. The govt. should issue a notification banning school buses for the use of CNG kit.

21. Statement: It is reported that during the last fortnight there has been three cases of near–miss situation involving aircraft that came perilously close to each other and could avoid collision as the pilots acted just in time.

Course of Action:

I. The pilots of all the six aircraft involved in this incident should be de-rostered immediately.

II. Some flights should be diverted to other airports for the next few months to decongest the sky over the city airport.

III. The traffic controllers of the city should be sent the refresher courses in batches to prepare themselves to handle such a pressure situation.

22. Statement: The Department of Education has recommended that the primary level admission to Government and Government aided schools should be done purely through random selection and not by admission tests. This is necessitated as the number of admission seekers is much more than the available seats.

Course of Action:

I. The Government should instruct the private schools to follow the same practice also.

II. The Government should set up an independent body to regulate the primary level admissions.

III. The schools should be asked to select student only from those who stay in the neighboring areas of the school.

23. Statement: A devastating earthquake has ravaged the city killing hundreds of people and rendering many more homeless.

Course of Action:

I. The entry of outsiders into the city should be stopped.

II. The civic administration should immediately make alternate temporary hours in engagement for the victim

III. The affected people should immediately be shifted to a safer place.

24. Statement: In one of the worst accidents on a railway level crossing, fifty people died when a bus carrying them collided with a running train.

Course of Action:

I. The train driver should immediately be suspended.

II. The driver of the bus should be tried in court for negligence on his part.

III. The railways authorities should be asked to man all its level crossings.

25. Statement: A mass mortality of shrimps in ponds on entire Andhra coast has recently been reported

Course of Action:

I. The water of the affected ponds should immediately be treated for identifying the nature of the virus.

II. The catching of shrimps from the ponds should temporarily be stopped.

III. The fishermen should be asked to watch for the on set of such phenomenon in nature.

2 Intermediate Level

Directions (Qs. 1-23): Each of the questions below contains a statement followed by two or more options for course of action. A course of action is a step for an administrative decision to be made for improvement, follow-up, or additional action in relation to a problem, policy, or other issue. Based on the information in the statement, you must assume that everything in the statement is true, and then decide which of the suggested courses of action is/are logically worth pursuing.

Give answer:

(A) If only course of action I is follows.

(B) If only course of action II is follows.

(C) If either course of action I or II is follows.

(D) If neither course of action I nor II is follows.

(E) If both course of action I and II are follows.

1. Statement: Nuclear power cannot make a country secure.

Course of Action:

I. We must stop further expenses on increasing our nuclear power.

II. We must concentrate on improving our diplomatic relations.

2. Statement: There has been an unprecedented increase in use of malpractices by the students during various examinations held in the country this year.

Course of Action:

I. All the concerned authorities conducting these examinations should immediately take effective measures to curb this menace.

II. All those students who are detected to have used unfair means should be debarred from appearing in any of these examinations for the next three years. **[Bank PO 2004]**

3. Statement: Japan is not likely to grant India's request for a $500 million fast disbursing loan for the current year.

Course of Action:

I. India should approach other countries to get a loan.

II. India should persuade Japan to grant the loan to meet its immediate demand of foreign exchange.

4. Statement: Large number of people have become critically ill after consuming spurious liquor from a local shop.

Course of Action:

I. The Government should immediately close down all the shops selling liquor till the stocks are tested for presence of toxicity.

II. The owner of the liquor shop should be asked to leave the town and open a shop elsewhere. **[Agriculture Officer 2005]**

5. **Statement:** Local villagers have reported that instances of illegal cutting of trees have increased over the last few months in the forest area.

Course of Action:

I. The local should be encouraged to report any such activities in the future as well.

II. Authorities should immediately look into the matter and put stop to such illegal activities. **[Bank PO 2004]**

6. **Statement:** The Librarian finds some cases in which the pages from certain books issued from the library, are torn.

Course of Action:

I. The Librarian should keep a record of books issued to each student and if the pages are found torn, strict measures should be taken against the child who had been issued that book.

II. Some funds should be collected from the children collectively to renovate the library.

7. **Statement:** Nearly 26% of all engineering graduates have been left unemployed owing to sever recession word-wide.

Course of Action:

I. All the unemployed students should be advised to take up jobs in foreign countries.

II. The unemployed students should be advised to take up jobs only after the recession is over.

8. **Statement:** Many private schools have been violating Government directives and have been charging more fee than the specified limits.

Course of Action:

I. The Government should identify such schools and stringent actions against them.

II. The Government should not limit school fees and keep it flexible for the schools to decide.

9. **Statement:** The cinema halls are incurring heavy losses these days as people prefer to watch movies in home on TV than to visit cinema halls.

Courses or action:

I. The cinema halls should be demolished and residential multistory buildings should be constructed there.

II. The cinema halls should be converted into shopping malls. **[RBI 2002]**

10. **Statement:**The availability of imported fruits has increased in the indigenous market and so the demand for indigenous fruits has been decreased.

Course of Action:

I. To help the indigenous producers of fruits, the Government should impose high import duty on these fruits, even if these are not of good quality.

II. The fruit vendors should stop selling imported fruits so that the demand for indigenous fruits would be increased. **[IBPS 2002]**

11. **Statement:** There has been an unprecedented increase in the number of successful candidates in this year's School Leaving Certificate Examination.

Course of Action:

I. The Government should make arrangements to increase number of seats of intermediate courses in existing colleges.

II. The Government should take active steps to open new colleges to accommodate all these successful candidates. **[Bank PO 2003]**

12. **Statement:** There have been many instances of derailment of trains due to landslide in the hilly areas which caused loss of many lives.

Course of Action:

I. The railway authority should arrange to deploy pilot engines before the movement of passenger trains in the hilly areas to alert the trains in case of any landslide.

II. The railway authority should strengthen the hill slopes by putting iron meshes so that the loose boulders do not fall on the track. **[Bank PO 2004]**

13. **Statement:** The sale of a particular product has gone down considerably causing great concern to the company.

Course of Action:

I. The company should make a proper study of rival products in the market.

II. The price of the product should be reduced and quality improved. **[RRB 2004]**

14. **Statement:** If the retired Professors of the same institutes are also invited to deliberate on restructuring of the organisation, their contribution may be beneficial to the Institute.

Course of Action:

I. Management may seek opinion of the employees before calling retired professors.

II. Management should involve experienced people for the systematic restructuring of the organization. **[MAT 2004]**

15. **Statement:** Every year large number of devotee's die due to severe cold on their way to the shrine located at the top of the mountain range.

Course of Action:

I. The devotees should be discouraged to visit the shrine without having proper warm clothes and other amenities.

II. The government should provide warm clothes and shelter to all the devotees visiting the shrine. **[Bank PO 2004]**

16. **Statement:** It is reported that though Vitamin E present in fresh fruits and vegetables is beneficial for human body, capsuled Vitamin E does not have the same effect on human body.

Course of Action:

I. The gale of capsuled Vitamin E should be banned.

II. People should be encouraged to take fresh fruits and vegetables to meet the body's requirement of Vitamin E. **[SBI PO 2000]**

17. Statement: A large number of people visiting India from Country X have been tested positive for carrying viruses of a killer disease.

Course of Action:

I. The Government of India should immediately put a complete ban on people coming to India from Country X including those Indians who are settled in Country X.

II. The Government of India should immediately set up detection centers at all its airports and seaport to identify and quarantine those who are tested positive. **[SBI PO 2003]**

18. Statement: As stated in the recent census report the female to male ratio is alarmingly low.

Course of Action:

I. The Government should conduct another census to verify the results.

II. The Government should immediately issue orders to all the departments to encourage people to improve the ratio. **[Bank PO 2004]**

19. Statement: Courts take too long in deciding important disputes of various departments.

Course of Action:

I. Courts should be ordered to speed up matters.

II. Special powers should be granted to officers to settle disputes concerning their department. **[MAT 2005]**

20. Statement: Some serious blunders were detected in the accounts section of a factory.

Course of Action:

I. An efficient team of auditors should be appointed to check the accounts.

II. A show cause notice should be issued to all the employees involved in the irregularity. **[RRB 2004]**

21. Statement: There has been an unprecedented increase in the number of requests for berths in most of the long distance trains during the current holiday season.

Course of Action:

I. The railway authority should immediately increase the capacity in each of these trains by attaching additional coaches.

II. The people seeking accommodation should be advised to make their travel plan after the holiday. **[SBI PO 2003]**

22. Statement: The Meteorology Department has forecast that a severe cyclonic storm would hit coastal Andhra Pradesh and Orissa in the next 48.

Course of Action:

I. The local administration should advise the fishermen not to go to dangerous area in the sea.

II. The local administration should alert the people of coastal areas of these two states and they should be prepared to shift to safer places. **[RBI 2003]**

23. Statement: Three persons were caught with huge arms and ammunition in the city.

Course of Action:

I. Police should be instructed for night patrolling.

II. The three persons should be set free and their movements should be carefully watched to nab the other criminals. **[SBI PO 2002]**

Directions (Qs. 24 & 25): Each of the questions below contains a statement followed by three options for action. A course of action is a step for an administrative decision to be made for improvement, follow-up, or additional action in relation to a problem, policy, or other issue. Based on the information in the statement, you must assume that everything in the statement is true, and then decide which of the suggested courses of action is/are logically worth pursuing.

Give answer:

(A) Only I follow

(B) Only II follow

(C) Only III follow

(D) Only II and III follow

(E) None of these

24. Statement: It is estimated that about twenty lakh people will visit the city during the ensuing festival.

Course of Action:

I. The civic authority should monitor the crowd and restrict entry of the people beyond a manageable number.

II. The local police authority should be put on high alert to maintain law and order during the festival.

III. All the hospitals in the city should be put on high alert in case of any eventuality. **[Bank PO 2003]**

25. Statement: The exodus from villages to cities is detrimental to both.

Course of Action:

I. Rural postings must be made mandatory.

II. There should be fewer trains linking cities to smaller places.

III. Employment generation scheme should be launched in rural areas. **[MAT 1999]**

Level 3 Expert

Directions (Qs. 1-15): Each of the questions below contains a statement followed by three options for course of action. A course of action is a step for an administrative decision to be made for improvement, follow-up, or additional action in relation to a problem, policy, or other issue. Based on the information in the statement, you must assume that everything in the statement is true, and then decide which of the suggested courses of action is/are logically worth pursuing.

Give answer:

(A) If only Course of Action I is follows.
(B) If only Course of Action II is follows.
(C) If either Course of Action I or II is follows.
(D) If all Course of Action follow.
(E) If both Course of Action I and II or II and III follow

1. **Statement:** The vehicular traffic has increased so much in the recent past that it takes at least two hours to travel between the city and the airport during peak hours.
   Course of Action:
   I. The local police station should immediately deploy police personnel round the clock on the main road.
   II. Those involved in fighting should be identified and put behind bars.
   III. The local administration should disband the management of the two clubs with immediate effect.

2. **Statement:** Many students of the local school fell ill for the fourth time in a row in the last sixth months after consuming food prepared by the school canteen.
   Course of Action:
   I. The school management should immediately terminate the contract of the canteen and ask for compensation.
   II. The school management should advise all the students not to eat food items from the canteen.
   III. The owner of the canteen should immediately be arrested for negligence.
   [RBI Grade B Exam 2009]

3. **Statement:** Many schools buses have fitted CNG kit without observing the safety guideline properly. This results into some instances of these buses catching fire due to short circuit and endangering the lives of the school children.
   Course of Action:
   I. The regional transport authority should immediately carry out checks of all the school buses fitted with CNG kit.
   II. The management of all the schools should stop hiring buses fitted with CNG kit.
   III. The Govt. should issue a notification banning school buses for use of CNG kit.
   [RBI Grade B Exam 2009]

4. **Statement:** A sudden cloud burst over the island city resulted into unpredicted rainfall causing flood like situation in the entire area. Large number of people were caught unaware and were stranded on the road.
   Course of Action:
   I. The local administration should immediately put in place an action plan for avoiding such situation in future.
   II. The local administration should immediately deploy personnel to help the stranded people to move to safer places.
   III. The local administration should advice all the citizens not to venture out on the road till situation improves. **[Grade B Exam 2009]**

5. **Statement:** It is reported that during the last fortnight there has been three eases of near miss situation involving two air crafts over the busy city airport. In all these cases both the aircrafts came perilously close to each other and could avoid collision as the pilots acted just in time.
   Course of Action:
   I. The pilots of all the six air crafts involved in these incidents should immediately be de-roistered.
   II. Some flights should be diverted to other airports for the next few months to decongest the sky over the city airport.
   III. Air traffic controllers of the city airport should be sent for refresher courses in batches to prepare themselves to handle such pressure situation.
   [RBI Grade B Exam 2009]

6. **Statement:** Many political activists have decided to stage demonstrations and block traffic movement in the city during peak hours to protest against the step rise in price of essential commodities.
   Course of Actions:
   I. The government should immediately ban all forms of agitations in the country.
   II. The police authority of the city should deploy additional forces all over the city to help traffic movement in the city.
   III. The state administration should carry out preventive arrests of the known criminals staying in the city. **[SBI PO Exam 2010]**

7. **Statement:** The school dropout rate in many districts in the state has increased sharply during the last few years as the parents of these children make them work in the fields owned by others to earn enough for them to get at least one meal a day.
   Course of Action:
   I. The Government should put up a mechanism to provided food grains to the poor people in these districts through public distribution system to encourage the parents to send their wards to school.

II. The Government should close down some of these schools in the district and deploy the teachers of these schools to nearby schools and also ask remaining students to join these schools.

III. The Government should issue arrest warrants for all the parents who force their children to work in fields instead of attending classes.

[SBI PO Exam 2010]

8. **Statement:** A large private bank has decided to retrench one third of its employees in view of the huge losses increased by it during the past three quarters.

Course of Action:

I. The Government should issue a notification to general public to immediately stop all transactions with the bank.

II. The Government should direct the bank to refrain from retrenching its employees.

III. The Government should ask the central bank of the country to initiate an enquiry into the bank's activities and submit its report.

[SBI PO Exam 2010]

9. **Statement:** One aspirant was killed due to stampede while participating in a recruitment drive of police constables.

Course of Action:

I. The officials in charge of the recruitment process should immediately be suspended.

II. A team of officials should be asked to find out the circumstances which led to the death of the aspirant and submit its report within a weak.

III. The Government should ask the home department to stagger the number of aspirants over more number of days to avoid such incidents in future. **[SBI PO Exam 2010]**

10. **Statement:** A heavy unseasonal downpour during the last two days has paralysed the normal life in the state in which five persons were killed but this has provided a huge relief to the problem of acute water crises in the state.

Course of Action:

I. The State Government should set up a committee to review the alarming situation.

II. The State Government should immediately remove all the restrictions on use of potable water in all the major cities in the state.

III. The State Government should send relief supplies to all the affected areas in the state.

11. **Statement:** There have been quite a few incidents of highway robbery on the super expressway between Cities A and B during recent months.

Course of Action:

I. The local administration should immediately set up police tickets along the expressway to prevent robbery.

II. The local administration should immediately close down the expressway till the robbers are apprehended.

III. More and more people should be given training on how to tackle with robbers. **[RBI 2003]**

12. **Statement:** It has been reported by one of the TV channels that the answer papers of Board examination of one state are evaluated by students studying in the same standard with the help of model answers as instructed by the examiners.

Course of Action:

I. All such examiners should be immediately suspended from their official positions.

II. All such papers evaluated by the students should be immediately confiscated and got evaluated by qualified teachers.

III. The board should explore possibilities even though they are remote, of getting the answer papers of this examination evaluated by computerised machines. **[Bank PO 2004]**

13. **Statement:** Major part of the Rabi crop in the district is damaged due to unseasonal heavy rains during the last few days.

Course of Action:

I. The Government should grant relief to the affected farmers to compensate their loss.

II. The Government should provide free seed and fertilizer to the farmers for the kharif season.

III. The Government should waive all the loans taken for the rabbi crop by the affected farmers.

[Bank PO 2005]

14. **Statement:** The day time temperatures in this summer have been four to five degree celsius above the normal temperature across the country.

Course of Action:

I. All the district headquarters should be alerted to send prompt reports of death due to heat waves in their jurisdiction.

II. The Government machinery should be put on high alert and provided with necessary equipment's to prevent any untoward incident.

III. The Government should make necessary arrangements to provide drinking water in all the areas affected due to extreme heat waves.

[Bank PO 2004]

15. **Statement:** The meteorological department has issued a notification forecasting less rainfall during next year's monsoon.

Course of Action:

I. The Government should immediately set up a water authority for proper management of water resources.

II. The water supply authorities should be asked to implement reduction in regular water supply to tackle the situation.

III. The farmers should be advised to cultivate alternate crops which require less water during the coming months. **[NABARD 2002]**

ANSWER KEY

Level-1: Beginner

1.	(B)	2.	(D)	3.	(E)	4.	(E)	5.	(E)	6.	(B)	7.	(D)	8.	(B)	9.	(B)	10.	(A)
11.	(D)	12.	(B)	13.	(A)	14.	(A)	15.	(B)	16.	(A)	17.	(E)	18.	(E)	19.	(D)	20.	(A)
21.	(C)	22.	(E)	23.	(E)	24.	(C)	25.	(A)										

Level-2: Intermediate

1.	(B)	2.	(E)	3.	(C)	4.	(A)	5.	(E)	6.	(A)	7.	(D)	8.	(A)	9.	(D)	10.	(D)
11.	(A)	12.	(C)	13.	(A)	14.	(B)	15.	(A)	16.	(B)	17.	(B)	18.	(B)	19.	(E)	20.	(E)
21.	(A)	22.	(E)	23.	(A)	24.	(E)	25.	(C)										

Level-3: Expert

1.	(B)	2.	(E)	3.	(E)	4.	(E)	5.	(B)	6.	(B)	7.	(A)	8.	(C)	9.	(E)	10.	(D)
11.	(A)	12.	(E)	13.	(E)	14.	(E)	15.	(E)										

Solutions with Detailed Explanations

Level-1: BEGINNER

1. **Option (B) is correct.**
Explanation: Course of action II is the preferred choice as it directly addresses the pressing issue of contaminated groundwater by providing a practical solution of ensuring the supply of safe drinking water to the affected locality. Shifting the population to another area, as suggested in course of action I, poses logistical challenges and does not address the root cause of the problem. By prioritizing the provision of safe drinking water, the government fulfills its duty to protect public health and ensures a sustainable solution to the issue of arsenic contamination in the locality.

2. **Option (D) is correct.**
Explanation: If neither Course of Action I nor II is followed, it indicates a need for a more nuanced approach to address the situation. Suspending the protesting employees, as suggested in Course of Action II, could escalate tensions and potentially worsen the relationship between the company and its workforce. On the other hand, immediately withdrawing the new recruitment policy, as proposed in Course of Action I, might not adequately address the underlying issues leading to the protest. Instead, the company could opt for dialogue and negotiation with the employees to understand their concerns and explore potential modifications to the policy that address both the company's needs and the employees' grievances. This approach emphasizes communication, collaboration, and finding a mutually agreeable solution, which could help mitigate tensions and foster a more positive work environment in the long term.

3. **Option (E) is correct.**
Explanation: The discovery of large cache of live ammunition in the scrap yard of a local steel factory demands a complete shut down of the steel factory and a close probe into the issue. Also, corrective measures to avoid such incidence in future need to be implemented. Thus, both the Course of Action I and II follow.

4. **Option (E) is correct.**
Explanation: Any act that breaks the protocol of a school is punishable, to set precedent to others, so that it is not repeated. Be it contacting the parents of those students, or taking disciplinary action against them. Thus, both the Course of Action I and II follow.

5. **Option (E) is correct.**
Explanation: The problem of blockage of both pairs of the railway tracks can be solved by sending men and equipment to the spot and diverting the trains running in both the directions. Thus, both the Course of Action I and II follow.

6. **Option (B) is correct.**
Explanation: If only Course of Action II is followed, it is because engaging in an all-out war, as suggested in Course of Action I, could escalate tensions further and lead to catastrophic consequences, including loss of lives and widespread destruction. On the other hand, opting for serious dialogue with neighboring countries, as proposed in Course of Action II, em-

phasizes diplomatic efforts to address the underlying issues causing the military threats. Dialogue offers a peaceful and constructive approach to reducing tensions at the borders, fostering understanding, cooperation, and potentially long-term solutions to regional conflicts. It aligns with India's interests in maintaining stability and promoting peaceful relations with its neighbors, demonstrating maturity and statesmanship in handling complex geopolitical challenges.

7. **Option (D) is correct.**

Explanation: Scrapping entire election processes in the pretext of inadequate representation of people is ridiculous, so is the decision to take away the voting rights of those who did not exercise their rights. So, neither I nor II follows.

8. **Option (B) is correct.**

Explanation: Following course, I would be an infringement of the right to freedom of individuals. if a committee finds out the reasons for these professionals taking up such jobs then it will solve the main problem of switching from their own fields to some other. Hence, only Course II follows.

9. **Option (B) is correct.**

Explanation: If only Course of Action II is followed, it is because setting up a fact-finding team to analyze the damages and take effective steps directly addresses the issue of water loss due to leakage in pipes supplying water. This action focuses on identifying the root causes of the problem and devising practical solutions to mitigate further loss. It allows for a systematic investigation into the extent of the damage, identifying areas where repairs or replacements are needed, and implementing measures to prevent future leakages. In opposition to it, while ordering an inquiry, as suggested in Course of Action I, provide some insights into the issue, setting up a fact-finding team is a more proactive and focused approach that facilitates timely and targeted interventions to restore and improve the drinking water supply to the affected parts of town.

10. **Option (A) is correct.**

Explanation: If only Course of Action I is followed, it is the correct approach because taking immediate steps to remove all unauthorized constructions on government land addresses the issue directly and legally. By doing so, the government upholds the rule of law and asserts its authority over public property, ensuring that it is utilized for its intended purposes. Removal of unauthorized constructions also prevents further encroachment and sets a precedent discouraging future illegal occupation of government land. Whereas, upon observing Course of Action II, which suggests putting all encroachers behind bars and imposing heavy fines, may not be feasible or practical for every case, and it could lead to social unrest or legal complications. It is more important to address the root cause of the issue by removing unauthorized constructions and preventing future encroachment through legal means.

11. **Option (D) is correct.**

Explanation: If neither Course of Action I nor II is followed, it is the correct answer because both proposed actions fail to address the root causes of the increasing dropout rates in government schools in urban areas. Closing down schools where dropout rates exceed 20 percent, as written in Course of Action I, does not tackle the underlying issues contributing to the dropout problem, such as inadequate infrastructure, poor quality of education, socioeconomic factors, or lack of support systems. Punishing parents of dropout students, as proposed in Course of Action II, is also to address the complex reasons behind dropout rates and further exacerbate social inequalities. Rather, the government should focus on identifying the specific factors contributing to dropout rates and implementing targeted interventions, such as improving the quality of education, providing support services for students at risk of dropping out, addressing socioeconomic barriers, and engaging with communities to promote the value of education. This approach prioritizes addressing the root causes of the issue and working towards sustainable solutions to improve retention rates in government schools.

12. **Option (B) is correct.**

Explanation: If only Course of Action II is followed, it is the correct approach because it addresses the systemic issue that led to the accident, which is the failure of the signaling system. Constituting a task force to review the functioning of the signaling system allows for a comprehensive assessment of the factors contributing to the failure and the implementation of measures to prevent similar incidents in the future. This action focuses on improving the safety and reliability of the railway infrastructure, benefiting not only the passengers but also the complete efficiency of the transportation system. On the other hand, terminating the services of the motorman, as suggested in Course of Action I, may be unjustified as it overlooks the possibility that the motorman may not have been at fault and fails to address the underlying issue of infrastructure failure.

13. **Option (A) is correct.**

Explanation: Course I follow the problem which is short circuit and it causes extensive damage to goods and property, so strict guidelines for all establishment regarding installation and maintenance of electrical fittings will definitely come to the aid. While Course II is extreme to follow.

14. **Option (A) is correct.**

Explanation: Course I is the obvious course of action. But Course II is absurd because for cases of theft of books from the library, all students cannot be held punishable.

15. **Option (B) is correct.**

Explanation: If only Course of Action II is followed, it is the correct approach because it addresses the root cause of the pollution problem by focusing on modifying the sewage system and finding alternative ways to dispose of the city's waste. This action aims to prevent further pollution of the river and improve its condition in the long term. By investing in upgrading the sewage system and implementing proper waste management practices, the government can mitigate the ongoing damage to the river ecosystem and protect public health. In contrast, penalizing individuals who dumped garbage and sewage into the river, as suggested in Course of Action I, may address immediate accountability but does not address the larger systemic issue of inadequate waste management infrastructure. Also, focusing solely on punishment may not be effective in preventing future pollution if the underlying causes are not addressed. Therefore, Course of Action II offers a more sustainable solution by tackling the problem at its source.

16. **Option (A) is correct.**
Explanation: If only Course of Action I is followed, it is the correct answer because it provides a proactive approach to address the suspicion of missing money from the safe. Recounting the money with the help of the staff and cross-checking it with the balance sheet allows for a thorough investigation within the company's internal procedures. This action helps to verify whether there is indeed any discrepancy and, if so, to identify the source of the problem. Also, involving the staff in the recounting process fosters transparency and accountability within the company. On the other hand, informing the police, as suggested in Course of Action II, may be premature and could potentially escalate the situation unnecessarily before confirming whether there is any actual wrongdoing. Therefore, Course of Action I is the appropriate first step in handling the situation effectively and efficiently.

17. **Option (E) is correct.**
Explanation: Implemention of both Course of Action I and II offers a comprehensive strategy to tackle the significant drop in water levels in the city's lakes. Imposing a partial cut in water supply, as suggested in Course of Action I, directly addresses the immediate urgency of the situation by conserving the remaining water resources and ensuring essential needs are met. Concurrently, appealing to residents through mass media for minimal water use, as proposed in Course of Action II, complements supply management efforts by fostering awareness about water conservation practices and encouraging responsible usage. This combined approach not only addresses the immediate crisis but also promotes long-term sustainability through public engagement and behavior change, contributing to effective water resource management in the city.

18. **Option (E) is correct.**
Explanation: By the implementation of both the Courses of Action I and II offers a comprehensive approach to addressing the alarming increase in malaria cases in the city. Advising government hospitals to store an adequate supply of malaria drugs ensures timely access to treatment for those affected, addressing the immediate healthcare needs. Also, by urging people to use mosquito repellants and maintain cleanliness targets the prevention of new infections by reducing mosquito breeding grounds and minimizing exposure to malaria-carrying mosquitoes. This combined strategy addresses both treatment and prevention aspects of the malaria problem, aiming to reduce the overall burden of malaria in the affected areas and contribute to long-term public health outcomes.

19. **Option (D) is correct.**
Explanation: Involving police personnel would scare the clubs and disbanding the management of the two club will curb the problem. Course II is the last resort, if preventive measures fail.

20. **Option (A) is correct.**
Explanation: Only Course of Action I is the correct answer because it directly addresses the issue of buses fitted with CNG kits not following safety guidelines. By conducting checks on all school buses fitted with CNG kits, the regional transport authority can identify and rectify any safety violations, ensuring that the buses meet the required safety standards. This approach prioritizes the safety of school children by addressing the root cause of the problem. Thus, only Course of Action I provides a targeted and practical response to the problem.

21. **Option (C) is correct.**
Explanation: Only Course of Action III is the correct answer because it directly addresses the issue by focusing on improving the skills and preparedness of the traffic controllers to handle pressure situations like near-miss incidents. By sending the traffic controllers for refresher courses, they can enhance their ability to manage air traffic effectively and respond appropriately during critical moments, by reducing the likelihood of similar incidents occurring in the future. This approach address the root cause of the problem by strengthening the capabilities of the personnel responsible for ensuring the safety of air traffic. Thus, only Course of Action III offers a targeted and practical response to the problem.

22. **Option (E) is correct.**
Explanation: Since the basic problem is that number of admission seekers are much more than the available seats hence Course of Action I and II will help to reduce the problem.

23. **Option (E) is correct.**
Explanation: None of the provided courses of action is the correct answer as they fail to address the immediate and urgent needs of the victims of the devastating earthquake effectively. Course of Action I's suggestion to stop the entry of outsiders into the city is impractical and could hinder crucial aid and support from reaching the affected area. Course of Action II lacks specificity and fails to outline concrete plans for providing alternate temporary arrange-

ments for the victims. Whereas, Course of Action III's proposal to immediately shift the affected people to a safer place overlooks the logistical challenges and complexities involved in large-scale relocation efforts. In reality, a comprehensive response to such a disaster would likely involve immediate search and rescue operations, provision of emergency medical care and shelter, and coordinated efforts to distribute essential supplies and assess the extent of damage for long-term recovery and rebuilding plans. Thus, none of the provided courses of action adequately address the urgent and multifaceted needs of the situation.

24. **Option (C) is correct.**

Explanation: Accidents at railways crossings can be averted by deploying men to regulate traffic and installing barriers to check traffic movements. So, only III follow.

25. **Option (A) is correct.**

Explanation: As a result of mass mortality of shrimps in ponds owing to to the presence of a virus, the nature of the virus needs to be identified for treatment. Even catching of shrimps from the ponds should temporarily be stopped, and any such phenomenon must be reported for prompt action. So only Course I follows.

Level-2: INTERMEDIATE

1. **Option (B) is correct.**

Explanation: The sentence implies that increasing defensive power does not ensure the safety of a country. There are other factors also that need to be given importance, like improving our diplomatic relations. This does not imply that the country should stop concentrating on increasing defensive power. So only II follows.

2. **Option (E) is correct.**

Explanation: Any malpractice can be curbed through effective measures and punishing the offenders. So both I and II follow.

3. **Option (C) is correct.**

Explanation: If there are slim chances of Japan granting India's request for a $500 million fast disbursing loan for the current year, it manifests India's need for that amount. So, India can approach other countries to get a loan or persuade Japan.

4. **Option (A) is correct.**

Explanation: The highlight is on 'critically ill after consuming spurious liquor'. This calls for a complete shut down of all the shops selling liquor till the stocks are tested for presence of toxicity. II course of action is illogical.

5. **Option (E) is correct.**

Explanation: With illegal cutting of trees, the most affected ones will be the locals and the wild habitat. So, locals must be endowed with the responsibility of reporting any such activities in the future. An immediate halt to such illegal activities is the need of the moment.

6. **Option (A) is correct.**

Explanation: The wrong practice ought to be checked, if the library is to be maintained. This is possible if precaution is taken to catch the guilty and punish him for the act. Thus, only I follow.

7. **Option (D) is correct.**

Explanation: If a country is facing unemployment owing to sever recession word-wide, provisions must be made to accommodate employees at a low wage. So neither I nor II is valid.

8. **Option (A) is correct.**

Explanation: If schools are found violating Government directives; it is justified for the Government to take action against those establishments. So I course of action is logical. II course of action is an opinion that favours schools. So it is not valid.

9. **Option (D) is correct.**

Explanation: Eliminating movie theatres is not a solution. Offering incentives and promotional schemes to cinema hall owners for marketing campaign can enable them to entice crowds to the halls.

10. **Option (D) is correct.**

Explanation: Both the suggestions in I and II are unfair ways to reduce competition. The right course of action would be to develop methods and procedures that would enable indigenous producers to produce fruits of higher quality and sell them on the market for prices that were on par with those of imported products. Because of this, neither I nor II follows.

11. **Option (A) is correct.**

Explanation: If only Course of Action I is followed, it is the correct answer because it presents a practical and feasible solution to the unprecedented increase in successful candidates in the School Leaving Certificate Examination. By making arrangements to increase the number of seats of intermediate courses in existing colleges, the government can efficiently utilize existing infrastructure and resources to accommodate the influx of students. This approach leverages the capacity of established educational institutions, minimizing the need for additional investments in new infrastructure and ensuring a more cost-effective and sustainable response to the increased demand for higher education. In opposite to it, Course of Action II, which suggests opening new colleges, may not be as immediately viable or efficient, as it involves significant time, resources, and administrative processes to establish new educational institutions. Thus, Course of Action I is the more appropriate and practical approach to address the situation.

12. **Option (C) is correct.**

Explanation: It is obvious that either precautions should be taken to warn trains far in advance of a landslide or measures should be taken to prevent track obstruction during landslides. As a result, course II follows.

13. **Option (A) is correct.**
Explanation: It is obvious that researching competitors' products will aid in determining the reason for the decline in sales, after which appropriate action can be taken. Thus, only I follow as a result.

14. **Option (B) is correct.**
Explanation: The central issue revolves around the retiring professors' contribution to the Institute. Consulting employees' opinions is deemed unnecessary due to the potential for conflicting views, which could complicate the decision-making process. Rather, it is argued that experienced individuals with their wealth of knowledge will significantly benefit the organization. This perspective is only reflected in Option II.

15. **Option (A) is correct.**
Explanation: It is obvious that the issue may be resolved by informing the pilgrims of the shrine's extreme weather to help make prior arrangements to maintain their health.
Therefore, I is the only one who follows.

16. **Option (B) is correct.**
Explanation: The assertion that Vitamin E present in fresh fruits and vegetables is beneficial for the human body than capsule Vitamin E implies that people should be encouraged to take fresh fruits and vegetables to meet the body's requirement of Vitamin E. Thus, only II follows.

17. **Option (B) is correct.**
Explanation: It is important to check the people coming to India if they are carrying such viruses. So detection centres are mandatory. While it is obvious that the non-infected people shouldn't be prohibited from travelling to India

18. **Option (B) is correct.**
Explanation: If only Course of Action II is followed, it is the correct answer because it presents a proactive approach to address the issue of the alarmingly low female-to-male ratio indicated in the recent census report. By issuing orders to all departments to encourage people to improve the ratio, the government can implement targeted initiatives and policies aimed at addressing gender imbalances. This action emphasizes the importance of societal and cultural changes to promote gender equality and female empowerment, which can lead to improvements in the female-to-male ratio over time. In contrast, Course of Action I, suggesting another census to verify the results, may not address the underlying causes of the low ratio and could delay the implementation of necessary interventions to address gender disparities. Therefore, Course of Action II is the more practical and effective approach to address the issue.

19. **Option (E) is correct.**
Explanation: To deliver prompt justice to the populace, either the work of the court has to be expedited or the system can be reorganised in such a way that problems can be resolved at the lower levels itself . Both courses I & II follows.

20. **Option (E) is correct.**
Explanation: Implementing both Course of Action I and II provides a comprehensive approach to addressing the serious blunders detected in the accounts section of the factory. Appointing an efficient team of auditors, as suggested in Course of Action I, ensures a thorough investigation into the financial records to identify the nature and extent of the blunders, facilitating the determination of corrective actions. Concurrently, issuing show cause notices to all employees involved in the irregularity, as proposed in Course of Action II, holds them accountable for their actions and prompts transparency in addressing the blunders. This combined approach emphasizes both investigation and accountability, fostering a culture of integrity and compliance within the organization while addressing the immediate need to rectify the irregularities.

21. **Option (A) is correct.**
Explanation: People cannot be prevented from travelling to a certain location due to a shortage of berths. Instead, it is the responsibility of the railway authorities to to increase the capacity in each of the trains. Course I alone follows.

22. **Option (E) is correct.**
Explanation: Implementing both Course of Action I and II provides a comprehensive strategy to mitigate the potential impact of the severe cyclonic storm forecasted for coastal Andhra Pradesh and Orissa. Advising fishermen to avoid dangerous areas at sea, as suggested in Course of Action I, prioritizes their safety and reduces the risk of maritime accidents during the storm. Simultaneously, alerting coastal residents and preparing them for evacuation, as proposed in Course of Action II, ensures that people are aware of the impending danger and have time to take necessary precautions, such as securing their homes and relocating to safer areas. By addressing both the safety of fishermen and coastal residents, these actions aim to minimize loss of life and damage from the cyclonic storm, thus offering a comprehensive approach to disaster preparedness and response.

23. **Option (A) is correct.**
Explanation: To avoid any unfavorable incident, the police should be immediately cautioned and placed on high alert. Also, once apprehended, such offenders shouldn't be freed. They might be questioned to look for further offenders. Course I alone follow, then.

24. **Option (E) is correct.**
Explanation: It is obvious that individuals cannot be prevented from taking part in the celebration due to inadequate planning. Also, police must be used to control large crowds and prevent any accidents during public events. Furthermore, alerting hospitals so they are prepared to offer immediate medical assistance to patients in case of an emergency costs nothing but may be beneficial. II and III therefore do. So, both II and III follow.

25. Option (C) is correct.

Explanation: It is obvious that course II refuses to follow because it is obvious that cutting back on trains will not stop the migration. The superior amenities and work prospects in the cities are the main causes of the exodus. Therefore, it may be stopped without using force by creating favorable conditions instead for those who live in villages. Course I thus do not follow while Course III does.

Level-3: EXPERT

1. **Option (B) is correct.**

Explanation: The problem is not about airport bound vehicle owners but all those vehicles that ply in that route. So convenience to all is necessary, this makes I illogical. If the load of vehicular traffic should be diverted through various link roads during peak hours, it will decongest the traffic at the said route. III is the most illogical and inconvenient option. So, only II follows.

2. **Option (E) is correct.**

Explanation: By implementing both Course of Action I and II offers a comprehensive response to the recurring incidents of students falling ill after consuming food from the school canteen. Terminating the canteen contract and seeking compensation Course of Action I addresses accountability by holding the canteen responsible for the safety of the food served. Advising students not to consume food from the canteen Course of Action II prioritizes their safety and prevents further incidents. Together, these actions ensure both immediate protection for the students and accountability for the canteen, thereby addressing the issue effectively.

3. **Option (E) is correct.**

Explanation: Both Courses of Action I and II follow because they collectively address the immediate and preventive measures necessary to ensure the safety of school children. The course of Action I involves the regional transport authority conducting immediate checks on all school buses with CNG kits, ensuring any safety violations are identified and rectified, thus reducing the risk of fire due to improper installations. The course of Action II requires school management to stop hiring buses with CNG kits, temporarily removing potential hazards until safety compliance is confirmed. This combined approach effectively mitigates current risks while preventing future incidents, ensuring a balanced and practical response without resorting to an outright ban, which could overlook the benefits of properly installed CNG kits.

4. **Option (E) is correct.**

Explanation: If both Course of Action II and III are followed, it would offer a comprehensive approach to addressing the sudden cloud burst and resulting flood-like situation in the island city. Deploying personnel to assist stranded people as in Course of Action II ensures immediate support and safety for those affected, while advising citizens not to venture out on the road as in Course of Action III prioritizes preventive measures to minimize further risk and potential harm. Together, these actions provide both immediate assistance and preventive measures to manage the emergency effectively, ensuring the well-being of the residents and reducing the impact of the adverse weather conditions.

5. **Option (B) is correct.**

Explanation: Course of Action II follows because it directly addresses the immediate problem of airspace congestion over the city airport, which is likely contributing to the near-miss incidents. By diverting some flights to other airports, the sky over the city airport will become less crowded, thereby reducing the risk of aircraft coming perilously close to each other. This measure provides an immediate solution to alleviate the congestion and enhance safety without disrupting the regular functioning of the airport. Courses of Action I and III, while potentially beneficial, are not as directly related to the immediate issue of congestion; de-rostering pilots without a thorough investigation might be premature, and sending air traffic controllers for refresher courses, though valuable, would take time and may not address the immediate need to reduce air traffic density.

6. **Option (B) is correct.**

Explanation: If only Course of Action II is followed, it is the correct answer because it provides a practical and targeted response to the situation without infringing on citizens' rights to peaceful protest. Deploying additional police forces throughout the city, as suggested in Course of Action II, addresses the immediate concern of maintaining traffic movement during peak hours while allowing political activists to exercise their right to protest. This action helps prevent potential disruptions and ensures public safety without resorting to extreme measures such as banning all forms of agitation or carrying out preventive arrests, as proposed in Courses of Action I and III, respectively. By focusing on maintaining order and facilitating traffic flow, Course of Action II strikes a balance between upholding public order and respecting citizens' democratic rights to express their grievances through peaceful demonstrations.

7. **Option (A) is correct.**

Explanation: If only Course of Action I is followed, it is the correct answer because it addresses the underlying socioeconomic issue contributing to the increase in school dropout rates. By implementing a mechanism to provide food grains to poor families in these districts through the public distribution system, Course of Action I aims to alleviate the economic pressure on parents, thereby encouraging them to prioritize their children's education over sending them to work in fields for sustenance. This approach recognizes the root cause of the problem and offers a practical solution to incentivize parents to send their children to school. In contrast, Courses of Action II and III may not effectively address the socioeconomic challenges faced by families and could potentially exacerbate the issue by either closing down schools or resorting to punitive measures against parents, without addressing the underlying economic factors. Therefore, Course of Action I provides a targeted and feasible approach to address the issue of increasing school dropout rates in the districts.

8. **Option (C) is correct.**
Explanation: If either Course of Action I or II is followed, it would constitute a reasonable response to the situation. Course of Action I proposes issuing a notification to the general public to immediately stop all transactions with the bank, which could potentially protect customers from further financial risk associated with the bank's losses. On the other hand, Course of Action II suggests directing the bank to refrain from retrenching its employees, which could mitigate the negative impact on the affected employees and their families. Both courses of action aim to address different aspects of the problem: Course of Action I focuses on protecting the interests of customers, while Course of Action II prioritizes the welfare of the bank's employees. Thus, either of these actions could be considered appropriate depending on the specific circumstances and priorities of the government.

9. **Option (E) is correct.**
Explanation: The actions in II & III are both sufficient. The aspirant's death was caused by a number of factors, which the committee should be required to address. Additionally, the home department needs to limit candidates' participation for a longer period of time.

10. **Option (D) is correct.**
Explanation: If all Course of Action I follows, IS the correct answer as it proposes an approach of addressing the aftermath of the heavy unseasonal downpour and its impact on the state. Setting up a committee to review the alarming situation in Course of Action I allows for a comprehensive assessment of the damage caused by the downpour and the effectiveness of existing measures to mitigate its effects. This review can inform future actions and policies to better prepare for and respond to similar situations in the future, ensuring more effective management of water crises and other emergencies. Thus, Course of Action I offers a systematic and strategic approach to addressing the challenges posed by the unseasonal downpour and its consequences.

11. **Option (A) is correct.**
Explanation: It is obvious that the only way to actually prevent robberies is to enhance security measures and increase police surveillance. Course I do as a result. Since neither of these is realistically feasible, neither II nor III follows.

12. **Option (E) is correct.**
Explanation: Students who study diligently throughout the year to achieve well on the Board test ought to be judged fairly by specialists rather than automatically or by persons with little expertise.
Also, examiners who neglect to evaluate the answers should be disciplined.
I and II both do as a result, but III does not.

13. **Option (E) is correct.**
Explanation: All the three suggested courses intend at extending as much relief to farmers as possible. So all I, II, and III follow.

14. **Option (E) is correct.**
Explanation: The situation calls for providing the ordinary people with as much assistance and relief as possible, so easing their adjustment to the extremely hot weather. So necessary arrangements to provide drinking water in all the affected areas and providing necessary equipments to prevent any untoward incident will tackle the issue at hand. Thus, only II and III continue.

15. **Option (E) is correct.**
Explanation: Having the knowledge well in advance shows that effective management and modest water supply reductions can preserve enough water for the emergency. Alternative crop cultivation could not be profitable for the farmers. So, only II and I continue.

■ ■ ■

Chapter 5

Statements and Conclusions

LEARNING OBJECTIVES:

- Understanding the concepts of Statements and Conclusions
- To determine the appropriate Sets of Conclusions
- Tips & Tricks to Solve Statement & conclusions Questions

CONCEPT:

- Questions from the statement and conclusions topic comprise a statement followed by a set of conclusions. Candidates need to choose the most appropriate conclusion regarding the statement given.
- Mostly the biggest mistake which is made by candidates while solving the statement–conclusion questions is that they make assumptions while answering questions which ultimately lead to marking the incorrect option as a conclusion for the given statement.
- No assumptions, facts or information can be used to answer questions based on this concept and the data given in the statement is the only fact.
- Candidates must know that to answer questions from this topic, they need to analyse the information given and then select the most logical conclusion based on the statement.

Tips and Tricks to Solve Statement and Conclusion Questions:

- If two or more sentences are used to frame a statement, then, the sentences must be interrelated, and mutual contradiction should be there.
- Do not look for truthful notions. The information provided in the statement is the only requirement for a candidate to answer the question. No assumptions should be made.
- Read the statement carefully and look for keywords which are common between the statement and the conclusions.
- If there is more than one conclusion applicable to the statement, candidates must ensure that the conclusions they opt for, have some relation with each other.
- Do not judge based on the length of the statement or statements. Make sure that you read the statement carefully before you make a conclusion.
- Candidates often lose marks due to negative marking in such questions. Therefore, ensure that you do not guess the answers in this topic.

SOLVED EXAMPLES

Example 1:

Statement: In a T20 match played between India and Australia, the total runs made by the Indian team were 200. 160 runs out of 200 runs were made by spinners.

Conclusion I: 80% of the team consists of spinners.

Conclusion II: The opening batsmen were spinners.

(a) Only conclusion I is true.
(b) Only conclusion II is true.
(c) Both conclusions I and II are true.
(d) Neither conclusion I nor II is true.
(e) Either conclusion I or II is true.

Sol. (d) Neither conclusion I nor II is true; neither conclusion is logically correct with regard to the statement.

Example 2:

Statement: The Team Manager humiliated Varun in front of his colleagues on a Monday morning.

Conclusion I: The Team Manager did not like Varun.

Conclusion II: Varun was not as popular as his other colleagues.

(a) Only conclusion I is true.
(b) Only conclusion II is true.
(c) Both conclusions I and II are true.
(d) Neither conclusion I nor II is true.
(e) Either conclusion I or II is true.

Sol. (d) Neither conclusion I nor II is true; none of the conclusions gives a valid reason for the statement to be correct.

Example 3:

Statement: A metal producing company in India has moved from a position where there was a shortage of metal production to a position where there is the self-sufficiency of metal.

Conclusion I: India was previously importing metal.

Conclusion II: At this speed of self-sufficiency, India can soon become a foreign exchange earner.

(a) Only conclusion I is true.
(b) Only conclusion II is true.
(c) Both conclusions I and II are true.
(d) Neither conclusion I nor II is true.
(e) Either conclusion I or II is true.

Sol. (c) Both conclusions I and II are true.

Example 4:

Statement: Only good dancers are invited to the competition. No one without dancing techniques is a good dancer.

Conclusion I: All invited dancers in the competition dance well.

Conclusion II: Those dancers who do not have good dancing techniques are not invited to the competition.

(a) Only conclusion I is true.
(b) Only conclusion II is true.
(c) Both conclusions I and II are true.
(d) Neither conclusion I nor II is true.
(e) Either conclusion I or II is true.

Sol. (c) Both conclusions I and II are true.

Level 1 Beginner

Directions (Qs. 1 to 25): In the question below is a statement followed by two conclusions numbered I and II. Assume everything in the statement to be true, then consider the two conclusions together and decide which of them logically follows beyond a reasonable doubt from the information given in the statement.

1. Statement: Electric supply in the upper parts of Fengling Valley has been shut down due to excessive snowfall in the month of February.

Conclusion:

I. Some parts of Fengling Valley receive snowfall more than other parts.

II. The common people in the upper part of Fengling Valley have to face a lot of problems in the winter season.

(A) Only conclusion I follows.
(B) Only conclusion II follows.
(C) Both conclusion I and conclusion II follow.
(D) Neither conclusion I nor conclusion II follows.

2. Statement: In one day match between Team X and Team Y, the score made by the losing Team X was 140/10.

Conclusion:

I. The bowling of Team Y was very good.

II. The batting of Team X was extremely poor.

(A) Only conclusion I follows.
(B) Only conclusion II follows.
(C) Both conclusion I and conclusion II follow.
(D) Either conclusion I or conclusion II follows.

3. Statement: Cycling daily for 1/2 hour or walking for 1 hour can increase a person's life span by one year.

Conclusion:

I. All people who are into desk jobs definitely suffer from several medical issues.

II. Moderate amount of physical exercise is helpful for leading a healthy life.

(A) Only conclusion I follows.
(B) Only conclusion II follows.
(C) Both conclusion I and conclusion II follow.
(D) Neither conclusion I nor conclusion II follows.

4. Statement: All apples are neither all good nor all bad; each type has its own properties.

Conclusion:

I. Some apples we find are quite good.

II. Some apples we find are not good.

(A) Only conclusion I follows.
(B) Only conclusion II follows.
(C) Both conclusion I and conclusion II follow.
(D) Neither conclusion I nor conclusion II follows.

5. Statement: Last year, the total accident count in Country A was 5,25,679 which caused 1,50,700 traffic-related deaths.

Conclusion:

I. Some of the traffic accidents were fatal.

II. The poor condition of the road was also responsible for such a high number of accidents.

(A) Only conclusion I follows.
(B) Only conclusion II follows.
(C) Both conclusion I and conclusion II follow.
(D) Neither conclusion I nor conclusion II follows.

6. Statement: All employees who do not work properly bring a bad name for themselves and also are a liability to an organisation.

Conclusion:

I. Such employees should be fired from the organisation.

II. Strict action is required in such cases.

(A) Only conclusion I follows.
(B) Only conclusion II follows.
(C) Both conclusion I and conclusion II follow.
(D) Neither conclusion I nor conclusion II follows.

7. Statement: Only arts students are permitted to attend the conference, other than arts students no one is permitted.

Conclusion:

I. All students present at the conference are arts students.

II. Those who do not have an arts background are not allowed in the conference.

(A) Only conclusion I follows.
(B) Only conclusion II follows.
(C) Both conclusion I and conclusion II follow.
(D) Neither conclusion I nor conclusion II follows.

8. **Statement:** PentaCell Fuel Company has moved Country B from a position of shortage to self-sufficiency in the Compressed Natural Gas.
Conclusion:
I. Previously Country B had to import Compressed Natural Gas.
II. In this regard, Country B can soon become a foreign exchange earner.
(A) Only conclusion I follows.
(B) Only conclusion II follows.
(C) Both conclusion I and conclusion II follow.
(D) Neither conclusion I nor conclusion II follows.

9. **Statement:** In a one day cricket match, the total runs made by a team were 230. Out of these 180 runs were made by spinners.
Conclusion:
I. 85% of the team consists of spinners.
II. The opening batsmen were definitely spinners.
(A) Only conclusion I follows.
(B) Only conclusion II follows.
(C) Both conclusion I and conclusion II follow.
(D) Neither conclusion I nor conclusion II follows.

10. **Statement:** The ever-growing population increase and depleting resources is going to be the common scenario of many developing countries in the near future.
Conclusion:
I. The population in the developing countries will decrease in the near future.
II. With the increasing population, it may soon be difficult for the Government in the developing countries to provide the common people with a proper quality of life.
(A) Only conclusion I follows.
(B) Only conclusion II follows.
(C) Both conclusion I and conclusion II follow.
(D) Neither conclusion I nor conclusion II follows.

11. **Statement:** There have been several deaths in the last one month due to several reasons in City Y.
Conclusion:
I. The mortality rate of the City Y has increased in the last month
II. There has been a leakage of poisonous gas in City Y.
(A) Only conclusion I follows.
(B) Only conclusion II follows.
(C) Both conclusion I and conclusion II follow.
(D) Neither conclusion I nor conclusion II follows.

12. **Statement:** Team A and Team B both have excellent players but team A scored more goals than team B and won the match.
Conclusion:
I. Team B has poor players who are not good in the game.
II. Team B has a weak defence with less number of expert defenders.
(A) Only conclusion I follows.
(B) Only conclusion II follows.
(C) Both conclusion I and conclusion II follow.
(D) Neither conclusion I nor conclusion II follows.

13. **Statement:** The water supply to Javni area has been cut and people are suffering.
Conclusion:
I. Residents of Javni area may have failed to pay the water tax.
II. Water is very precious and its supply should be cut off for areas alternately to preserve it.
(A) Only conclusion I follows.
(B) Only conclusion II follows.
(C) Both conclusion I and conclusion II follow.
(D) Neither conclusion I nor conclusion II follows.

14. **Statement:** More houses in Baguihati area have lifts as compared to the houses in Salt Lake area.
Conclusion:
I. The residents of Baguihati are very lazy.
II. The residents of Baguihati are very rich.
(A) Only conclusion I follows.
(B) Only conclusion II follows.
(C) Both conclusion I and conclusion II follow.
(D) Neither conclusion I nor conclusion II follows.

15. **Statement:** In Country X, there have been several cases of colon cancer. But when some citizens of Country X moved to Country Y, the cases of colon cancer were less. The food habits of both the countries are completely different.
Conclusion:
I. Food habit of Country X may be responsible for colon cancer there.
II. Food habit of Country Y may be different and that is why there were lesser cases of colon cancer of those residents who moved from Country X to Country Y.
(A) Only conclusion I follows.
(B) Only conclusion II follows.
(C) Both conclusion I and conclusion II follow.
(D) Neither conclusion I nor conclusion II follows.

16. **Statement:** The T.V. programmes on almost all channels, telecast specially for men are packed with a variety of health and fitness tips and workout plans. A major portion of magazines for men also contains the items mentioned above.
Conclusion:
I. A man's primary interest lies in health and fitness only.
II. Men are not interested in other things.
(A) Only conclusion I follows.
(B) Only conclusion II follows.
(C) Both conclusion I and conclusion II follow.
(D) Neither conclusion I nor conclusion II follows.

17. Statement: The distance of 600 km by road between Xadin city and Pandora city will be reduced to 230 km by sea. This will lead to a saving of ₹ 5 crores per annum on fuel.

Conclusion:

I. Fuel must be preserved to the greatest extent possible for the future generations as it is non-renewable.

II. Transportation by sea is cheaper than transportation by road in the given case.

(A) Only conclusion I follows.
(B) Only conclusion II follows.
(C) Both conclusion I and conclusion II follow.
(D) Neither conclusion I nor conclusion II follows.

18. Statement: The manager of Pharma X humiliated Rajeev in the presence of his colleagues.

Conclusion:

I. The manager did not like Rajeev at all.

II. Rajeev was not popular with his colleagues.

(A) Only conclusion I follows.
(B) Only conclusion II follows.
(C) Both conclusion I and conclusion II follow.
(D) Neither conclusion I nor conclusion II follows.

19. Statement: Country X has been blacklisted on Global Forum for financing terrorism.

Conclusion:

I. Country Y has seen rise in terrorism caused by terrorist organisations belonging Country X, which is an enemy nation of Country Y.

II. Country X is being ruled by a dictator.

(A) Only conclusion I follows.
(B) Only conclusion II follows.
(C) Both conclusion I and conclusion II follow.
(D) Neither conclusion I nor conclusion II follows.

20. Statement: Mr Ramesh Singh has been experiencing hallucinations for the past two days.

Conclusion:

I. Mr Ramesh Singh is a regular drinker.

II. Mr Ramesh Singh recently had a divorce.

(A) Only conclusion I follows.
(B) Only conclusion II follows.
(C) Both conclusion I and conclusion II follow.
(D) Neither conclusion I nor conclusion II follows.

21. Statement: The Bank of England's to auction 25 metric tons of gold drew plenty of bidders looking for a bargain, but was criticised by major gold producers worldwide.

Conclusion:

I. The Bank of England should not auction gold which it possesses to keep steady international prices of gold.

II. Bidders should quote higher gold prices to retain present value of gold in the international markets.

(A) If only conclusion I follows.
(B) If only conclusion II follows.
(C) If either I or II follows.
(D) If neither I nor II follows.
(E) If both I and II follow.

22. Statement: The use of non-conventional sources of energy will eliminate the energy crisis in the world.

Conclusion:

I. Modern technology is gradually replacing the conventional sources of energy.

II. The excessive exploitation of environment has led to depletion of conventional sources of energy.

(A) If only conclusion I follows.
(B) If only conclusion II follows.
(C) If either I or II follows.
(D) If neither I nor II follows.
(E) If both I and II follow.

23. Statement: Good voice is a natural gift but one has to keep practicing to improve and excel well in the field of music.

Conclusion:

I. Natural gifts need nurturing and care.

II. Even though your voice is not good, one can keep practising.

(A) If only conclusion I follows.
(B) If only conclusion II follows.
(C) If either I or II follows.
(D) If neither I nor II follows.
(E) If both I and II follow.

24. Statement: India's economy depends mainly on forests.

Conclusion:

I. Trees should be preserved to improve Indian economy.

II. India wants only maintenance of forests to improve economic conditions.

(A) If only conclusion I follows.
(B) If only conclusion II follows.
(C) If either I or II follows.
(D) If neither I nor II follows.
(E) If both I and II follow.

25. Statement: In Japan, the incidence of stomach cancer is very high, while that of bowel cancer is very low. But Japanese emigrate to Hawaii, this is reversed – the rate of bowel cancer increases but the rate of stomach cancer is reduced in the next generation. All this is related to nutrition – the diets of Japanese in Hawaii are different than those in Japan.

Conclusion:

I. The same diet as in Hawaii should be propagated in Japan also.

II. Bowel cancer is less severe than stomach cancer.

(A) If only conclusion I follows.
(B) If only conclusion II follows.
(C) If either I or II follows.
(D) If neither I nor II follows.
(E) If both I and II follow.

Level 2 Intermediate

Directions (Qs. 1-25): In the question below is a statement followed by two conclusions numbered I and II. Assume everything in the statement to be true, then consider the two conclusions together and decide which of them logically follows beyond a reasonable doubt from the information given in the statement.

1. The price of Hilsa fish is always very high.

Conclusion:

I. People want to pay high prices for the tasty fish.

II. The demand of Hilsa may be higher than its supply that leads to the rise in price.

(A) Only conclusion I follows.
(B) Only conclusion II follows.
(C) Both conclusion I and conclusion II follow.
(D) Neither conclusion I nor conclusion II follows.

2. Statement: There have been a number of murders in Xingpi Town during the last three weeks.

Conclusion:

I. Xingpi town is situated in the middle of a dense forest.

II. Xingpi town has less population as compared to other towns.

(A) Only conclusion I follows.
(B) Only conclusion II follows.
(C) Both conclusion I and conclusion II follow.
(D) Neither conclusion I nor conclusion II follows.

3. Statement: The price of commodities has started increasing after a new political party came to power.

Conclusion:

I. Corruption and black markets may have led to the rise in prices.

II. The political party wants to take revenge against the common people for causing them to lose in the last election

(A) Only conclusion I follows.
(B) Only conclusion II follows.
(C) Both conclusion I and conclusion II follow.
(D) Neither conclusion I nor conclusion II follows.

4. Statement: Recently in a serious accident where an old woman and her daughter were run over by a truck has again laid great focus on the condition of roads in the city.

Conclusion:

I. The woman was not cautious while walking on the road.

II. Due to poor condition of roads several accidents had taken place earlier also.

(A) Only conclusion I follows.
(B) Only conclusion II follows.
(C) Both conclusion I and conclusion II follow.
(D) Neither conclusion I nor conclusion II follows.

5. Statement: Smoking causes severe health hazards in pregnant women.

Conclusion:

I. Pregnant women are always under stress and hence they smoke a lot.

II. Researchers have established facts that smoking has earlier caused several pregnancy related problems in pregnant women.

(A) Only conclusion I follows.
(B) Only conclusion II follows.
(C) Both conclusion I and conclusion II follow.
(D) Neither conclusion I nor conclusion II follows.

6. Statement: After his gall bladder stone operation where his gall bladder had to be removed, he experiences indigestion every now and then whenever he takes oily foods and fries.

Conclusion:

I. Removal of the gall bladder causes problem if someone takes oily and fried foods.

II. Gall bladder is one of the essential organs of the body.

(A) Only conclusion I follows.
(B) Only conclusion II follows.
(C) Both conclusion I and conclusion II follow.
(D) Neither conclusion I nor conclusion II follows.

7. Statement: Recently the CBI has asked the employees of HiFi Techno Solutions to declare their undisclosed assets but none of the employees is ready to disclose their assets.

Conclusion:

I. The employees are ready to go to court for false allegations.

II. The employees are very honest and do not have any undisclosed asset.

(A) Only conclusion I follows.
(B) Only conclusion II follows.
(C) Both conclusion I and conclusion II follow.
(D) Neither conclusion I nor conclusion II follows.

8. Statement: People in Country M wear woollen garments all over the year.

Conclusion:

I. Residents of Country M love wearing woollen garments.

II. The normal climate of Country M is extremely cold all throughout the year.

(A) Only conclusion I follows.
(B) Only conclusion II follows.
(C) Both conclusion I and conclusion II follow.
(D) Neither conclusion I nor conclusion II follows.

9. Statement: Residents of Country B suffer from various diseases as compared to residents of Country A.

Residents of Country B eat everything such as, worms, caterpillars, bats and many unhealthy food items and that too not properly cooked. Residents of

Country A have a proper food habit and most of them eat healthy foods that are cooked properly.

Conclusion:

I. Cooking a food item properly is very essential to maintain a healthy lifestyle.

II. Residents of Country B are very rich.

(A) Only conclusion I follows.

(B) Only conclusion II follows.

(C) Both conclusion I and conclusion II follow.

(D) Neither conclusion I nor conclusion II follows.

10. Statement: After the collision of Gangayaan and Rosie, two cruise ships, none of the passengers could be found and they have been declared missing.

Conclusion:

I. All passengers are dead.

II. Some passengers may have survived and are still missing.

(A) Only conclusion I follows.

(B) Only conclusion II follows.

(C) Both conclusion I and conclusion II follow.

(D) Neither conclusion I nor conclusion II follows.

11. Statement: Hospitals in City A have no more beds to admit new patients who are suffering from COVID 19.

Conclusion:

I. There have been many cases of COVID 19 affected patients.

II. Number of hospitals in City A may be less.

(A) Only conclusion I follows.

(B) Only conclusion II follows.

(C) Both conclusion I and conclusion II follow.

(D) Neither conclusion I nor conclusion II follows.

12. Statement: The government wants to privatise the Railways.

Conclusion:

I. Privatisation is extremely bad for any sector.

II. The government wants to earn by privatising the sector.

(A) Only conclusion I follows.

(B) Only conclusion II follows.

(C) Both conclusion I and conclusion II follow.

(D) Neither conclusion I nor conclusion II follows.

13. Statement: An Indian origin nurse has been awarded by the Government for her work during a pandemic outbreak.

Conclusion:

I. The nurse must be having big links to politicians.

II. The nurse dedicated her time in helping and looking after many patients during the sudden crisis of the pandemic.

(A) Only conclusion I follows.

(B) Only conclusion II follows.

(C) Both conclusion I and conclusion II follow.

(D) Neither conclusion I nor conclusion II follows.

14. Statement: There have been 30 accidents involving MX 2 model helicopters which is the highest till date in a single month.

Conclusion:

I. The company wants to risk the lives of the passengers and test the model.

II. The MX 2 model helicopters may have a manufacturing defect.

(A) Only conclusion I follows.

(B) Only conclusion II follows.

(C) Both conclusion I and conclusion II follow.

(D) Neither conclusion I nor conclusion II follows.

15. Statement: The government has extended the work from home initiative during the nationwide lockdown during the pandemic.

Conclusion:

I. The government gets commission from the companies who in turn are paying less to the employees. This is helping the companies to grow in this crisis.

II. The situation has not yet turned normal so that office goers can resume their work by going to their offices.

(A) Only conclusion I follows.

(B) Only conclusion II follows.

(C) Both conclusion I and conclusion II follow.

(D) Neither conclusion I nor conclusion II follows.

16. Statement: The minister questioned the utility of the space research programme and suggested its replacement by areas of felt national needs.

Conclusion:

I. Exploring the space does not contribute to critical national needs.

II. Research should be oriented to national needs.

(A) If only conclusion I follows.

(B) If only conclusion II follows.

(C) If either I or II follows.

(D) If neither I nor II follows.

(E) If both I and II follow.

17. Statement: The commissioner of police has appealed people not to put up banners which obstruct pedestrian or motor traffic.

Conclusion:

I. Some of the people may respond and will not put up such banners.

II. Policemen will have to keep a watchful eye on the new banners which are being put up on the roads.

(A) If only conclusion I follows.

(B) If only conclusion II follows.

(C) If either I or II follows.

(D) If neither I nor II follows.

(E) If both I and II follow.

18. Statement: Jade plant has thick leaves and it requires little water.

Conclusion:

I. All plants with thick leaves requires little water.

II. Jade plants may be grown in places where water is not in abundance.

(A) If only conclusion I follows.

(B) If only conclusion II follows.

(C) If either I or II follows.
(D) If neither I nor II follows.
(E) If both I and II follow.

19. Statement: I know nothing except the fact of my ignorance.

Conclusion:

I. Writer knowledge is very poor.
II. The world of knowledge is too vast to be explored by a single person.

(A) If only conclusion I follows.
(B) If only conclusion II follows.
(C) If either I or II follows.
(D) If neither I nor II follows.
(E) If both I and II follow.

20. Statement: A man must be wise to be a good wrangler. Good wranglers are talkative and boring.

Conclusion:

I. All the wise persons are boring.
II. All the wise persons are good wranglers.

(A) If only conclusion I follows.
(B) If only conclusion II follows.
(C) If either I or II follows.
(D) If neither I nor II follows.
(E) If both I and II follow.

21. Statement: Morning walks are good for health.

Conclusion:

I. All healthy people go for morning walks.
II. Evening walks are harmful.

(A) If only conclusion I follows.
(B) If only conclusion II follows.
(C) If either I or II follows.
(D) If neither I nor II follows.
(E) If both I and II follow.

22. Statement: Parents are prepared to pay any price for an elite education to their children.

Conclusion:

I. All parents these days are very well off.
II. Parents have an obsessive passion for a perfect development of their children through good schooling.

(A) If only conclusion I follows.
(B) If only conclusion II follows.
(C) If either I or II follows.
(D) If neither I nor II follows.
(E) If both I and II follow.

23. Statement: Industrial revolution which first of all started in Europe has brought about modern age.

Conclusions:

I. Disparity between rich and poor results in revolution.
II. Revolution overhauls society.

(A) If only conclusion I follows.
(B) If only conclusion II follows.
(C) If either I or II follows.
(D) If neither I nor II follows and
(E) If both I and II follow.

24. Statement: This book is the only book which focuses its attention to the problem of poverty in India between 1950 and 1980.

Conclusion:

I. There was no question of poverty before 1950.
II. No other book deals with poverty in India during 1950 to 1980.

(A) If only conclusion I follows.
(B) If only conclusion II follows.
(C) If either I or II follows.
(D) If neither I nor II follows and
(E) If both I and II follow.

25. Statement: Government has spoiled many top ranking financial institutions by appointing bureaucrats as Directors of these institutions.

Conclusion:

I. Government should appoint Directors of the financial institutes taking into consideration the expertise of the person in the area of finance.
II. The Director of the financial institute should have expertise commensurate with the financial work carried out by the institute.

(A) If only conclusion I follows.
(B) If only conclusion II follows.
(C) If either I or II follows.
(D) If neither I nor II follows and
(E) If both I and II follow.

Level 3 Expert

Directions (Qs. 1-15): In the question below is a statement followed by two conclusions numbered I and II. Assume everything in the statement to be true, then consider the two conclusions together and decide which of them logically follows beyond a reasonable doubt from the information given in the statement.

1. Statement: Fake news spread on social media has led to deaths of 14 people in the last month.

Conclusion:

I. Fake news arises from genuine sources and there is no such thing called fake news.
II. Fake news is unethical and has severe negative consequences.

(A) Only conclusion I follows.
(B) Only conclusion II follows.
(C) Both conclusion I and conclusion II follow.
(D) Neither conclusion I nor conclusion II follows.

2. Statement: Company X has decided to give laptops and personal mobile phones to all its employees in order to increase their efficiency.

Conclusion:

I. Company X can afford to give laptops and personal mobile phone to the employees.

II. Having personal laptops and mobile phones may help in better communication and more efficient output from the employees.

(A) Only conclusion I follows.
(B) Only conclusion II follows.
(C) Both conclusion I and conclusion II follow.
(D) Neither conclusion I nor conclusion II follows.

3. Statement: N95 masks with valved respirators cannot stop the virus from entering.

Conclusion:

I. Researchers have found that the provision of a valved respirator allows the entry of viruses due to their openings.

II. N95 masks without valved respirators may prevent the virus from penetrating the mask.

(A) Only conclusion I follows.
(B) Only conclusion II follows.
(C) Both conclusion I and conclusion II follow.
(D) Neither conclusion I nor conclusion II follows.

4. Statement: Information regarding the raid on a gangster's house by Dingla City Police has been leaked. But except the 10 policemen, who were supposed to go on the raid, nobody knew of this.

Conclusion:

I. There might be a mole within the 10 policemen who has leaked the information.

II. The entire police department has becomes corrupt and it was just a publicity stunt.

(A) Only conclusion I follows.
(B) Only conclusion II follows.
(C) Both conclusion I and conclusion II follow.
(D) Neither conclusion I nor conclusion II follows.

5. Statement: After the outbreak of a global pandemic there has been a severe economic crisis all across the globe.

Conclusion:

I. Many people might have lost their jobs.

II. Share markets may have crashed due to a global economic crisis.

(A) Only conclusion I follows.
(B) Only conclusion II follows.
(C) Both conclusion I and conclusion II follow.
(D) Neither conclusion I nor conclusion II follows.

6. Statement: Gangadhar is a great right arm bowler and a famous person when it comes to cricket. But in yesterday's match he bowled using his left arm which shocked everyone.

Conclusion:

I. Gangadhar knows bowling in both arms.

II. There is a possibility that he was having some problem in his right arm.

(A) Only conclusion I follows.
(B) Only conclusion II follows.
(C) Both conclusion I and conclusion II follow.
(D) Neither conclusion I nor conclusion II follows.

7. Statement: After the cyclone Aamphan there has been a severe issue in the network of mobile phones.

Conclusion:

I. Many mobile towers may have been destroyed during the cyclone.

II. The mobile network providers were busy in their relief works, as volunteers.

(A) Only conclusion I follows.
(B) Only conclusion II follows.
(C) Both conclusion I and conclusion II follow.
(D) Neither conclusion I nor conclusion II follows.

8. Statement: Most people who smoke get cancer.

Conclusion:

I. Smoking cause cancer in smokers.

II. Smoking is the only cause of cancer.

(A) Only conclusion I follows.
(B) Only conclusion II follows.
(C) Both conclusion I and conclusion II follow.
(D) Neither conclusion I nor conclusion II follows.

9. Statement: Company X has planned to shut down its office in City A and set up a new office in City B.

Conclusion:

I. City A is definitely a city with less population.

II. City B has many rich people.

(A) Only conclusion I follows.
(B) Only conclusion II follows.
(C) Both conclusion I and conclusion II follow.
(D) Neither conclusion I nor conclusion II follows.

10. Statement: There has been several cases of food poisoning after people ate foods from Shaandar restaurant.

Conclusion:

I. The quality of food was bad which led to the food poisoning.

II. Shaandar restaurant definitely has employees who all are very careless.

(A) Only conclusion I follows.
(B) Only conclusion II follows.
(C) Both conclusion I and conclusion II follow.
(D) Neither conclusion I nor conclusion II follows.

11. Statement: Company X is being forced to sell 100% of its stake in Company Y and it will be taken over completely by the latter.

Conclusion:

I. Company X might be bankrupt.

II. Company X must be facing serious issues in management and repayment of loans.

(A) Only conclusion I follows.
(B) Only conclusion II follows.
(C) Both conclusion I and conclusion II follow.
(D) Neither conclusion I nor conclusion II follows.

12. Statement: The Z+ Model of the Santro cars have led to several deaths due to accidents.

Conclusion:

I. There might be a serious issue regarding the safety of the Z+ Model.

II. The company might have committed a mistake while checking the model for its safety before launching it in the market.

(A) Only conclusion I follows.
(B) Only conclusion II follows.
(C) Both conclusion I and conclusion II follow.
(D) Neither conclusion I nor conclusion II follows.

13. **Statement:** Even after getting a bullet wound, Detective Byomkesh Bakshi ran after the armed gangster and at the dead end of the road, took him down.

Conclusion:

I. Detective Byomkesh Bakshi is a courageous man.
II. The gangster was a foolish person.

(A) Only conclusion I follows.
(B) Only conclusion II follows.
(C) Both conclusion I and conclusion II follow.
(D) Neither conclusion I nor conclusion II follows.

14. **Statement:** Surdeep Rajput's body was found hanging from the ceiling fan at a height of 8 feet from the ground in his study room. Surdeep was 6 feet tall and no stool or bed was present in the study room. A suicide note was found on the mattress where he used to sleep and study.

Conclusion:

I. Surdeep Rajput might have been murdered.
II. The suicide note might be fake.

(A) Only conclusion I follows.
(B) Only conclusion II follows.
(C) Both conclusion I and conclusion II follow.
(D) Neither conclusion I nor conclusion II follows.

15. **Statement:** New CNG and battery driven cars have been launched in City X, which are 5 times costlier than petrol and diesel cars. And after the launch, only 10 cars have been sold in a month, whereas the population of the city is 1 lakh.

Conclusion:

I. The purchasing capacity of the residents of City X might not be high and so they cannot afford to buy them.
II. The new battery and CNG cars are defective.

(A) Only conclusion I follows.
(B) Only conclusion II follows.
(C) Both conclusion I and conclusion II follow.
(D) Neither conclusion I nor conclusion II follows.

ANSWER KEY

Level-1: Beginner

1.	(C)	2.	(D)	3.	(B)	4.	(C)	5.	(A)	6.	(B)	7.	(C)	8.	(A)	9.	(D)	10.	(B)
11.	(A)	12.	(B)	13.	(A)	14.	(D)	15.	(C)	16.	(D)	17.	(C)	18.	(D)	19.	(A)	20.	(D)
21.	(D)	22.	(A)	23.	(E)	24.	(A)	25.	(D)										

Level-2: Intermediate

1.	(B)	2.	(D)	3.	(A)	4.	(B)	5.	(B)	6.	(C)	7.	(D)	8.	(B)	9.	(A)	10.	(B)
11.	(C)	12.	(D)	13.	(B)	14.	(B)	15.	(B)	16.	(E)	17.	(A)	18.	(B)	19.	(B)	20.	(D)
21.	(D)	22.	(B)	23.	(B)	24.	(B)	25.	(E)										

Level-3: Expert

1.	(B)	2.	(C)	3.	(B)	4.	(A)	5.	(C)	6.	(C)	7.	(A)	8.	(A)	9.	(D)	10.	(A)
11.	(A)	12.	(C)	13.	(A)	14.	(C)	15.	(A)										

Solutions with Detailed Explanations

Level-1: BEGINNER

1. **Option (C) is correct.**

Explanation: Here, we have to assume everything in the statement to be true, then consider the two conclusions together and decide which of them becomes logically valid.

Conclusion I is drawn from the statement, which makes it quite evident that not all of Fernging Valley's electricity has been turned off owing to severe snowfall, but just some areas have.

2. **Option (D) is correct.**

Explanation: Here, we have to assume everything in the statement to be true, then consider the two conclusions together and decide which of them becomes logically valid.

The above statement shows that, prior to losing every wicket, the losing Team X scored 140 runs in total. Therefore, either Team X's hitting was subpar or Team Y's bowling was excellent. Therefore, I or II is true.

3. **Option (B) is correct.**

Explanation: Here, we have to assume everything in the statement to be true, then consider the two conclusions together and decide which of them becomes logically valid. The statement mentions the health benefits of walking and cycling, but it is unclear what exactly is meant to be said about the health of someone who has a desk job. Thus, we can't draw such a conclusion. Therefore, only conclusion II follows.

4. **Option (C) is correct.**

Explanation: Here, we have to assume everything in the statement to be true, then consider the two conclusions together and decide which of them becomes logically valid. The statement mentions that the all apples are neither all good nor all bad that makes both the assumptions correct.

5. **Option (A) is correct.**

Explanation: Here, we have to assume everything in the statement to be true, then consider the two conclusions together and decide which of them becomes logically valid. In the statement given here, it is clearly mentioned that there were traffic-related deaths. But no clear information is given regarding the bad condition of the road, therefore only conclusion I follows.

6. **Option (B) is correct.**

Explanation: Here, we have to assume everything in the statement to be true, then consider the two conclusions together and decide which of them becomes logically valid. Conclusion I is a too strict action to take and can send negative message to the rest of the employees. Such strict action should be taken only after warnings. Thus, I is not the correct conclusion. But if employees are not working, the organisation may get impacted. Thus, strict warning is required. So, conclusion II is followed.

7. **Option (C) is correct.**

Explanation: Here, we have to assume everything in the statement to be true, then consider the two conclusions together and decide which of them becomes logically valid. It is clear from the statement that only students studying arts are allowed to attend the conference. It follows that all of the pupils in attendance have an art background, and those who do not will not be allowed in. As a result, conclusions I and II are also followed.

8. **Option (A) is correct.**

Explanation: Here, we have to assume everything in the statement to be true, then consider the two conclusions together and decide which of them becomes logically valid. As stated in the statement: "Country B is now self-sufficient in compressed natural gas, having moved from a state of shortage thanks to PentaCell Fuel Company." Therefore, we may draw the conclusion that Country B formerly experienced a compressed natural gas deficit and had to import compressed natural gas. However, nothing in the sentence indicates that Country B could gain foreign exchange in the future; so, conclusion II is not supported. Only conclusion I is implied.

9. **Option (D) is correct.**

Explanation: Here, we have to assume everything in the statement to be true, then consider the two conclusions together and decide which of them becomes logically valid. As per the given statement, 85% of the total runs were made by spinners. But this doesn't indicate that the team consists majorly of spinners. It is a possibility that few players had made majority of the runs.

Nothing about the opening batsman is mentioned in the statement. So, conclusion II also does not follow too.

10. **Option (B) is correct.**

Explanation: Here, we have to assume everything in the statement to be true, then consider the two conclusions together and decide which of them becomes logically valid. The information presented in conclusion I is in direct contradiction to the fact given in the statement. Thus, I does not agree with the conclusion. The direct consequences of the condition mentioned in the statement is stated in Conclusion II in a clear and concise manner.

11. **Option (A) is correct.**

Explanation: Here, we have to assume everything in the statement to be true, then consider the two conclusions together and decide which of them becomes logically valid. It makes sense to draw conclusion I. Nevertheless, we're not sure if a gas leak caused the fatalities. As a result, conclusion I follows while conclusion II does not.

12. **Option (B) is correct.**

Explanation: Here, we have to assume everything in the statement to be true, then consider the two conclusions together and decide which of them becomes logically valid.

Since the statement says that both have excellent players, option I is ruled out. Despite this team A scored more goals against team B, this shows that the defence of team B must be weak. Hence, option II is valid.

13. **Option (A) is correct.**

Explanation: Here, we have to assume everything in the statement to be true, then consider the two conclusions together and decide which of them becomes logically valid.

Since the statement mentions that the water supply is disconnected thus option I can be deduced. The use of 'may' makes Conclusion I a dependable option. Option II is neither hinted nor derived. Thus, it is incorrect.

14. **Option (D) is correct.**

Explanation: Here, we have to assume everything in the statement to be true, then consider the two conclusions together and decide which of them becomes logically valid.

Both conclusions are invalid and are extremely illogical. There may be difference in the average heights of the buildings. Even there may be difference in the number of storeys. So, we cannot conclude the given conclusions from the given statement.

15. Option (C) is correct.
Explanation: Here, we have to assume everything in the statement to be true, then consider the two conclusions together and decide which of them becomes logically valid.
Here, it may be taken into consideration that food habit is the main reason behind the cause of colon cancer in Country X because only after the residents of X move to country Y (which has a completely different food habit) , do the people face less chances of colon cancer.
So, both the conclusions are true in this case.

16. Option (D) is correct.
Explanation: Here, we have to assume everything in the statement to be true, then consider the two conclusions together and decide which of them becomes logically valid. We cannot easily conclude that a man's area of interest is only health and fitness. Hence, conclusion I is false here.
Conclusion II is also false because it says something that is illogical.

17. Option (C) is correct.
Explanation: Here, we have to assume everything in the statement to be true, then consider the two conclusions together and decide which of them becomes logically valid.
According to the statement, sea transport is cheaper than road transport in the case of route from Xadin city and Pandora city, not in all the cases. So, conclusion I does follow for this case only. The statement stresses on the saving of fuel, which is indeed a non-renewable source of energy. So, conclusion II follows.

18. Option (D) is correct.
Explanation: Here, we have to assume everything in the statement to be true, then consider the two conclusions together and decide which of them becomes logically valid. It's possible that the manager degraded Rajeev due to some of his own carelessness rather than his dislike for him. It's unclear to us if Rajeev was loved or despised by the manager. Thus, I do not agree with the conclusion. Additionally, nothing in the statement suggests that Raveev is well-liked by his peers. Therefore, conclusion II is not followed.

19. Option (A) is correct.
Explanation: Here, we have to assume everything in the statement to be true, then consider the two conclusions together and decide which of them becomes logically valid. Because Country X and Y are foes, Conclusion I can be considered legitimate. Thus, it is possible that Country Y was funding terrorism.
Conclusion II is erroneous and does not hold true.

20. Option (D) is correct.
Explanation: Here, we have to assume everything in the statement to be true, then consider the two conclusions together and decide which of them becomes logically valid.
According to the statement provided, we are unable to determine whether or not he drinks frequently or whether or not he just went through a divorce.

21. Option (D) is correct.
Explanation: The announcement simply discusses the reaction it got from the bidders and gold miners; it makes no mention of the auction itself. So, I does not follow the conclusion. The statement "many bidders searching for a deal" runs directly against conclusion II. Thus, conclusion II is likewise non-following.

22. Option (A) is correct.
Explanation: From the part of the statement: "but one has to keep practicing to improve and excel well in the field of music." we can derive statement I. Since, it is not mentioned that there is any kind of restriction upon practicing if one's voice is not good. Both conclusions I and II directly follow from the given statement. However, conclusion II is not related to the given statement and so does not follow.

23. Option (E) is correct.
Explanation: Clearly conclusion I follows directly from the given statement. However, conclusion II is not related to the given statement and so does not follow.

24. Option (A) is correct.
Explanation: The assertion that India's economy is largely dependent on its forests is made. This implies that it is important to protect forests. So, conclusion I follows. It is not indicated, however, that the economy can only be strengthened by maintaining forests. Thus, conclusion II is not supported.

25. Option (D) is correct.
Explanation: The assertion does not promote a particular nation's diet or make a comparison between the two forms of cancer which are prevalent in both the said countries. So neither of the country's diet can be propagated. As a result, neither conclusion I nor conclusion II are justified.

Level-2: INTERMEDIATE

1. Option (B) is correct.
Explanation: Here, we have to assume everything in the statement to be true, then consider the two conclusions together and decide which of them becomes logically valid. The statement asserts that the price of Hilsa fish is always high. High demand and low supply leads to high price. Thus, conclusion II is a valid argument. People are willing to pay high price is not the valid conclusion.

2. Option (D) is correct.
Explanation: Here, we have to assume everything in the statement to be true, then consider the two conclusions together and decide which of them becomes logically valid. None of the conclusions I and II can be deduced from the given statement. There is no mention of population in the given statement also.

3. Option (A) is correct.
Explanation: Here, we have to assume everything in the statement to be true, then consider the two conclusions together and decide which of them becomes logically valid. Conclusion I is a valid point. We can deduce that the price is rising as a result of corruption and black markets. However, conclusion II is not at all reasonable.

4. **Option (B) is correct.**
Explanation: Here, we have to assume everything in the statement to be true, then consider the two conclusions together and decide which of them becomes logically valid. We do not know whether the woman was careless on the road. But we know the fact that the condition of the road was very poor and hence conclusion II can be easily established from that.

5. **Option (B) is correct.**
Explanation: Here, we have to assume everything in the statement to be true, then consider the two conclusions together and decide which of them becomes logically valid. We are not aware of the fact mentioned in conclusion I. But conclusion II can be a valid conclusion because the statement draws a relation between health hazards of smoking and pregnant women and the conclusion supports the assertion.

6. **Option (C) is correct.**
Explanation: Here, we have to assume everything in the statement to be true, then consider the two conclusions together and decide which of them becomes logically valid. The statement clearly states that after removal of the gall bladder, and while eating oily foods and fries stuff the person faced indigestion. So it is quite clear that the absence of gall bladder causes digestion issues and that it is an important organ of the human body. Thus, both the conclusions are true and valid.

7. **Option (D) is correct.**
Explanation: Here, we have to assume everything in the statement to be true, then consider the two conclusions together and decide which of them becomes logically valid. In the given statement it has already been mentioned that the CBI has asked the employees to declare their undisclosed assets. It clearly means that they must be having some undisclosed assets. And there is no mention of allegations here. Thus, neither of the conclusions is true.

8. **Option (B) is correct.**
Explanation: Here, we have to assume everything in the statement to be true, then consider the two conclusions together and decide which of them becomes logically valid. Conclusion II only holds true. Unless the climate is extremely cold none would wear woollen garments.

9. **Option (A) is correct.**
Explanation: Here, we have to assume everything in the statement to be true, then consider the two conclusions together and decide which of them becomes logically valid. Conclusion I only holds true and is actually a valid point. The statement mentions clearly that the residents of the city A eat properly cooked food and they don't face major health issues. But conclusion II is invalid because the statement doesn't hint any connection between food and wealth of the residents.

10. **Option (B) is correct.**
Explanation: Here, we have to assume everything in the statement to be true, then consider the two conclusions together and decide which of them becomes logically valid. Conclusion II only holds true and is actually a valid point. Some passengers who have been declared missing may be still alive.

11. **Option (C) is correct.**
Explanation: Here, we have to assume everything in the statement to be true, then consider the two conclusions together and decide which of them becomes logically valid. The statement claims that there are no more beds to admit patients suffering from COVID 19. Thus, conclusion I and II both hold true and are actually valid points.

12. **Option (D) is correct.**
Explanation: Here, we have to assume everything in the statement to be true, then consider the two conclusions together and decide which of them becomes logically valid. The only information given in the statement is that the government wants to privatize the Railways. From this we can't conclude the reason behind the intent of the government. Thus, conclusion I and II both hold illogical and cannot be valid conclusions to the given statement.

13. **Option (B) is correct.**
Explanation: Here, we have to assume everything in the statement to be true, then consider the two conclusions together and decide which of them becomes logically valid. Conclusion I is baseless, only conclusion II presents a valid conclusion that may be the cause of her getting the award.

14. **Option (B) is correct.**
Explanation: Here, we have to assume everything in the statement to be true, then consider the two conclusions together and decide which of them becomes logically valid. Only conclusion II presents a valid conclusion that may be the cause of so many accidents involving that model.

15. **Option (B) is correct.**
Explanation: Here, we have to assume everything in the statement to be true, then consider the two conclusions together and decide which of them becomes logically valid. Conclusion I is not valid and is unethical.
Conclusion II holds true here, as it can be clearly inferred from the given statement that the situation post COVID 19 has not normalized yet for asking the employees to start working from office.

16. **Option (E) is correct.**
Explanation: The statement unmistakably emphasises how much more crucial it is to pay attention to national demands than space research projects, which divert the attention of the relevant authorities. Consequently, conclusions I and II are drawn.

17. **Option (A) is correct.**
Explanation: It is obvious that the request was made with the intention of raising awareness and having some impact. Thus, I will make a valid conclusion. Nonetheless, the remark refers to a broad appeal rather than specific guidelines. Thus, conclusion II is not supported.

18. Option (B) is correct.

Explanation: The assertion only refers to jade plants—not other plants with thick leaves. So, I do not follow the conclusion. Furthermore, because jade plants don't need a lot of water, they may be cultivated in areas without an excess of it. Thus, conclusion II comes next.

19. Option (B) is correct.

Explanation: The statement is a symbolic one and only conclusion II correctly explains it.

20. Option (D) is correct.

Explanation: According to the statement, good wranglers are wise men. But it does not mean that all wise men are good wranglers. So, neither conclusion I nor conclusion II follows.

21. Option (D) is correct.

Explanation: The statement mentions that morning walks improve health. But this does not mean that all healthy people go for morning walks. So, conclusion I does not follow. Also, nothing is mentioned about evening walks in the statement. So, conclusion II also does not follow.

22. Option (B) is correct.

Explanation: The statement implies that people are inclined towards giving their children good education. So, only conclusion II follows while conclusion I does not.

23. Option (B) is correct.

Explanation: The cause of revolution cannot be deduced from the given statement. So, conclusion I does not follow. However, the statement mentions that Industrial Revolution brought about modern age. This means that revolution overhauls society. So, conclusion II follows.

24. Option (B) is correct.

Explanation: The statement's use of the term "only book" implies conclusion II. It is impossible to infer anything about the level of poverty before 1950 from the statement. Thus, I is not the apt conclusion.

25. Option (E) is correct.

Explanation: The statement claims that by designating bureaucrats as directors, the government has ruined financial firms. This implies that only those having a background in finance and familiarity with the institutes's financial operations should be nominated as Directors. Thus, findings I and II are correct conclusions.

Level-3: EXPERT

1. Option (B) is correct.

Explanation: Here, we have to assume everything in the statement to be true, then consider the two conclusions together and decide which of them becomes logically valid. Conclusion II is a valid conclusion. It is quite evident from the statement that the fake news let to the death of 14 people, so it is apparent that fake new is harmful. Conclusion I is just contrary, thus should be ruled out.

2. Option (C) is correct.

Explanation: Here, we have to assume everything in the statement to be true, then consider the two conclusions together and decide which of them becomes logically valid. Here, both the conclusions are valid. If the company could not afford the laptops and mobiles it would not have given them. Moreover, having personal laptops and mobiles will help in better work and efficiency of the employees since the lack of these gadgets causes inefficiency, as is quite evident from the given statement.

3. Option (B) is correct.

Explanation: Here, we have to assume everything in the statement to be true, then consider the two conclusions together and decide which of them becomes logically valid. The assertion mentions that N95 masks with valved respirators cannot stop the virus from entering. Conclusion I is not the apt conclusion to draw as it is a fact upon which the assertion is based. Conclusion II can be safely derived.

4. Option (A) is correct.

Explanation: Here, we have to assume everything in the statement to be true, then consider the two conclusions together and decide which of them becomes logically valid. Conclusion I is true and because except those 10 policemen, no one knew about this. There might be a mole or informer within those 10 policemen. Conclusion II is illogical and cannot be held valid.

5. Option (C) is correct.

Explanation: Here, we have to assume everything in the statement to be true, then consider the two conclusions together and decide which of them becomes logically valid.

Both the conclusions are valid and true because the word 'may' has been used, which means there is a possibility.

6. Option (C) is correct.

Explanation: Here, we have to assume everything in the statement to be true, then consider the two conclusions together and decide which of them becomes logically valid.

Here, both the conclusions are true. First one is true because if he had known bowling using left arm he would not have done so. And again, he would not have done so, if his right arm had been fine.

7. Option (A) is correct.

Explanation: Here, we have to assume everything in the statement to be true, then consider the two conclusions together and decide which of them becomes logically valid. Conclusion I is absolutely valid which is one of the after effects of a cyclone. Conclusion II is out of the track and irrelevant.

8. Option (A) is correct.

Explanation: Here, we have to assume everything in the statement to be true, then consider the two conclusions together and decide which of them becomes logically valid. Since the statement mentions that most people who smoke gets cancer, we can deduce that smoking can be one of the reasons for getting cancer. But conclusion II is an absolute statement and we can't say that smoking is the only reason for cancer.

9. **Option (D) is correct.**

Explanation: Here, we have to assume everything in the statement to be true, then consider the two conclusions together and decide which of them becomes logically valid. Because a company has planned to shut down its office in City A and set up a new office in City B, we can't derive anything about any of the cities' population or the status of wealth. Neither of the conclusions given here is relevant and valid.

10. **Option (A) is correct.**

Explanation: Here, we have to assume everything in the statement to be true, then consider the two conclusions together and decide which of them becomes logically valid. Since the food was not good it led to food poisoning. But we cannot be sure if all the employees were definitely careless. Maybe it was due to carelessness of a few employees.

11. **Option (A) is correct.**

Explanation: Here, we have to assume everything in the statement to be true, then consider the two conclusions together and decide which of them becomes logically valid. Company X may go bankrupt as it is being taken over and all of its holdings are being sold. However, we are unsure if Company X is really having significant problems with debt payback and administration.

12. **Option (C) is correct.**

Explanation: Here, we have to assume everything in the statement to be true, then consider the two conclusions together and decide which of them becomes logically valid. Both the conclusions are equally valid. It is quite likely that the Z+ Model's safety was not verified by the firm before its commercial release.

13. **Option (A) is correct.**

Explanation: Here, we have to assume everything in the statement to be true, then consider the two conclusions together and decide which of them becomes logically valid. From the given data that Bakshi pinned doen a gangster despite a bullet wound, evinces that Detective Byomkesh Bakshi is a courageous man.

14. **Option (C) is correct.**

Explanation: Here, we have to assume everything in the statement to be true, then consider the two conclusions together and decide which of them becomes logically valid. Both the conclusions here are valid. In this instance, there is a good chance that it is not a suicide. Without a stool or other elevated item to stand on, no one could have just leaped to the ceiling and hung himself.

15. **Option (A) is correct.**

Explanation: Here, we have to assume everything in the statement to be true, then consider the two conclusions together and decide which of them becomes logically valid. Conclusion I mentions a valid point. But without buying one cannot know if the car is defective. So conclusion II is wrong. Therefore, option A is the correct answer choice here.

Chapter 6

Deriving Conclusions and Passages

LEARNING OBJECTIVES:

- To test your comprehension power
- To determine the conclusions
- How to solve questions pertaining to Deriving conclusions.

This type of question undoubtedly tests your comprehension power of the given passage; it also requires your reasoning power so as to arrive at the correct conclusion among the given options. We can learn about it through practice.

➤ **How to Make Inferences?**

Aspirants must merge the clues in the given text with their prior knowledge and determine the answers to the questions that lead to conclusions about the underlying ideas.

➤ **Tips to Solve the Question Pertaining to Deriving Conclusions:**

- Comprehend the given passage.
- Summarize the gist.
- Weigh in the given options with close scrutiny.
- Apply reasoning as to which option would be the correct answer.
- The candidate has to apply the implied/inferred meaning of the paragraph and the statements provided in the options and then derive at the most appropriate conclusion.
- Eliminate options that do not support the evidence provided in the passage.
- The inference can be understood by understanding the inherent meaning, i.e., a method of reading between the lines.

Level 1 Beginner

Directions (Qs. 1 & 2): Read the passage and answer the questions.

Ram took a deep breath and dried his sweaty palms on his jeans. He looked down the ramp and shivered. It was a steep drop. But he had to go through with it. Everyone was staring straight at him. He put his skateboard down and got ready. He could do it!

1. What evidence helps you to infer that Ram was nervous?

(A) He put his skateboard down and got ready.
(B) His palms were sweaty.
(C) He looked down the ramp.
(D) He could do it.

2. Based on the evidence, it can be concluded that Ram will do what?

(A) He is probably not going down.
(B) He is probably going to get on his skateboard and go down the ramp.
(C) He is probably going to look at his friends and ask them what to do.
(D) He is probably going to fix his skateboard.

Directions (Qs. 3 to 6): Read the passage and answer the questions.

A tiger, when killing its natural prey, which it does either by stalking or lying in wait for it, depends for the success of its attack on its speed and, to a lesser extent, on the condition of its teeth and claws. When, therefore, a tiger is suffering from one or more painful wounds or when its teeth are missing or defective and its claws worn down, and it is unable to catch animals it has been accustomed to eating, it is driven by the necessity to killing human beings.

3. Tiger kills man only when it has been incapacitated through wounds.

(A) If the inference is 'definitely true', i.e., it directly follows from the facts given in the passage.
(B) If the inference is 'probably true' though not definitely true in the light of the facts given.
(C) If you think the data are inadequate, i.e., you

cannot determine from the given facts whether the inference is likely to be true or false.

(D) If you think the interference is 'probably false' though not definitely false in the light of the facts given.

(E) If you think the inference is 'definitely false', i.e., it contradicts the given facts.

4. Human beings are the natural prey of tigers.

(A) If the inference is 'definitely true', i.e., it directly follows from the facts given in the passage.

(B) If the inference is 'probably true', though not definitely true in the light of the facts given.

(C) If you think the data are inadequate, i.e., you cannot determine from the given facts whether the inference is likely to be true or false.

(D) If you think the interference is 'probably false' though not definitely false in the light of the facts given.

(E) If you think the inference is 'definitely false', i.e., it contradicts the given facts.

5. Sharp claws are needed by the tigers to kill animals in the forest.

(A) If the inference is 'definitely true', i.e., it directly follows from the facts given in the passage.

(B) If the inference is 'probably true' though not definitely true in the light of the facts given.

(C) If you think the data are inadequate, i.e., you cannot determine from the given facts whether the inference is likely to be true or false.

(D) If you think the interference is 'probably false' though not definitely false in the light of the facts given.

(E) If you think the inference is 'definitely false', i.e., it contradicts the given facts.

6. Old age propels tigers to take to man eating.

(A) If the inference is 'definitely true', i.e., it directly follows from the facts given in the passage.

(B) If the inference is 'probably true', though not definitely true in the light of the facts given.

(C) If you think the data are inadequate i.e., you cannot determine from the given facts whether the inference is likely to be true or false.

(D) If you think the interference is 'probably false' though not definitely false in the light of the facts given.

(E) If you think the inference is 'definitely false', i.e., it contradicts the givten facts.

Directions (Qs. 7 to 11): Read the passage and answer the questions.

Forest Policy and Impact: In her book Ecology and the Politics of Survival, Vandana Shiva (1991) argues that tropical forest resources are undergoing the world's most severe ecological and economic crisis. The food security of the entire world depends upon linkages between the ecological stability and the economic well-being of the majority of the world's people who live in the tropics or the Third World. Shiva explains the crisis of tropical forestry in the light of the conflicting demands for biomass by the three fundamental economies associated with forests:

1. Nature's economy of essential ecological processes.

2. The survival economy of basic needs satisfaction for people.

3. The market economy of industrial–commercial demands. Nature's economy of essential ecological processes generates a demand on the products of the forest in terms of the maintenance of soil systems and the hydrological balance of the forest ecosystems. The survival economy of basic needs satisfaction reflects the requirement of forest biomass (wood fuel, fodder, fruits, nuts, green manure, small timber, etc.) by people living in and around forests. The market economy of industrial–commercial demand converts forest biomass into items of the formal market economy, such as pulpwood, plywood, furniture, housing timber, wood fuel, etc., for the urban market. Nature's economy and survival economy have always overlapped in India. They functioned simultaneously without conflict as the survival needs of local people were satisfied through conservation-oriented utilisation. The colonial rule introduced dramatic breaks in usage. The former perception of the multiple functions of a forest ecosystem was replaced with one-dimensional scientific forestry whose only objective was maximising the production of commercially valuable timber. Market logging eliminated the utilisation of forest resources for ecological or economic objectives. Post-colonial forest policy further aggravated utilisation conflicts and forest degradation. The system of clear-cutting (with artificial regeneration) was adopted. Shiva concludes that converting natural forests to pulpwood plantations further eroded biomass needed for fuel, fodder, fertilisers, etc. Monoculture plantations of eucalyptus, pine, etc., severely undermined ecological processes in mountain catchments like the Himalayas and the Western Ghats.

7. Which conclusions can be derived from the passage?

(a) Conservation of forests and use of forests are interdependent processes.

(b) We should not cultivate more pine and Nilgiri trees.

(c) Colonial policy has caused the reduction of forests.

(d) Market economy based on trade demand does not depend on forests.

(A) Only (a) **(B)** Only (b)

(C) Only (a), (b) and (c) **(D)** Only (b), (c) and (d)

8. What is the central idea of this passage?

(A) Environmental degradation and reduction in forest wealth.

(B) Wrong environment policy and reduction in forest wealth.

(C) Place of forests in Indian culture.

(D) Benefits of monoculture tree plantation.

9. What are the effects of colonialism?

(a) Forests considered only for market benefits.

(b) Conflicts generated due to forest wealth.

(c) Monoculture objectives of forestry were implemented.

(d) Loss of biodiversity in the forests.

(A) Only (a) **(B)** Only (d)

(C) Only (a), (b) and (c) **(D)** All of these

10. Which approach of a community related to forests in India, do you understand from the given passage?
(A) Conservation and use of forests
(B) Excess use of trees in the forests
(C) Forests for expansion of trade
(D) Forests only for tribal people

11. According to the given passage, food security depends on ______.
(a) food production
(b) ecological stability
(c) monsoon
(d) economic welfare of the people living in tropical region
(A) Only (a) (B) Only (b) and (c)
(C) Only (b) and (d) (D) Only (a) and (d)

Directions (Qs 12 & 13): Read the passage and answer the questions.

Many people who live near to mobile phone masts are worried that radiation from these masts will damage their health. Mobile phones themselves have also been suspected of emitting dangerous levels of radiation, and a report recommended that children should be discouraged from making non-essential calls. Emission of radiation from the masts is much lower than that from a mobile phone. A few seconds of making a phone call are comparable to 24 hours of exposure from a mast. Radiation from both these sources is below the international guidelines as to what is a dangerous level, but no one can yet be certain if these guidelines accurately reflect the level of risk.

12. Select the statement that can be drawn as the most appropriate conclusion from the above passage.
(A) People who use mobile phones are putting their health at risk.
(B) If extensive use of mobile phones is not harmful to health, radiation from a mast is unlikely to be a risk.
(C) The International guidelines underestimate the risk to health from low levels of radiation.
(D) The health risk from living near a phone mast is lower than that from using a mobile phone.

13. A study of native born residents in Newland found that two-thirds of the children developed considerable levels of nearsightedness after starting school. In contrast, their illiterate parents and grandparents, who had no opportunity for formal schooling, showed no signs of this disability. If the above statements are true, which of the following conclusions is most strongly supported by them?
(A) Only people who have the opportunity for formal schooling develop nearsightedness.
(B) The nearsightedness in the children is caused by the visual stress required by reading and other class work.
(C) Both (A) and (B)
(D) None of these.

Directions (Qs 14 to 18): Read the passage and answer the questions.

Economic liberalisation and globalisation have put pressure on Indian industry, particularly on the service sector, to offer quality product and services at low costs and with high speed. Organisations have to compete with high speed. Organisations have to compete with unequal partners from abroad. It is well recognised that developing countries like India are already behind other countries technologically, in many areas, although some of them, particularly India, boast of huge scientific and technical manpower. In addition to this, if an entrepreneur or industrialist has to spend a lot of the time, money and energy dealing with unpredictable services and negotiating with the local bureaucracy, it can have a significant dampening effect on business.

14. Official formalities are less cumbersome in almost all the countries except India.
(A) If the inference is 'definitely true', i.e., it directly follows from the facts given in the passage.
(B) If the inference is 'probably true' though not definitely true in the light of the facts given.
(C) If you think the data are inadequate, i.e., you cannot determine from the given facts whether the inference is likely to be true or false.
(D) If you think the interference is 'probably false' though not definitely false in the light of the facts given.
(E) If you think the inference is 'definitely false', i.e., it contradicts the given facts.

15. No, other developing country except India claims that they have highly trained technical manpower
(A) If the inference is 'definitely true', i.e., it directly follows from the facts given in the passage.
(B) If the inference is 'probably true' though not definitely true in the light of the facts given.
(C) If you think the data are inadequate, i.e., you cannot determine from the given facts whether the inference is likely to be true or false.
(D) If you think the interference is 'probably false' though not definitely false in the light of the facts given.
(E) If you think the inference is 'definitely false', i.e., it contradicts the given facts.

16. Indian service industry was more comfortable before economic liberalisation.
(A) If the inference is 'definitely true', i.e., it directly follows from the facts given in the passage.
(B) If the inference is 'probably true' though not definitely true in the light of the facts given.
(C) If you think the data are inadequate, i.e., you cannot determine from the given facts whether the inference is likely to be true or false.
(D) If you think the interference is 'probably false' though not definitely false in the light of the facts given.
(E) If you think the inference is 'definitely false', i.e., it contradicts the given facts.

17. India at present is to some extent at par with the developed countries in terms of technological development.

(A) If the inference is 'definitely true', i.e., it directly follows from the facts given in the passage.

(B) If the inference is 'probably true' though not definitely true in the light of the facts given.

(C) If you think the data are inadequate, i.e., you cannot determine from the given facts whether the inference is likely to be true or false.

(D) If you think the interference is 'probably false' though not definitely false in the light of the facts given.

(E) If you think the inference is 'definitely false', i.e., it contradicts the given facts.

18. Foreign companies are more equipped than domestic companies to provide quality services in good time.

(A) If the inference is 'definitely true', i.e., it directly follows from the facts given in the passage.

(B) If the inference is 'probably true', though not definitely true in the light of the facts given.

(C) If you think the data are inadequate, i.e., you cannot determine from the given facts whether the inference is likely to be true or false.

(D) If you think the interference is 'probably false' though not definitely false in the light of the facts given.

(E) if you think the inference is 'definitely false', i.e., it contradicts the given facts.

Directions (Qs. 19 to 23): Read the passage and answer the questions.

One of the greatest advantages a company has over its competitors is a system of distribution and product support, i.e., the dealer network. Dealers play a vital role in helping a company build and maintain close relationships with customers and gain insights into how they can improve their products and services to fulfill customer needs. And a company can achieve customer loyalty through dealer loyalty. Therefore, it must make efforts to build their competence, for more effective performance. Dealers who are long established members of a company can get close to customers but to tap the full potential of such dealers, a company must forge extremely close ties with them and integrate them into its critical business systems. When treated this way dealers can serve as a source of market intelligence, as proxies for customers, as consultants and the dealers. Although these investments take the usual form of money, it also includes softer aspects such as training and development.

19. The customers are more forthright in giving their feedback about a product or a service.

(A) If the inference is 'definitely true', i.e., it directly follows from the facts given in the passage.

(B) If the inference is 'probably true', though not definitely true in the light of the facts given.

(C) If you think the data are inadequate, i.e., you cannot determine from the given facts whether the inference is likely to be true or false.

(D) If you think the interference is 'probably false' though not definitely false in the light of the facts given.

(E) If you think the inference is 'definitely false', i.e., it contradicts the given facts.

20. Trusted dealers are the direct link between the company and the customers.

(A) If the inference is 'definitely true' i.e., it directly follows from the facts given in the passage.

(B) If the inference is 'probably true', though not definitely true in the light of the facts given.

(C) If you think the data are inadequate, i.e., you cannot determine from the given facts whether the inference is likely to be true or false.

(D) If you think the interference is 'probably false' though not definitely false in the light of the facts given.

(E) If you think the inference is 'definitely false', i.e., it contradicts the given facts.

21. Developing a network of dealers is more useful while launching a new product or service.

(A) If the inference is 'definitely true', i.e., it directly follows from the facts given in the passage.

(B) If the inference is 'probably true', though not definitely true in the light of the facts given.

(C) If you think the data are inadequate, i.e., you cannot determine from the given facts whether the inference is likely to be true or false.

(D) If you think the interference is 'probably false' though not definitely false in the light of the facts given.

(E) If you think the inference is 'definitely false', i.e., it contradicts the given facts.

22. The company should insist dealer loyalty to the extent that the dealer will not sell similar products of any other company

(A) If the inference is 'definitely true' i.e., it directly follows from the facts given in the passage.

(B) if the inference is 'probably true', though not definitely true in the light of the facts given.

(C) If you think the data are inadequate, i.e., you cannot determine from the given facts whether the inference is likely to be true or false.

(D) If you think the interference is 'probably false' though not definitely false in the light of the facts given.

(E) If you think the inference is 'definitely false', i.e., it contradicts the given facts.

23. A company which has a good chain of loyal dealers need not spend money on advertising.

(A) If the inference is 'definitely true' i.e., it directly follows from the facts given in the passage.

(B) if the inference is 'probably true', though not definitely true in the light of the facts given.

(C) If you think the data are inadequate, i.e., you cannot determine from the given facts whether the inference is likely to be true or false.

(D) If you think the interference is 'probably false' though not definitely false in the light of the facts given.

(E) If you think the inference is 'definitely false', i.e., it contradicts the given facts.

2 Level Intermediate

Directions (Qs 1 to 3) : Read each passage and answer the questions.

1. No national productivity measures are available for underground industries that may exist but remain unreported. On the other hand, at least some industries that are run entirely by self-employed industrialists are included in national productivity measures. If the above statements are true, which of the following conclusions is most strongly supported by them?

(A) There are at least some industries run entirely by self-employed industrialists that are underground industries.

(B) No industries that are run entirely by self-employed industrialists operate underground.

(C) There are at least some industries other than those run entirely by self-employed industrialists that are underground industries.

(D) There are at least some industries run entirely by self-employed industrialists that are not underground industries.

2. The basic thrust, of the Government's policy is to provide price incentives to farmers to make them produce more food. But is a price-incentive system, always efficient in ensuring incremental yields? Our contention is that this incentive works only in persuading farmers to shift cultivation from one crop to another depending on which crop is more profitable at) the given prices. But it would not be a sufficient condition in ensuring incremental output of all crops which is what is required. If the above statements are true, which of the following conclusions is most strongly supported by them?

(A) If you think the inference is "Definitely True".

(B) If you think that the inference is "Probably True" although not definitely true in the light of the facts given.

(C) If the data given is inadequate, i.e. from the statements given above, you cannot say whether the inference is likely to be true or likely to be false.

(D) If you think that the inference is "Probably False" although not definitely false in the light of the facts given.

3. Cataract blindness is the disease which begins with clouding of the eyes and can lead to loss of vision, will probably afflict 12 million more people by 2020, as a result of shortage of skilled doctors limits access to care in developing nations. In the clinical way of training, it takes years to create a good surgeon. It is impossible to train all the doctors needed and then put them in developing countries at this rate. A non-profit organisation 'HelpMeSee', committed to fighting cataract blindness, wants to train 30,000 people for a procedure to remove the impairment using a virtual reality simulator that replicates the human eye and feel the live surgery. The simulator is a major development because it can make a great surgeon in less than three months.

Select the most appropriate statement which can be inferred from the above information.

(A) Now there is no need of trained surgeons for doing cataract surgery as virtual reality simulators for removing impairment are available.

(B) Now it is possible to train any person to remove cataract impairment using a virtual-reality simulator that replicates the human eye and feel the live surgery.

(C) Now virtual reality simulator can make a person a great surgeon in less than three months for removing cataract impairment.

(D) Now problem of cataract blindness can be eradicated using virtually reality simulators.

Directions (Qs 4 to 8): Read the passage and answer the questions.

Primary education in Bihar is in a poor shape. Pupils in over 50 per cent of the schools read in the open throughout the year. Over six million children born to lower income group parents remain unlettered. Not even one per cent of the 63,000 primary schools has facilities of furniture, toilet, drinking and games. 3,113 new teachers have been appointed in the current financial year out of which 2,747 are women. Now each of the 13,270 primary schools has at least two teachers .

4. 630 primary schools in Bihar have all the facilities like furniture, toilet, drinking water, games.

(A) If the inference is 'definitely true', i.e., it directly follows from the facts given in the passage.

(B) If the inference is 'probably true', though not definitely true in the light of the facts given.

(C) If you think the data are inadequate, i.e., you cannot determine from the given facts whether the inference is likely to be true or false.

(D) If you think the interference is 'probably false' though not definitely false in the light of the facts given.

(E) If you think the inference is 'definitely false', i.e., it contradicts the given facts.

5. In Bihar, 50 per cent of the primary teachers are women.

(A) If the inference is 'definitely true' i.e., it directly follows from the facts given in the passage.

(B) If the inference is 'probably true', though not definitely true in the light of the facts given.

(C) If you think the data are inadequate, i.e., you cannot determine from the given facts whether the inference is likely to be true or false.

(D) If you think the interference is 'probably false' though not def initely false in the light of the facts given.

(E) If you think the inference is 'definitely false', i.e., it contradicts the given facts.

6. A large number of primary schools in Bihar are one teacher schools.

(A) If the inference is 'definitely true' i.e., it directly follows from the facts given in the passage.

(B) If the inference is 'probably true', though not definitely true in the light of the facts given.

(C) If you think the data are inadequate, i.e., you cannot determine from the given facts whether the inference is likely to be true or false.

(D) If you think the inference is 'probably false' though not def initely false in the light of the facts given.

(E) If you think the inference is 'definitely false', i.e., it contradicts the given facts.

7. There are six million belonging to lower income groups in Bihar.

(A) If the inference is 'definitely true' i.e., it directly follows from the facts given in the passage.

(B) If the inference is 'probably true', though not definitely true in the light of the facts given.

(C) If you think the data are inadequate, i.e., you cannot determine from the given facts whether the inference is likely to be true or false.

(D) If you think the inference is 'probably false' though not def initely false in the light of the facts given.

(E) If you think the inference is 'definitely false', i.e., it contradicts the given facts.

8. Classrooms of most of the primary schools in Bihar are inadequate.

(A) If the inference is 'definitely true' i.e., it directly follows from the facts given in the passage.

(B) If the inference is 'probably true', though not definitely true in the light of the facts given.

(C) If you think the data are inadequate, i.e., you cannot determine from the given facts whether the inference is likely to be true or false.

(D) If you think the inference is 'probably false' though not definitely false in the light of the facts given.

(E) If you think the inference is 'definitely false', i.e., it contradicts the given facts.

Directions (Qs 9 to 13): Read the passage and answer the questions.

India needs higher investment in the port sector and still lags far behind the international ports in container traffic, though there has been considerable growth in this segment over the past few years. There is a need to continually benchmark Indian ports against the best ports worldwide and continue to engage in policy efforts so as to attain prices per container of port services which are the lowest in the world. The average turn-around time for ships docking at most of the ports in India has been falling for the past three years. However, pre-berthing time has been marginally increasing over the years.

9. The best port in the world is located in the United States of America.

(A) If the inference is 'definitely true' i.e., it directly follows from the facts given in the passage.

(B) If the inference is 'probably true', though not definitely true in the light of the facts given.

(C) If you think the data are inadequate, i.e., you cannot determine from the given facts whether the inference is likely to be true or false.

(D) If you think the inference is 'probably false' though not definitely false in the light of the facts given.

(E) If you think the inference is 'definitely false', i.e., it contradicts the given facts.

10. Indian ports have not been graded so far on the international standard.

(A) If the inference is 'definitely true' i.e., it directly follows from the facts given in the passage.

(B) If the inference is 'probably true', though not definitely true in the light of the facts given.

(C) If you think the data are inadequate, i.e., you cannot determine from the given facts whether the inference is likely to be true or false.

(D) If you think the inference is 'probably false' though not definitely false in the light of the facts given.

(E) If you think the inference is 'definitely false', i.e., it contradicts the given facts.

11. Indian ports need considerable development to match with the best ports in the world.

(A) If the inference is 'definitely true' i.e., it directly follows from the facts given in the passage.

(B) If the inference is 'probably true', though not definitely true in the light of the facts given.

(C) If you think the data are inadequate, i.e., you cannot determine from the given facts whether the inference is likely to be true or false.

(D) If you think the inference is 'probably false' though not definitely false in the light of the facts given.

(E) If you think the inference is 'definitely false', i.e., it contradicts the given facts.

12. Pre-berthing time is gradually decreasing over the years.

(A) If the inference is 'definitely true' i.e., it directly follows from the facts given in the passage.

(B) If the inference is 'probably true', though not definitely true in the light of the facts given.

(C) If you think the data are inadequate, i.e., you cannot determine from the given facts whether the inference is likely to be true or false.

(D) If you think the inference is 'probably false' though not definitely false in the light of the facts given.

(E) If you think the inference is 'definitely false', i.e., it contradicts the given facts.

13. Indian ports offer the lowest price per container as service charges.

(A) If the inference is 'definitely true' i.e., it directly follows from the facts given in the passage.

(B) If the inference is 'probably true', though not definitely true in the light of the facts given.

(C) If you think the data are inadequate, i.e., you cannot determine from the given facts whether the inference is likely to be true or false.

(D) If you think the inference is 'probably false' though not definitely false in the light of the facts given.

(E) If you think the inference is 'definitely false', i.e., it contradicts the given facts.

Directions (Qs 14 to 18): Read the passage and answer the questions.

Laws governing the cooperative societies are uniform in all states. These laws give the member of a housing society the right to nomination during his life time. This is quite unlike the rule in other property related cases where nomination comes into force after the demise of the member. The question then arises that, can the nominee get full proprietorial rights over a flat merely because he has been nominated by a decreased member of the society. Many people are under the wrong impression that once a nomination form has been filled, their responsibility is over and that the nominee would have no problem acquiring the property. And, that the legal heirs of the member will pose no problem for the nominee.

14. Nomination to property right need not be legal heirs only.

(A) If the inference is 'definitely true' i.e., it directly follows from the facts given in the passage.

(B) if the inference is 'probably true', though not definitely true in the light of the facts given.

(C) If you think the data are inadequate i.e., from the facts given you cannot say whether the inference is likely to be true or false.

(D) If you think the interference is 'probably false' though not definitely false in the light of the facts given.

(E) If you think the inference is 'definitely false', i.e., it contradicts the given facts.

15. Cooperative movement had started with cooperative housing societies.

(A) If the inference is 'definitely true' i.e., it directly follows from the facts given in the passage.

(B) If the inference is 'probably true', though not definitely true in the light of the facts given.

(C) If you think the data are inadequate, i.e., you cannot determine from the given facts whether the inference is likely to be true or false.

(D) If you think the interference is 'probably false' though not definitely false in the light of the facts given.

(E) If you think the inference is 'definitely false', i.e., it contradicts the given facts.

16. Property related laws are more or less same in all the states.

(A) If the inference is 'definitely true' i.e., it directly follows from the facts given in the passage.

(B) If the inference is 'probably true', though not definitely true in the light of the facts given.

(C) If you think the data are inadequate, i.e., you cannot determine from the given facts whether the inference is likely to be true or false.

(D) If you think the interference is 'probably false' though not definitely false in the light of the facts given.

(E) If you think the inference is 'definitely false', i.e., it contradicts the given facts.

17. There is a need to educate the people on all aspects of laws governing the cooperative societies.

(A) If the inference is 'definitely true' i.e., it directly follows from the facts given in the passage.

(B) If the inference is 'probably true', though not definitely true in the light of the facts given.

(C) If you think the data are inadequate, i.e., you cannot determine from the given facts whether the inference is likely to be true or false.

(D) If you think the interference is 'probably false' though not definitely false in the light of the facts given.

(E) If you think the inference is 'definitely false', i.e., it contradicts the given facts.

18. The law that considers whether a person is a legal heir or not has lacunae.

(A) If the inference is 'definitely true' i.e., it directly follows from the facts given in the passage.

(B) If the inference is 'probably true', though not definitely true in the light of the facts given.

(C) If you think the data are inadequate, i.e., you cannot determine from the given facts whether the inference is likely to be true or false.

(D) If you think the interference is 'probably false' though not definitely false in the light of the facts given.

(E) If you think the inference is 'definitely false', i.e., it contradicts the given facts.

Directions (Qs 19 to 23): Read the passage and answer the questions.

The space exploration has been done mainly by using unmanned satellites called space probes containing a large variety of latest scientific instruments on board. These space probes have provided us the close up pictures and other data about planets and other bodies in the outer space. The climax of the intensive American space programme came when Neil Armstrong became the first man to set foot on the moon on July 20, 1969. Originally, the artificial satellites were launched for studying the upper atmosphere of earth.

19. The space probes have increased our knowledge about space and the bodies in it.

(A) If the inference is 'definitely true' i.e., it directly follows from the facts given in the passage.

(B) If the inference is 'probably true', though not definitely true in the light of the facts given.

(C) If you think the data are inadequate, i.e., you cannot determine from the given facts whether the inference is likely to be true or false.

(D) If you think the interference is 'probably false' though not definitely false in the light of the facts given.

(E) If you think the inference is 'definitely false', i.e., it contradicts the given facts.

20. Space probes are meant to study the upper atmosphere of earth only.
(A) If the inference is 'definitely true' i.e., it directly follows from the facts given in the passage.
(B) If the inference is 'probably true', though not definitely true in the light of the facts given.
(C) If you think the data are inadequate, i.e., you cannot determine from the given facts whether the inference is likely to be true or false.
(D) If you think the interference is 'probably false' though not definitely false in the light of the facts given.
(E) If you think the inference is 'definitely false', i.e., it contradicts the given facts.

21. Neil Armstrong was the first man to go into space.
(A) If the inference is 'definitely true' i.e., it directly follows from the facts given in the passage.
(B) If the inference is 'probably true', though not definitely true in the light of the facts given.
(C) If you think the data are inadequate, i.e., you cannot determine from the given facts whether the inference is likely to be true or false.
(D) If you think the interference is 'probably false' though not definitely false in the light of the facts given.
(E) If you think the inference is 'definitely false', i.e., it contradicts the given facts.

22. Space probes are provided with computers.
(A) If the inference is 'definitely true' i.e., it directly follows from the facts given in the passage.
(B) If the inference is 'probably true', though not definitely true in the light of the facts given.
(C) If you think the data are inadequate, i.e., you cannot determine from the given facts whether the inference is likely to be true or false.
(D) If you think the interference is 'probably false' though not definitely false in the light of the facts given.
(E) If you think the inference is 'definitely false', i.e., it contradicts the given facts.

23. Moon has been explored by man.
(A) If the inference is 'definitely true' i.e., it directly follows from the facts given in the passage.
(B) If the inference is 'probably true', though not definitely true in the light of the facts given.
(C) If you think the data are inadequate, i.e., you cannot determine from the given facts whether the inference is likely to be true or false.
(D) If you think the interference is 'probably false' though not definitely false in the light of the facts given.
(E) If you think the inference is 'definitely false', i.e., it contradicts the given facts.

Directions (Qs 24 to 28): Read the passage and answer the questions.

India needs higher investment in the port sector and still lags far behind the international ports in container traffic, though there has been considerable growth in this segment over the past few years. There is a need to continually benchmark Indian ports against the best ports worldwide and continue to engage in policy efforts so as to attain prices per container of port services which are the lowest in the world. The average turn-around time for ships docking at most of the ports in India has been falling for the past three years. However, pre-berthing time has been marginally increasing over the years.

24. The best port in the world is located in the United States of America.
(A) If the inference is 'definitely true' i.e., it directly follows from the facts given in the passage.
(B) If the inference is 'probably true', though not definitely true in the light of the facts given.
(C) If you think the data are inadequate, i.e., you cannot determine from the given facts whether the inference is likely to be true or false.
(D) If you think the interference is 'probably false' though not definitely false in the light of the facts given.
(E) If you think the inference is 'definitely false', i.e., it contradicts the given facts.

25. Indian ports have not been graded so far on the international standard.
(A) If the inference is 'definitely true' i.e., it directly follows from the facts given in the passage.
(B) If the inference is 'probably true', though not definitely true in the light of the facts given.
(C) If you think the data are inadequate, i.e., you cannot determine from the given facts whether the inference is likely to be true or false.
(D) If you think the interference is 'probably false' though not definitely false in the light of the facts given.
(E) If you think the inference is 'definitely false', i.e., it contradicts the given facts.

26. Indian ports need considerable development to match with the best ports in the world.
(A) If the inference is 'definitely true' i.e., it directly follows from the facts given in the passage.
(B) If the inference is 'probably true', though not definitely true in the light of the facts given.
(C) If you think the data are inadequate, i.e., you cannot determine from the given facts whether the inference is likely to be true or false.
(D) If you think the interference is 'probably false' though not definitely false in the light of the facts given.
(E) If you think the inference is 'definitely false', i.e., it contradicts the given facts.

27. Pre-berthing time is gradually decreasing over the years.
(A) If the inference is 'definitely true' i.e., it directly follows from the facts given in the passage.
(B) If the inference is 'probably true', though not definitely true in the light of the facts given.
(C) If you think the data are inadequate, i.e., you cannot determine from the given facts whether the inference is likely to be true or false.

(D) If you think the interference is 'probably false' though not definitely false in the light of the facts given.

(E) If you think the inference is 'definitely false', i.e., it contradicts the given facts.

28. Indian ports offer the lowest price per container as service charges.

(A) If the inference is 'definitely true' i.e., it directly follows from the facts given in the passage.

(B) If the inference is 'probably true', though not definitely true in the light of the facts given.

(C) If you think the data are inadequate, i.e., you cannot determine from the given facts whether the inference is likely to be true or false.

(D) If you think the interference is 'probably false' though not definitely false in the light of the facts given.

(E) If you think the inference is 'definitely false', i.e., it contradicts the given facts.

Level 3 Expert

Directions (Qs 1 to 5): Read the passages and answer the questions.

Logically, there are rules of conduct. Every country has laid down comprehensive series of practical rules for citizens for resolving mutual contradictory rights and interests. Most of these rules have been laid down to sustain social activities. For instance, many countries have laid down rules to protest against such unsocial activities as theft, attack and murder. These rules are backed by judicial system and executor institutions, which look after the people who obey the rules and also who violate the rules. Wherever the human behaviour is involved such rules are not only for namesake there but are necessary also.

1. Human beings are susceptible to violate rules.

(A) If the inference is 'definitely true' i.e., it directly follows from the facts given in the passage.

(B) If the inference is 'probably true', though not definitely true in the light of the facts given.

(C) If you think the data are inadequate, i.e., you cannot determine from the given facts whether the inference is likely to be true or false.

(D) If you think the inference is 'probably false' though not definitely false in the light of the facts given.

(E) If you think the inference is 'definitely false', i.e., it contradicts the given facts.

2. There are no rules in countries where citizens interests and rights do not contradict.

(A) If the inference is 'definitely true' i.e., it directly follows from the facts given in the passage.

(B) If the inference is 'probably true', though not definitely true in the light of the facts given.

(C) If you think the data are inadequate, i.e., you cannot determine from the given facts whether the inference is likely to be true or false.

(D) If you think the inference is 'probably false' though not definitely false in the light of the facts given.

(E) If you think the inference is 'definitely false', i.e., it contradicts the given facts.

3. There is no need to have any machinery to ensure strict adherence to the rules by citizens.

(A) If the inference is 'definitely true' i.e., it directly follows from the facts given in the passage.

(B) If the inference is 'probably true', though not definitely true in the light of the facts given.

(C) If you think the data are inadequate, i.e., you cannot determine from the given facts whether the inference is likely to be true or false.

(D) If you think the inference is 'probably false' though not definitely false in the light of the facts given.

(E) If you think the inference is 'definitely false', i.e., it contradicts the given facts.

4. Without rules, human behavior degenerates into anarchy.

(A) If the inference is 'definitely true' i.e., it directly follows from the facts given in the passage.

(B) If the inference is 'probably true', though not definitely true in the light of the facts given.

(C) If you think the data are inadequate, i.e., you cannot determine from the given facts whether the inference is likely to be true or false.

(D) If you think the inference is 'probably false' though not definitely false in the light of the facts given.

(E) If you think the inference is 'definitely false', i.e., it contradicts the given facts.

5. There is no need of any rules if individuals do not have to interact with each other.

(A) If the inference is 'definitely true' i.e., it directly follows from the facts given in the passage.

(B) If the inference is 'probably true', though not definitely true in the light of the facts given.

(C) If you think the data are inadequate, i.e., you cannot determine from the given facts whether the inference is likely to be true or false.

(D) If you think the inference is 'probably false' though not definitely false in the light of the facts given.

(E) If you think the inference is 'definitely false', i.e., it contradicts the given facts.

Directions (Qs 6 to 10): Read the passages and answer the questions.

One of the greatest advantages a company has over its competitors is a system of distribution and product support, i.e., the dealer network. Dealers play a vital role in helping a company build and maintain close relationships with customers and gain insights into how they can improve their products and services to fulfill customer needs. And a company can achieve customer loyalty through dealer loyalty. Therefore, it must make efforts to build their competence, for more effective performance. Dealers who are long established members of a company can get close to customers but to tap the full potential of such dealers, a company must forge extremely close ties with them and integrate them into its critical business systems. When treated this way dealers can serve as a source of market intelligence, as proxies for customers, as consultants and the dealers. Although these investments take the usual form of money, it also includes softer aspects such as training and development.

6. The customers are more forthright in giving their feedback about a product or a service.
(A) If the inference is 'definitely true' i.e., it directly follows from the facts given in the passage.
(B) If the inference is 'probably true', though not definitely true in the light of the facts given.
(C) If you think the data are inadequate, i.e., you cannot determine from the given facts whether the inference is likely to be true or false.
(D) If you think the inference is 'probably false' though not definitely false in the light of the facts given.
(E) If you think the inference is 'definitely false', i.e., it contradicts the given facts.

7. Trusted dealers are the direct link between the company and the customers.
(A) If the inference is 'definitely true' i.e., it directly follows from the facts given in the passage.
(B) If the inference is 'probably true', though not definitely true in the light of the facts given.
(C) If you think the data are inadequate, i.e., you cannot determine from the given facts whether the inference is likely to be true or false.
(D) If you think the inference is 'probably false' though not definitely false in the light of the facts given.
(E) If you think the inference is 'definitely false', i.e., it contradicts the given facts.

8. Developing a network of dealers is more useful while launching a new product or service.
(A) If the inference is 'definitely true' i.e., it directly follows from the facts given in the passage.
(B) If the inference is 'probably true', though not definitely true in the light of the facts given.
(C) If you think the data are inadequate, i.e., you cannot determine from the given facts whether the inference is likely to be true or false.
(D) If you think the inference is 'probably false' though not definitely false in the light of the facts given.
(E) If you think the inference is 'definitely false', i.e., it contradicts the given facts.

9. The company should insist dealer loyalty to the extent that the dealer will not sell similar products of any other company.
(A) If the inference is 'definitely true' i.e., it directly follows from the facts given in the passage.
(B) If the inference is 'probably true', though not definitely true in the light of the facts given.
(C) If you think the data are inadequate, i.e., you cannot determine from the given facts whether the inference is likely to be true or false.
(D) If you think the inference is 'probably false' though not definitely false in the light of the facts given.
(E) If you think the inference is 'definitely false', i.e., it contradicts the given facts.

10. A company which has a good chain of loyal dealers need not spend money on advertising.
(A) If the inference is 'definitely true' i.e., it directly follows from the facts given in the passage.
(B) If the inference is 'probably true', though not definitely true in the light of the facts given.
(C) If you think the data are inadequate, i.e., you cannot determine from the given facts whether the inference is likely to be true or false.
(D) If you think the inference is 'probably false' though not definitely false in the light of the facts given.
(E) If you think the inference is 'definitely false', i.e., it contradicts the given facts.

Directions (Qs 11 to 15): Read the passages and answer the questions.

Cotton Acreage in India during the current year has fallen by 10% as cotton growers had moved on cultivation of other cash crops. This is the result of the cotton glut in world markets in Post September 11 and the consequent slowdown in the world economy. But this scenario brought with it benefits to one segment of the industry yarn manufactures, as they get higher prices for their produce. Some yarn manufactures too had stocked up on low priced cotton last year. The combined effect of all this is evident in the rise in net profits and net margins of yarn manufactures.

11. Land used for growing cotton in India is conducive to grow other cash crops.
(A) If the inference is 'definitely true' i.e., it directly follows from the facts given in the passage.
(B) If the inference is 'probably true', though not definitely true in the light of the facts given.
(C) If you think the data are inadequate, i.e., you cannot determine from the given facts whether the inference is likely to be true or false.
(D) If you think the interference is 'probably false' though not definitely false in the light of the facts given.
(E) If you think the inference is 'definitely false', i.e., it contradicts the given facts.

12. The farmers will again grow cotton next year due to increased price of cotton yarn.
(A) If the inference is 'definitely true' i.e., it directly follows from the facts given in the passage.
(B) If the inference is 'probably true', though not definitely true in the light of the facts given.
(C) If you think the data are inadequate, i.e., you cannot determine from the given facts whether the inference is likely to be true or false.

(D) If you think the interference is 'probably false' though not definitely false in the light of the facts given.
(E) If you think the inference is 'definitely false', i.e., it contradicts the given facts.

13. There has been shortage of cotton in the world market last year.
(A) If the inference is 'definitely true' i.e., it directly follows from the facts given in the passage.
(B) If the inference is 'probably true', though not definitely true in the light of the facts given.
(C) If you think the data are inadequate, i.e., you cannot determine from the given facts whether the inference is likely to be true or false.
(D) If you think the interference is 'probably false' though not definitely false in the light of the facts given.
(E) If you think the inference is 'definitely false', i.e., it contradicts the given facts.

14. There has been a huge drop in the supply of cotton during the current year.
(A) If the inference is 'definitely true' i.e., it directly follows from the facts given in the passage.
(B) If the inference is 'probably true', though not definitely true in the light of the facts given.
(C) If you think the data are inadequate, i.e., you cannot determine from the given facts whether the inference is likely to be true or false.
(D) If you think the interference is 'probably false' though not definitely false in the light of the facts given.
(E) If you think the inference is 'definitely false', i.e., it contradicts the given facts.

15. World economy witnessed an upward trend during pre-September 11 period.
(A) If the inference is 'definitely true' i.e., it directly follows from the facts given in the passage.
(B) If the inference is 'probably true', though not definitely true in the light of the facts given.
(C) If you think the data are inadequate, i.e., you cannot determine from the given facts whether the inference is likely to be true or false.
(D) If you think the interference is 'probably false' though not definitely false in the light of the facts given.
(E) If you think the inference is 'definitely false', i.e., it contradicts the given facts.

ANSWER KEY

Level-1: Beginner

1.	(B)	2.	(B)	3.	(A)	4.	(E)	5.	(A)	6.	(C)	7.	(C)	8.	(B)	9.	(D)	10.	(A)
11.	(C)	12.	(B)	13.	(B)	14.	(C)	15.	(E)	16.	(B)	17.	(D)	18.	(A)	19.	(A)	20.	(A)
21.	(B)	22.	(A)	23.	(C)														

Level-2: Intermediate

1.	(D)	2.	(A)	3.	(C)	4.	(E)	5.	(C)	6.	(E)	7.	(A)	8.	(B)	9.	(C)	10.	(C)
11.	(A)	12.	(E)	13.	(E)	14.	(A)	15.	(C)	16.	(C)	17.	(A)	18.	(B)	19.	(A)	20.	(E)
21.	(C)	22.	(B)	23.	(A)	24.	(C)	25.	(C)	26.	(A)	27.	(E)	28.	(E)				

Level-3: Expert

1.	(A)	2.	(E)	3.	(E)	4.	(A)	5.	(E)	6.	(A)	7.	(A)	8.	(B)	9.	(A)	10.	(C)
11.	(A)	12.	(B)	13.	(E)	14.	(B)	15.	(B)										

Solutions with Detailed Explanations

Level-1: BEGINNER

1. **Option (B) is correct.**
Explanation: A and D are positive statements which mean that he was not nervous. B and C statements seem to be the correct answer choices but statement C only says that he looked down which cannot be the correct fact to infer. Hence, statement B is the only fact to infer that Ram was nervous.

2. **Option (B) is correct.**
Explanation: Based on the circumstances presented above, it may be inferred that he will take the next logical step, or the ramp.

3. **Option (A) is correct.**
Explanation: According to the passage, a tiger takes to killing man only when certain wounds render it

incapable to kill its natural prey - the animals in the forest.

4. **Option (E) is correct.**
Explanation: The paragraph indicates that when tigers are unable to obtain the prey they are accustomed to eating, they turn to killing humans. This is against the reality stated in the inquiry.

5. **Option (A) is correct.**
Explanation: The text claims that a tiger's ability to kill its victim is dependent upon the health of its claws. The stated fact is implied by this.

6. **Option (C) is correct.**
Explanation: Old age is not necessarily equal to incapaciated body for hunting. Thus, the given fact is neither mentioned in nor can be derived from the given passage.

7. **Option (C) is correct.**
Explanation: The market economy of industrial–commercial demands is part of the three fundamental economies associated with forests. So, statement (d) is incorrect.

8. **Option (B) is correct.**
Explanation: Wrong environment policy and reduction in forest wealth.
Passaged is discussed "Forest Policy and Impact" and pointed out wrong environment policy and reduction in forest wealth.

9. **Option (D) is correct.**
Explanation: As written in the paragraph, "The colonial rule introduced...." we can conclude that deforestation and conflicts for market benefit, monoculture and ecological deprivation (that includes biodiversity losses) were the effects of colonialism.

10. **Option (A) is correct.**
Explanation: Conservation and use of forests nature's economy and survival economy have always overlapped in India. They functioned simultaneously without conflict as the survival needs of local people were satisfied through conservation-oriented utilisation.

11. **Option (C) is correct.**
Explanation: Global food security depends on the relationships that exist between ecological stability and the economic prosperity of the vast majority of people who live in tropical or Third World countries. The paragraph affirms the veracity of Statements (b) and (d).

12. **Option (B) is correct.**
Explanation: People who use mobile phones are putting their health at risk.
Detailed solution for the given passage: We can conclude that:
(A) *People who use mobile phones are putting their health at risk.*
This is stronger than the passage allows. It never says mobile phone users are definitely at risk—it only mentions suspicion, uncertainty, and guidelines. So (A) goes beyond the passage.
(B) *If extensive use of mobile phones is not harmful to health, radiation from a mast is unlikely to be a risk.*
This follows directly: mast radiation is much less than phone radiation, so if the greater exposure isn't harmful, the lesser one logically shouldn't be either.
(C) *The International guidelines underestimate the risk to health from low levels of radiation.*
The passage says "no one can yet be certain." That means we cannot conclude underestimation.
(D) *The health risk from living near a phone mast is lower than that from using a mobile phone.*
This is true based on the numbers given. But it's more of a factual restatement, not the strongest conclusion.

13. **Option (B) is correct.**
Explanation: The argument mentions that two-thirds of the children developed considerable levels of nearsightedness. From this we can derive that visual stress required by reading and other class work is the reason for nearsightness among the students. Thus, conclusion II follows. Conclusion I is not correct because only people who have the opportunity for formal schooling develop nearsightedness is an extreme statement to derive at.

14. **Option (C) is correct.**
Explanation: The final sentence of the passage hints at lumbering official customs in India, but nothing can be concluded about India's status in comparison to other nations.

15. **Option (E) is correct.**
Explanation: The reference to although some of them, refutes the given fact on the ground that not only India, but other nations too make such claims.

16. **Option (B) is correct.**
Explanation: It is specified within the passage that the passage of remote companies as a result of financial liberalization has put weight on Indian industry. Hence, the given fact appears very plausible.

17. **Option (D) is correct.**
Explanation: It is specified within the passage that the passage of remote companies as a result of financial liberalization has put weight on Indian industry. Hence, the given fact appears very plausible.

18. **Option (A) is correct.**
Explanation: The fact clearly follows from the first two sentences of the passage.

19. **Option (A) is correct.**
Explanation: It is mentioned in the passage that only the dealers can serve as good proxies for customers. This implies the given fact.

20. **Option (A) is correct.**
Explanation: The given inference directly follows from the second sentence of the passage.

21. **Option (B) is correct.**
Explanation: The passage proposes that merchants offer assistance a company reach out to the clients and get their input. The given deduction appears to be likely genuine within the light of this fact.

22. **Option (A) is correct.**
Explanation: The given inference directly follows from the statement and a company can achieve customer loyalty through dealer loyalty, in the passage.

23. **Option (C) is correct.**

Explanation: The significance of dealers for a company has been talked about within the passage. But there's no mention of significance or need of promotions within the passage.

Level-2: INTERMEDIATE

1. **Option (D) is correct.**
Explanation: As the paragraph discusses about the underground industries. Of the given four options, the most appropriate option seems to be (D).
2. **Option (A) is correct.**
Explanation: The author is examining in detail the Government's policy of providing incentives to farmers to form them deliver more nourishment including the negative aspects. Here the alternative (A) shows up to be the right reply since the induction drawn shows up to be "Definitely True".
3. **Option (C) is correct.**
Explanation: A person may now become a skilled surgeon in less than three months by using a virtual reality simulator to remove cataract impairment.
Based on the statements provided:
Option (A): Thanks to the availability of virtual reality simulators that remove impairment, skilled surgeons are no longer required to perform cataract surgery. Not implied
(Because for make any surgery, we must require a trained doctor, as machine is also run by a person).
Option (B): With a virtual reality simulator that mimics the human eye and allows users to experience the sensation of a live surgery, anybody can now be trained to erase cataract impairment—not assumed. (It is impossible to train everyone; instead, we must train doctors since they are surgical specialists who have put in a great deal of preparation.)
Option (C) is the safest option that enables a qualified doctor to get trained through a virtual simulator for removing cataract impairment.
4. **Option (E) is correct.**
Explanation: The passage mentions that not even one per cent of the 63,000 primary schools has facilities of furniture, toilet, drinking and games. One percent of 63,000 is 630. This translates that not even 630 schools have facilities of furniture, toilet, drinking and games.
5. **Option (C) is correct.**
Explanation: The passage mentions that out of 3,113 newly appointed teachers 2,747 are women. But nothing is mentioned about the percent of total women teachers in Bihar.
6. **Option (E) is correct.**
Explanation: It is mentioned in the passage that each of the 13,270 primary schools has at least two teachers.
7. **Option (A) is correct.**
Explanation: The passage mentions that approximately six million children are born to parents of lower socioeconomic status.
This implicitly suggests the stated fact.
8. **Option (B) is correct.**
Explanation: The paragraph indicates that over 50% of schools' students read aloud to themselves. Maybe this is a result of the inadequate classes offered.
9. **Option (C) is correct.**
Explanation: There is no such mention in the passage.
10. **Option (C) is correct.**
Explanation: The paragraph makes no mention of earlier attempts to improve Indian ports development.
11. **Option (A) is correct.**
Explanation: The sentence directly supports the inference that has been drawn. It is imperative to consistently compare Indian ports with the world's top ports in the passage.
12. **Option (E) is correct.**
Explanation: The last sentence of the passage contradicts the fact given statement.
13. **Option (E) is correct.**
Explanation: The paragraph makes reference to the necessity of pursuing legislative initiatives in order to achieve the lowest port service charges per container globally. This suggests that these service fees are not currently the lowest.
14. **Option (A) is correct.**
Explanation: The paragraph mentions that the legal heirs may provide some challenges for the nominee while trying to obtain the property. The given fact is implied by this.
15. **Option (C) is correct.**
Explanation: The text makes no mention of how the cooperative movement got its start.
16. **Option (C) is correct.**
Explanation: The paragraph discusses how cooperative society laws are identical throughout all states, not just laws pertaining to property.
17. **Option (A) is correct.**
Explanation: It is obvious that such training is required in order for individuals to support nominations and resolve issues that arise for legal heirs.
18. **Option (B) is correct.**
Explanation: The text claims that the nominee has trouble obtaining property from the legal heirs even after the deceased has completed the nomination form. Thus, the stated fact is very likely.
19. **Option (A) is correct.**
Explanation: The passage mentions that images and specific data about the celestial bodies and outer space have been sent back by space probes. As a result, they have contributed to our growing understanding of space and its inhabitants.
20. **Option (E) is correct.**
Explanation: The paragraph states that the space probes' original purpose was to investigate Earth's upper atmosphere. However, they are currently employed to investigate space and gather additional data about it.
21. **Option (C) is correct.**
Explanation: The paragraph states that Neil Armstrong was the first person to set foot on the moon. However, there is no talking about the first man to travel into space.
22. **Option (B) is correct.**

Explanation: The passage claims that space probes are outfitted with a wide range of cutting-edge scientific equipment. Computers may therefore also be present. It is evident that man has explored the moon since Neil Armstrong was the first person to set foot on it.

23. **Option (A) is correct.**
Explanation: The fact mentioned in the passage that Neil Armstrong was the first man to set foot on the Moon clearly proves that moon has been explored by man.

24. **Option (C) is correct.**
Explanation: There is no such mention in the passage.

25. **Option (C) is correct.**
Explanation: In this paragraph, there is no mention of earlier attempts to improve Indian ports.

26. **Option (A) is correct.**
Explanation: The sentence directly supports the inference that has been drawn. It is imperative to consistently compare Indian ports with the world's top ports in the passage.

27. **Option (E) is correct.**
Explanation: The last sentence of the passage contradicts the given statement.

28. **Option (E) is correct.**
Explanation: The passage mentions the necessity of pursuing legislative initiatives to achieve the lowest port service charges per container globally. This suggests that these service fees are not currently the lowest.

Level-3: EXPERT

1. **Option (A) is correct.**
Explanation: The given inference directly follows from the last sentence of the passage.

2. **Option (E) is correct.**
Explanation: The passage indicates that every nation has established codes of behaviour. This goes against the information provided in the statement.

3. **Option (E) is correct.**
Explanation: It is mentioned in the passage that rules of conduct are essential to ensure peace among citizens, which also hints at the necessity of the machinery that can scrutinize the citizens who violate these rules.

4. **Option (A) is correct.**
Explanation: The given inference follows from the last sentence of the passage.

5. **Option (E) is correct.**
Explanation: The passage emphasizes the necessity of moral guidelines to stop antisocial behaviours like stealing that don't include social connection. As a result, following the rules is essential in all situations.

6. **Option (A) is correct.**
Explanation: The paragraph indicates that the only people who can effectively represent clients in place of them are the dealers, who serve as proxies for customers. Therefore, it can be concluded that customers are more forthright in giving their feedback about a product or a service. This suggests the specified reality.

7. **Option (A) is correct.**
Explanation: Since, dealers who are long established members of a company can get close to customers. Thus the writer recommends that a company must forge extremely close ties with them and integrate them into its critical business systems.

8. **Option (B) is correct.**
Explanation: According to the passage, dealers can assist a business in contacting clients and getting their input. Moreover, a company can achieve customer loyalty through dealer loyalty. It is likely that the offered inference is accurate.

9. **Option (A) is correct.**
Explanation: The passage's assertion that a business may gain consumer loyalty through dealer loyalty supports the stated inference.

10. **Option (C) is correct.**
Explanation: The importance of dealers for a company has been discussed in the passage. But there is no mention of importance or necessity of advertisements in the passage.

11. **Option (A) is correct.**
Explanation: The aforementioned conclusion is evidently implied by the fact that cotton producers have shifted to the production of other cash crops.

12. **Option (B) is correct.**
Explanation: It is quite probable that the profitability of the yarn manufacturers may impel the farmers to grow cotton again next year.

13. **Option (E) is correct.**
Explanation: The passage's second sentence, "the cotton glut in the world markets," makes it very evident that there was an abundance of cotton on hand. This goes against the stated reality.

14. **Option (B) is correct.**
Explanation: The fact that yarn manufacturers who had piled up on cheap cotton have made enormous profits suggests that cotton prices have increased, most likely as a result of a decrease in supply.

15. **Option (B) is correct.**
Explanation: The passage mentions that following September 11, there was a downturn in the global economy. This lends much credence to the stated reality.

■ ■ ■

Chapter 7

Theme Detection

LEARNING OBJECTIVES:

- ❖ The concepts of Theme Detection
- ❖ Tips for Solving Logical Analogies
- ❖ The Effective Test-taking strategies

In every competitive exam, one of the most important sections is Reasoning. According to logic and type, reasoning is basically divided into a few sections. Theme detection is one of them.

In theme detection, the problems are related to the passages. From the passage, read the data carefully and decide the primary point the creator is attempting to make. What conclusion can be drawn from the contention? Every passage is trailed by five or four statements. One statement supports the creator's contention than the others do.

While reading, you need to identify argument in order to properly understand the main point. Stated claim: In paragraphs, topic sentence often identifies the main claim or idea of the paragraph. This is usually first sentence but not always.

How to find stated claim:

- Read the paragraph.
- Ask "what is the paragraph about?".
- Summarise the content in own words.
- Find the sentence within the paragraph that best matches the summary.

TIPS FOR SOLVING LOGICAL ANALOGIES

The following tips can be kept in mind while solving such questions.

1. **Skim the options one by one:** Quickly read the given options one by one and detect the theme of given option before moving to the second option. It is not advisable to move to the second option without comprehending the theme of the first option as it can lead to confusion. You can even consider writing the theme of each option before moving to the next.
2. **Avoid facts and details and stick to an overall idea:** A theme can be comprehended just by analysing the overall idea and there is no need to go into details such as facts, data, etc.
3. **Do not get discouraged by seeing difficult vocabulary** Sometimes, terms related to finance or research, are used in such questions which make understanding of the context difficult. However, in some cases such words do not contribute much to the theme and can easily be avoided as a theme of the context is related to an overall idea and not to individual words.

MIND IT !

These effective test-taking strategy tips and tricks are well worth remembering before you take the actual logical reasoning tests:

- Practice, practice and practice some more to ace your assessment and aptitude tests!
- Read the question and instructions properly. Even though this seems logical, often candidates miss out very important information. Multiple-choice tests use so called 'distractors' as answer possibilities. These distractors are answers options which are deliberately similar to the right answer; in other words, the answer possibilities are designed to test if you read the question and provided information properly.
- Therefore, take your time to carefully read the information provided.
- Be prepared with a pen and a piece of paper when doing the online test.
- It can be useful to develop a (mental) checklist of strategies to solve the questions. Remember the list of possible rules discussed above. This can help you to work more methodically in the test. If needed, write the discovered rules down.
- Try to focus on one rule at a time.

1 Beginner Level

Directions (Qs 1 to 25): Each of the following questions contains a small paragraph followed by a question on it. Read each paragraph carefully and answer the question given below it.

1. In the novel "To Kill a Mockingbird" by Harper Lee, the central theme revolves around racial injustice and discrimination in a small Southern town. The story follows the experiences of a young girl named Scout Finch and her family, who become entangled in a racially charged trial. Throughout the narrative, the author highlights the deep-seated prejudices and biases that exist within society.
   What is the central theme of "To Kill a Mockingbird"?
   (A) Cooking recipes
   (B) Adventure and exploration
   (C) Racial injustice and discrimination
   (D) Time travel escapades
2. "The Shawshank Redemption" is a classic film that explores the theme of hope and redemption. The story is set within the confines of a maximum-security prison and follows the journey of Andy Dufresne, a banker who maintains his hope and ultimately finds redemption through an unexpected friendship.
   What is the primary theme of "The Shawshank Redemption"?
   (A) Gardening techniques
   (B) Fear and isolation
   (C) Hope and redemption
   (D) Financial success
3. In Shakespeare's famous play "Hamlet," the central theme revolves around the concept of revenge. Hamlet, the protagonist, seeks to avenge his father's murder by his uncle, King Claudius. The play delves into the moral and psychological complexities of revenge.
   What is the primary theme explored in "Hamlet"?
   (A) Love and marriage
   (B) Time travel adventures
   (C) Revenge
   (D) Magic and sorcery
4. Maya Angelou's poem "Still I Rise" is a powerful expression of the theme of resilience and strength. Through her verses, Angelou celebrates the indomitable human spirit that can overcome adversity and discrimination.
   What is the central theme of Maya Angelou's poem "Still I Rise"?
   (A) Space exploration
   (B) Resilience and strength
   (C) Cooking and recipes
   (D) Scientific discoveries
5. George Orwell's novel "1984" is a dystopian masterpiece that primarily addresses the theme of totalitarianism and the dangers of a surveillance state. The story is set in a bleak future where the government exercises total control over its citizens.
   What is the central theme explored in George Orwell's "1984"?
   (A) Happiness and contentment
   (B) Totalitarianism and surveillance
   (C) Travel and adventure
   (D) Fashion trends
6. In Shirley Jackson's short story "The Lottery," the central theme criticises blind conformity within a small town's tradition of a deadly annual lottery. The chilling narrative highlights the dangers of unquestioningly following tradition.
   What is the primary theme criticised in "The Lottery"?
   (A) Environmental conservation
   (B) Blind conformity and tradition
   (C) Financial planning
   (D) Political activism
7. Martin Luther King Jr.'s "I Have a Dream" speech is a historic address that centres on the theme of civil rights and racial equality. King passionately articulates his vision for a racially integrated and just America.
   What is the central theme of Martin Luther King Jr.'s "I Have a Dream" speech?
   (A) Sports and athletics
   (B) Civil rights and racial equality
   (C) Culinary arts
   (D) Modern technology
8. F. Scott Fitzgerald's novel "The Great Gatsby" explores the theme of the American Dream and its corruption. Through the enigmatic character of Jay Gatsby, the author delves into the pursuit of wealth and success.
   What is the central theme of "The Great Gatsby"?
   (A) Space exploration
   (B) The American Dream and its corruption
   (C) World history
   (D) Scientific inventions
9. In E.B. White's children's book "Charlotte's Web," the primary theme revolves around friendship and the circle of life. The story follows the bond between a spider named Charlotte and a pig named Wilbur.
   What is the central theme of "Charlotte's Web"?
   (A) Adventure and exploration
   (B) Friendship and the circle of life
   (C) Advanced mathematics
   (D) Social media trends
10. Logical detection is a valuable skill that involves recognising patterns, making connections, and identifying recurring ideas or messages within various forms of communication.
    What does logical detection primarily involve?
    (A) Solving crossword puzzles
    (B) Cooking gourmet meals

(C) Identifying patterns and recurring ideas

(D) Playing musical instruments

11. People say that it is a bad habit to sleep in the afternoon but a slight modification in the method can largely affect your productivity. Instead of sleeping for long hours, you can take rest for few minutes by closing your eyes. Research says that a small nap of 10 minutes is powerful enough to re-energise you.

From the passage, the statement that best supports the theme of the passage is:

(A) Taking power nap can help in increasing your productivity.

(B) Do not sleep for longer hours in afternoon.

(C) Try to sleep not more than 10 minutes in the afternoon.

(D) None of the above.

12. Yoga is very beneficial in eradicating life-threatening diseases of the human body. Simultaneously, if not done according to the procedure, it can have adverse effects on the body too. Many people have complained about their disease becoming more serious after performing yoga. It was later found that the way they practised was wrong.

From the passage, the statement that best supports the theme of the passage is

(A) Yoga should be avoided.

(B) Yoga should be practised under the guidance of an expert.

(C) Meditation is better than yoga.

(D) None of the above.

13. Swami Vivekananda has said that "If you are not talking to yourself daily, then you are missing a great person". It is true in the context that by talking to yourself daily you can realise your strong and weak points. This will let you keep a track of your personality.

From the passage, the statement that best supports the theme of the passage is

(A) It is good to put a habit of talking to yourself daily.

(B) It is not good to keep silence with yourself.

(C) Vivekananda has told to talk more.

(D) None of the above.

14. Writers are those free birds who have the liberty of expressing their thoughts against the different sections of society, including government. But nowadays, they are reaming under the political pressure. Some do not even fear to be bribed.

From the passage, the statement that best supports the theme of the passage is:

(A) Writers should not work under anyone's order.

(B) Those writers who are accepting bribe should be jailed.

(C) Bribe is not good.

(D) None of the above.

15. The basic principle to expand your business is that, the company should be more service-oriented rather than focusing only on the production. This requires active participation of the managers with the other people rather than the products and the assemblies.

The passage well describes:

(A) Focus on service not on production

(B) In the upcoming days, the most important factor will be interpersonal skills.

(C) Managers should be good at talking to people.

(D) None of the above

16. Gone are the days where you used to score good marks by reading your books and subjects prescribed in your course of syllabus. Now every board of education is changing their style of education and exam format. Nowadays, to get good marks, you have to read the out of the regular course of syllabus and also take help of the Internet if needed.

The passage well describes the fact:

(A) Internet is necessary nowadays.

(B) You need to focus less on outside activities and more on study.

(C) Knowledge of a particular subject in all aspects is important.

(D) Study has become so important that all extracurricular activities should be curbed.

17. Industrial exhibitions play a major role in a country's economy. Such exhibitions, now regularly held in Delhi, enable us to measure the extent of our own less advanced industrial progress and the mighty industrial power and progress of countries like the U.K., U.S.A. and Russia whose pavilions are the centres of the greatest attention and attractions.

The passage best supports the statement that the industrial exhibitions:

(A) boost up production qualitatively and quantitatively by analytical comparison of a country's products with those of the developed countries.

(B) are not of much use to the countries who are industrially backward.

(C) are more useful for the developed countries like U.S.A. whose products stand out superior to those of the developing countries.

(D) greatly tax the poor economics.

18. Exports and imports, a swelling favourable balance of trade, investments and bank balances, are not an index or a balance sheet of national prosperity. Till the beginning of the Second World War. English exports were noticeably greater than what they are today. And yet England has greater national prosperity today than it ever had. Because the income of average Englishmen, working as field and factory labourers, clerks, policemen, petty shopkeepers and shop assistants, domestic workers and other low paid workers, has gone up.

The passage best supports the statement that:

(A) English trade has continually increased since the Second World War.

(B) a nations economy strengthens with the increase in exports.

(C) a countrys economic standard can be best adjudged by the per capita income.

(D) a countrys balance of trade is the main criteria of determining its economic prosperity.

19. There is a shift in our economy from a manufacturing to a service orientation. The increase in service sector will require the managers to work more with people rather than with objects and things from the assembly line. This passage best supports the statements that:

(A) interpersonal skills will become more important in the future work place.

(B) assembly line will exist in serve organisations.

(C) manufacturing organisations ignore importance of people.

(D) managers should have a balanced mind.

20. Satisfaction with co-workers, promotion opportunities, the nature of work and pay is associated with high performance among those with strong growth needs. Among those with weak growth needs, no such relationship is present and in fact, satisfaction with promotion opportunities goes with low performance.

This passage best supports the statement that:

(A) every organisation has few employees having weak growth need.

(B) relationship between job satisfication and performance is moderated by growth need.

(C) job satisfaction and performance are directly and closely related.

(D) satisfaction is an inevitable organisational variable.

21. The press should not be afraid of upholding and supporting a just and righteous cause. It should not be afraid of criticising the government in a healthy manner. The press has to be eternally vigilant to protect the rights of the workers, backward and suppressed sections of the society. It should also give a balanced view of the things so that people can be helped in the formation of a healthy public opinion.

The passage best supports the statements that:

(A) the press has a great role to play in a democracy.

(B) the press can be used by the government as an effective media for the upliftment of the backward sections of a society.

(C) the press is the only means to project to the masses the policies of the government.

(D) the freedom of press is essential for the proper functioning of democracy.

22. Emerson said that the poet was landlord, sealord, airlord. The flight of imagination made the poet master of land sea and air. But a poet's dream of yesterday becomes today an actual achievement and a reality for all men. Even those who invented, improved and perfected the aeroplane could hardly have dreamt of the possibility of flight into outer space.

The passage best supports the statements that:

(A) man has reached the climax of technologies development with the exploration into outer space.

(B) what man imagined has never been impossible; he has always turned it a reality through his conception of ideas and sheer hard labour.

(C) seemingly impossible imagination makes one a good poet.

(D) all imaginations become a reality some day.

23. The virtue of art does not allow the work to be interfered with or immediately ruled by anything other than itself. It insists that it alone shall touch the work in order to bring it into being. Art requires that nothing shall attain the work except through art itself.

This passage best supports the statement that

(A) artist should use his art for the sake of society.

(B) art is for the sake of art alone.

(C) art is for the sake of art and life.

(D) art is governed by external rules and conditions.

24. The future of women in India is quite bright and let us hope that they will justify their abilities by rising to the occasion. Napolean was right when he declared that by educating the women we can educate the whole nation. Because a country can never rise without the contribution of 50% of their population.

The passage best supports the statement that:

(A) women ought to be imparted full freedom to prove their worth and contribute to the progress of the nation.

(B) a nation can progress only when women are given equal rights and opportunities as men.

(C) all women should be well educated.

(D) India is striving hard for the emancipation of women.

25. Though the waste of time or the expenditure on fashions is very large, yet fashions have come to stay. They will not go, come what may. However, what is now required is that strong efforts should be made to displace the excessive craze for fashion from the minds of these youngsters.

The passage best supports the statements that:

(A) the hoard for fashion should be done away with so as not to let down the constructive development.

(B) work and other activities should be valued more than the outward appearance.

(C) the excessive craze for fashion is detrimental to one's personality.

(D) fashion is the need of the day.

Level 2 Intermediate

Directions (Qs 1 to 22): Each of the following questions contains a small paragraph followed by a question on it. Read each paragraph carefully and answer the question given below it.

1. There is a thin line that separates the two words — "relationship" and "friendship". If one boy and girl are closely associated with each other mentally and emotionally, that does not mean that they are in relationship. Good friends can also share this strong emotional bond.

This passage is trying to convince the fact that:

(A) friends can also share strong mental and emotional attachment.

(B) relationship is more complex than friendship.

(C) the persons who are good friends are in relationship with each other.

(D) the persons who are in relationships are good friends.

2. Through heavy industrial revolution, the businessman has changed the whole gesture of people. They have provided the people with world class luxury items and have introduced them to the modern standard of living. Past few centuries the standard of people has been changed by the businessman.

The passage clearly talks about:

(A) in the past few years, business has increased rapidly.

(B) everybody should do business.

(C) people need to thank the businessman

(D) when it comes to the growth of civilisation and the standards of people, the contribution of the businessman is more.

3. There are two types of brain tumour; one that grows very fast and other one is just opposite. Most doctors suggest, surgery as the primary option but unless the tumour is removed completely, there is a fair chance of re-growing of the tumour. Thanks to the advance technology, like cyberknife treatment, that provides the option of complete removal of tumour through radiation therapy. It is painless procedure and during treatment patient can continue his/her regular duty.

(A) Surgery is not the primary solution for every tumour.

(B) Not every doctor is upgraded with latest technology.

(C) Both A and B are true.

(D) None of the above

4. Tablets are making people crazy. They are wasting their valuable time chatting with others, surfing on net, and playing games but still there are many advantages of having a smartphone.

What is the theme of the passage?

(A) Author is optimistic on using tablets.

(B) Author is pessimistic on using tablets.

(C) Author is neutral on using tablets.

(D) None of the above

5. Storyboarding is not only an act of creating a PPT file with text, it also requires putting relevant image files and to animate them in accordance with the theme and content of the passage.

(A) Storyboarding is a creative work.

(B) Storyboarding is a layman's work.

(C) Relevant image is the main part of storyboarding.

(D) None of the above

6. If any person is doing a wrong deed then, he /she should be hanged if that crime is a critical one. This will lead the other people to think 100 times before committing such crime. Those who are against it, do not want the system to be strong enough to build fear in the heart of the criminals.

Through this passage, the author is trying to say that capital punishment:

(A) should be abolished.

(B) should not be abolished.

(C) may or may not be abolished.

(D) cannot be judged from the passage.

7. Even after being given legal status by the honourable Supreme Court, gay relationships will still be considered taboo in India. People here think of it as a crime and think it is against the etiquette of their respective religious beliefs. No matter how hard people will show support from the outside but at their heart they will have the same disrespect towards these couples.

What can be inferred from the above passage?

(A) India is a good place for gay couples to live in.

(B) India is a worst place for the gay couples to live in.

(C) Beliefs of the people can be changed with the due course of time.

(D) None of the above.

8. Social media has now become the addiction of general public. In their spare time, you can see a lot of people wasting their time in commenting on other's pictures or making some illogical virtual status updates. However; social media is sometimes helpful too. To gather public attention regarding any important message or to do an online campaign of your business and product, this is the best platform.

Through this passage, one thing can be inferred that:

(A) social media should be banned as it is making people mentally sick.

(B) do the online campaign of your business on social media.

(C) there is both positive and negative sides of using social media.

(D) None of the above

9. Often, people run after the money and higher increment without gaining adequate knowledge of the work they are handling. They should focus on their job first and later gain expertise over it. Money will follow your success. But in the act of balancing both, one should also not neglect his/her family due to which his/her existence is there in the present.

If we prioritise the job, money and family in descending order, it will be:

(A) job, money, family **(B)** family, money, job

(C) job, family, money **(D)** family, job, money

10. Unemployment is a major problem being faced by our nation at present. This is so worst in condition that good technical graduates even from IITs are sitting unemployed. This is due to the poor mentality of our people to depend upon jobs in other organisations rather than creating one for themselves and for others through entrepreneurships.

This statement that supports the passage is:

(A) India should create more jobs for youngsters.
(B) India is behind other countries in terms of employment.
(C) people of India should focus more on entrepreneurships.
(D) None of the above.

11. A popular Indian automobile company has decided to enter into African market by launching its new product in Kenya. It has also set up an assembly unit for the same in Kenya to foster selling process.
Through this passage, one thing can be concluded:
(A) Indian companies are interested in African market.
(B) Africa always encourages companies from different countries.
(C) The Indian company is going in loss.
(D) Next year some more Indian companies will launch themselves in Africa.

12. 78 people were buried alive under the ground yesterday evening when the 15-storey Idrani building collapsed in just a blink of eye in Sikendrabad. This was a five-decade-old building structure, built with strong mortar elements in the year 1998.
From the passage, the statement that best supports the theme of the passage is:
(A) the municipality and development authority should be aware about those buildings which are not strong enough to stand because Sikendrabad is an old city.
(B) all the old buildings must be destroyed.
(C) Sikendrabad is not safe for visitors.
(D) Idrani hotels architecture is not good in our country.

13. One of the important humanitarian by-products of technology is the greater dignity and value that it imparts to human labour. In a highly industrialised society, there is no essential difference between Brahmin and Dalit, Muslim and Hindu; they are equally useful and hence equally valuable in the industrial society. Individual productivity fixes the size of the pay cheque and this fixes social status.
The passage best supports the statement that:
(A) all individuals, irrespective of caste and creed are born equal.
(B) human labour has dignity and value.
(C) technology decides individual social status.
(D) industrial society is a greater leveler of men.

14. Due to enormous profits involved in smuggling, hundreds of persons have been attracted towards this anti-national activity. Some of them became millionaires overnight. India has a vast coast line both on the Eastern and Western Coast. It has been a heaven for smugglers who have been carrying on their activities with great impunity. There is no doubt, that from time to time, certain seizures were made by the enforcement authorities during raids and ambush but even allowing these losses the smugglers made huge profits.
The passage best supports the statement that:
(A) smuggling is fast increasing in our country owing to the quick profit in entails.
(B) authorities are taking strict measures to curb smuggling.
(C) smuggling ought to be curbed.
(D) smuggling hampers the economic development of a nation.

15. The only true education comes through the stimulation of the child's powers by the demands of the social situations in which he finds himself. Through these demands he is stimulated to act as a member of a unity, to emerge from his original narrowness of action and feeling, and to conceive himself from the stand point of the welfare of the group to which he belongs.
The passage best supports the statement that real education:
(A) comes from the self-centred approach of the students.
(B) comes through the interaction with social situations.
(C) is not provided in our schools today.
(D) will take place if the children imbibe action and feeling.

16. Throughout the ages, the businessmen have helped build civilisation's great cities, provided people with luxuries and supported artists with patronage, and lift his fellow citizens to understand the standard of living. In the last few centuries the businessmen have seeded the Industrial Revolution around the world.
The passage best supports the statement that the businessmen:
(A) have contributed to the growth of civilisation.
(B) are the beneficiary of the Industrial Revolution.
(C) live luxurious and comfortable life.
(D) are accountable to the society.

17. The attainment of individual and organisational goals is mutually interdependent and linked by a common denominator: employee work motivation. Organisational members are activated to satisfy their personal goals, and they contribute their efforts to the attainment of organisational objectives as means of achieving these personal goals.
The passage best supports the statement that motivation:
(A) is crucial for the survival of an individual and organisation.
(B) encourages an individual to give priority to personal goals over organisational goals.
(C) is the external force which induces an individual to contribute his efforts.
(D) makes organisation and society inseparable.

18. The prevention of accidents makes it necessary not only for safety devices to be used to guard exposed machinery but also for mechanics to be instructed in safety rules, which they must follow for their own protection, and for the lighting in the plant to be adequate.
The passage best supports the statement that industrial accidents:

(A) are always avoidable.

(B) may be due to ignorance.

(C) can be eliminated with the help of safety rules.

(D) usually result from inadequate machinery.

19. The consumption of harmful drugs by the people can be prevented not only by banning their sale in the market but also by instructing users about their dangerous effects which they must understand for their safety. Drug addicts may also be provided with the proper medical facilities for their rehabilitation. This will help in scaling down the use of drugs.

The passage best supports the statement that consumption of harmful drugs:

(A) can be eliminated with the help of banning their sale.

(B) is due to lack of medical facilities.

(C) can always be reduced.

(D) are no increase in the society.

20. The school has always been the most important means of transferring the wealth of tradition from one generation to the next. This applies today in an even higher degree than in former times for; through the modern development of economy, the family as bearer of tradition and education has become weakend.

This passage best supports the statement that for transferring the wealth of tradition from one generation to the next:

(A) there are means other than the school.

(B) several different sources must be tried.

(C) economic development plays a crucial role.

(D) modern technology must be put to use.

21. To forgive an injury is often considered to be a sign of weakness; it is really a sign of strength. It is easy to allow oneself to be carried away by resentment and hate into an act of vengeance; but it takes a strong character to restrain those natural passions. The man who forgives an injury proves himself to be the superior of the man who wronged himself and puts the wrong doer to shame.

The passage best supports the statements that:

(A) mercy is the noblest form of revenge.

(B) a person with calm and composed nature has depth of thought and vision.

(C) the sufferer alone knows the intensity of his sufferings.

(D) people tend to forgive the things happened in the past.

22. Through advertising, manufacturing exercises a high degree of control over consumers' desires. However, all manufacturers assume enormous risks in attempting to predict what consumers will want and in producing goods in quantity and distributing them in advance of final selection by the consumers.

The paragraph best supports the statement that manufacturers:

(A) must depend upon the final consumers for the success of their undertakings.

(B) can predict with great accuracy the success of any product they put on the market.

(C) distribute goods directly to the consumers.

(D) can eliminate the risk of overproduction by advertising.

Level 3 Expert

Directions (Qs 1 to 10): Each of the following questions contains a small paragraph followed by a question on it. Read each paragraph carefully and answer the question given below it.

1. Shoojit Sicar's sensational movie PINK has gathered positive words of mouth from all generation of Indian audience. Prior to its release from its trailer, it was expected to focus only a particular mass of audience but its record breaking box office success proved that all wrong

(A) PINK has gained audience support but not critic's support.

(B) Film has not yet recovered its cost.

(C) Taste of Indian cinema audience is changing gradually.

(D) Box-office success can be fake too.

2. India is well known globally for its finest art that one can witness in many famous temples present over here but it is a matter of shame that we are soon going to lose that credit too. By this statement, what does writer prefer to say?

(A) Indian government should stop focusing on other matters, rather should give primary importance to this.

(B) India has already lost some other credits like this too in past.

(C) People of India should argue with their government for the same.

(D) None of the above

3. Exports and imports, a swelling favourable balance of trade, investments and bank- balances, are not an index or a balance sheet of national prosperity. Till the beginning of the Second World War, English exports were noticeably greater than what they are today. And yet England has greater national prosperity today than it ever had. Because the income of average Englishmen, working as field and factory labourers, clerks, policemen, petty shopkeepers and shop assistants, domestic workers and other low-paid workers, has gone up.

The passage best supports the statement that:

(A) a country's economic standard can be best adjudged by per capital income.

(B) a country's balance of trade is the main criteria of determining its economic prosperity.

(C) a nation's economy strengthens with the increase

in exports.

(D) English trade has continually increased since the Second World War.

4. It is up to our government and planners to devise ways and means for the mobilisation of about ten crore workers whose families total up about forty crore men, women and children. Our agriculture is over-manned. A lesser number of agriculturists would mean more purchasing or spending power to every agriculturist. This will result in the shortage of man-power for many commodities to be produced for which there will be a new demand from a prosperous agrarian class. This shortage will be removed by surplus man-power released from agriculture as suggested above.

The passage best supports the statement that:

(A) employment in production is more fruitful than employment in agriculture.

(B) Indian economy is in a poor shape basically due to improper mobilisation of man-power.

(C) a shift of labour from agricultural sector to the industrial sector would uplift the living standard.

(D) the industrial sector is labour-deficient while the agricultural sector is over- manned in our country.

5. Nowadays, it is difficult to sit comfortably in your seat in the train although you have a confirmed reservations. People with general reservation tickets are also boarding the reserved compartments and are making it difficult for the reserved passengers. The T.T. also takes it as an opportunity of earning some extra unofficial money.

From the passage, we can infer that

(A) Confirm reservation cannot guarantee you a comfortable journey.

(B) Strict action should be taken against the T.T.

(C) Railway administration should interfere in the matter.

(D) None of the above

6. Many argue that art cannot be defined. Art is often considered the process or product of deliberately arranging elements in a way that appeals to the senses or emotions. It encompasses a diverse range of human activities, creations and ways of expression, including music, literature, film, sculpture and paintings.

(A) Art is defined as a form of human expression of a creative nature.

(B) Artist realizes his dreams through his artistic creation.

(C) Art is governed by external rules and conditions.

(D) Art requires that nothing shall attain the work except through art itself.

7. The model was extended to establish a relationship between financial development and economic growth. Co-integration results show that capital–output ratio and rate of growth of human capital have positive effects on real rate of growth of GDP, irrespective of the indicator of stock market development. An increase in the market capitalization dampens economic growth, whereas turnover has no significant effect, and an increase in the money market rate of interest has a positive effect on economic growth in India.

(A) Reform measures on the market rate of interest that were introduced in the Indian banking system appear to have promoted economic growth significantly.

(B) The impact of the developments in the financial sector on economic growth in India.

(C) There is a shift in our economy from a manufacturing to a service orientation.

(D) Real wealth, real effective exchange rate and the rate of growth of labour have negative effects.

8. Most social network services are web-based and provide means for users to interact over the Internet, such as e-mail and instant messaging. Online community services are sometimes considered as a social network service, though in a broader sense, social network service usually means an individual-centered service whereas online community services are group-centered. Social networking sites allow users to share ideas, pictures, posts, activities, events, and interests with people in their network.

(A) Facebook service consists of a representation of each user (often a profile), his/her social links, and a variety of additional services.

(B) A social networking service is a platform to build social networks or social relations among people who, for example, share interests, activities, backgrounds, or real-life connections.

(C) Several websites are beginning to tap into the power of the social networking model for philanthropy.

(D) Companies have begun to merge business technologies and solutions, such as cloud computing, with social networking concepts.

9. Industrial exhibitions play a major role in a country's economy. Such exhibitions, now regularly held in Delhi, enable us to measure the extent of our own less advanced industrial progress and the mighty industrial power and progress of countries like the U.K., U.S.A. and Russia whose pavilions are the centres of the greatest attention and attractions.

The passage best supports the statement that industrial exhibitions:

(A) greatly tax the poor economies.

(B) are more useful for the developed countries like U.S.A. whose products stand out superior to those of the developing countries.

(C) are not of much use to the countries who are industrially backward.

(D) boost up production qualitatively and quantitatively by analytical comparison of a country's products with those of the developed countries.

10. Most of the child labourers are engaged in agriculture and allied subject like livestock, foresting and fisheries. In the urban areas, children work in dhabas, eateries helpers or cleaners in trucks and as domestic servants etc. They have long working hours, bad and unhygienic working conditions and fewer wages. The main reason behind child labour is poverty.

(A) Child Labour is a social evil in every nation.
(B) Awareness of the people and Government also compels poor parents to make their children employed as laborers.
(C) Almost every country in the world has laws relating to and aimed at preventing child labour.
(D) Parties recognise the right of the child to be protected from economic exploitation and from performing any work.

ANSWER KEY

Level-1: Beginner

1.	(C)	2.	(C)	3.	(C)	4.	(B)	5.	(B)	6.	(B)	7.	(B)	8.	(B)	9.	(B)	10.	(C)
11.	(A)	12.	(B)	13.	(A)	14.	(A)	15.	(B)	16.	(C)	17.	(A)	18.	(C)	19.	(A)	20.	(B)
21.	(D)	22.	(B)	23.	(B)	24.	(A)	25.	(A)										

Level-2: Intermediate

1.	(A)	2.	(D)	3.	(A)	4.	(A)	5.	(A)	6.	(B)	7.	(B)	8.	(C)	9.	(D)	10.	(C)
11.	(A)	12.	(A)	13.	(B)	14.	(A)	15.	(B)	16.	(A)	17.	(B)	18.	(C)	19.	(A)	20.	(C)
21.	(A)	22.	(D)																

Level-3: Expert

1.	(C)	2.	(B)	3.	(A)	4.	(B)	5.	(A)	6.	(A)	7.	(B)	8.	(B)	9.	(D)	10.	(A)

Solutions with Detailed Explanations

Level-1: BEGINNER

1. **Option (C) is correct.**
Explanation: Prejudice and racial injustice.
The main topic of "To Kill a Mockingbird" is racial injustice and prejudice in a tiny Southern town, as stated clearly in the facts supplied. The narrative draws attention to the pervasive biases and prejudices in society.

2. **Option (C) is correct.**
Explanation: Hope and redemption.
The paragraph states that the central theme of "The Shawshank Redemption" is hope and redemption. Andy Dufresne's journey in a maximum-security prison and his ultimate redemption through an unexpected friendship emphasise this theme.

3. **Option (C) is correct.**
Explanation: The information given makes it clear that the idea of retribution serves as the main subject in Shakespeare's "Hamlet." The play's main plot is around Hamlet's attempt to get revenge on King Claudius for killing his father.

4. **Option (B) is correct.**
Explanation: The passage notes that resilience and courage are the main themes of Maya Angelou's poem "Still I Rise." The poem honours the resilience of the human spirit in the face of injustice and misfortune.

5. **Option (B) is correct.**
Explanation: According to the information given, the main themes of George Orwell's book "1984" are authoritarianism and the perils of a surveillance state. The narrative takes place in a dystopian future where themes of governmental monitoring and control predominate.

6. **Option (B) is correct.**
Explanation: The paragraph indicates that the central theme criticised in Shirley Jackson's "The Lottery" is blind conformity within a town's tradition of a deadly annual lottery. The story highlights the dangers of unquestioningly following tradition.

7. **Option (B) is correct.**
Explanation: According to the information provided, racial equality as well as civil rights is the primary focus of Martin Luther King Jr.'s "I Have a Dream" speech. King's vision for an America that is equitable and racially integrated is eloquently expressed in this address.

8. **Option (B) is correct.**
Explanation: The passage suggests that the American Dream and its corruption serve as the main themes of F. Scott Fitzgerald's book "The Great Gatsby."
The narrative examines the corrosive effects of pursuing success and fortune.

9. **Option (B) is correct.**
Explanation: The provided information states that the primary theme of E.B. White's "Charlotte's Web" is friendship and the circle of life. The story centres around the bond between a spider named Charlotte and a pig named Wilbur.

10. **Option (C) is correct.**
Explanation: The paragraph explains that logical detection primarily involves recognising patterns, making connections, and identifying recurring ideas or messages within various forms of communication.

11. **Option (A) is correct.**
Explanation: Option A best describes the theme of the passage. The paragraph is about quality sleep in the noon and its impact on productivity. Researchers conclude the efficacy of 10 minutes nap as equally productive.

12. **Option (B) is correct.**
Explanation: Since, if not done according to the procedure, yoga can have adverse effects on the body, it is best to perform yoga under the expert guidance. Option B best describes the theme of the passage.

13. **Option (A) is correct.**
Explanation: Option A best describes the theme of the passage.

14. **Option (A) is correct.**
Explanation: Since, writers are those free birds who have the liberty of expressing their thoughts against the different sections of society, it is safe to comprehend that they must not take anyone's orders or be bribed. Option A best describes the theme of the passage.

15. **Option (B) is correct.**
Explanation: If you don't possess interpersonal skills, it will be challenging to keep the production running smoothly.

16. **Option (C) is correct.**
Explanation: The passage is clearly depicting the importance of gaining the knowledge on overall front for a particular subject.

17. **Option (A) is correct.**
Explanation: Boost up production qualitatively and quantitatively by analytical comparison of a country's products with those of the developed countries.

18. **Option (C) is correct.**
Explanation: A country's economic standard can be best adjudged by the per capita income. It is evident from the para that as and when the country's (England) national prosperity reached heights, subsequently the income of any working man in that country has also sot up.

19. **Option (A) is correct.**
Explanation: Interpersonal skills will become more important in the future work place. That is so because with the increase in service sector will require the managers to work more with people rather than with objects and things from the assembly line.

20. **Option (B) is correct.**
Explanation: Relationship between job satisfication and performance is moderated by growth need.

21. **Option (D) is correct.**
Explanation: The paragraph is about the role of press in a democracy in protecting the rights of the workers, backward and suppressed sections of the society and in the formation of a healthy public opinion. So, the freedom of press is essential for the proper functioning of democracy.

22. **Option (B) is correct.**
Explanation: Man has always been able to bring his visions of the unattainable into reality via his creative thoughts and unceasing work.

23. **Option (B) is correct.**
Explanation: It is established in the paragraph that Art requires that nothing shall attain the work except through art itself. So, the correct theme is : Art is for the sake of art alone.

24. **Option (A) is correct.**
Explanation: Women should be granted complete freedom to establish their value and advance the country. This is reverberated in the words of Napolean, when he declared that by educating the women we can educate the whole nation. Because a country can never rise without the contribution of 50% of their population.

25. **Option (A) is correct.**
Explanation: The hoard for fashion should be done away with so as not to let down the constructive development.

Level-2: INTERMEDIATE

1. **Option (A) is correct.**
Explanation: This passage is clearly describing the fact that friends can also share the same emotional and mental attachment as done by people in relationships.

2. **Option (D) is correct.**
Explanation: The answer can be best understood by reading the passage well.

3. **Option (A) is correct.**
Explanation: Option (A) is correct because cyberknife is providing an alternative to surgery .

4. **Option (A) is correct.**
Explanation: According to author, despite of dark sides, there are many brighter sides of using a smartphone.

5. **Option (A) is correct.**
Explanation: According to the passage, it is a creative endeavour as it calls for a thoughtful selection of images and their animation in line with the topic.

6. **Option (B) is correct.**
Explanation: The author is clearly saying not to abolish the capital punishments

7. **Option (B) is correct.**
Explanation: The author expresses little optimism regarding the acceptance of homosexual couples in India and says nothing about how people's views of the future will alter in the near future.

8. **Option (C) is correct.**
Explanation: Here, social media is presented with both pros and cons. A simple reading of the passage can lead us to the correct answer.

9. **Option (D) is correct.**
Explanation: Option D best describes the theme of the passage.
10. **Option (C) is correct.**
Explanation: Option C best describes the theme of the passage.
11. **Option (A) is correct.**
Explanation: Africa is a big continent so, India is interested there.
12. **Option (A) is correct.**
Explanation: It is the responsibility of development authority and municipality to look into old buildings with shaky infrastructure.
13. **Option (B) is correct.**
Explanation: The very first sentence of the paragraph reiterates the answer. Human labour has dignity and value.
14. **Option (A) is correct.**
Explanation: The reason behind the swift increase in smuggling is enormous profits in a small amount of time. Smuggling is fast increasing in our country owing to the quick profit in entails.
15. **Option (B) is correct.**
Explanation: Comes through the interaction with social situations.
16. **Option (A) is correct.**
Explanation: Owing to the building of civilization's great cities, and uplifting the standard of living of fellow citizens, it is true that businessmen have contributed to the growth of civilisation.
17. **Option (B) is correct.**
Explanation: The passage makes it quite apparent that employee work motivation is the common denominator that links the achievement of individual and organisational goals. Individuals are driven to achieve their own objectives and demands. In order to accomplish these personal aims, they give it their all to reach the organisational goals.
18. **Option (C) is correct.**
Explanation: The entire passage focuses on the safety regulations that need to be observed to prevent mishaps. Thus, option C accurately captures the topic.
(A) is incorrect because adopting preventative measures can reduce the number of accidents. The paragraph makes no mention of these always being preventable.
While (B) is inaccurate, it does not capture the essence of the text because the whole paragraph focuses on taking preventative action to avoid accidents rather than analysing the causes of accidents. (D) is incorrect as poor illumination and technician ineptitude both contribute to accidents.
19. **Option (A) is correct.**
Explanation: The paragraph states that discouraging drug sales and educating consumers about their adverse consequences are two ways to stop the use of toxic medications. Drug abusers may also get a range of medical services to aid in their quick recovery. Thus, choice A is correct.
20. **Option (C) is correct.**
Explanation: The passage's final sentence states that the family's role as the guardian of tradition and education has diminished as a result of economic growth. Because families' and people's behaviour to uphold their cultural values are the most important factors, economic growth is thus inevitably involved in the passing down of traditions from one generation to the next. Thus, choice C is accurate.
21. **Option (A) is correct.**
Explanation: According to the passage, a man who shows forgiveness for an injury demonstrates his superiority over the one who caused it. Thus, the purest form of retaliation is kindness.
22. **Option (D) is correct.**
Explanation: Manufacturers have significant influence on the demands of customers via advertising. However, by trying to guess what customers will want and by creating things in bulk and distributing them before the customers make their final decision, the producer takes on a great deal of risk. Thus, can eliminate the risk of overproduction.

Level-3: EXPERT

1. **Option (C) is correct.**
Explanation: Prediction by the experts about the movie went wrong proves because the movie garnered appreciation from all kinds of audience, not only women(as expected).
2. **Option (B) is correct.**
Explanation: The use of word "too" in the sentence does say that India has lost some similar credits in past.
3. **Option (A) is correct.**
Explanation: Countries economic standard can be best adjudged by the per capita income.
4. **Option (B) is correct.**
Explanation: Indian economy is in a poor shape basically due to improper mobilisation of man-power.
5. **Option (A) is correct.**
Explanation: The assertion that people with general reservation tickets are also boarding the reserved compartments and are making it difficult for the reserved passengers, hence this confirms the authenticity of option (A).
6. **Option (A) is correct.**
Explanation: As per the passage the definition of art is any creative form of human expression in diverse forms. The last line of the paragraph sets the theme of the extract.
7. **Option (B) is correct.**
Explanation: The impact of the developments in the financial sector on economic growth in India.
8. **Option (B) is correct.**
Explanation: A social networking service is a platform to build social networks or social relations among people who, for example, share interests, activities, backgrounds, or real life connection.
9. **Option (D) is correct.**
Explanation: Boost up production qualitatively and quantitatively by analytical comparison of a country's products with those of the developed countries.
10. **Option (A) is correct.**
Explanation: Child Labour is a social evil in every nation because children are exploited and overworked and underpaid. This is all because of poverty. So, it is a social evil.

■ ■ ■

Chapter 8

Cause and Effect Reasoning

LEARNING OBJECTIVES:

- Identifying the cause and effect relationship.
- What are the goals of cause and effect reasoning
- To curate the logical conclusions by examining cause & effect.

Cause and effect reasoning is a type of logical reasoning that entails comprehending the relationship between events or phenomena. It investigates the idea that one event or action, known as the cause, leads to another event or outcome, known as the effect. Individuals use this type of reasoning to examine how specific causes result in specific effects or how specific effects result from specific causes.

The cause is the reason or factor that initiates or brings about a specific event or situation. It is the action or condition that occurs before the effect and is thought to have a causal influence. The outcome or consequence that occurs as a result of the cause, on the other hand, is referred to as the effect.

The goal of cause and effect reasoning is to establish a link or relationship between these causes and effects. It entails identifying and comprehending the factors that lead to specific outcomes, recognising patterns, and forecasting the outcomes of specific actions or events. By observing and analysing cause and effect relationships, one can gain insights into the underlying mechanisms of various phenomena and make informed decisions based on this knowledge.

Cause and effect reasoning is essential in many fields, including science, history, economics and everyday life. It enables us to explain events, make predictions, solve problems and comprehend the consequences of our actions. We can unravel complex systems and phenomena and draw logical conclusions about the world around us by examining cause and effect relationships.

Example 1:

I. There is a sharp decline in the production of oil seeds this year.

II. The government decided to increase the import quantum of edible oil.

(A) If statement I is the cause and statement II is its effect.

(B) If statement II is the cause and statement I is its effect.

(C) If both the statements I and II are independent causes.

(D) If both the statements I and II are effects of independent causes.

(E) If both the statements I and II are effects of some common cause.

Sol. (A) Oil supply will inevitably be reduced by a rapid decrease in oilseed output; the only way to replenish the necessary supply is through oil imports.

Example 2:

I. The life today is too fast, demanding and full of variety in all aspect, which at time leads to stressful situation.

II. Number of suicide cases among teenagers is on increase.

(A) If statement I is the cause and statement II is its effect.

(B) If statement II is the cause and statement, I is its effect.

(C) If both the statements, I and II are independent causes.

(D) If both the statements I and II are effects of independent causes.

(E) If both the statements, I and II are effects of some common cause.

Sol. (A) Stress is predominant in life today, and hence a major cause of frustration among the youth and is bound to lead them to take harsh steps as suicide.

1 Level Beginner

Directions (Qs 1 to 15): In each of the following questions, two statements numbered I and II are given. There may be cause and effect relationship between the two statements. These two statements may be the effect of the same cause or independent causes. These statements may be independent courses without having any relationship. Read both statements in each question and mark your answer as:

(A) If statement I is the cause and, statement II is its effect.
(B) If statement II is the cause and statement, I is its effect.
(C) If both the statements I and II are independent causes.
(D) If both the statements I and II are effects of independent causes.
(E) If both the statements I and II are effects of some common cause.

1. I. The prices of vegetables have been increased considerably during this summer.
II. There is tremendous increase in the temperature during this summer thereby damaging crops greatly. **[Bank PO 2003]**

2. I. Police resorted to lathi-charge to disperse the unlawful gathering of large number of people.
II. The citizens' forum called a general strike in protest against the police atrocities. **[SSC PO 2005]**

3. I. It is the aim of the city's civic authority to get the air pollution reduced by 20% in the next two months.
II. The number of asthma cases in the city is constantly increasing. **[RBI 2005]**

4. I. The police authority has recently caught a group of house breakers.
II. The citizens group in the locality have started night vigil in the area. **[Bank PO 2006]**

5. I. The university authority has instructed all the colleges under its jurisdiction to ban use of all phones inside the college premises.
II. Majority of the teachers of the colleges sighted a joint petition to the university complaining the disturbances caused by cell phone ringtones inside the classrooms. **[Bank PO 2005]**

6. I. The government has recently fixed the fees for professional courses offered by the unaided institutions which are much lower than the fees charged last year.
II. The parents of the aspiring students launched a severe agitation last year protesting against the high fees charged by the unaided institutions. **[Bank PO 2004]**

7. I. Large number of people living in the low-lying areas have been evacuated during the last few days to safer places.
II. The government has rushed in relief supplies to the people living in the affected areas. **[SBI PO 2005]**

8. I. The performance of most of the students in final exam of class X in the schools run by the government was excellent.
II. Many teachers of the government schools left the school and joined private school. **[Asst. Manager 2005]**

9. I. Majority of the citizens in the locality belong to higher income group.
II. The sales in the local super market are comparatively much higher than in other localities. **[Bank PO 2007]**

10. I. There is considerable reduction in the number of people affected by water-borne diseases in city A during this rainy season.
II. The government has opened four new civil hospitals in city A in the beginning of the year. **[Bank PO 2003]**

11. I. The life today is too fast, demanding and full of variety in all aspects which at times leads to stressful situations.
II. Number of suicide cases among teenagers is on increase. **[Bank PO 2006]**

12. I. In the university examination, overall performance of students from college 'X' was better than that of students from college 'Y'
II. Majority of the students depend upon coaching classes for university examinations. **[IRMA 2005]**

13. I. The farmers have decided against selling their kharif crops to the government agencies.
II. The government has reduced the procurement price of kharif crops starting from the last month to the next six months. **[SBI PO 2005]**

14. I. The school authority has asked the X Std. students to attend special classes to be conducted on Sundays.
II. The parents of the X Std. students have withdrawn their wards from attending private tuitions conducted on Sundays. **[Bank PO 2006]**

15. I. The employees of the biggest bank in the country have given an indefinite strike call starting from third of the next month.
II. The employees of the Central Government have with drawn their week long demonstrations. **[Special Officer 2006]**

2 Level Intermediate

Directions (Qs 1 to 15): In each of the following questions, two statements numbered I and II are given. There may be cause and effect relationship between the two statements. These two statements may be the effect of the same cause or independent causes. These statements may be independent courses without having any relationship. Read both statements in each question and mark your answer as:

(A) If statement I is the cause and, statement II is its effect.
(B) If statement II is the cause and statement, I is its effect.
(C) If both the statements I and II are independent causes.
(D) If both the statements I and II are effects of independent causes.
(E) If both the statements I and II are effects of some common cause.

1. I. Rural and semi-urban areas in the country have been suffering due to load shedding for quite some time.
II. If the government is not able to overcome the power crisis, load shedding will be extended even to the urban area. **[Bank PO 2006]**

2. I. Most of the steel producing companies in the country have made considerable profit during the last financial year.
II. Many Asian countries have been importing huge quantities of steel from India. **[Bank PO 2005]**

3. I. The literacy rate in the district has been increasing for the last four years.
II. The district administration has conducted extensive training programme for the workers involved in the literacy drive. **[SBI PO 2005]**

4. I. There is unprecedented increase in the number of young unemployed in comparison to the previous year.
II. A large number of candidates submitted applications against an advertisement for the post of manager is issued by bank. **[Bank PO 2003]**

5. I. All the schools in the area had to be kept closed for the most of part of week.
II. Many parents have withdrawn their children from the local schools. **[SBI PO 2005]**

6. I. The Reserve Bank of India has recently put restrictions on few small banks in the country.
II. The small banks in the private and co-operative sector in India are not in a position to with stand the competitions of the bigger in the public sector. **[SBI PO 2005]**

7. I. The private medical colleges have increased the tuition fees in the current year by 200 per cent over the last year's fees to meet the expenses.
II. The government medical colleges have not increased their fees in spite of price escalation. **[RBI 2004]**

8. I. Majority of students in college expressed their opinion against the college of its decision to break away from university and became autonomous.
II. The university authorities have expressed their inability to provide grants to its constituent colleges. **[Bank PO 2005]**

9. I. There has been an increase in water level of all the water tanks supplying drinking water to city during the last fortnight.
II. Most of the trains were cancelled last week due to water logging on tracks. **[Bank PO 2003]**

10. I. India has surpassed the value of tea exports this year over all the earlier years due to an increase in demand for quality tea in the European market.
II. There is an increase in demand of coffee in the domestic market during the last two year. **[RBI 2004]**

11. I. The police authority has recently caught a group of house breakers.
II. The citizens group in the locality have started night vigil in the area.

12. I. The government has recently fixed the fees for professional courses offered by the unaided institutions which are much lower than the fees charged last year.
II. The parents of the aspiring students launched a severe aligation last year protesting against the high fees charged by the unaided institutions.

13. I. The government of India applied strict traffic rules for citizens of India.
II. All citizens of India should follow the traffic rules.

14. I. Majority of the employees of an office are present at the office on Monday.
II. Majority of the employees of an office are absent at the office on Saturday.

15. I. The zoo authority will close down the week for next one week.
II. A renovation will be done at the zoo in the next week.

3 Level Expert

Directions (Qs 1 to 6): In each of the following questions, two statements numbered I and II are given. There may be cause and effect relationship between the two statements. These two statements may be the effect of the same cause or independent causes. These statements may be independent causes without having any relationship.

Read both statements in each question and mark your answer as

(A) If statement I is the cause and statement II is its effect.
(B) If statement II is the cause and statement I is its effect.
(C) If both the statements I and II are independent causes.
(D) If both the statements I and II are effects of independent causes.
(E) If both the statements I and II are effects of some common cause.

1. I. The local traders' association urged all its members to close down their shops for a day to protest against the government's new tax policy.
II. Many shopkeepers decided to close down their shops for the day and gave a day off to their employees. [Bank PO 2005]

2. I. The prices of petroleum products dropped marginally last week.
II. The State Government reduced the tax on petroleum products last week. [Bank PO 2007]

3. I. The university authority has decided to conduct all terminal examinations in March/April every year to enable them to declare results in time.
II. There has been considerable delay in declaring results in the past due to shortage of teachers evaluating the answer sheets of the examination conducted by the university. [RBI 2004]

4. I. The staff of Airport authorities called off the strike they were observing in protest against privatisation.
II. The staff of Airport authorities went on strike anticipating a threat to their jobs. [Bank PO 2006]

5. I. Many people visited the religious place during the weekend.
II. Few people visited the religious place during the week days. [Specialist Officer's 2006]

Directions (Qs 6 to 15): In each of the following questions, two statements numbered I and II are given. There may be cause and effect relationship between the two statements. These two statements may be the effect of the same cause or independent causes. These statements may be independent causes without having any relationship. Read both statements in each question and mark your answer as

(A) Statement II is the cause, I and III are its effects.
(B) Statement I is the cause, I and III are its effects.
(C) Statement III is the cause, I and II are its effects.
(D) Statement III is the cause and II is its effects while Statement I is an effect of some independent cause.
(E) None of the above

6. I. In urban areas, the poor bear the brunt of environmental effects such as water or air pollution.
II. The rapid urban development has outpaced the development of environmental infrastructure in many large cities.
III. Just for the own sake of profit, builders in urban areas are indulging in construction work without considering about the environment and urban poor, who mostly die from chronical diseases. [IBPS PO Mains Exam 2019]

7. **Statement:** Prime Minister Narendra Modi launched three mega flagship schemes aimed at transforming Urban India, including the much talked about Smart Cities proposal with a whopping lakh crore kitty having been lined up for the projects. He also unveiled logo of the housing mission, which has his personal touch in the finalisation of its design. Speaking at the event, Modi said, "The decision to make cities smart will be taken not by governments but by the people of the city, the local administration. Let there be competition between cities in development so that smart cities come up."
Which of the following will be an effect of the initiative taken by the government?
(A) Ensuring water supply to each household, sewer connections, sanitation and solid waste management in rural and urban governance would be the focus under the scheme.
(B) Quality of life will improve in rural and urban areas.
(C) Provision of roads and public transportation besides implementation of reforms in urban governance would be the focus under the scheme.
(D) Millions of jobs will be created and scarcity of houses will be removed in urban and rural areas.
(E) All of the above [IBPS PO Mains Exam 2019]

8. I. Despite giving their best performance, more than 100 employees of XYZ Pvt. Ltd. have been laid off.
II. More than 40% employees of XYZ Pvt. Ltd. who have crossed the age of 50 years have been asked to take voluntary retirement from their services.
(A) Statement I is the cause and statement If is the effect.
(B) Statement I is the cause and statement I is its effect.
(C) Both statements I and II are effects of independent causes.
(D) Both statements I and II are independent causes.
(E) Both statements I and II are effects of some common cause. [Andhra Bank PO Exam 2015]

9. **Effect:** At least twenty school children were seriously injured while going for a school picnic during the weekend.
Which of the following can be a possible cause of the above effect?
(A) The teacher accompanying the school children fell ill during the journey.
(B) The bus in which the children were travelling met with an accident during journey.
(C) The driver of the bus in which the children were travelling did not report after the break at the halting place on their journey.
(D) The school authority banned all school picnics for the next six months with immediate effect.
(E) None of the above [RBI Grade B Exam 2009]

10. Cause: Government has recently decided to hike the procurement price of paddy for the rabbi crops.
Which of the following will be a possible effect of the above cause?
(A) The farmers may be encouraged to cultivate paddy for the Rabi season.
(B) The farmers may switch over to other cash crops in their paddy fields.
(C) There was a drop in production of paddy during Kharif season.
(D) Government may not increase the procurement price of paddy during the next Kharif season.
(E) Government will buy paddy from the open market during the next few months.
[Grade B Exam 2009]

11. I. The government has decided to make all the information related to primary education available to the general public.
II. In the past, the general public did not have access to all this information related to primary education.
(A) Statement I is the cause and statement If is the effect.
(B) Statement I is the cause and statement I is its effect.
(C) Both statements I and II are effects of independent causes.
(D) Both statements I and II are independent causes.
(E) Both statements I and II are effects of some common cause.

12. I. There has been a high increase in the incidents of atrocities against women in the city during the past few months.
II. The police authority has been unable to nab the culprits who are committing crime against women. **[Bank PO Exam 2004]**
(A) Statement I is the cause and statement If is the effect.
(B) Statement I is the cause and statement I is its effect.
(C) Both statements I and II are effects of independent causes.
(D) Both statements I and II are independent causes.
(E) Both statements I and II are effects of some common cause.

13. I. The prices of petrol and diesel in the domestic market have remained unchanged for the past few months.
II. The crude oil prices in the international market have gone up substantially in the last few monhs.
[Bank PO Exam 2004]
(A) Statement I is the cause and statement If is the effect.
(B) Statement I is the cause and statement I is its effect.
(C) Both statements I and II are effects of independent causes.
(D) Both statements I and II are independent causes.
(E) Both statements I and II are effects of some common cause.

14. I. The local co-operative credit society has decided to stop giving loans to farmers with immediate effect.
II. A large number of credit society members have withdrawn major part of their deposits from the credit society. **[MBA 2005]**
(A) Statement I is the cause and statement If is the effect.
(B) Statement I is the cause and statement I is its effect.
(C) Both statements I and II are effects of independent causes.
(D) Both statements I and II are independent causes.
(E) Both statements I and II are effects of some common cause.

15. I. The Government has imported large quantities of sugar as per trade agreement with other countries.
II. The prices of sugar in the domestic market have fallen sharply in the recent months.
[Specialist Officer 2006]
(A) Statement I is the cause and statement If is the effect.
(B) Statement I is the cause and statement I is its effect.
(C) Both statements I and II are effects of independent causes.
(D) Both statements I and II are independent causes.
(E) Both statements I and II are effects of some common cause.

ANSWER KEY

Level-1: Beginner

1.	(B)	2.	(A)	3.	(B)	4.	(E)	5.	(B)	6.	(B)	7.	(E)	8.	(D)	9.	(A)	10.	(C)
11.	(A)	12.	(C)	13.	(B)	14.	(A)	15.	(D)										

Level-2: Intermediate

1.	(E)	2.	(B)	3.	(B)	4.	(A)	5.	(D)	6.	(B)	7.	(C)	8.	(B)	9.	(E)	10.	(C)
11.	(C)	12.	(B)	13.	(C)	14.	(E)	15.	(B)										

Level-3: Expert

1.	(A)	2.	(B)	3.	(B)	4.	(D)	5.	(E)	6.	(C)	7.	(C)	8.	(C)	9.	(B)	10.	(A)
11.	(B)	12.	(C)	13.	(D)	14.	(B)	15.	(A)										

Solutions with Detailed Explanations

Level-1: BEGINNER

1. **Option (B) is correct.**
Explanation: It is obvious that crop damage caused by high temperatures may have resulted in a shortage of vegetables and an increase in their price.
2. **Option (A) is correct.**
Explanation: It is obvious that the police used a lathi-charge to disperse the crowd in response to the widespread public protest.
3. **Option (B) is correct.**
Explanation: The increased number of asthma cases must have prompted the government to take action to reduce the air pollution that causes the disease.
4. **Option (E) is correct.**
Explanation: Both claims are amply supported by a common cause, which is undeniably an increase in thefts in the area.
5. **Option (B) is correct.**
Explanation: The university's decision was clearly in response to college professors' protests about the use of mobile phones on university property.
6. **Option (B) is correct.**
Explanation: As a result of the parents' protests about the institutions' exorbitant fees, the government intervened and set the fee at a more reasonable level.
7. **Option (E) is correct.**
Explanation: Flooding has occurred in the area, as evidenced by the evacuation of low-lying areas and the rush of aid to affected communities.
8. **Option (D) is correct.**
Explanation: There must have been various reasons for both government school teachers leaving to work in private schools and government school students performing well in final exams.
9. **Option (A) is correct.**
Explanation: Since the residents of a certain locality have a high earning potential; therefore, the sales in the local supermarket are comparatively higher than in other localities.
10. **Option (C) is correct.**
Explanation: The following sentences are complete in themselves and portray distinct occurrences.
11. **Option (A) is correct.**
Explanation: Stress from daily life is a significant source of young dissatisfaction and is likely to drive them to extreme measures such as suicide.
12. **Option (C) is correct.**
Explanation: Here, both the statements I and II are independent causes. The reason for the overall performance of students from college 'X' being better than that of students from college 'Y', may be that college X is a superior college compared to Y. II may be the offshoot of the inadequacy of college teaching.
13. **Option (B) is correct.**
Explanation: Farmers must have been discouraged from selling to government organisations as agricultural procurement prices fell.
14. **Option (A) is correct.**
Explanation: It is clear that the parents have instructed their children to attend school-sponsored special sessions on Sundays rather than private tuitions.
15. **Option (D) is correct.**
Explanation: The bank strike and the end of the government workers' protest appear to be two separate incidents caused by different factors.

Level-2: INTERMEDIATE

1. **Option (E) is correct.**
Explanation: Both statements contain information that is clearly the result of a major power outage.
2. **Option (B) is correct.**
Explanation: Increased global demand for steel will inevitably boost Indian steel companies' sales and, ultimately, profits.
3. **Option (B) is correct.**
Explanation: Clearly, the district administration's unwavering efforts in this area can be directly attributed to the increase in literacy rates.
4. **Option (A) is correct.**
Explanation: An increase in the number of unemployed young people would inevitably result in large crowds vying for a single opening.
5. **Option (D) is correct.**
Explanation: The decision to close the schools for a week and the parents' decision to withdraw their children from the neighbourhood schools are two distinct issues that must have been triggered by a variety of individual factors.
6. **Option (B) is correct.**
Explanation: If the small banks in the private and co-operative sector in India are not in a position to withstand the competitions of the bigger in the public sector, they will not be able to ensure good service to the customers. So, to ensure smooth operation of the financial services, the Reserve Bank of India has recently put restrictions on few small banks in the country.
7. **Option (C) is correct.**

Explanation: The increase in private college fees, as well as the fact that it has not increased in government colleges, appears to be policy concerns addressed by the respective determining bodies at the two levels.

8. **Option (B) is correct.**

Explanation: It is obvious that the university's decision to deny grants to colleges must have caused the constituent colleges to become autonomous.

9. **Option (E) is correct.**

Explanation: The issues raised in both comments are undoubtedly the result of the region's frequent downpours.

10. **Option (C) is correct.**

Explanation: The two sentences cover two distinct generalised statistical outcomes.

11. **Option (C) is correct.**

Explanation: Both the statements are linked by a common cause- an increase in the number of thefts in the locality.

12. **Option (B) is correct.**

Explanation: As a result of the parents' protests about the institutions' exorbitant fees, the government intervened and set the prices at a more affordable level.

13. **Option (C) is correct.**

Explanation: Because the administration of traffic laws by the government is a separate cause from residents' adherence to the laws, assertions I and II are independent causes in this case.

14. **Option (E) is correct.**

Explanation: Statements I and II are both effects of independent causes in this case, because statement I refers to the presence of employees at the office and statement II refers to the absence of employees at the office. As a result, both Statements are the result of two distinct causes.

15. **Option (B) is correct.**

Explanation: Just because renovation will be done at the zoo in the next week, the zoo authority has decided to shut down the zoo for one week. So, II is the cause for I.

Level-3: EXPERT

1. **Option (A) is correct.**

Explanation: Clearly, the association's decision to stage a massive 'bandh' in protest of the government's new policy would have prompted shopkeepers to close their doors. As a result, I mentions the direct cause of the effect in II.

2. **Option (B) is correct.**

Explanation: It goes without saying that lowering the tax or tariff on a specific product will always result in lowering of the price for that product. As a result, II is the source of the impact in I.

3. **Option (B) is correct.**

Explanation: As a result of the delayed declaration of results by university, it has been decided to conduct the examination in March/April in order to announce the result at proper time.

4. **Option (D) is correct.**

Explanation: It is obvious that calling off a strike and starting one are actions that may or may not be motivated by the same reason.

As a result, they must be the result of distinct independent causes.

5. **Option (E) is correct.**

Explanation: It is obvious that fewer people visiting a location during the week and more people visiting on the weekend are related occurrences that must have occurred as a result of a common cause, such as a weekend holiday.

6. **Option (C) is correct.**

Explanation: Environmental progress has stalled due to profit-driven developers who don't care about the poor, who suffer and die the most from pollution, or the environment, as well as increasing urbanisation.

7. **Option (C) is correct.**

Explanation: Because we are discussing the Smart Cities Mission, everything related to rural areas is off-limits. Option (C), on the other hand, focuses on urban development.

8. **Option (C) is correct.**

Explanation: Both the layoffs at XYZ Pvt. Ltd. and the request for more than 40% of employees to choose voluntary retirement are distinct events that must have been precipitated by separate factors.

9. **Option (B) is correct.**

Explanation: The best reason for the stated effect is option (B).

10. **Option (A) is correct.**

Explanation: The government decided to raise the price of paddy to encourage farmers to cultivate it. So, the farmers may be encouraged to cultivate paddy for the rabi season.

11. **Option (B) is correct.**

Explanation: The government must have regarded the populace's ignorance as a major reason for the failure of the elementary education plan. As a result, a cure must have been sought in the form of the action mentioned in I.

12. **Option (C) is correct.**

Explanation: There has been an increase in incidents of violence against women, but the police have been unable to apprehend those responsible. These two are about the same issue, but are related to independent causes.

13. **Option (D) is correct.**

Explanation: The stagnation of petrol and diesel prices in the domestic market, as well as their increase in the international market, must be supported by independent causes.

14. **Option (B) is correct.**

Explanation: Clearly, withdrawal of funds by society members will reduce the society's lending power.

15. **Option (A) is correct.**

Explanation: Price decreases when supply increases.

■ ■ ■

Chapter

9

Assertion and Reason

LEARNING OBJECTIVES:

- Identifying the correct and incorrect assertion and reason.
- To evaluate the logical relationships.

In analytical reasoning, assertions and reasons play a crucial role in evaluating the logical relationships between statements or premises. An assertion is a statement or claim made within an argument or logical reasoning process. It is often presented as a fact or belief that is being put forward for consideration. On the other hand, a reason is a supporting statement or evidence provided to justify or explain the assertion.

The relationship between assertions and reasons is typically structured in the form of an argument or logical framework. The assertion serves as the main claim, while the reason supports or provides evidence for that assertion. The reason aims to establish the validity of the assertion or strengthen the overall argument being presented.

IDENTIFYING THE CORRECT AND INCORRECT ASSERTION AND REASON:

- Let's use an example to illustrate the application of assertions and reasons in analytical reasoning:

  Assertion: "Regular exercise improves cardiovascular health."

  Reason: "Studies have consistently shown that engaging in physical activity increases heart strength and reduces the risk of heart disease."

  In this example, the assertion is that regular exercise improves cardiovascular health. The reason provided is that studies have consistently demonstrated the positive effects of physical activity on heart health. The reason supports the assertion by providing evidence and logical support for the claim.

  When analysing assertions and reasons, it is essential to evaluate the logical connection between them. The reason should be relevant and sufficiently strong to support the assertion. There should be a clear logical relationship between the two, where the reason provides logical support or evidence for the assertion being made. It is important to employ critical thinking skills to assess the validity and soundness of the argument presented.

To elaborate further, the use of assertions and reasons allows individuals to construct logical arguments and evaluate the strength of their claims. Assertions represent the main ideas or claims being put forth, while reasons serve to support those assertions and provide evidence or logical reasoning.

The strength of an argument relies on the quality of the reasons given to support the assertions. A strong reason should be based on reliable evidence, expert opinions or well-established facts. It should directly relate to the assertion being made and provide a logical and persuasive connection. Additionally, the reason should address potential counter arguments and anticipate possible objections.

Critical thinking skills are vital when analysing assertions and reasons. It involves carefully examining the logical structure of an argument, identifying any flaws or fallacies and assessing the overall strength and validity of the reasoning provided. This process helps individuals evaluate the soundness of an argument and make informed judgments about its credibility.

By understanding the relationship between assertions and reasons, individuals can engage in effective analytical reasoning. They can construct well-supported arguments, identify the strengths and weaknesses of various positions, and make informed decisions based on logical and evidence-based thinking.

Example 1:

Assertion (A): Most of the Himalayan Rivers are perennial.

Reason (R): They are fed by melting snow.

Mark your answer as:

(a) Both A and R are true and R is the explanation of A.

(b) Both A and R are true but R is not the correct explanation of A.

(c) A is true but R is false.

(d) A is false and R is true.

(e) Both A and R is false.

Sol. (a) Most Himalayan Rivers are perennial because they are fed by the melting snow throughout the year. Thus, R correctly explains A.

Example 2:

Assertion (A): Bangladesh imports jute from India.
Reason(R): Bangladesh has most of the jute mills.
Mark your answer as:
(a) Both A and R are true and R is the explanation of A.
(b) Both A and R are true but R is not the correct explanation of A.
(c) A is true but R is false.
(d) A is false and R is true.
(e) Both A and R is false.

Sol. (e) When Bangladesh was created after partition of India, the areas of jute production went to Bangladesh while the jute mills were left in India. So, India imports raw jute from Bangladesh. Thus, both A and R are false.

Level 1 Beginner

Directions (Qs 1 to 25): In each of the questions given below, there are two statements labelled as Assertion (A) and Reason (R). Mark your answer as per the codes provided below:
(A) Both A and R are true and R is the correct explanation of A.
(B) Both A and R are true but R is not the correct explanation of A.
(C) A is true but R is false.
(D) A is false R is true.

1. **Assertion (A):** India is a democratic country.
Reason (R): People elect their own representatives who form the government. **[MAT 2018]**
2. **Assertion (A):** Methane gas released by some industries lends to global warming.
Reason (R): Methane is a heavy gas and it settles in the lower regions of the atmosphere. **[UPSSSC Mandi Parishad 2018]**
3. **Assertion (A):** Rainwater harvesting reduces soil erosion.
Reason (R): Rainwater harvesting is not important for conservation of water. **[RRB NTPC, 2016]**
4. **Assertion (A):** The steam engine was invented by James Watt.
Reason (R): There was a problem of taking out water from flooded mines. **[CMAT 2016]**
5. **Assertion (A):** Cut fruits and vegetables should not be kept in open for long.
Reason (R): Their vitamin content is ruined.
6. **Assertion (A):** Baking soda creates acidity in the stomach.
Reason (R): Baking soda is alkaline.
7. **Assertion (A):** The escape velocity from the surface of the moon is less than that from the Earth's surface.
Reason (R): The moon has no atmosphere. **[MAT 2011]**
8. **Assertion (A):** The British sovereignty continued to exist in India.
Reason (R): The British sovereign appointed the last Governor–General of free India. **[MAT 2004]**
9. **Assertion (A):** Increase in carbon dioxide would melt polar ice.
Reason (R): Global temperature would rise. **[NIFT UG 2014]**
10. **Assertion (A):** Areas near the Equator receive rainfall throughout the year.
Reason (R): High temperature and high humid cause conventional rain in afternoons near the Equator. **[MBA 2004]**
11. **Assertion (A):** In upper course, work of the river is erosion.
Reason (R): River flows swiftly in the upper course.
12. **Assertion (A):** We prefer to wear white clothes in winter.
Reason (R): White clothes are good reflectors of heat. **[RRB NTPC 2016]**
13. **Assertion (A):** Forest cutting is undesirable from the point of view of soil erosion.
Reason (R): Cutting of forests reduces the interception of rain water. **[MAT 2008]**
14. **Assertion (A):** Mercury is the farthest planet from the Sun.
Reason (R): Mercury is the smallest planet in the entire solar system. **[MAT 2005]**
15. **Assertion (A):** Venus is placed distant from the Sun as compared to Mercury, yet it is the hottest.
Reason (R): Immense carbon dioxide in the atmosphere of Venus creates a greenhouse effect.
16. **Assertion (A):** Graphite is slippery and used as a lubricant.
Reason (R): Graphite has free electrons. **[NIFT (PG) 2014]**
17. **Assertion (A):** India's 'Republic Day' falls on 26th January.
Reason (R): Constitution of India, declaring India as a 'Republic', came into force on 26th January 1950. **[MAT 2013]**
18. **Assertion (A):** In India, the judiciary is independent of the executive.
Reason (R): Judiciary favours the government and helps in the implementation of its plans. **[NIFT (PG) 2014]**
19. **Assertion (A):** India is a secular country.
Reason (R): Indian people can practice any faith they like. **[MAT 2013]**
20. **Assertion (A):** Tamil Nadu gets most of the rainfall in

winter.

Reason (R): Tamil Nadu gets rainfall from retreating monsoons. [NIFT (PG) 2014]

21. **Assertion (A):** Clothes are not washed properly in hard water.

Reason (R): Hard water contains many minerals. [NIFT (PG) 2014]

22. **Assertion (A):** Mahatma Gandhi is considered as 'Father of the Nation' in India.

Reason (R): Mahatma Gandhi was the first Governor General of Independent India. [MAT 2014]

23. **Assertion (A):** Too much work causes stress.

Reason (R): It disturbs the body balance between its capacity and the demand. [MAT 2012]

24. **Assertion (A):** Perennial rivers mostly originate from the Himalayas.

Reason (R): The fountains in the Himalayas feed the rivers. [RRB NTPC 2016]

25. **Assertion (A):** An apple a day keeps the doctor away.

Reason (R): Apples are very costly. [MAT 2012]

Level 2 Intermediate

Directions (Qs 1 to 21): In each of the questions given below, there are two statements labelled as Assertion and Reason. Mark your answer as per the codes provided below:

(A) Both A and R are true and R is the correct explanation of A.

(B) Both A and R are true but R is not the correct explanation of A.

(C) A is true but R is false.

(D) A is false but R is true.

(E) Both A and R are false.

1. **Assertion (A):** We feel comfortable in hot and humid climate.

Reason (R): Sweat evaporates faster in humid climate.

2. **Assertion (A):** Ventilators are provided near the roof.

Reason (R): Conduction takes place better near the roof.

3. **Assertion (A):** Pluto is the coldest planet.

Reason (R): It receives slant rays of the Sun.

4. **Assertion (A):** Glass tumbler breaks in winter when hot water is poured in it.

Reason (R): When hot water is poured, the outer surface of glass expands.

5. **Assertion (A):** Carbohydrates provide energy to the body.

Reason (R): Obesity is caused by excessive intake of carbohydrates.

6. **Assertion (A):** There is a rainbow in the sky only after rains.

Reason (R): Water drops suspended in the air break up sun's rays into seven colours.

7. **Assertion (A):** River Narmada flows westward.

Reason (R): Narmada falls into the Bay of Bengal.

8. **Assertion (A):** India has a tropical monsoon type climate.

Reason (R): India is located exactly between the tropical latitudes. [MAT 2005]

9. **Assertion (A):** When common salt is kept open, it absorbs moisture from the air.

Reason (R): Common salt contains magnesium chloride.

10. **Assertion (A):** A salt water fish drinks sea water whereas a fresh water fish never drinks water.

Reason (R): A salt water fish is hypertonic to its environment while a fresh water fish is not hypertonic to its environment.

11. **Assertion (A):** Himalayas once laid under the sea.

Reason (R): Fossils of marine creatures are traded on the Himalayas.

12. **Assertion (A):** Eskimos reside in igloos.

Reason (R): No other material except snow is available.

13. **Assertion (A):** India celebrates its Independence Day on 15th August, 1947.

Reason (R): India become independent on 15th August 1947.

14. **Assertion (A):** Silver is not used to make wires.

Reason (R): Silver is a bad conductor.

15. **Assertion (A):** A body weighs less when immersed in water.

Reason (R): Newton's law explains the above phenomenon. [MAT 2013]

16. **Assertion (A):** The colour of light with the shortest wavelength is violet.

Reason (R): One can notice this colour of light on one end of the rainbow which has seven colours of different wavelengths. [MAT 2011]

17. **Assertion (A):** We feel colder on mountains than on plains.

Reason (R): Temperature decreases with altitude. [NIFT LIG 2014]

18. **Assertion (A):** Buddha preached four noble truths.

Reason (R): He wanted to remove desire, which is the cause of human sorrow and misery.

19. **Assertion (A):** Moon cannot be used as a satellite for communication.

Reason (R): Moon does not move in the equatorial plane of the earth.

20. **Assertion (A):** Leakages in household gas cylinders can be detected.

Reason (R): LPG has a strong smell. [RRB NTPC 2016]

21. **Assertion (A):** Autism is a developmental disability.

Reason (R): Heredity and lower development of brain are the causes of the Autism. [SSC CGL 2014]

3 Level Expert

Directions (Qs 1 to 13): In each of the following questions, there are two statements labelled as Assertion and Reason.

(A) Both A and R are true and R is the correct explanation of A.
(B) Both A and R are true but R is not the correct explanation of A.
(C) A is true but R is false.
(D) A is false but R is true.
(E) Both A and R are false.

1. **Assertion (A):** The filament in an electric bulb does not burn up although its temperature is about 2700°C when it glows.
Reason (R): Bulb filament is made of tungsten.
2. **Assertion (A):** An iron ball floats on mercury but gets immersed in water.
Reason (R): The specific gravity of Iron is more than that of mercury.
3. **Assertion (A):** Beriberi is a viral infection.
Reason (R): Vitamin deficiency causes diseases.
4. **Assertion (A):** A ship rises as it enters the sea from a river.
Reason (R): The density of sea water is higher as compared to river water.
5. **Assertion (A):** Uranium undergoes nuclear fusion reaction.
Reason (R): It has a big, unstable nucleus.
6. **Assertion (A):** Diamond is used for cutting glass.
Reason (R): Diamond has a high refractive index.
7. **Assertion (A):** Goiter is a common disease in mountainous regions.
Reason (R): The diet of the people in mountain slacks iodine content.
8. **Assertion (A):** Carbon monoxide when inhaled causes death.
Reason (R): Carbon monoxide combines with hemoglobin.
9. **Assertion (A):** Weeds should not be allowed to grow along with the crops.
Reason (R): Weeds leave no space for plants to grow.
10. **Assertion (A):** Buddha left home after his marriage.
Reason (R): He wished to be free from all worldly ties and become an ascetic.
11. **Assertion (A):** Winds are deflected to their right in Northern Hemisphere and to the left in the Southern Hemisphere.
Reason (R): Rotation of earth causes a change in wind direction.
12. **Assertion (A):** Photosynthesis takes place in all green plants.
Reason (R): Chlorophyll is essential for photosynthesis.
13. **Assertion (A):** When a person standing in a lift which is either at rest or moving up or moving down with uniform speed, he does not find any apparent change in his weight.
Reason (R): Reaction of the floor of the lift is equal to his weight.

ANSWER KEY

Level-1: Beginner

1.	(A)	2.	(A)	3.	(C)	4.	(A)	5.	(A)	6.	(D)	7.	(B)	8.	(D)	9.	(A)	10.	(A)
11.	(A)	12.	(D)	13.	(A)	14.	(D)	15.	(A)	16.	(B)	17.	(A)	18.	(C)	19.	(A)	20.	(A)
21.	(B)	22.	(C)	23.	(A)	24.	(C)	25.	(C)										

Level-2: Intermediate

1.	(E)	2.	(C)	3.	(C)	4.	(C)	5.	(C)	6.	(A)	7.	(C)	8.	(C)	9.	(A)	10.	(A)
11.	(A)	12.	(C)	13.	(A)	14.	(C)	15.	(C)	16.	(B)	17.	(A)	18.	(A)	19.	(A)	20.	(A)
21.	(A)																		

Level-3: Expert

1.	(B)	2.	(C)	3.	(D)	4.	(A)	5.	(D)	6.	(B)	7.	(A)	8.	(A)	9.	(C)	10.	(A)
11.	(A)	12.	(A)	13.	(A)														

Solutions with Detailed Explanations

Level-1: BEGINNER

1. **Option (A) is correct.**
Explanation: India is a democratic country, which is evident from the fact that its citizens have the power to elect their representatives. These elected officials are responsible for forming the government, thus the reason directly explains the assertion.
2. **Option (A) is correct.**
Explanation: Methane gas contributes to global warming due to its greenhouse effect, not because it is heavy and settles in the lower atmosphere. The assertion is true, but the reason does not correctly explain why methane leads to global warming.
3. **Option (C) is correct.**
Explanation: Rainwater harvesting indeed reduces soil erosion by minimizing runoff. However, the reason given is false because rainwater harvesting is very important for the conservation of water.
4. **Option (A) is correct.**
Explanation: James Watt made significant improvements to the steam engine, which was crucial for solving the problem of water removal from flooded mines. The assertion is true, but the reason provided is not the direct explanation for Watt's invention.
5. **Option (A) is correct.**
Explanation: Cut fruits and vegetables should not be kept open for long as their exposure to air can lead to oxidation, which degrades their vitamin content. The reason is a direct explanation of the assertion.
6. **Option (D) is correct.**
Explanation: Baking soda is indeed alkaline and it neutralizes acidity in the stomach rather than creating it. Therefore, the assertion is false while the reason is true.
7. **Option (B) is correct.**
Explanation: The escape velocity from the moon is less than from Earth due to the moon's lower gravitational pull, which is a result of its smaller mass. The absence of an atmosphere on the moon is not the reason for this difference..
8. **Option (D) is correct.**
Explanation: British sovereignty in India ended with independence. The appointment of the last Governor-General by the British sovereign does not imply the continuation of British sovereignty, making the assertion false and the reason true.
9. **Option (A) is correct.**
Explanation: An increase in carbon dioxide levels would lead to a rise in global temperatures, which could cause polar ice to melt. The reason provided is a direct explanation for the assertion.
10. **Option (A) is correct.**
Explanation: Areas near the Equator experience rainfall throughout the year due to high temperatures and humidity, which lead to convectional rainfall. The reason correctly explains the assertion.
11. **Option (A) is correct.**
Explanation: In the upper course, the river's swift flow due to the steep gradient causes significant erosion, which is the primary work of the river in this region.
12. **Option (D) is correct.**
Explanation: We actually prefer to wear dark clothes in winter because they absorb heat. White clothes reflect heat and are better suited for summer.
13. **Option (A) is correct.**
Explanation: Deforestation leads to reduced interception of rainwater, which can exacerbate soil erosion, making forest cutting undesirable from an environmental standpoint.
14. **Option (D) is correct.**
Explanation: Mercury is not the farthest planet from the Sun; it is the closest. The reason is incorrect as Mercury's size is not related to its proximity to the Sun.
15. **Option (A) is correct.**
Explanation: Venus is indeed hotter than Mercury despite being further from the Sun, primarily due to the thick carbon dioxide in the atmosphere that creates a strong greenhouse effect.
16. **Option (B) is correct.**
Explanation: Graphite's slipperiness is due to its layered structure, where weak van der Waals forces allow layers to slide over each other, not directly because of free electrons.
17. **Option (A) is correct.**
Explanation: India's Constitution came into effect on January 26, 1950, making it a republic, which is why we celebrate Republic Day on this date.
18. **Option (C) is correct.**
Explanation: The judiciary in India is independent of the executive and does not favor the government in implementing its plans.
19. **Option (A) is correct.**
Explanation: India is a secular country, and the freedom for Indian people to practice any faith they like is a testament to this secularism.
20. **Option (A) is correct.**
Explanation: Tamil Nadu receives most of its rainfall during the winter season from the northeast retreating monsoons.
21. **Option (B) is correct.**
Explanation: Clothes are not washed properly in hard water due to the presence of minerals like calcium and magnesium, which interfere with the action of soap.
22. **Option (C) is correct.**
Explanation: R is untrue whereas A is true. Mahatma Gandhi was not the first Governor General of

Independent India, despite the fact that he is regarded as the "Father of the Nation" in India.

23. **Option (A) is correct.**

Explanation: Stress is brought on by too much effort because it upsets the body's ability to balance its capacity and demand.

As a result, both A and R are true, and R is the appropriate justification for A.

24. **Option (C) is correct.**

Explanation: R is untrue, while A is true. Most perennial rivers have their beginnings in glaciers or hilly, snowy areas.

25. **Option (C) is correct.**

Explanation: The adage "An apple a day keeps the doctor away" is unquestionably accurate, yet the assertion R is debatably true.

As a result, R is false while A is true.

Level-2: INTERMEDIATE

1. **Option (E) is correct.**

Explanation: Contrary to the assertion, hot and humid climates are uncomfortable because sweat does not evaporate efficiently in high humidity, preventing the body from cooling effectively, which is essential for comfort.

2. **Option (C) is correct.**

Explanation: Ventilators are strategically placed near the roof because hot air, being less dense, rises and can be more effectively expelled from the room, ensuring better air circulation and temperature regulation within the space.

3. **Option (C) is correct.**

Explanation: Pluto's extreme coldness is attributed to its significant distance from the Sun, which results in minimal solar radiation reaching the planet. The angle of the Sun's rays is less relevant than the sheer distance.

4. **Option (C) is correct.**

Explanation: A glass tumbler may break when hot water is poured into it during winter because the rapid temperature change causes differential expansion between the inner and outer surfaces, leading to stress fractures.

5. **Option (C) is correct.**

Explanation: Carbohydrates are indeed a vital source of energy for bodily functions, but obesity is caused by an overall excess caloric intake from various sources, not just carbohydrates, and includes factors like metabolism and physical activity.

6. **Option (A) is correct.**

Explanation: Rainbows occur after rain due to the dispersion of sunlight by water droplets acting as prisms. This process separates light into its constituent colors, creating the spectrum we see as a rainbow.

7. **Option (C) is correct.**

Explanation: The River Narmada is unique among Indian rivers as it flows westward, forming a rift valley and ultimately draining into the Arabian Sea, contrary to the assertion that it falls into the Bay of Bengal.

8. **Option (C) is correct.**

Explanation: India's tropical monsoon climate is influenced by its topography and the Himalayas, which block cold winds, and the Indian Ocean's moisture. The Tropic of Cancer's position affects only part of the country's climate.

9. **Option (A) is correct.**

Explanation: Common salt can absorb moisture from the air due to the presence of hygroscopic substances like magnesium chloride, which attract and retain water molecules, leading to the salt becoming damp.

10. **Option (A) is correct.**

Explanation: Saltwater fish drink seawater to balance the osmotic pressure, as their bodies are hypertonic compared to their environment, while freshwater fish do not need to drink water for this balance.

11. **Option (A) is correct.**

Explanation: The presence of marine fossils in the Himalayas supports the theory that this region was once under the sea, indicating a dramatic geological shift that led to the formation of these mountains.

12. **Option (C) is correct.**

Explanation: Eskimos use snow to build igloos not just due to a lack of materials but because snow acts as an excellent insulator, trapping heat inside and providing a warm shelter in the harsh Arctic environment

13. **Option (A) is correct.**

Explanation: India celebrates Independence Day on August 15th to commemorate the day in 1947 when it achieved independence from British colonial rule, marking the end of nearly two centuries of British presence.

14. **Option (C) is correct.**

Explanation: In addition, it is a good conductor of electricity.

Due of its high cost, silver is not utilised to build electrical lines. Hence, Reason is false, Assertion is true.

15. **Option (C) is correct.**

Explanation: Both A and R are true. The force is discussed by Newton's law. While a body that is submerged in water weighs less due to buoyancy.

16. **Option (B) is correct.**

Explanation: Violet light has the shortest wavelength in the visible spectrum, which is why it appears at one end of a rainbow. However, the reason provided does not explain the assertion about the color's wavelength.

17. **Option (A) is correct.**

Explanation: A is correctly explained by saying that both are true. Superior to sea level. Mountain summits become cooler because temperature drops as altitude increases.

18. Option (A) is correct.

Explanation: Buddha taught the eight-fold path of enlightenment, which has the power to put an end to all human suffering, as well as the four noble truths, which are the reasons for human pain and desire. R therefore completely explains A.

19. Option (A) is correct.

Explanation: The Moon's orbit does not allow it to be used as a geostationary satellite for communication purposes, as it does not maintain a fixed position relative to the Earth's surface.

20. Option (A) is correct.

Explanation: The smelly ingredient ethyl mercaptan is present in solution of LPC. This makes scent leaks in domestic gas cylinders detectable.

21. Option (A) is correct.

Explanation: Autism is indeed a developmental disability, and while genetic and neurological factors are believed to play a role, the exact causes are complex and not fully understood.

Level-3: EXPERT

1. Option (B) is correct.

Explanation: The filament in an electric bulb is made of tungsten, which has a very high melting point. The bulb is filled with inert gases like argon or helium, which prevent the filament from burning even at high temperatures due to the absence of oxygen.

2. Option (C) is correct.

Explanation: An iron ball floats on mercury because the density of mercury is higher than that of iron, allowing the iron ball to float. However, in water, the density of iron is greater than that of water, causing the iron ball to sink.

3. Option (D) is correct.

Explanation: Beriberi is not a viral infection; it is a disease caused by a deficiency of Vitamin B1 (thiamine). Vitamin deficiencies do cause diseases, making the reason correct but the assertion incorrect.

4. Option (A) is correct.

Explanation: The up thrust produced by sea water on the ship is more than that produced by river water due to the higher density of sea water.

5. Option (D) is correct.

Explanation: Uranium does not undergo nuclear fusion; it undergoes nuclear fission. The large, unstable nucleus of uranium makes it susceptible to fission, not fusion.

6. Option (B) is correct.

Explanation: Diamond is used to cut glass because of its hardness and rigid three-dimensional structure. Diamonds have a high refractive index, which increases their transparency and brightness.

7. Option (A) is correct.

Explanation: Goiter is common in mountainous regions due to a lack of iodine in the diet. Iodine is essential for the production of thyroid hormones, and its deficiency leads to the enlargement of the thyroid gland, known as goiter.

8. Option (A) is correct.

Explanation: When carbon monoxide is breathed, it reacts with blood's hemoglobin to generate haemoglobin, which prevents oxygen from being transported.

9. Option (C) is correct.

Explanation: Weeds compete with crops for nutrients, water, and light, which can hinder the growth of crops. Therefore, it is important to control weeds to ensure that crops can grow properly.

10. Option (A) is correct.

Explanation: Buddha left his house even after he was married because he wanted to cut himself off from the outside world and live as a hermit.

11. Option (A) is correct.

Explanation: The deflection of winds to the right in the Northern Hemisphere and to the left in the Southern Hemisphere is due to the Coriolis effect, which is caused by the rotation of the Earth.

12. Option (A) is correct.

Explanation: Photosynthesis occurs in all green plants because chlorophyll, the green pigment in plants, is essential for capturing light energy and converting it into chemical energy during photosynthesis.

13. Option (A) is correct.

Explanation: When a person is in a lift moving with uniform speed or at rest, there is no apparent change in weight because the reaction force from the floor of the lift is equal to the person's weight.

■ ■ ■

Chapter 10

Syllogism

LEARNING OBJECTIVES:

- Basic concept of syllogism.
- Types of syllogism.

Syllogism is an essential concept in logical and analytical reasoning that enables us to draw conclusions through deductive reasoning. It follows a specific structure comprising three components: the major premise, the minor premise, and the conclusion.

The major premise serves as the initial statement, establishing a general principle or relationship. It often takes the form of a categorical statement or a broad generalisation. For example, "All mammals are warm-blooded animals."

The minor premise follows as the second statement, providing a specific case or instance that relates to the major premise. It focuses on a particular subject and adds more specific information. For example, "Dogs are mammals."

The conclusion is the logical outcome derived from the major and minor premises. It reveals the relationship between the two premises and generates new information based on their combination. For instance, based on the previously mentioned major and minor premises, the conclusion would be "Dogs are warm-blooded animals."

In a valid syllogism, if the major and minor premises are true, then the conclusion must also be true. Syllogistic reasoning relies on the principles of logical inference, where the conclusion logically follows from the premises. There are various forms of syllogisms, including categorical syllogisms, hypothetical syllogisms, and disjunctive syllogisms.

TYPES OF SYLLOGISM:

- In analytical reasoning, syllogisms are logical arguments consisting of two premises and a conclusion. There are various types of syllogisms based on their structure and form. Here are the main types of syllogisms in analytical reasoning:

1. **Categorical Syllogism:** This is the most common type of syllogism. It involves categorical statements that use categorical propositions such as "All A are B" or "Some A are B." Categorical syllogisms consists of three categorical propositions: two premises and a conclusion.
2. **Hypothetical Syllogism:** In this type of syllogism, the premises and the conclusion are conditional statements. The premises consist of hypothetical propositions ("If A, then B") and the conclusion follows logically from these conditional statements.
3. **Disjunctive Syllogism:** This type of syllogism involves disjunctive propositions, which present two or more mutually exclusive options. The premises state that either one option is true or another option is true, and the conclusion determines which option must be true based on the premises.
4. **Causal Syllogism:** Causal syllogisms involve premises that establish a cause-and-effect relationship between two events or phenomena. The conclusion of a causal syllogism asserts a cause-effect relationship based on the premises.
5. **Statistical Syllogism:** In this type of syllogism, the premises involve statistical or probabilistic information. The conclusion of a statistical syllogism relies on statistical data or generalisations to make an inference.
6. **Dilemma:** A dilemma is a syllogism that presents a situation with two or more alternatives, each leading to a different outcome. The conclusion of a dilemma syllogism asserts that one of the alternatives must be true, leading to a particular outcome.

These are the main types of syllogisms in analytical reasoning. Each type has its own rules and forms, and they are commonly used to test logical reasoning and deductive thinking skills.

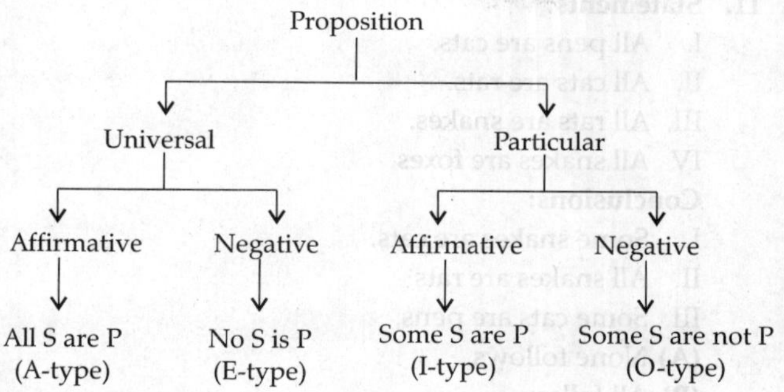

Example 1: Statements:

I. Some dogs are pens.
II. All pens are pots.

Conclusions:

I. Some pens are dogs.
II. Some pens are pots.
III. Some pots are pens.
IV. Some dogs are pots.
V. Some pots are dogs.

Sol. Conclusion I is the conversion of Statement I.
Conclusion II is the implication of Statement II.
Conclusion III is the conversion of Statement II.
Conclusion IV is the mediate inference of Statements I and II.
Conclusion V is the conversion of Conclusion IV.

Example 2: Statements:

I. Some cars are scooters.
II. Some scooters are buses.

Conclusions:

I. Some cars are buses.
II. No cars are buses.

Sol. Both the conclusions are invalid individually. However, we can say that either of Conclusion I or II is true.

Hence, both the conclusions make a complementary pair of conclusions.

1 Level Beginner

Directions (Qs. 1–7): In each question below are four statements followed by two conclusions numbered I and II. You have to take the four given statements to be true even if they seem to be at variance with commonly known facts and then decide which of the given conclusions logically follows from the four statements disregarding commonly known facts. Give answer:

(A) If only Conclusion I follows.
(B) If only Conclusion II follows.
(C) If either Conclusion I or II follows.
(D) If neither Conclusion I nor II follows.
(E) If both Conclusions I and II follow.

1. Statements:

I. Some apples are orange.
II. Some orange are pineapples.
III. Some pineapples are not coconuts.
IV. Some coconuts are black forests.

Conclusions:

I. Some apples are pineapples.
II. Some pineapples are coconuts. **[SBI PO 2015]**

2. Statements:

I. All mobiles are tablets.
II. All tablets are smartphones.
III. All smartphones are laptops.
IV. All laptops are computers.

Conclusions:

I. Some tablets are laptops.
II. Some laptops are not tablets. **[SBI PO 2015]**

3. Statements:

I. All mobiles are tablets.
II. All tablets are smartphones.
III. All smartphones are laptops.
IV. All laptops are computers.

Conclusions:

I. All computers being mobiles is a possibility.
II. All tablets being computers is a possibility.

[SBI PO 2015]

4. Statements:

I. Some tablets are capsules.
II. All capsules are syrups.
III. Some syrups are medicines.
IV. All medicines are powders.

Conclusions:

I. Some syrups are powders.
II. Some syrups are tablets.

[Andhra Bank PO 2008]

5. Statements:

I. All jungles are trees.
II. All trees are roads.
III. All roads are houses.
IV. All houses are building.

Conclusions:

I. All trees are houses.
II. Some building are roads. **[LIC ADO 2007]**

6. Statements:

I. All books are pens.
II. Some pens are desks.
III. Some desks are chairs.
IV. Some chairs are tables.

Conclusions:

I. Some tables are desks.
II. Some chairs are pens. **[NIACL 2014]**

7. Statements:

I. All trousers are pants.
II. Some pants are shirts.

III. All shirts are buttons.
IV. Some buttons are threads.

Conclusions:

I. Some threads are pants.
II. Some buttons are trousers. **[LIC ADO 2007]**

Directions (Qs. 8–15): In each of the questions below are given four statements followed by three conclusions numbered I, II, and III. You have to take the given statements to be true even if they seem to be at variance with commonly known facts. Read all the conclusion(s) and then decide which of the given conclusions logically follow(s) from the given statements disregarding commonly known facts.

8. Statements:

I. All boxes are cups.
II. All chairs are cups.
III. All cups are mirrors.
IV. All tables are mirrors.

Conclusions:

I. Some tables are chairs.
II. Some mirrors are boxes.
III. Some mirrors are chairs.

(A) Only I follows
(B) Only II follows
(C) Only III follows
(D) All follow
(E) II and III follow **[IDBI Executive 2018]**

9. Statements:

I. Some fruits are flowers.
II. Some flowers are buds.
III. No bud is leaf.
IV. All leaves are plants.

Conclusions:

I. No plant is bud.
II. Some plants are flowers.
III. Some buds are fruits.

(A) None follows
(B) Only I follows
(C) II and III follows
(D) Only III follows
(E) None of these **[IDBI Bank PO 2008]**

10. Statements:

I. Some pearls are gems.
II. Some gems are diamonds.
III. All diamonds are rings.
IV. All rings are bangles.

Conclusions:

I. Some bangles are rings.
II. All rings are diamonds.
III. All diamonds are bangles.

(A) Only I follows
(B) I and II follow
(C) I and III follow
(D) All follow
(E) None of these

[Punjab and Sindh Bank PO 2008]

11. Statements:

I. All pens are cats.
II. All cats are rats.
III. All rats are snakes.
IV. All snakes are foxes.

Conclusions:

I. Some snakes are cats.
II. All snakes are rats.
III. Some cats are pens.

(A) None follows
(B) All follow
(C) Only II follows
(D) I and III follow
(E) None of these

[Punjab and Sindh Bank Clerk 2011]

12. Statements:

I. Some shirts are pants.
II. All pants are caps.
III. All caps are ties.
IV. No tie is socks.

Conclusions:

I. No cap is socks.
II. Some pants are shirts.
III. All caps are pants.

(A) I and II follow
(B) Only II follows
(C) Only III follows
(D) None follows
(E) All follow **[UBI PO 2010]**

13. Statements:

I. Some leaves are flowers.
II. No flower is fruit.
III. Some fruits are branches.
IV. Some branches are stems

Conclusions:

I. Some leaves are stems.
II. All leaves are either stems or fruits.
III. All stems are either branches or fruits.

(A) Only I follows
(B) II and III follow
(C) Only III follows
(D) All follow
(E) None of these **[OBC PO 2007]**

14. Statements:

I. Some fans are coolers.
II. Some coolers are machines.
III. Some machines are computers.
IV. All computers are televisions.

Conclusions:

I. Some televisions are machines.
II. Some machines are fans.
III. No machine is a fan.

(A) None follows
(B) Only I follows
(C) Only either II or III follows

(D) Only I and either II or III follow
(E) All follow **[OBC PO 2007]**

15. Statements:
All keys are staplers.
All staplers are blades.
Some blades are erasers.
Some erasers are sharpeners.
Conclusions:
I. Some sharpeners are keys.
II. All keys are blades.
III. Some erasers are keys.
(A) I and II follow
(B) Only I follows
(C) Only II follows
(D) All follow
(E) None of these **[OBC PO 2007]**

Directions (Qs. 16–20): In each of the questions below are given four statements followed by four conclusions numbered I, II, III and IV. You have to take the given statements to be true even if they seem to be at variance with commonly known facts. Read all the conclusions and then decide which of the given conclusion(s) logically follow(s) the given statements disregarding commonly known facts.

16. Statements:
Some trains are cars.
All cars are branches.
All branches are nets.
Some nets are dresses.
Conclusions:
I. Some dresses are cars.
II. Some nets are trains.
III. Some branches are trains.
IV. Some dresses are trains.
(A) I and III follow **(B)** II and III follow
(C) I and IV follow **(D)** II, III and IV follow
(E) None of these **[Syndicate Bank PO 2010]**

17. Statements:
Some benches are walls.
All walls are houses.
Some houses are jungles.
All jungles are roads.
Conclusions:
I. Some roads are benches.
II. Some jungles are walls.
III. Some houses are benches.
IV. Some roads are houses.
(A) I and III follow **(B)** III and IV follow
(C) II, III, and IV follow **(D)** None of these
[PNB PO 2010]

18. Statements:
Some baskets are glasses.
All glasses are pots.
Some pots are plates.
All plates are cups.
Conclusions:
I. No glasses are pots
II. All glasses are baskets.
III. At least some pots are baskets
IV. Some plates being glasses is a possibility.
(A) III and IV follow **(B)** Only IV follows
(C) I and II follow **(D)** None follows
(E) All follow

19. Statements:
All snakes are eagles.
Some eagles are rabbits.
All rabbits are birds.
Some birds are animals.
Conclusions:
I. Some animals are snakes.
II. Some birds are snakes.
III. Some birds are eagles.
IV. All birds are rabbits
(A) None follows
(B) Only II follows
(C) Only III follows
(D) Both II and III follow
(E) None of these

20. Statements: Some books are journals.
All journals are papers.
Some papers are cards.
All cards are boards.
Conclusions:
I. Some papers are books.
II. Some papers are boards
III. Some boards are journals.
IV. Some boards are books
(A) I and II follow
(B) Only I follows
(C) I, II and III follow
(D) All follow
(E) None of these **[IDBI Bank PO 2009]**

Directions (Qs. 21–25): In each of the questions below. Some statements are given followed by conclusions/group of conclusions. You have to assume all the statements to be true even if they seem to be at variance from the commonly known facts and then decide which of the given conclusions logically does not follows from the information given in the statements.

21. Statements: All plastic is rubber.
Some plastic is teflon.
Some teflon is cotton.
All cotton is woolen.
Conclusions:
(A) All rubber is plastic.
(B) No plastic is woolen is a possibility.
(C) All teflon can be woollen.
(D) Some teflon is rubber.
(E) Some woolen is teflon.

22. Statements:
Some air is ball.
No ball is cat.

Some cat is dog.
All dogs are egg.

Conclusions:

(A) Some dogs are not ball
(B) All egg can be ball
(C) All air is egg is a possibility
(D) Some egg is not ball
(E) Some air is dog is a possibility.

23. Statements:

All watch is clock.
All clock is table.
No watch is pen.
No clock is chair.

Conclusions:

(A) Some table can be chair.
(B) Some table are watch.
(C) No watch is chair.
(D) Some table is not pen.
(E) No pen is chair.

24. Statements:

Some pepsi are coca cola.
No coca cola is a miranda.
All miranda are dew.

Conclusions:

I. Some coca cola not being miranda is a possibility.
II. Some dew is not coca cola.
III. All pepsi are miranda.
IV. Some pepsi can be dew.

(A) Only I and II do not follow
(B) Only III and IV do not follow
(C) Only III does not follow
(D) All follow except IV
(E) None of these

25. Statements:

Some tibet are china.
All china are nepal.
No nepal is bhutan.

Conclusions:

I. Some bhutan's are not tibet.
II. All tibet being nepal is a possibility.
III. At least some bhutan's are nepal.
IV. All china can be nepal.

(A) II and IV do not follow.
(B) I and IV do not follow.
(C) I and III does not follow.
(D) II and III do not follow.
(E) None of these

2 Level Intermediate

1. Read the given statements and conclusions carefully. Assuming that the information given in the statements is true, even if it appears to be at variance with commonly known facts, decide which of the given conclusions logically follow(s) from the statements.

Statements:

All dogs are lions.
No elephant is a lion.

Conclusions:

I. No dog is an elephant.
II. No lion is a dog.
III. Some elephants are dogs.

(A) Conclusions II and III follow.
(B) Only Conclusion II follows.
(C) Conclusions I and III follow.
(D) Only Conclusion I follows. **[SSC CGL 2020]**

2. Study the following statements carefully and decide which of the conclusions logically follows disregarding the commonly known facts.

Statements:

All aeroplanes are trains.
Some trains are chairs.

Conclusions:

I. Some aeroplanes are chairs.
II. Some chairs are aeroplanes.
III. Some chairs are trains.
IV. Some trains are aeroplanes.

(A) None follows **(B)** I and II follow
(C) II and III follow **(D)** III and IV follow

[SSC Stenographer 2016]

Directions (Qs. 3–12): In the questions below are given two statements followed by two conclusions. You have to take the given statements to be true even if they seem to be at variance from commonly known facts and decide which of the conclusion(s) logically follows from the two given statements.

Give answer

(A) If only Conclusion I follows
(B) If only Conclusion II follows
(C) If both Conclusions I and II follow
(D) If neither Conclusion I nor II follows

3. Statements:

All clouds are fog.
All fog are white.

Conclusions:

I. Some white are clouds.
II. Some fog are clouds. **[SSC CGL 2017]**

4. Statements:

All poets are daydreamers.
All painters are daydreamers.

Conclusions:

I. All painters are poets.
II. Some daydreamers are not painters.

[SSC CGL 2015]

5. Statements:
Some wagons are buggies.
All wagons are carts.
Conclusions:
I. All buggies are carts.
II. Some carts are buggies. **[RRBs ALP 2019]**

6. Statements:
Some camels are ships.
No ship is a boat.
Conclusions:
I. Some ships are camels.
II. Some camels are not boats. **[SSC 10+2 2017]**

7. Statements:
No squares are rectangles.
All rectangles are triangles.
Conclusions:
I. Some triangles are squares.
II. Some triangles are rectangles.

8. Statements:
I. All women are girls.
II. Some girls are painters.
Conclusions:
I. All girls are women.
II. Some women are painters. **[SSC GD 2018]**

9. Statements:
All sticks are canes.
Some wands are sticks.
Conclusion:
I. Some canes are wands.
II. No wands are canes. **[SSC 10+2 2018]**

10. Statements:
Some pencil are sticks.
All sticks are trees.
Conclusions:
I. All sticks are pencil.
II. All pencil are trees.
[UPSSSC VDO 2018]

11. Statements:
All leaves are green.
Some leaves are hard.
Conclusions:
I. Some hard are green.
II. All green are leaves.
[SSC Delhi Police Constable 2017]

12. Statements:
All pink are doors.
All male are doors.
Conclusions:
I. Some males are pink.
II. All doors are pink.
[SSC Delhi Police Constable 2017]

13. Study the following statement carefully and decide which of the conclusions logically follows disregarding the commonly known facts.

Statements:
I. All politicians are honest person.
II. All honest persons are fair.
Conclusions:
I. Some honest persons are politicians.
II. No honest person is politician.
III. Some fair persons are politicians.
IV. All fair persons are politicians.
(A) II and IV **(B)** I and III
(C) I, II and IV **(D)** II and III
[UGC NET 2018]

Direction (Qs. 14–15): In each question/ set of questions below are two/ three statements followed by two conclusions numbered I and II. You have to take the two/ three given statements to be true even if they seem to be at variance from commonly known facts and then decide which of the given conclusions logically follows from the given statements disregarding commonly known facts.

Give answer
(A) If only Conclusion I follows.
(B) If only Conclusion II follows.
(C) If either Conclusion I or II follows.
(D) If neither Conclusion I nor II follows.
(E) If both Conclusions I and II follow.

14. Statements:
Some lights are rays.
All rays are optics.
Conclusions:
I. Some lights are definitely not optics.
II. Some rays are definitely not lights
[Bihar Kshatriya (GBO) 2012]

15. Statements:
All vacancies are jobs.
Some jobs are occupations.
Conclusions:
I. All vacancies are occupations.
II. All occupations being vacancies is a possibility.
[IBPS PO 2012]

16. Statements:
I. All contracts are agreements.
II. All agreements are accepted offers.
Which of the following derivations is correct?
[CLAT 2014]
(A) All accepted offers are contracts.
(B) All agreements are contracts.
(C) All contracts are accepted offers.
(D) None of the above

Directions (Qs. 17–25): Two/three statements are given below followed by two/three conclusions (I, II and III). You have to consider the two/three statements to be true even if they seem to be at variance with commonly known facts. You have to decide which of the conclusions, if any follow from the given statements.

Give answer
(A) Only I follows
(B) Only II follows

(C) Both I and II follow
(D) Neither I nor II follow
(E) Either I or II follows

17. Statements:
All trains are buses.
All buses are jeeps.
All jeeps are aeroplanes.
Conclusions:
I. Some buses are not aeroplanes.
II. All jeeps are trains. **[SBI Clerk 2016]**

18. Statements:
No bank is a locker.
All banks are stores.
No store is a panel.
Conclusions:
I. No store is a locker.
II. No panel is a bank. **[BPS PO/MT 2015]**

19. Statements:
Some stands are racks.
No rack is a box.
All boxes are cartons.
Conclusions:
I. All stands can never be boxes.
II. All racks being cartons is a possibility. **[LIC AAO 2016]**

20. Statements:
Some roads are houses.
Some houses are bungalows.
No bungalow is an apartment.
Conclusions:
I. All roads being apartments is a possibility.
II. No apartment is a house. **[NABARD Grade A&B 2016]**

21. Statements:
Some ratios are percent.
All percent are fractions.
No fraction is a section.
Conclusions:
I. All sections being ratios is a possibility.
II. At least some fractions are ratios. **[IBPS RRB Officer Grade B 2017]**

22. Statements:
Some sketches are paintings.
All paintings are drawings.
Some drawings are letters.
Conclusions:
I. All sketches can never be drawings.
II. No painting is a letter. **[RBI Assistant 2017]**

23. Statements:
All packets are envelopes.
No envelope is a gift.
Some gifts are boxes.
Conclusions:
I. All envelopes are packets.
II. All boxes can never be envelopes. **[IBPS PO/ MT 2017]**

24. Statements:
No rain is game.
Some games are chain.
No chain is lane.
Conclusions:
I. Some chains are not rain.
II. Some games are lane. **[IBPS Clerk 2017]**

25. Statements:
All Indians are Americans.
All Americans are Pakistanis.
No British is Americans.
Conclusions:
I. All Indians are Pakistani.
II. Some Pakistani are British.
III. No Indian is British. **[MP Police Sub Inspector 2017]**
(A) Only I and III follow
(B) All follow
(C) Only III follows
(D) Only II follows

3 Level Expert

1. Statements:
All aids are devices.
No device is a tool.
All tools are machines.
Some machines are electronics.
Conclusions:
(A) Some aids are definitely not electronics.
(B) No tool is an electronic.
(C) All aids are machines.
(D) All electronics can never be devices.
(E) All electronics being aids is a possibility. **[MHT MBA 2017]**

2. Statements:
Some villages are towns.
Some towns are huts.
All huts are rivers.
Some rivers are tents.
Conclusions:
I. Some tents are towns.
II. Some rivers are towns.
III. Some huts are villages.
(A) Only I follows
(B) Only II follows
(C) Only III follows
(D) I and II follow
(E) None of these

[IDBI Executive 2018]

3. **Statements:**
Some dolls are barbie.
Some barbie are famous.
All famous are player.
No famous is actor.
Some actors are barbie.
Conclusions:
I. Some barbie are not actors.
II. Some barbie are players.
III. Some players are famous.
(A) Only I follows
(B) Only II and III follow
(C) Only I and III follow
(D) All follow
(E) None of these

[IBPS Clerk Mains 2019]

4. **Statements:**
All good are bad.
All bad are best.
All best are worst.
Some worst is fair.
No best is normal.
Some normal are worst.
Conclusions:
I. All fair being normal is a possibility.
II. Some best are fair.
III. Some bad to be good is a possibility.
(A) Only I follows
(B) Only II and III follow
(C) Only I and III follow
(D) All follow
(E) None of the above [IBPS Clerk Mains 2019]

5. **Statements:**
All eyes are legs.
No eyes are nose.
All noses are hands.
Some hands are legs.
No legs are ears.
Conclusions:
I. Some hands are ears.
II. Some hands are not nose.
III. Some hands are not ears.
(A) Only I follows
(B) Either I or II and III follow
(C) Either I or III and II follow
(D) All follow
(E) None of the above

[IBPS Clerk 2019]

Directions (Qs. 6–7): Each question given below consists of five or six statements followed by options consisting of three statements put together in a specific order. Choose the option which indicates a valid argument containing logically related statements that is, where the third statement is a conclusion drawn from the preceding two statements. [CMAT 2014]

6. A. All synopses are poets.
B. Some synopses are mentors.
C. Some X are not mentors.
D. All X are poets.
E. All synopses are mentors.
F. All synopses are X.
(A) ACB **(B)** AEC **(C)** FEC **(D)** DFA

7. A. All heroines are pretty.
B. Some heroines are popular.
C. Shweta is pretty.
D. Shweta is a popular heroine.
E. Some popular heroines are pretty.
(A) ABE **(B)** ACD **(C)** DCA **(D)** EDC

8. **Conclusions:**
Some reds being black is a possibility.
Some blue being red is a possibility.
Statements:
I. All black are pink. Some red are pink. No blue is red.
II. All black is pink. No red is pink. All blue is black.
III. Some black are pink. Some red are pink. No blue is red.
IV. Some black are pink. Some red are pink. No pink is blue.
V. Some black are pink. Some red are pink. All blues are black.
(A) Only Statement I
(B) Both Statements IV and V
(C) Only Statement IV
(D) Both Statements II and III
(E) Only Statement V

9. **Statements:**
All papers are mills.
All mills are factories.
Conclusions:
I. All mills are papers.
II. All papers are factories.
(A) Only I follows
(B) Only II follows
(C) Both I and II follow
(D) Neither I nor II follow
(E) Either I or II follows [LIC AAO 2016]

10. **Statements:**
Some ratios are percent.
All percent are fractions.
No fraction is a section.
Conclusions:
I. All sections being ratios is a possibility.
II. At least some fractions are ratios.
(A) Only I follows
(B) Only II follows
(C) Both I and II follow
(D) Neither I nor II follow
(E) Either I or II follows

[IBPS RRB Officer Grade B 2017]

11. Statements:

I. Some red are yellow.

II. No yellow is green.

Conclusions:

I. Some yellow are red.

II. Some green are red.

III. Some red are not green.

IV. All green are red.

(A) II and III follow.

(B) I and II follow.

(C) Either III or IV follows.

(D) Only I follows. **[CG PSC 2013]**

12. Statements:

All apples are oranges.

Some oranges are papayas.

Conclusions:

I. Some apples are papayas.

II. Some papayas are apples.

(A) If only conclusion I follows.

(B) If only conclusion II follows.

(C) If both conclusions I and II follow.

(D) If neither conclusion I nor II follows.

13. Statements:

I. Some beautiful women are actresses.

II. All actresses are good dancers.

Which of the following derivations is correct?

(A) Some beautiful women are good dancers.

(B) All good dancers are actresses.

(C) Both (A) and (B) follow.

(D) None of the above

ANSWER KEY

Level-1: Beginner

1.	(D)	2.	(A)	3.	(B)	4.	(E)	5.	(E)	6.	(D)	7.	(D)	8.	(E)	9.	(A)	10.	(C)
11.	(D)	12.	(A)	13.	(E)	14.	(D)	15.	(C)	16.	(B)	17.	(B)	18.	(A)	19.	(C)	20.	(A)
21.	(A)	22.	(B)	23.	(E)	24.	(E)	25.	(E)										

Level-2: Intermediate

1.	(D)	2.	(D)	3.	(C)	4.	(D)	5.	(B)	6.	(C)	7.	(B)	8.	(D)	9.	(A)	10.	(D)
11.	(A)	12.	(D)	13.	(B)	14.	(D)	15.	(B)	16.	(C)	17.	(D)	18.	(B)	19.	(C)	20.	(A)
21.	(C)	22.	(D)	23.	(B)	24.	(A)	25.	(A)										

Level-3: Expert

1.	(D)	2.	(B)	3.	(D)	4.	(A)	5.	(E)	6.	(D)	7.	(A)	8.	(B)	9.	(B)	10.	(B)
11.	(D)	12.	(D)	13.	(A)														

Solutions with Detailed Explanations

Level-1: BEGINNER

1. Option (D) is correct.

Explanation:

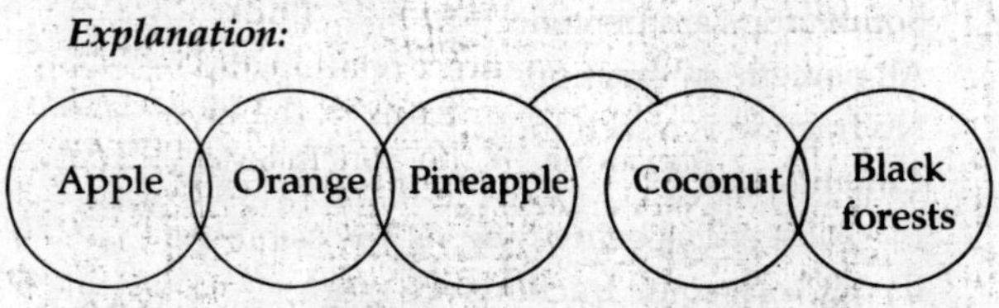

Conclusions: There is no direct or indirect link between apples and pineapples or pineapples and coconuts in the given statements. Therefore, neither conclusion I nor II follows

Sol. (2-3):

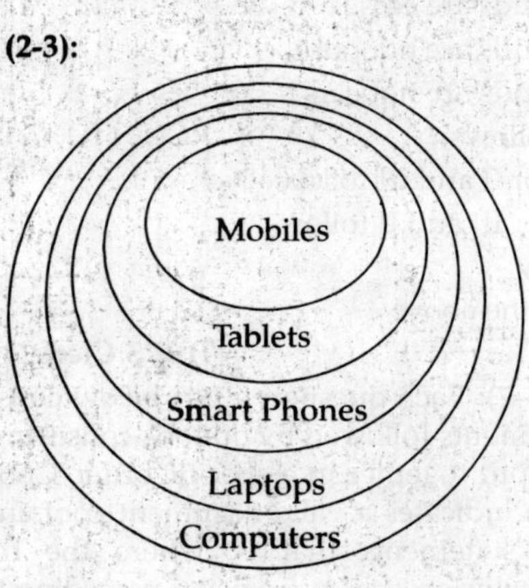

2. **Option (A) is correct.**

Explanation: Since all mobiles are tablets, and all tablets are smartphones, which in turn are all laptops, and all laptops are computers, it follows that some tablets are indeed laptops, making conclusion I correct. Conclusion II is incorrect because it contradicts the given statements; hence, it does not follow.

3. **Option (B) is correct.**

Explanation: Since there is no relation between computers and tablets, so some tablets being computers is only a possibility. So, Conclusion I is incorrect. While some smartphones are definitely computers. Conclusion I follows.

4. **Option (E) is correct.**

Explanation: Since some tablets are capsules, and all capsules are syrups, which in turn are some medicines, and all medicines are powders, it follows that some syrups are powders (conclusion I) and some syrups are tablets (conclusion II)

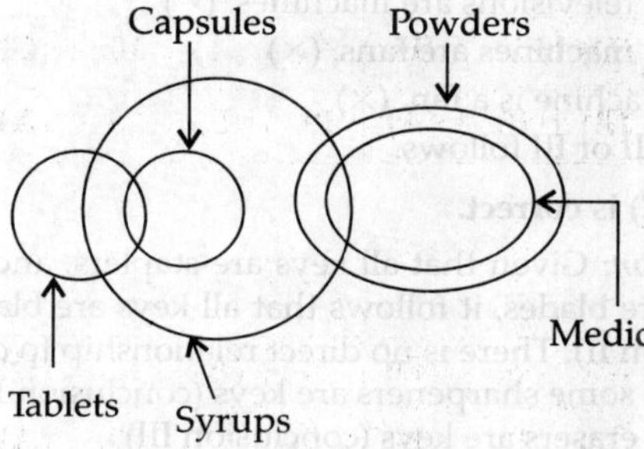

Conclusions:

I. Some syrups are powders. (✓)

II. Some syrups are tablets. (✓)

5. **Option (E) is correct.**

Explanation:

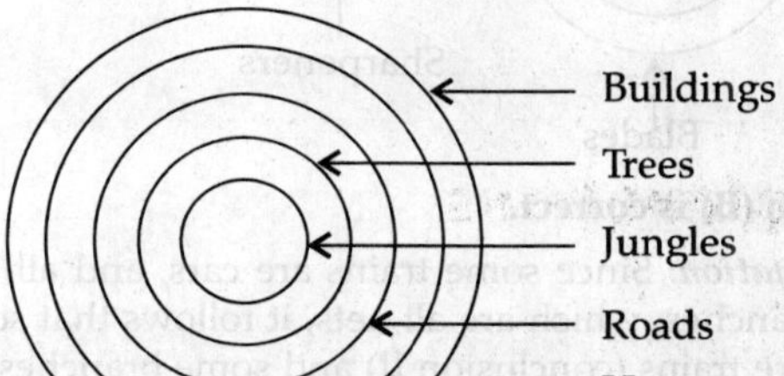

Conclusions:

I. All trees are houses. (✓)

II. Some buildings are roads. (✓)

6. **Option (D) is correct.**

Explanation: There is no direct relationship between tables and desks or chairs and pens in the given statements. Therefore, neither conclusion I nor II follows.

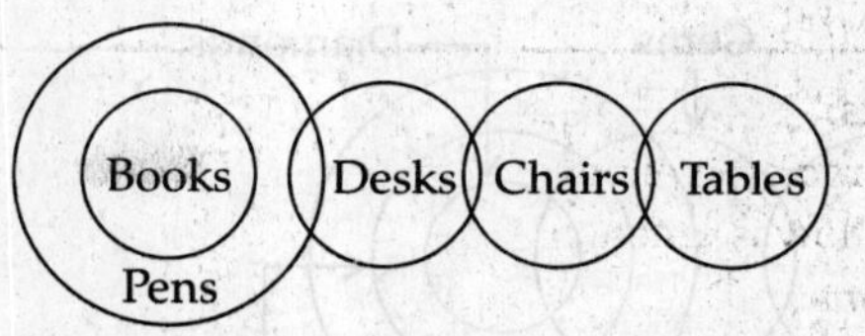

7. **Option (D) is correct.**

Explanation:

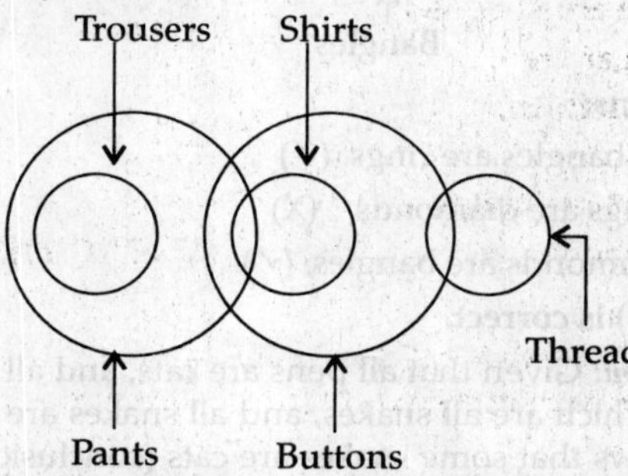

Conclusions: There is no direct relationship between threads and pants or buttons and trousers in the given statements. Therefore, neither conclusion I nor II follows.

8. **Option (E) is correct.**

Explanation:

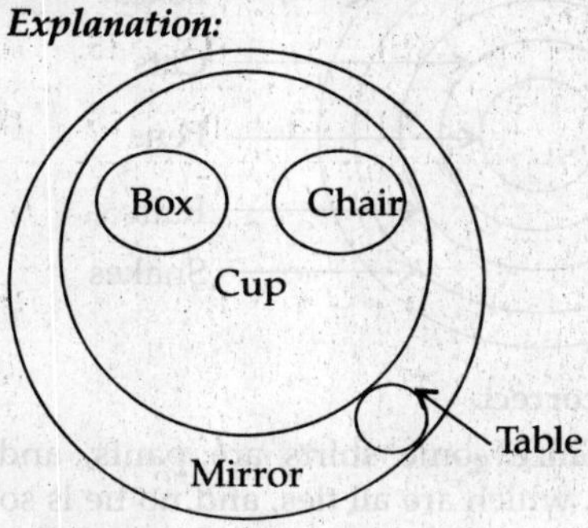

Conclusions:

I. Some tables are chairs. (×)

II. Some mirrors are boxes. (✓)

III. Some mirrors are chairs. (✓)

9. **Option (A) is correct.**

Explanation:

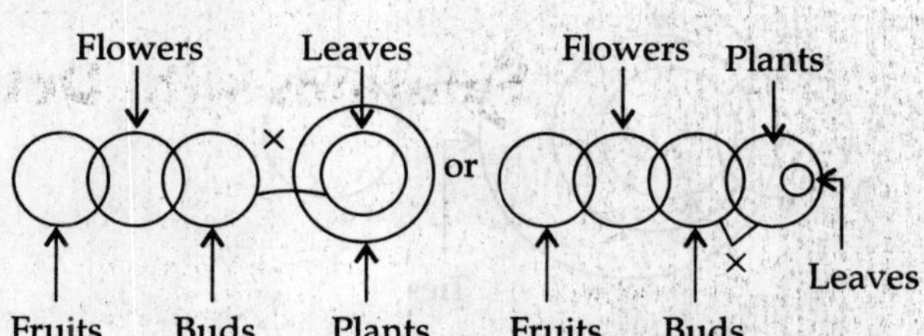

Conclusions: There is no direct relationship between plants and buds, flowers, or fruits in the given statements. Therefore, none of the conclusions logically follow from the statements.

10. **Option (C) is correct.**

Explanation:

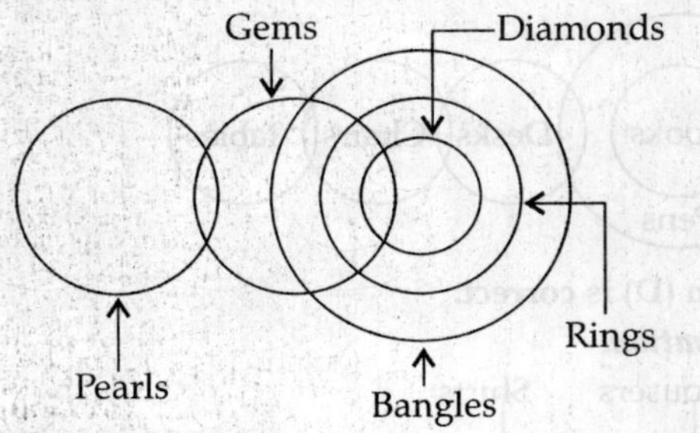

Conclusions:

I. Some bangles are rings. (✓)
II. All rings are diamonds. (X)
III. All diamonds are bangles. (✓)

11. Option (D) is correct.

Explanation: Given that all pens are cats, and all cats are rats, which are all snakes, and all snakes are foxes, it follows that some snakes are cats (conclusion I) and some cats are pens (conclusion III). Conclusion II does not follow because it is not stated that all snakes are rats.

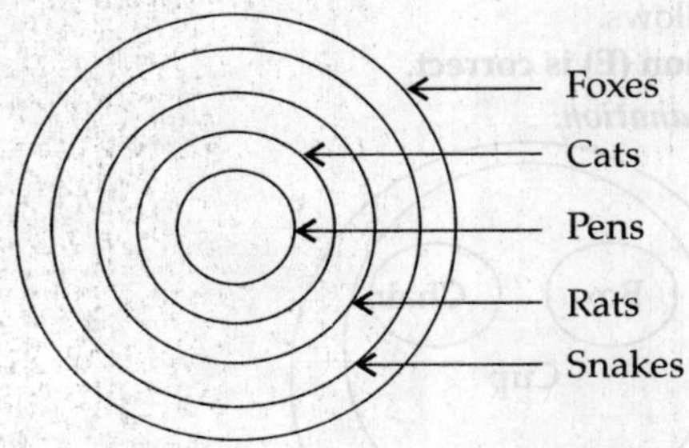

12. Option (A) is correct.

Explanation: Since some shirts are pants, and all pants are caps, which are all ties, and no tie is socks, it follows that no cap is socks (conclusion I) and some pants are shirts (conclusion II). Conclusion III does not follow because it is not stated that all caps are pants

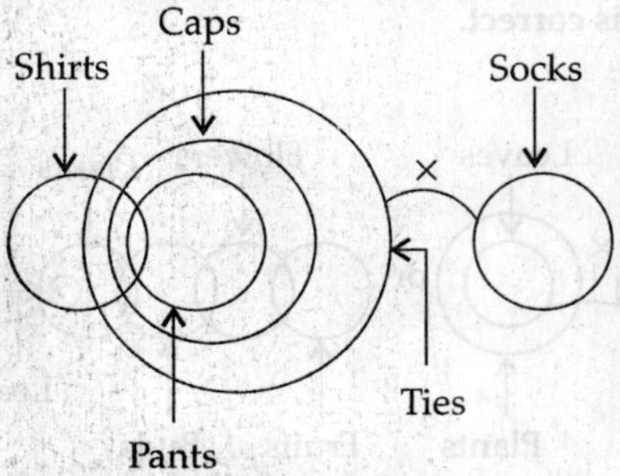

13. Option (E) is correct.

Explanation: There is no direct relationship that allows us to conclude that some leaves are stems (conclusion I), nor can we deduce that all leaves are either stems or fruits (conclusion II), or that all stems are either branches or fruits (conclusion III)

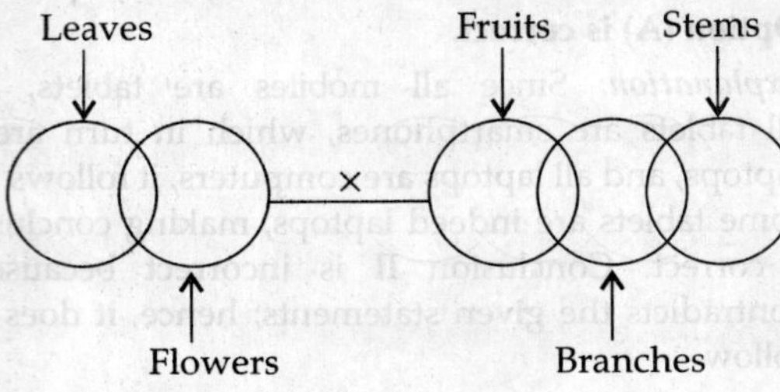

14. Option (D) is correct.

Explanation:

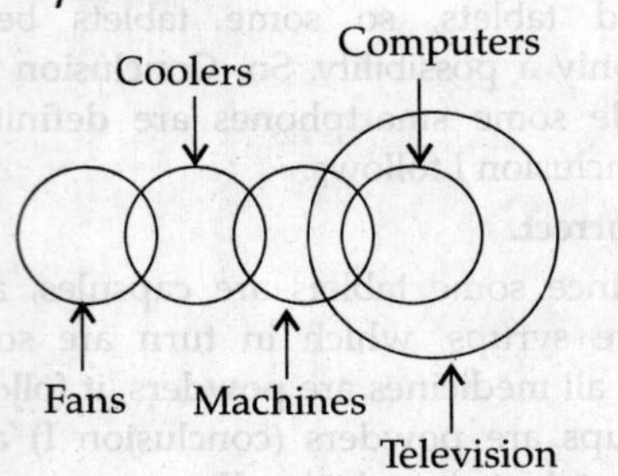

Conclusions:

I. Some televisions are machines. (✓)
II. Some machines are fans. (×)
III. No machine is a fan. (×)

So, either II or III follows.

15. Option (C) is correct.

Explanation: Given that all keys are staplers, and all staplers are blades, it follows that all keys are blades (conclusion II). There is no direct relationship to conclude that some sharpeners are keys (conclusion I) or that some erasers are keys (conclusion III)

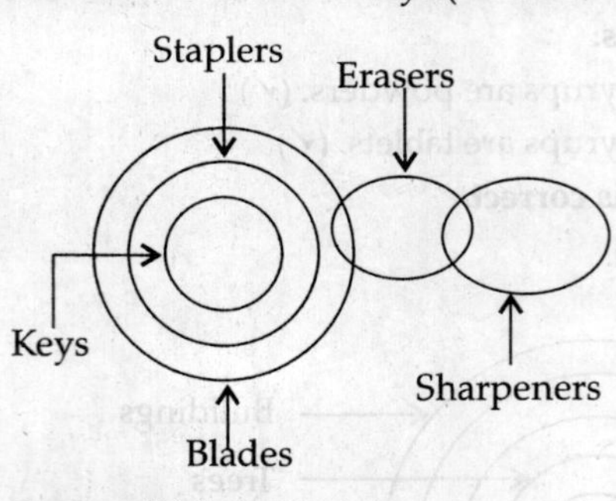

16. Option (B) is correct.

Explanation: Since some trains are cars, and all cars are branches, which are all nets, it follows that some nets are trains (conclusion II) and some branches are trains (conclusion III). Conclusions I and IV do not follow because there is no direct relationship between dresses and cars or trains.

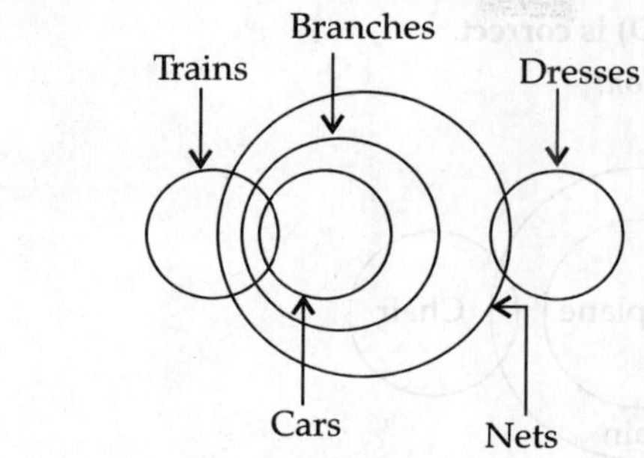

17. Option (B) is correct.

Explanation:

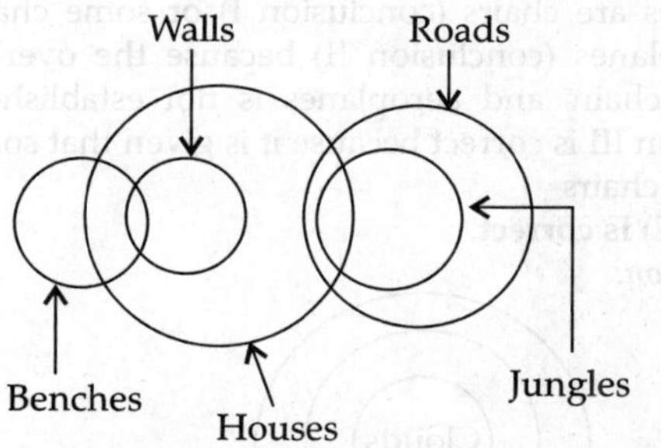

Conclusions: Given that some benches are walls, and all walls are houses, which are some jungles, and all jungles are roads, it follows that some houses are benches (conclusion III) and some roads are houses (conclusion IV). Conclusions I and II do not follow because there is no direct relationship between roads and benches or jungles and walls

18. Option (A) is correct.

Explanation: Since some baskets are glasses, and all glasses are pots, which are some plates, and all plates are cups, it follows that at least some pots are baskets (conclusion III) and it's possible that some plates are glasses (conclusion IV). Conclusions I and II do not follow because they contradict the given statements.

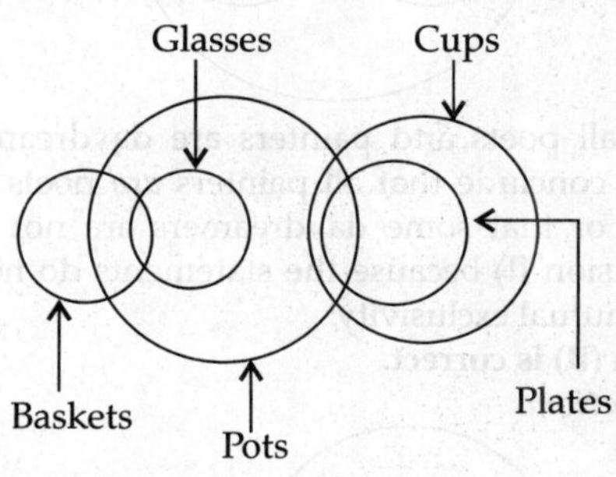

19. Option (C) is correct.

Explanation: All snakes are eagles, and some eagles are rabbits, which are all birds, and some birds are animals. It follows that some birds are eagles (conclusion III). Conclusions I, II, and IV do not follow because there is no direct relationship that supports these conclusions.

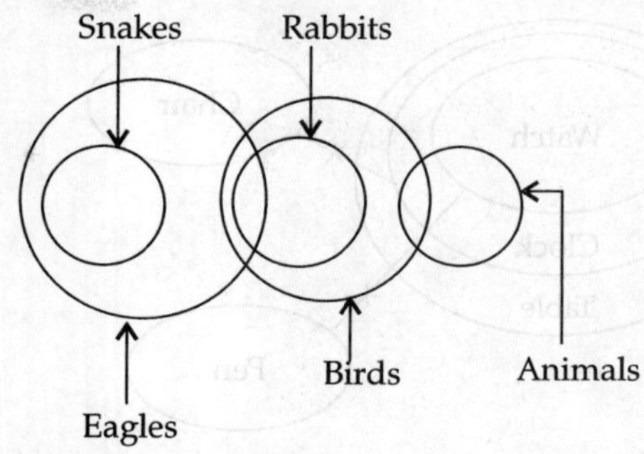

20. Option (A) is correct.

Explanation: Some books are journals, and all journals are papers, which are some cards, and all cards are boards. It follows that some papers are books (conclusion I) and some papers are boards (conclusion II). Conclusions III and IV do not follow because there is no direct relationship that supports these conclusions

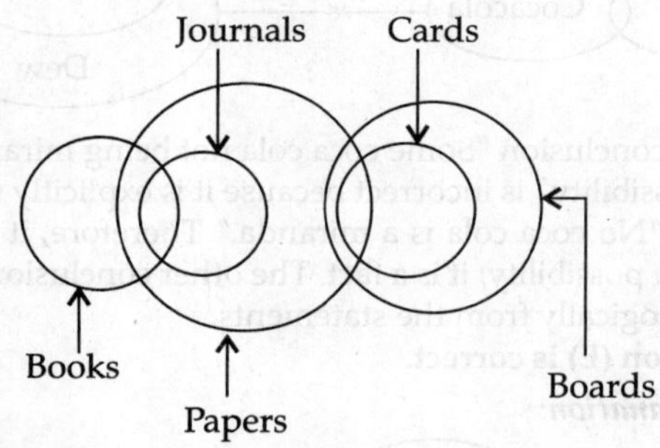

21. Option (A) is correct.

Explanation:

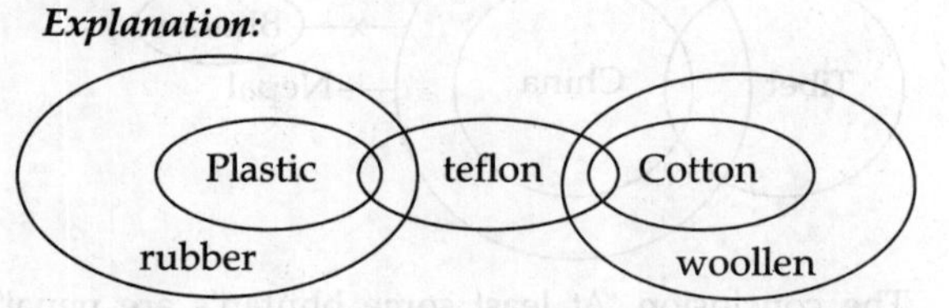

In this case, Conclusion (A) cannot be drawn since while some rubber is unquestionably plastic, it is impossible to say that all rubber is plastic.

22. Option (B) is correct.

Explanation:

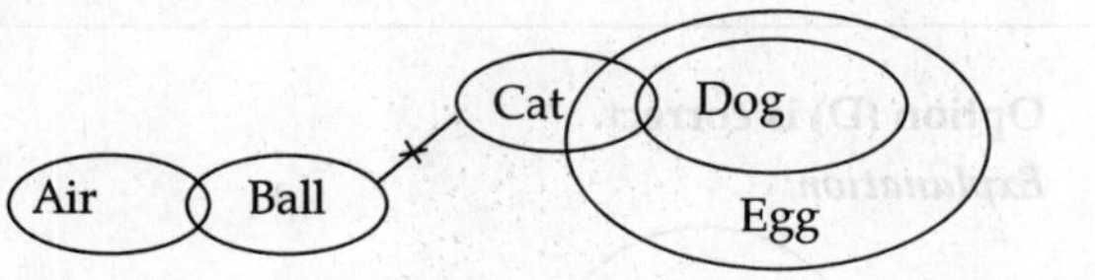

Here, Conclusion (B) is not supported because a portion of the egg is a cat and the ball is not a cat. As a result, not all eggs can be balls.

23. Option (E) is correct.

Explanation:

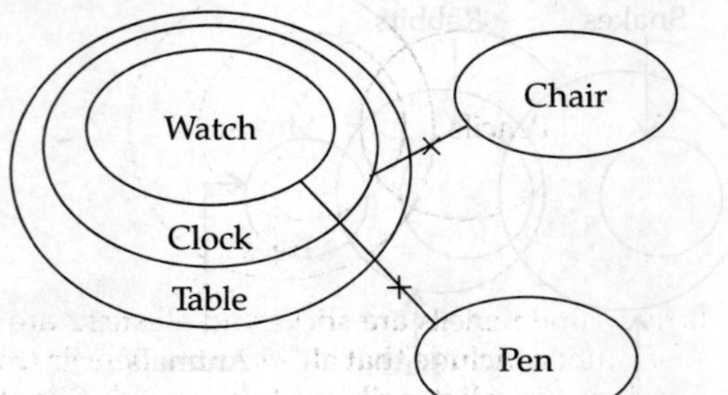

Because there is no direct connection between the items pen and chair in this situation, conclusion (E) cannot be drawn. Therefore, we cannot claim that a chair is not a pen.

24. Option (E) is correct.

Explanation:

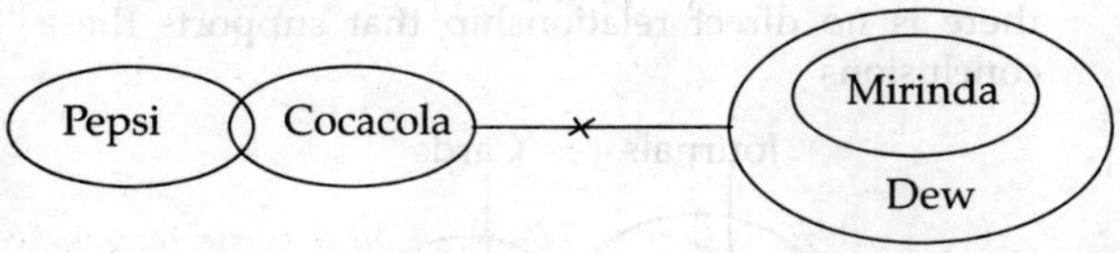

The conclusion "Some coca cola not being miranda is a possibility" is incorrect because it is explicitly stated that "No coca cola is a miranda." Therefore, it is not just a possibility; it is a fact. The other conclusions follow logically from the statements.

25. Option (E) is correct.

Explanation:

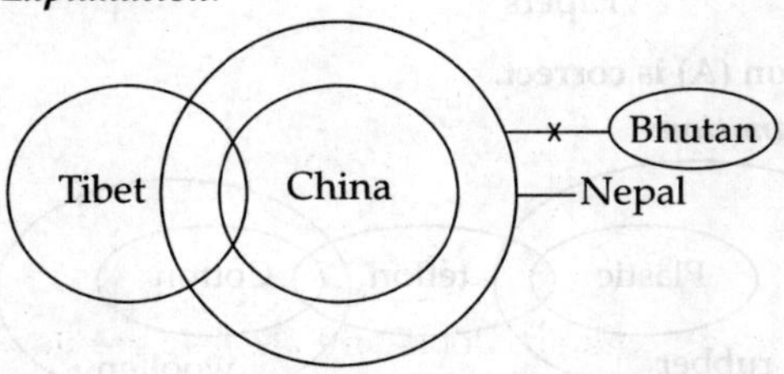

The conclusion "At least some bhutan's are nepal" cannot be drawn because it is stated that "No nepal is bhutan." Therefore, it is not possible for any part of Bhutan to be Nepal. The other conclusions are possible based on the given statements

Level-2: INTERMEDIATE

1. Option (D) is correct.

Explanation:

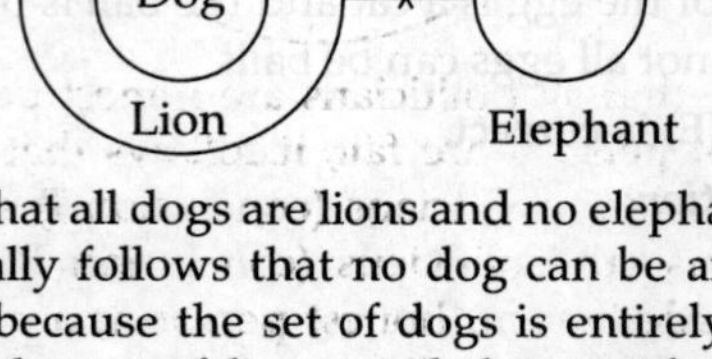

Given that all dogs are lions and no elephant is a lion, it logically follows that no dog can be an elephant. This is because the set of dogs is entirely contained within the set of lions, and the set of elephants is completely separate from the set of lions. Therefore, conclusion I is correct. Conclusions II and III are incorrect because they contradict the given statements

2. Option (D) is correct.

Explanation:

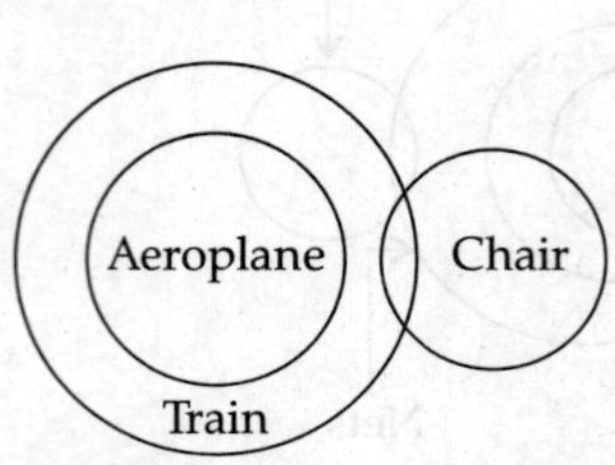

Since all aeroplanes are trains, and some trains are chairs, it follows that some trains are aeroplanes (conclusion IV). However, we cannot conclude that some aeroplanes are chairs (conclusion I) or some chairs are aeroplanes (conclusion II) because the overlap between chairs and aeroplanes is not established. Conclusion III is correct because it is given that some trains are chairs

3. Option (C) is correct.

Explanation:

Since all clouds are fog and all fog are white, it logically follows that some white are clouds (conclusion I) and some fog are clouds (conclusion II).

4. Option (D) is correct.

Explanation:

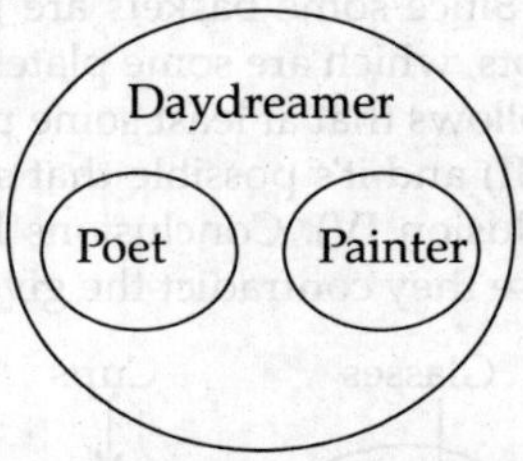

While all poets and painters are daydreamers, we cannot conclude that all painters are poets (conclusion I) or that some daydreamers are not painters (conclusion II) because the statements do not establish a mutual exclusivity.

5. Option (B) is correct.

Explanation:

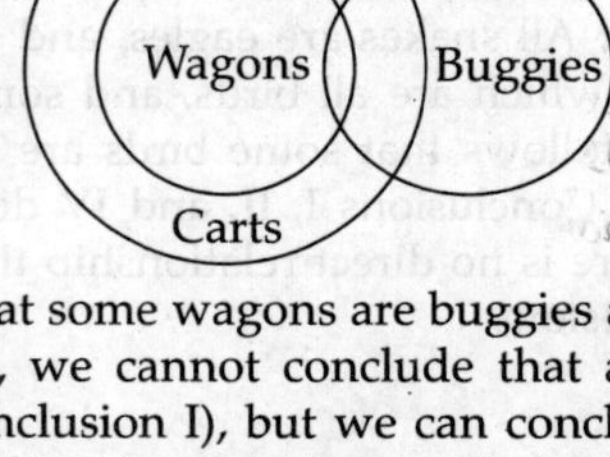

Given that some wagons are buggies and all wagons are carts, we cannot conclude that all buggies are carts (conclusion I), but we can conclude that some carts are buggies (conclusion II) due to the overlap between wagons and buggies.

6. Option (C) is correct.

Explanation:

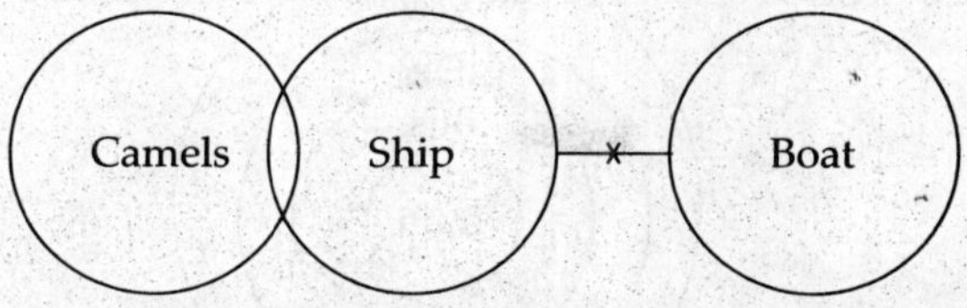

Since some camels are ships and no ship is a boat, it follows that some ships are camels (conclusion I) and some camels are not boats (conclusion II).

7. **Option (B) is correct.**
Explanation:

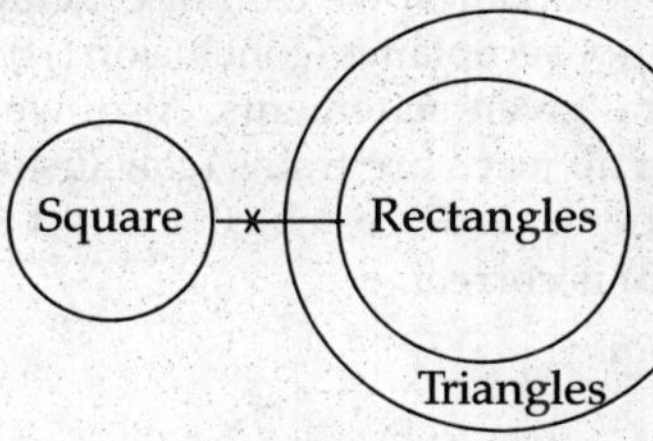

Given that no squares are rectangles and all rectangles are triangles, we cannot conclude that some triangles are squares (conclusion I), but we can conclude that some triangles are rectangles (conclusion II).

8. **Option (D) is correct.**
Explanation:

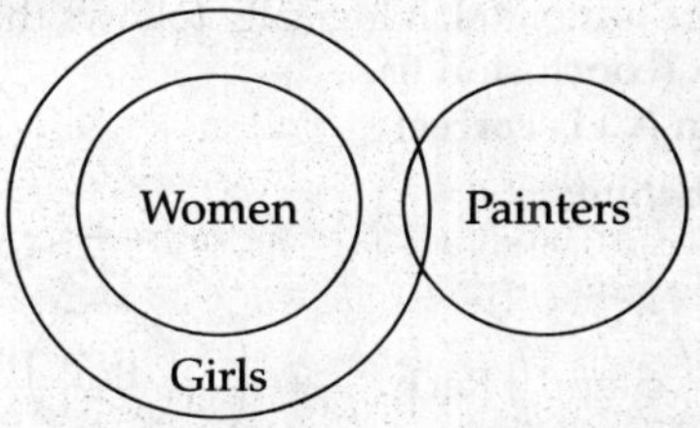

Although all women are girls, we cannot conclude that all girls are women (conclusion I). However, since some girls are painters, it follows that some women are painters (conclusion II).

9. **Option (A) is correct.**
Explanation:

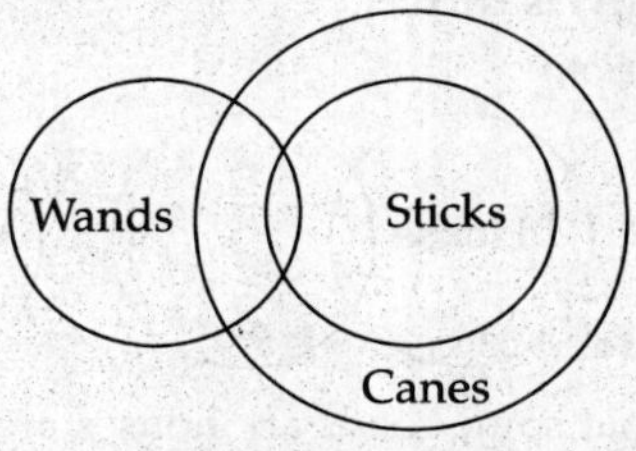

Since all sticks are canes and some wands are sticks, it follows that some canes are wands (conclusion I). We cannot conclude that no wands are canes (conclusion II) because it contradicts the given statements.

10. **Option (D) is correct.**
Explanation:

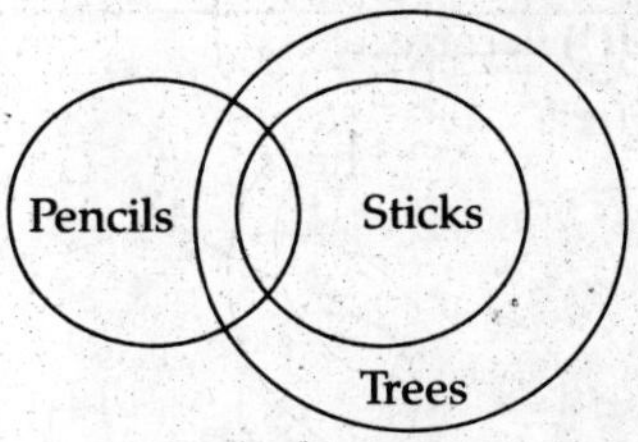

While some pencils are sticks and all sticks are trees, we cannot conclude that all sticks are pencils (conclusion I) or that all pencils are trees (conclusion II) due to the lack of a direct relationship.

11. **Option (A) is correct.**
Explanation:

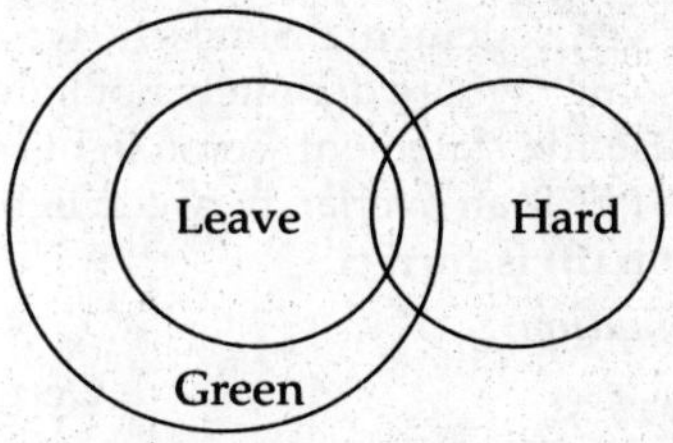

Given that all leaves are green and some leaves are hard, it follows that some hard are green (conclusion I). We cannot conclude that all green are leaves (conclusion II) because the statements do not establish exclusivity.

12. **Option (D) is correct.**
Explanation:

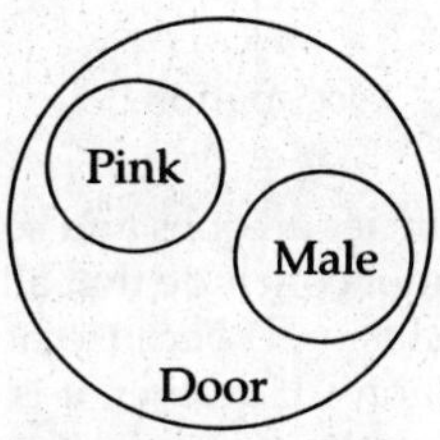

Since all pink are doors and all male are doors, we cannot conclude that some males are pink (conclusion I) or that all doors are pink (conclusion II) because the statements do not establish a direct relationship.

13. **Option (B) is correct.**
Explanation:

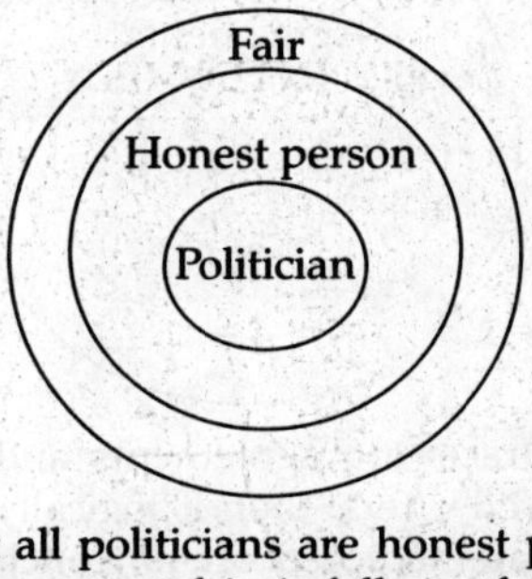

Given that all politicians are honest persons and all honest persons are fair, it follows that some honest persons are politicians (conclusion I) and some fair persons are politicians (conclusion III). We cannot conclude that no honest person is a politician (conclusion II) or that all fair persons are politicians (conclusion IV) because the statements do not support these conclusions.

14. Option (D) is correct.

Explanation:

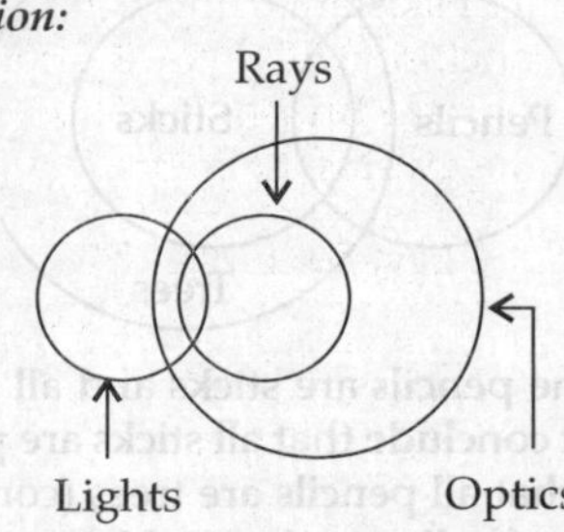

Given that some lights are rays and all rays are optics, we cannot conclude that some lights are definitely not optics (conclusion I) because it contradicts the given statements. Similarly, we cannot conclude that some rays are definitely not lights (conclusion II) because the statement "some lights are rays" implies that there is an overlap between lights and rays.

15. Option (B) is correct.

Explanation:

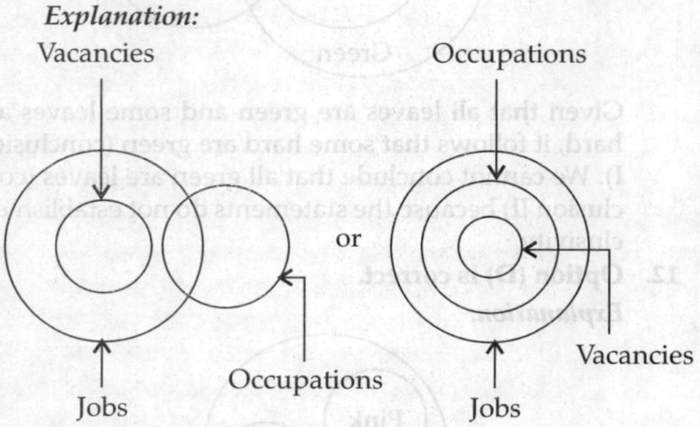

Since all vacancies are jobs and some jobs are occupations, we cannot conclude that all vacancies are occupations (conclusion I) because not all jobs are stated to be occupations. However, it is possible that all occupations could be vacancies (conclusion II) because the statement does not exclude this possibility.

16. Option (C) is correct.

Explanation:

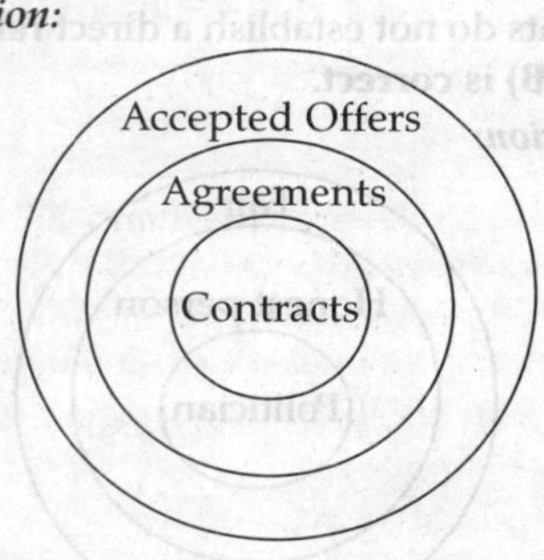

If all contracts are agreements and all agreements are accepted offers, then it logically follows that all contracts are accepted offers (conclusion C). This is because the set of contracts is contained within the set of agreements, which in turn is contained within the set of accepted offers.

17. Option (D) is correct.

Explanation:

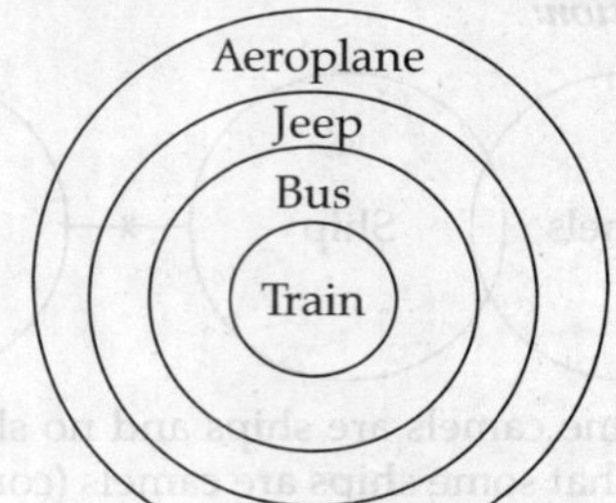

Since all trains are buses, all buses are jeeps, and all jeeps are aeroplanes, we cannot conclude that some buses are not aeroplanes (conclusion I) because it contradicts the given statements. Also, we cannot conclude that all jeeps are trains (conclusion II) because the statements do not establish a direct relationship.

18. Option (B) is correct.

Explanation:

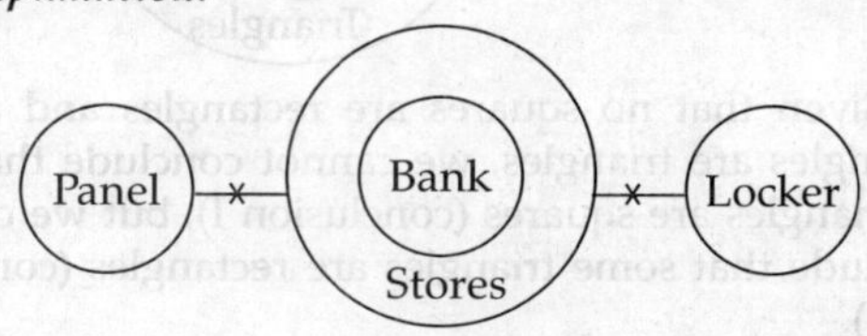

Given that no bank is a locker and all banks are stores, it follows that no store is a locker (conclusion I). Since no store is a panel, it logically follows that no panel is a bank (conclusion II).

19. Option (C) is correct.

Explanation:

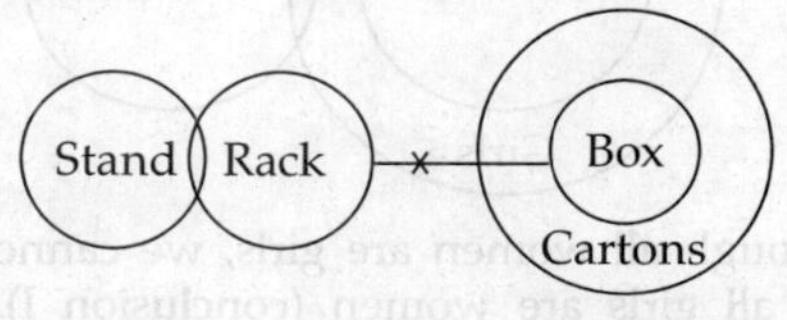

Since some stands are racks and no rack is a box, it follows that all stands can never be boxes (conclusion I). And since all boxes are cartons, it is possible that all racks being cartons is a possibility (conclusion II).

20. Option (A) is correct.

Explanation:

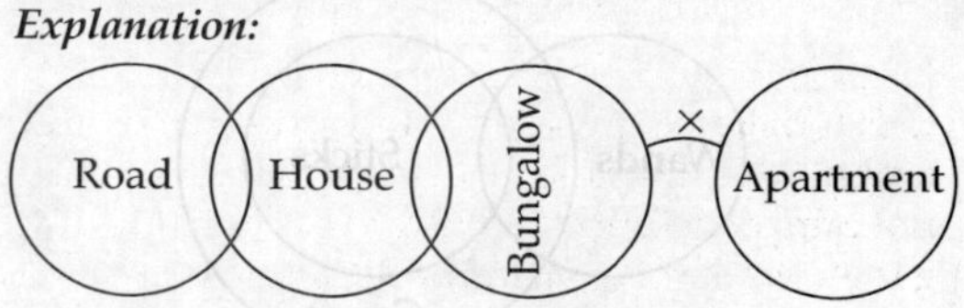

Given that some roads are houses and some houses are bungalows, and no bungalow is an apartment, we cannot conclude that no apartment is a house (conclusion II). However, it is possible that all roads could be apartments (conclusion I) because the statements do not exclude this possibility.

21. Option (C) is correct.

Explanation:

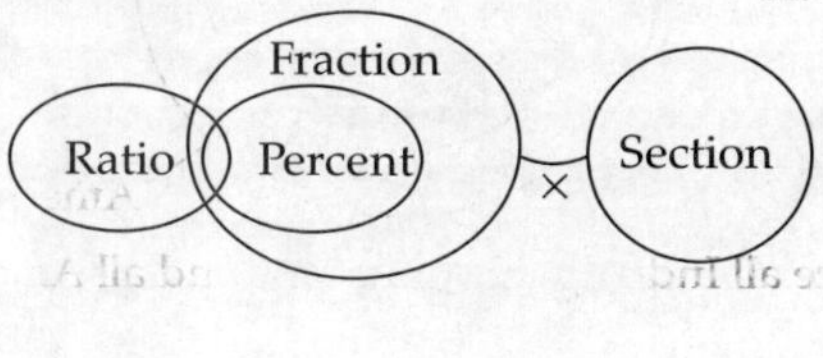

Since some ratios are percent and all percent are fractions, and no fraction is a section, it follows that all sections being ratios is a possibility (conclusion I). It also follows that at least some fractions are ratios (conclusion II).

22. Option (D) is correct.

Explanation:

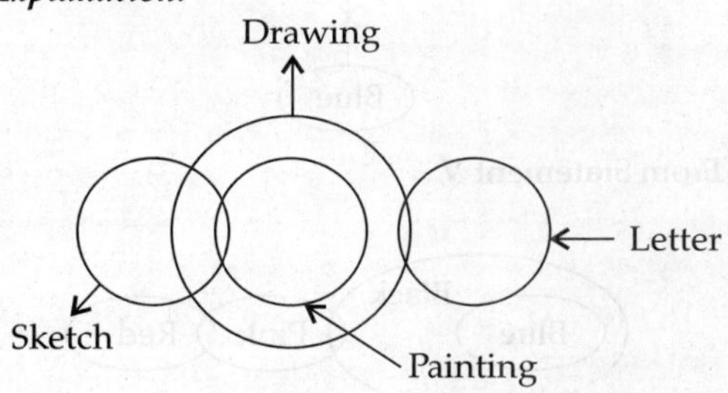

While some sketches are paintings and all paintings are drawings, we cannot conclude that all sketches can never be drawings (conclusion I) because the statements do not establish exclusivity. Also, we cannot conclude that no painting is a letter (conclusion II) because some drawings are letters.

23. Option (B) is correct.

Explanation:

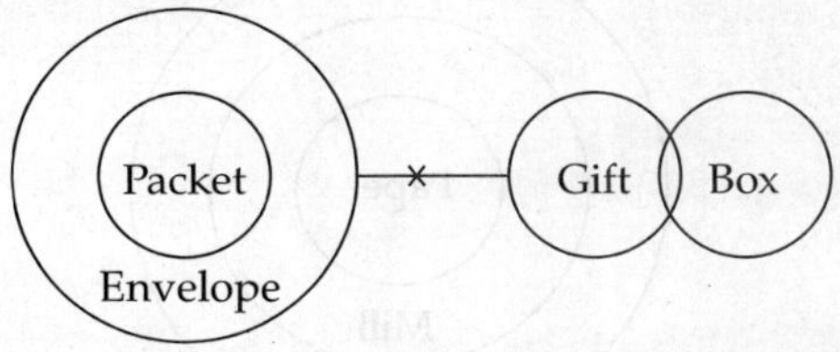

Since all packets are envelopes and no envelope is a gift, and some gifts are boxes, it follows that all boxes can never be envelopes (conclusion II). We cannot conclude that all envelopes are packets (conclusion I) because the statements do not establish a direct relationship.

24. Option (A) is correct.

Explanation:

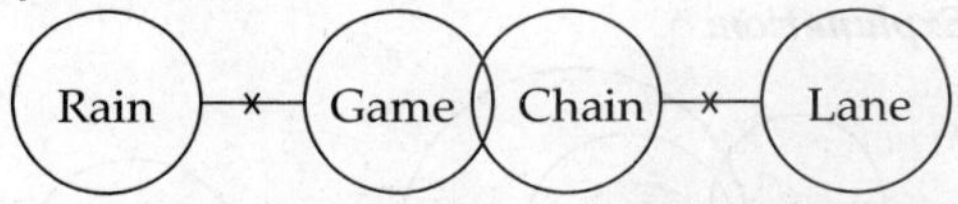

Given that no rain is game and some games are chain, and no chain is lane, it follows that some chains are not rain (conclusion I). We cannot conclude that some games are lane (conclusion II) because it contradicts the given statements.

25. Option (A) is correct.

Explanation:

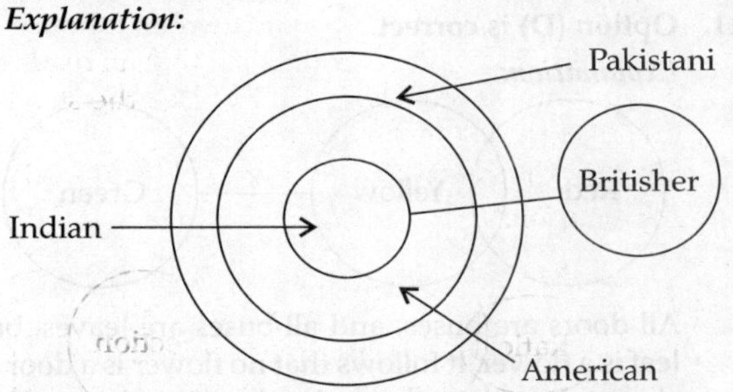

Since all Indians are Americans and all Americans are Pakistanis, and no British is American, it follows that all Indians are Pakistani (conclusion I) and no Indian is British (conclusion III). We cannot conclude that some Pakistani are British (conclusion II) because it contradicts the given statements.

Level-3: EXPERT

1. Option (D) is correct.

Explanation:

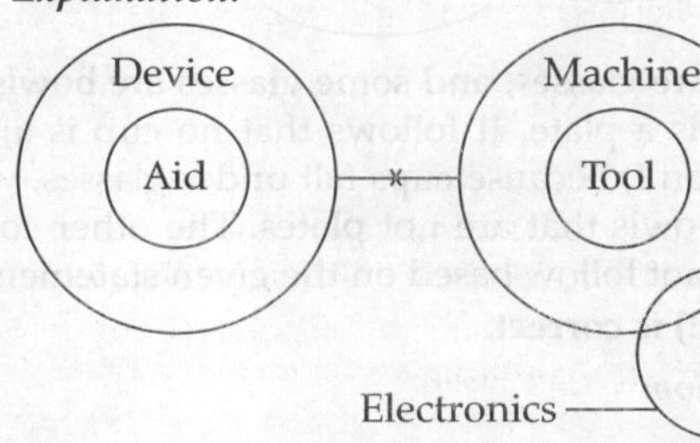

Since all benches are desks, and some desks are roads, which in turn are all pillars, it follows that some pillars are desks (conclusion II). However, we cannot conclude that some pillars are benches (conclusion I) or no pillar is a bench (conclusion IV) because the statements do not establish a direct relationship between benches and pillars.

2. Option (B) is correct.

Explanation:

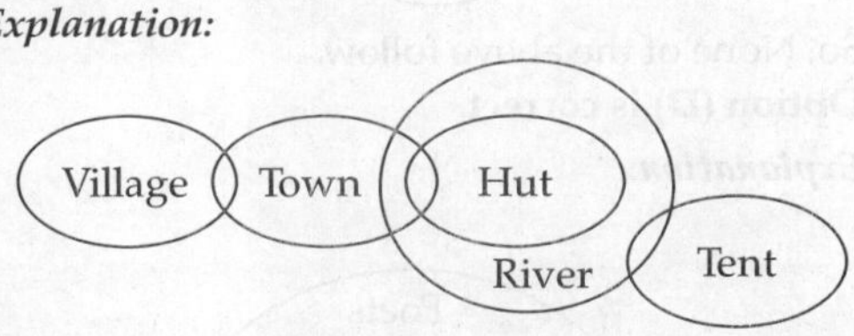

As evident from the diagram, Some rivers are towns.

3. Option (D) is correct.

Explanation:

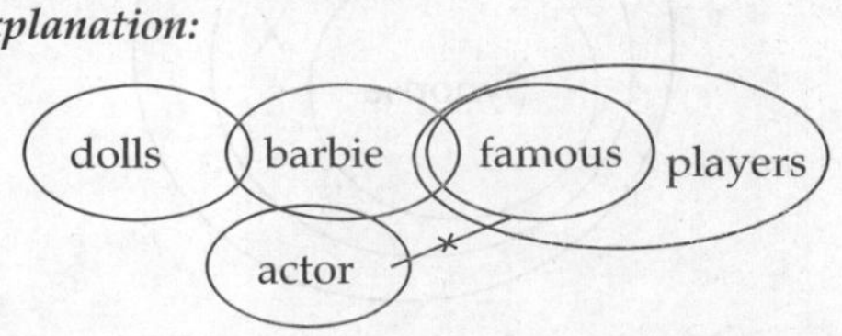

Since some bricks are trees, and all trees are pens, which in turn are all boats, it follows that some boats are bricks (conclusion I) and some pens are bricks (conclusion II). The other conclusions also follow due to the transitive relationship established through the statements.

4. Option (A) is correct.

Explanation:

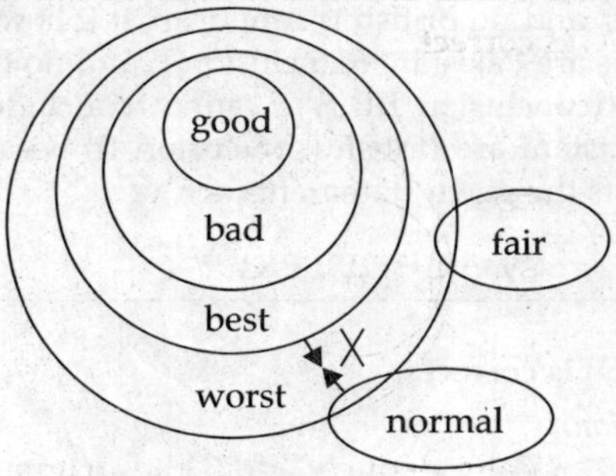

All cups are glasses, and some glasses are bowls, but no bowl is a plate. It follows that no cup is a plate (conclusion I) because cups fall under glasses, which include bowls that are not plates. The other conclusions do not follow based on the given statements.

5. **Option (E) is correct.**

Explanation:

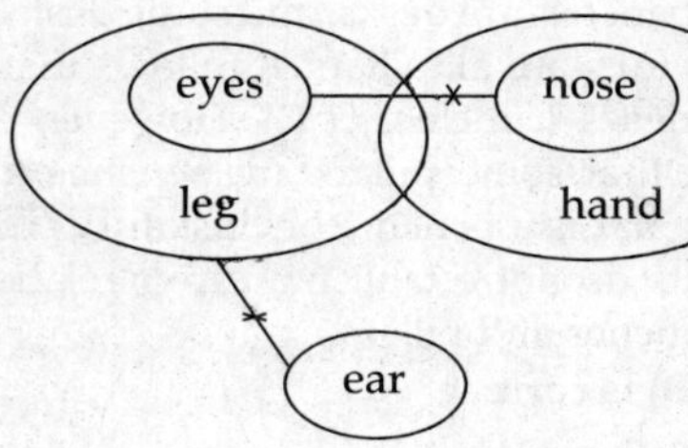

So, None of the above follow.

6. **Option (D) is correct.**

Explanation:

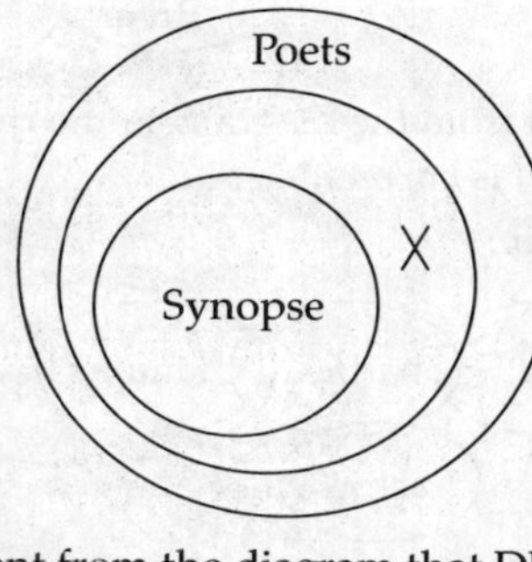

It is evident from the diagram that DFA is the correct pattern.

7. **Option (A) is correct.**

Explanation:

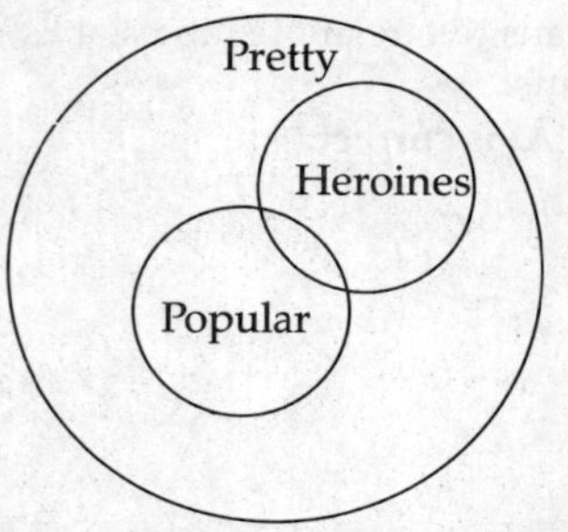

No man is sky, and no sky is road. It follows that no road is sky (conclusion II). However, we cannot conclude that no road is man (conclusion I) or some skies are men (conclusion III) because the statements do not establish a direct relationship.

8. **Option (B) is correct.**

Explanation:

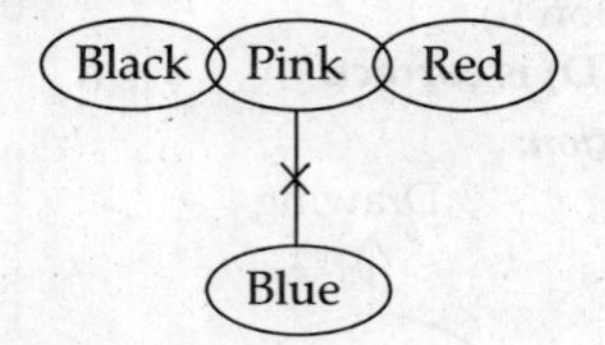

From Statement V,

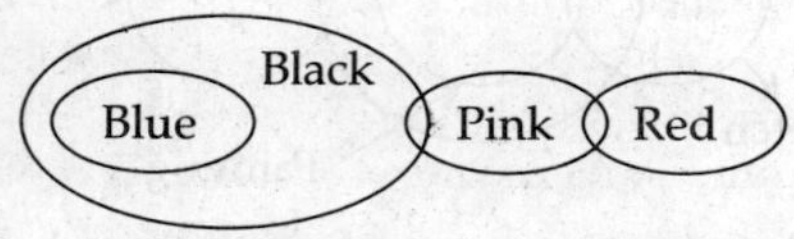

All myths are fictions, and no fiction is a novel, while all novels are stories. It follows that no myth is a novel (conclusion I). The other conclusions do not follow based on the given statements.

9. **Option (B) is correct.**

Explanation:

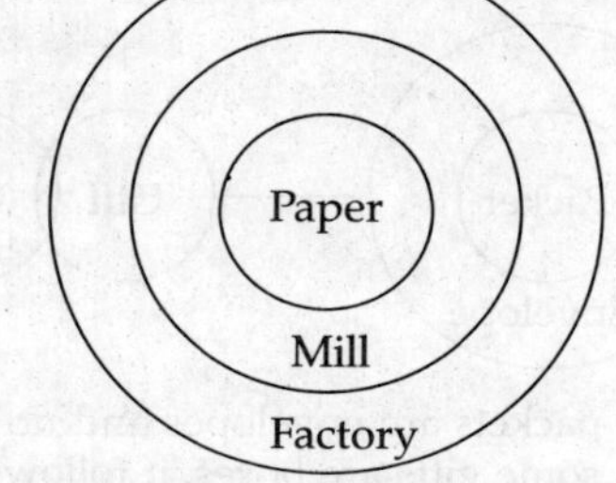

All rods are bricks, and some bricks are ropes, which in turn are all doors. It follows that some rods are doors (conclusion I) and some doors are bricks (conclusion II). The other conclusions do not follow based on the given statements.

10. **Option (B) is correct.**

Explanation:

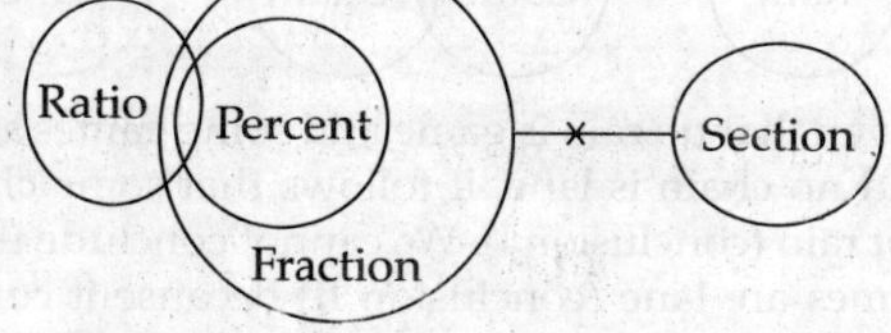

The diagram makes it clear that at least some fractions are ratios.

11. **Option (D) is correct.**

Explanation:

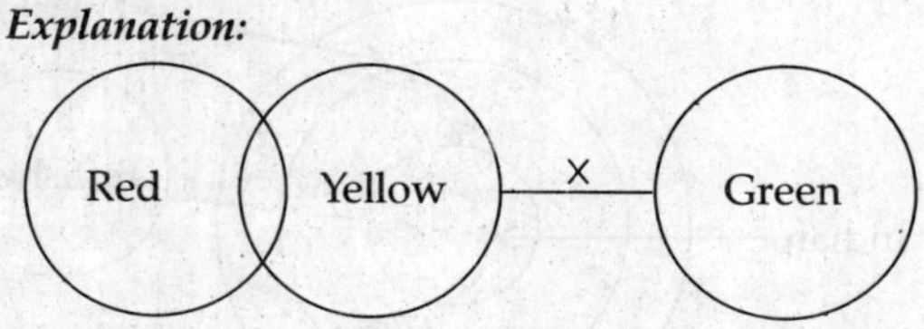

All doors are buses, and all buses are leaves, but no leaf is a flower. It follows that no flower is a door (conclusion I) and no flower is a bus (conclusion II). The other conclusions also follow due to the transitive relationship established through the statements.

12. Option (D) is correct.

Explanation:

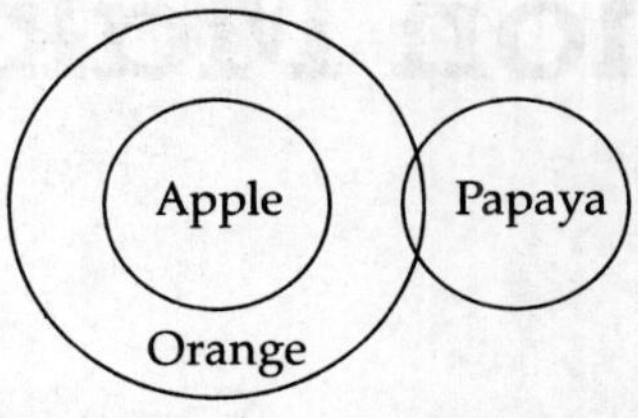

All pencils are birds, and all birds are skies, which in turn are all hills. It follows that all pencils are hills (conclusion I) and all birds are hills (conclusion IV). The other conclusions also follow due to the transitive relationship established through the statements.

13. Option (A) is correct.

Explanation:

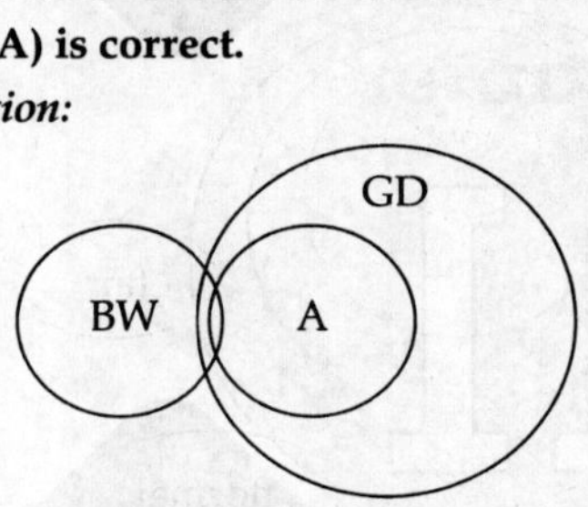

It can be logically deduced from the diagram that Some beautiful women are good dancers.

■ ■ ■

Chapter 11

Decision Making

LEARNING OBJECTIVES:

- Identifying the correct and incorrect decisions.

Chapter decision making in analytical reasoning involves determining the appropriate sequence to present the chapters or sections of a report, study, or analysis. Its goal is to organise information and ideas in a structured manner to effectively communicate key findings, arguments or recommendations to the intended audience.

IDENTIFYING THE CORRECT AND INCORRECT DECISIONS:

- Identifying correct and incorrect decisions in reasoning chapter decision making involves assessing whether the chosen order and structure of chapters effectively support the objectives and core message of the analysis. Here are some factors to consider when evaluating the decisions made in chapter decision making:

CORRECT DECISIONS:

- **Logical Progression:** The chapters should flow logically, with each chapter building upon the information presented in the previous one. The order should make sense and help the audience understand the analysis coherently.
- **Relevance and Significance:** The prioritisation of information should be based on the importance and relevance of each element in supporting the core message or argument. The most critical information should be given prominence.
- **Clear Relationships:** The logical relationships among elements should be accurately identified and presented in the order that best conveys those relationships. Dependencies and hierarchical relationships should be properly addressed.
- **Smooth Transitions:** The flow of information between chapters should be smooth, ensuring a seamless transition from one topic to another. The reader should be able to follow the analysis without confusion or abrupt shifts in focus.

INCORRECT DECISIONS:

- **Illogical Order:** If the chosen order of chapters does not follow a logical progression or does not effectively build upon previous information, it can lead to confusion and hinder the reader's understanding.
- **Lack of Relevance:** If less significant or unrelated information is given more prominence, it can distract from the core message or argument, making the analysis less effective.
- **Inaccurate Relationships:** Incorrectly identifying or presenting the logical relationships between elements can disrupt the coherence of the analysis and undermine the logical flow of ideas.
- **Disjointed Transitions:** Poorly executed transitions between chapters can result in a fragmented analysis, making it difficult for the reader to grasp the overall narrative or follow the line of reasoning.

Evaluating the correctness of chapter decision making requires careful consideration of the purpose, objectives, logical relationships, relevance, and flow of information. It may be helpful to gather feedback from peers or subject matter experts to identify any potential issues or areas for improvement in the chapter structure and order.

Example 1: Read the following information and answer the questions given below it.

The following are the conditions for selecting a "Management trainee for a reputed public sector company". The candidate must

(a) be a post-graduate in commerce with marks 60 % or CA.

(b) not more than 25 years old and less than 20 years old.

(c) have fluency in English and Hindi.

(d) be in a position to pay ₹ 10,000/- as deposit to the company.

(e) give an undertaking to work for at least 5 years for the company.

However,

(i) If a person satisfies all the conditions except (a) above he should be referred to the Managing Director of the company.

(ii) If a person satisfies all the conditions except (d) should be referred to the Chairman of the company.

On the basis of the above criteria and the information provided, you have to decide each case. You are not to assume anything which is beyond what's given in the questions. The alternative courses of decision and the method of indicating the same are as follows.

1. If data provided is not complete in the case of any of the candidates.
2. If the candidate cannot be selected as a Management Trainee.
3. If the candidate can be selected as a Management Trainee.
4. If the candidate is to be referred to the Managing Director.
5. If the candidate is to be referred to the Chairman.

(A) 22-year-old Raju is a Post-Graduate in commerce with 60% marks. He is fluent in Hindi Only. He can pay the required deposit and is also ready to give 5 years undertaking.

(B) 21-year-old Vijay has obtained 63% marks in Post-Graduation with commerce. He is fluent in Hindi and English and can pay the required deposit. He is willing to give 5 years' undertaking.

Sol. (A) Answer is 2.

(B) Answer is 3.

1 Beginner Level

Directions (Qs. 1–10): Read the following information and answer the questions given below it.

The following are the criteria for the admission into medical college.

The student must:

(a) have passed XII Standard examination in Science with at least 50% marks.

(b) be at least 18 years old as on 1.4.1991.

(c) have scored at least 65% marks in the entrance examination.

(d) to pay the monthly tuition fee of ₹ 400, and

(e) able to pay one-time deposit of ₹ 15,000 to the Institute.

(f) The case of student who satisfies all other criteria but can pay the one time deposit only upto ₹ 10,000, is to be referred to the director of the institute.

(g) The case of a candidate who satisfies all other criteria apart from the percentage of marks in XII Standard is to be referred to the Chairman for admission.

(h) A student who has satisfied all other criteria but has not yet received the result of the final examination of XIIth Std. may be provisionally admitted.

On basis of the above criteria and the information given in each of the following questions you have to take decisions as regards admittance of the student. Please note you did not assume anything in case of any student.

(A) If the student is not to be admitted.

(B) If the student is to be admitted.

(C) If the student is to be referred to the Director.

(D) If the student is to be referred to the Chairman, Admission.

(E) If the student is to be provisionally admitted.

1. Irene Fernand have passed XII Standard exam in Science with 70% marks. She has secured 75% marks in the entrance exam and was 18 years old on 01.07.1990. She can pay tuition fee of ₹400 per month but can pay one-time and deposit of only ₹10,000.

2. Prabir Singhal secured 60% marks in the XII Standard exam with Science. He was 19 years old on 01.03.1990 and has secured 70% marks in the entrance test. He can pay the stipulated one-time deposit of ₹15,000 and the monthly tuition fee of ₹400.

3. Sharad Joshi has passed his XII Standard exam with 52% marks and will be 20 years old, as on 8th December 1991. He has secured 68% marks in the entrance test. He is able to pay one-time deposit of ₹15,000 and the monthly tuition fee of ₹400.

4. Utpal Ghosh has passed XII Standard in Science with first class and was 18 years old in Jan. 1991. He has secured 70% marks in the entrance test and can pay monthly tuition fee of ₹400 and one-time deposit of ₹15,000.

5. Devan Varma has passed X and XI Standard exam in Science with 48% marks and was born on 25th July, 1972. He has secured marks in the entrance examination. He is able to pay one-time deposit of ₹15,000 and monthly tuition fee of ₹400.

6. Prashant Kohli has passed XII Standard exam in Science with 45% of marks. He was 19 years old as on 01.02.1991. He has secured 70% in the entrance examination. He is able to pay stipulated one-time deposit and monthly tuition fees.

7. Nitish Sharma has secured 72% marks in the entrance exam. He was born 17th September 1971. He is yet to receive his mark sheet of his XII Standard final exam in Science stream. He is able to pay the one-time deposit of ₹15,000 and the monthly tuition fee of ₹400.

8. Avinash Mundra passed XII Standard in Science with 55% marks and was born on 01.03.1973. He has secured 60% marks in the entrance exam and he can pay the monthly tuition fee of ₹400. He can pay one-time deposit of ₹9,000 only.

9. Jyoti Deshmukh has appeared for the final exam of XII in Science stream. She was 19 years old on 20.3.1991. She has secured 75% in the entrance examination. She is able to pay the one-time deposit of ₹15,000 and the monthly tuition fee of ₹400.

10. Prakash Swami secured 50% and 65% marks in the XII Standard and entrance exam respectively. He will be 18 years and 6 months old on 01.06.1991. He pays the stipulated one-time deposit and monthly tuition fees.

Directions (Qs. 11–20): Read the following information and answer the questions given below it.

The following are the conditions for selecting a "Management trainee for a reputed public sector company." The candidate:

(a) be a post-graduate in commerce with marks 60 % or CA.

(b) not be more than 25 years old and less than 20 years' old as on.

(c) have fluency in English and Hindi.

(d) be in a position to pay ₹ 10,000/- as deposit to the company.

(e) give an undertaking to work for at least 5 years for the company.

However,

(i) If a person satisfies all the conditions except (a) above he should be referred to the Managing Director of the company.

(ii) If a person satisfies all the conditions except (d) should be referred to the Chairman of the company.

On the basis of the above criteria and the information provided, you have to decide each case. You are not to assume anything which is beyond what's given in the questions. The alternative courses of decision and the method of indicating the same are as follows.

(A) If data provided is not complete in case of any of the candidates.

(B) If the candidate cannot be selected as a Management Trainee.

(C) If the candidate can be selected as a Management Trainee.

(D) If the candidate is to be referred to the Managing Director.

(E) If the candidate is to be referred to the Chairman.

11. 22-year-old Raju is a Post-Graduate in commerce with 60% marks. He is fluent in Hindi only. He can pay the required deposit and is also ready to give 5 years undertaking.

12. 21-year-old Vijay has obtained 63% marks in Post-Graduation with commerce. He is fluent in Hindi and English and can pay the required deposit. He is willing to give 5 years' undertaking

13. 23-year-old Suresh is a CA. with fluency in Hindi and English. He can pay ₹8,000 as deposit and will give 5 years' undertaking.

14. Amar is a Post Graduate with 59% marks in Commerce. He is fluent in Hindi and English and also willing to give an undertaking of-5 years and he can pay the required deposit.

15. Rajan is a Post-Graduate in Commerce with 70% marks. He is fluent in Hindi and English. He can pay the required deposit and is ready to pay 5 years' undertaking. His date of birth is 01.11.1973.

16. Anil whose date of birth is 01.09.1972, has obtained 70% marks in Post-graduation and also completed his CA. He can pay the required deposit is fluent in Hindi and English and also has no objection to giving 5 years undertaking to the company.

17. 24-year-old Saurabh is post graduate in commerce with 64% marks. He is fluent in Hindi and English. He can pay the required deposit and is willing to give 5 years' undertakings.

18. Neelan Garg whose date of birth 01.08.1963 has a C.A. degree. She is fluent in Hindi and English can pay the deposit and also has no objection to giving 4-year undertaking.

19. 24 years old Madan has got 62% in graduation with Commerce. He has fluency in Hindi and English. He can pay the required deposit and is also to give 5 year' undertaking.

20. Sujan Ray is a Post-Graduate with 65% marks, is fluent in Hindi and English and has done CA also. He is 23 years old and willing to give an undertaking of 5 years.

Direction (Qs. 21–25): The following are the directions to be followed for the selection of music directors for a recording company.

I. Candidate must be over 35 years of age as on 01.06.1996.

II. The candidate must at least a graduate in music.

III. The candidate must have at least one recorded Cassette of his or her music.

IV. Candidate must have given music for at least two T.V. serials.

If the candidate fulfils all these criteria, he or she will be selected as a director. However, if a candidate fulfils all these criteria except

(a) IV above, his or her case will be referred to the Producer.

(b) I above, his or her case will be referred to the Director.

(c) II above, but has given music for some films (feature film only), he she will be selected as a Music Director.

On the basis of these conditions decide what course of action to be taken in the case of the following candidates. Give answer

(A) If the candidate is to be selected as a Music Director.

(B) If the candidate is not to be selected as a Music Director.

(C) If his or her case is to be referred to the Producer'

(D) If his or her case is to be referred to the Director.

(E) If the data given about the candidate are inadequate to give a definite course of action.

21. Paratha Shah is 37 years old as on 01.01.1995. He is a graduate in music. He has given music for several T.V. serials (three serials). He has given music in some feature films.

22. Manju Mujumdar was born on 07.02.1960. She has given music in five T.V. serials. She has given music in two feature films and has seven cassettes of her music.

23. Manu Srivastava has several cassettes of his music. He has given music in four T.V. serials and three feature films. He is a graduate in music and he is older than Manju Mujumdar.

24. Shravan Mohapatra has a graduate degree in music. He is 40 years old. He has not given music in either any T. V. serial or any film. He has recorded some cassettes of his music.

25. Mohit Saxena has given music in several T.V. serials. He was born on 07.08.1969. He is a graduate in music and has recorded ten cassettes of his music. He has also given music in five documentary films.

Level 2 Intermediate

Directions (Qs. 1–10): The following are the criteria laid down by the College, University of Boston, for admission-seekers.

I. The student must not be less than 21 years of age and more than 33 Years of age, as on 1st August, 1995.

II. The student must possess a passport and an educational visa.

III. The student must possess a TOEFL score of at least 550.

IV. The student must be prepared to make a statutory deposit of $25,000 towards expenses (equal to ₹ 8 lakhs.

V. Student must not have any criminal record or any fatal or infectious disease. A student who has obtained eligibility certificate from the Law College will be deemed to have fulfilled this criterion, otherwise he or she would need to show a character certificate and a health certificate.

If a candidate fulfils all these criteria, he or she would be granted admission into the college. However, if a candidate fulfils all these criteria except.

(a) II above, he may be granted provisional admission into the college.

(b) I above, the case may be referred to the Dean of the college.

(c) IV above, but is sponsored by a company having a minimum equity capital of $ 2 million (₹6 crore), he or she will be granted admission.

On the basis of the conditions mentioned above, decide upon the course of action that should be taken in the case of each of the candidates mentioned answer:

(A) If the candidate is to be granted admission.

(B) If the candidate is not to be granted admission.

(C) If the candidate is to be granted provisional admission.

(D) If the case is to be referred to the Dean.

(E) If the data are inadequate to predict what course of action needs to be.

1. Sudhir Kashyap was born on 1st July, 1969. He is sponsored by a company Voltaic India Ltd. He possesses a passport, a visa and an eligibility certificate. He is prepared to make a statutory and deposit of $25,000.

2. Anju Kulshreshtha possesses an eligibility certificate. She was born on 2nd August, 1974. She has a passport and a visa. She is willing to make the required statutory deposit.

3. Rakesh Yadav is a B. Tech. and possess a character certificate as well as a health certificate. He is sponsored by O. A. P. India limited, a company having an equity base of 12.5 crore rupees. He has, a TOEFAL score of 720. He possesses a passport and a visa. He is 26-year-old.

4. Pranav Das gupta has a TOEFL score of 570. He is ready to make a statuary deposit of $25,000. He has a passport but not a visa. He does have the eligibility certificate and is 24-year-old.

5. Shantanu Mukherjee is 27 years old. He cannot deposit $25,000 on his own; nor he is sponsored by any company. He has a TOEFL score of 600. He possesses a passport, visa and an eligibility Certificate.

6. Rana Kumar Bhadra Singh is willing to make the required statuary deposit. His TOEFL score is 600. He was born on 2nd August 1973. He possesses a passport but not a visa. Similarly, he has the required health certificate but not the character certificate.

7. Umesh Unnikrishnan was born on 2nd September, 1974. He has a TOEFAL score of 660. He is not capable of making the required deposit, but he is sponsored by a Company having an equity capital of ₹10 crore. He has all the relevant certificates as required by the Law College.

8. Rakesh Mohapatra is a 27-year-old student sponsored by a company having an equity base of ₹12 crore. He possesses all the relevant certificates as required. His TOEFL score is 546.

9. Madan Varshneya was born on 2nd September, 1963. He is willing the required statutory deposit. He possesses a passport and a visa. He is yet to receive any health certificate although he has a character certificate. He has a TOEFL score of 600.

10. Ranjan Madhusudan is 28 years old. He is willing to make a statuary deposit of up to ₹9 lakh. He possesses a passport and a visa. He also has the required character certificate. His TOEFL score is 620.

Directions (Qs. 11–20): Study the following information and answer the questions given below it.

Given here are the conditions to become the members of a Resort company Club. A person must:

1. be in the age group of 18–50 years as on August 3, 1993.
2. be drawing a minimum salary of ₹ 1 lakh per annum.
3. own a house.

4. not have a family of more than four members including himself.
5. have exhibited excellence in any field of arts and sports.

However, if a person

(i) satisfies all the conditions except (3) above, the case may be referred to the Club Secretary.

(ii) satisfies all the conditions except (4) above, but draws a salary of more than ₹ 2 lakhs per annum, the case may be referred to the club president.

On the basis of the above conditions and the information provided for each person in the questions given below, decide which of the following courses of action should be taken regarding each candidate. Mark answer

(A) If the person is eligible to be a member;
(B) If the person cannot be allowed the membership;
(C) If the data provided is inadequate;
(D) If the case is to be referred to the Club Secretary; and
(E) If the case is to be referred to the Club President.

11. Mr. Sanjeev Rana, an IAS. Officer, draws a salary of ₹6,500 per month. His date of birth is 19th June, 1964. He holds a certificate of being the volleyball player in his college. He lives with his wife and daughter. He stays in government accommodation.

12. Ms. Sangeeta Seth, living with her mother and father, is a college professor earning ₹8,500 monthly. The house she lives in is on her name. She has a good record in the field of fine arts.

13. Mr. Ashoka Taneja, a bachelor lives in a private house owned by him with his parents and grandparents (all alive). He is a Senior Manager in a private firm drawing a salary of above ₹2 lakh per annum. He has won Trophy in badminton. He is 25 years old.

14. Mr. Radha Kapoor living with his husband IS a senior official in a company receiving ₹10,000 per month. She completed 10 years of service in the company on 9th January, 1992.

15. Mr. Kantians completed 32 years' in April 1991. He stays in his own with his wife and three sons. He works as a supervisor in a company and draws ₹ 1,12,000 per month. He has exhibited excellence in the field of arts.

16. Mr. Vipin Chandra who has 35 years old, works as a superintendent in a fertilizer plant. He lives as a tenant with his wife and two Sons. He draws a monthly salary of ₹8,700. He holds a certificate of merit in modem arts.

17. Mr. Rajan Khanna was born in October 1958. He is the Chairman of a Company and draws ₹ 10,500 per annum. He has been the captain of Basketball team of his office and lives in his own house with his wife.

18. Mr. Vivek Chandrawal is 43 years old. He lives alone in his own house.

He works as a supervisor in a textile mill and earns ₹9,000 every month.

19. Mr. Ajay Bhatnagar is a Branch Manager in a bank and draws a salary of ₹2,08,000 per annum. He lives in a flat owned by him, along with his parents, wife and a son. He holds a certificate of excellence in Tennis. His date of birth is 16th November, 1968.

20. Mr. Pankaj Mehta lives in his own house with his wife and a daughter. He gets a monthly salary of ₹7,500. He is a good painter and owns a gallery. He is 37 years of age.

Directions (Qs. 21–25): Study the following information carefully and answer the questions given below it.

The following are the qualifications necessary for the recruitment of a Librarian in a State University.

The candidate must:

1. have a Master's degree in Library Science with at least 55% marks or its equivalent grade and a consistently good academic record.
2. have a one-year specialisation or Master's Degree in an area of Information Technology in Archives and Manuscript-keeping.
3. have at least ten years' experience as a Deputy Librarian in a University.
4. bear an evidence of innovative library service and organisation of published work.

In case of a candidate who

5. has 15 years' experience as a College Librarian, the case may be referred to the Vice-Chancellor.
6. has obtained less than 55% marks in Library Science but has 13 years' experience as a Deputy Librarian in a University the case may be reform to the register of the university of his consideration.
7. Have M.Phil Ph.D. degree in Library science/ Information science/ Documentation/ Archives and Manuscript-keeping but has only few years' experience as a College Librarian, the condition at 1 may be waived.

Based on the above conditions and the information provided against each of the candidates in the questions given below, decide courses of action should be taken in the case of each candidate. Give answer:

(A) If the candidate is to be selected;
(B) If the candidate is not to be selected;
(C) If the data are inadequate;
(D) If the case is to be referred to the Registrar, and
(E) If the case is to be referred to the Vice-Chancellor.

21. Amit Shanna, having Master's Degree in Library Science with 70% marks and a one-year specialisation in an area of Information Technology joined as a Librarian in the Indian College on 22nd January, 1977. He also holds a certificate of innovative library service in the college.

22. Rahul Sehgal, an M.Phil in Library Science, has been a deputy librarian in the Rohilkhand University since 27th August. 1980. He also has master's Degree in Archives and Manuscript-keeping. He holds an evidence of innovative organisation of published work of the college student doing PhD.

23. Sanjay Verna has been a Deputy Librarian in the IMS University since 1973. He holds an evidence of contributing library service in the same institution. He has a Master's Degree in Library Science with 53% marks.

24. Ramesh Singhani, holding a Ph.D. in Library Science, has one-year specialisation in Archives and Manuscript-keeping. He has been Deputy Librarian in the Assam University since 11th April, 1982. He also has a certificate of innovative library service in a public library for three years.

25. Sunil Grewal has been a College Librarian since 15th December, 1975. He holds an M.Phil. Degree in Library Science.

3 Expert
Level

Directions (Qs. 1–10): The following are the criteria laid down by a government agency to accept or reject a proposal for foreign investment by a foreign company:

I. The company should be willing to employ only Indians in its cadre except for the post of chairman.

II. The company must have a business proposal of at least $ 1 million (₹ 3.5 crore).

III. The company should have a global turnover of at least $ 100 million (₹ 350 crore).

IV. The company's business offer must not cover the privileged category (bulk drugs, oil, defence and space research).

If a company fulfils all these criteria, the agency would clear a proposal However, if a company fulfils all these criteria except:

(a) I above, but is willing to export at least 80% of its production, its will be cleared.

(b) II above, the case will be referred to the finance ministry.

(c) III above, the case will be referred to the commerce ministry.

You have to read the details of all the proposals given below and there decide the course of action that would be taken by the agency. Give answer:

(A) If the proposal will be cleared.

(B) If the proposal will be referred to the finance ministry.

(C) If the proposal will be referred to the commerce ministry.

(D) If the data is inadequate to come to a definite conclusion.

(E) If the proposal will not be cleared.

1. Aiwa of S. Korea has proposed to manufactured audio equipment in India. It has a global turnover of $2000 million and proposed to invest $20 million in India. It is willing to employ in all Indian staff.

2. Sotiza of Japan proposed to invest $1000s in India for the production of terry towel. This company has a global turnover of $120 million. It is willing to employ only Indians except for the post of Chairman.

3. PHILIPSIC of Holland has a global turnover of over $680 million. It proposed to invest $15 million in India. It is willing to employ only Indians in the company.

4. STERLING INC. of USA proposes to invest 160 million in India in a project of power generation. The company has given an undertaking to the effect that it will employ only Indians in its Indian subsidiary.

5. HAZARAT-UL-SULEMAN is willing to invest 150 million dollars in a project of space-research equipment's. It proposes to employ an all-Indian staff. If has a global turnover of $1500 million.

6. PETERPAN of Holland proposes to have an all-Indians staff in project ofterry-towel manufacturing. It has a global turnover of180 million rupees and it proposes to invest ₹50 million in India.

7. STANDARD ORGANIC of Australia proposes to manufacture car accessories in India. It does not agree to have Indian workers the project. It has a global turnover of $120 million and its proposed investment outlay India is of $800,000.

8. CIPLA of U.A.E. is not willing to have Indian workers in its proposed business of manufacturing synthetic dye in India. It has a global turnover of $1200 million and proposes to invest $80 million in India.

9. SOMU ELECTRONICS INC. of U.A.E. has a turnover of $160 million. It proposes to invest $3,000,000 in a project to manufacture ball-point pens and is willing to export 80% of its production. It does not disagree to the condition of having an all-Indian staff.

10. SECADA INC. of U.K. is not willing to employ Indian workers in a project to manufacture cigarettes. It proposes to invest $10 million in the project and is willing to export 100% of its production. The global turnover of the company is $1600 million.

Directions (Qs. 11–15): The following are the criteria laid down by Sip Management Services Company Limited for the selection of Marine

I. The candidate must be between 21 and 30 years of age as on 01.01.1995.

II. The candidate must possess a passport.

III. The candidate must have an eyesight of 2.5 with no color

IV. The candidate must be a B.E. or a B.Tech in Mechanical Engineering.

V. The candidate must possess a work experience of 3 years in industry in the capacity of a Mechanical Engineer.

If a candidate fulfils all these criteria, he or she will be selected for the job. However, if a candidate fulfils all other criteria except:

(a) II above, he or she may be provisionally selected.

(b) I above, but is less than 35 years of age and has a working experience of at least 5 years as marine engineer, he or she may be selected.

(c) V above, the case may be referred to the chairman of the company.

Read the information given about a candidate and decide the course of that should be taken in his or her case. Give answer

(A) If the candidate is to be selected.

(B) If the candidate is to be selected provisionally.

(C) If the candidate is to be referred to the Chairman.

(D) If the date given about the candidate are inadequate to say which course of action would be taken.

(E) If the candidate is not to be selected.

11. Ran Jana Sabhmaval has an eyesight of 2.5 with no color. She is a B. TECH and has served as a Mechanical Engineer for five years. She was born on 07.01.1967.

12. Shan tan Chavarria was born on 02.01.1965. He has an eyesight of 2.5 with no color. He is a BE. in Mechanical Engineer. He has a worked as a mechanical engineer for four years and has a passport.

13. Ranjan Srinivasan has the eyesight as required by-the company. He was born on 25.07.1964. He is B.Tech in mechanical engineering and he has working experience of seven years as marine engineer. He has applied for a passport and is yet to get it.

14. Manu Srivastava is a diploma holder in Mechanical Engineer. His eyesight is within the limits stipulated by the company and has worked as a Mechanical Engineer for 4 years. On 1st January 1993, he was 23 years old.

15. Sunita Vadhawar is a B.Tech. in Mechanical Engineering. She has a work experience of 28 months in the capacity of Mechanical Engineer. Born on Aug, 1969, she has the eyesight within the stipulated limit and also a passport.

ANSWER KEY

Level-1: Beginner

1.	(C)	2.	(B)	3.	(B)	4.	(B)	5.	(A)	6.	(D)	7.	(E)	8.	(A)	9.	(E)	10.	(B)
11.	(B)	12.	(C)	13.	(E)	14.	(A)	15.	(B)	16.	(C)	17.	(C)	18.	(B)	19.	(A)	20.	(C)
21.	(E)	22.	(A)	23.	(A)	24.	(C)	25.	(D)										

Level-2: Intermediate

1.	(E)	2.	(E)	3.	(A)	4.	(C)	5.	(B)	6.	(B)	7.	(C)	8.	(B)	9.	(B)	10.	(E)
11.	(B)	12.	(C)	13.	(E)	14.	(C)	15.	(B)	16.	(D)	17.	(A)	18.	(C)	19.	(E)	20.	(B)
21.	(E)	22.	(A)	23.	(B)	24.	(A)	25.	(C)										

Level-3: Expert

1.	(A)	2.	(B)	3.	(D)	4.	(D)	5.	(E)	6.	(A)	7.	(E)	8.	(D)	9.	(A)	10.	(A)
11.	(D)	12.	(A)	13.	(E)	14.	(E)	15.	(C)										

Solutions with Detailed Explanations

Level-1: BEGINNER

1. Option (C) is correct.

Explanation: Irene Fernand meets the criteria (a), (b), and (c) but can only pay a one-time deposit of ₹10,000. As per condition (f), she should be referred to the director.

2. Option (B) is correct.

Explanation: Prabir Singhal satisfies all the criteria for admission.

3. Option (B) is correct.

Explanation: Sharad Joshi fulfills all the criteria for admission.

4. Option (B) is correct.

Explanation: Utpal Ghosh meets all the criteria for admission.

5. Option (A) is correct.

Explanation: Devan Varma does not meet the criteria (a) as he has less than 50% marks in XII Standard.

6. Option (D) is correct.

Explanation: Prashant Kohli does not meet the criteria (a) as he has less than 50% marks in XII Standard. So, he is to be referred to the Chairman for admission.

7. Option (E) is correct.

Explanation: Nitish Sharma meets all criteria except for (h), as he has not yet received the result of the final examination of XIIth Std. He may be provisionally admitted.

8. **Option (A) is correct.**
Explanation: Avinash Mundra meets all criteria except for (f), as he can only pay a one-time deposit of ₹ 9,000. Apart from this, he does not meet criteria (b) and (c). so he will not be admitted.

9. **Option (E) is correct.**
Explanation: Jyoti Deshmukh meets all criteria except for (h), as she has not yet received the result of the final examination of XIIth Std. She may be provisionally admitted.

10. **Option (B) is correct.**
Explanation: Prakash Swami meets all the criteria for admission.

11. **Option (B) is correct.**
Explanation: Raju is a 22-year-old post-graduate in commerce with 60% marks and can pay the required deposit. He is ready to give a 5-year undertaking but is fluent in Hindi only, not meeting criterion (c).

12. **Option (C) is correct.**
Explanation: Vijay, 21 years old, has obtained 63% marks in post-graduation with commerce. He is fluent in both Hindi and English, can pay the required deposit, and is willing to give a 5-year undertaking, meeting all criteria.

13. **Option (E) is correct.**
Explanation: Suresh, a 23-year-old CA, is fluent in Hindi and English but can only pay ₹ 8,000 as a deposit. He is willing to give a 5-year undertaking. He meets all criteria except (d).

14. **Option (A) is correct.**
Explanation: Amar is a post-graduate with 59% marks in commerce and is fluent in both Hindi and English. He is willing to give a 5-year undertaking and can pay the required deposit. However, there is no information about his age, so the data is inadequate for admission.

15. **Option (B) is correct.**
Explanation: Rajan is a post-graduate in commerce with 70% marks, fluent in Hindi and English, can pay the required deposit, and is ready to give a 5-year undertaking. His date of birth is 01.11.1973, which makes him over 25 years old.

16. **Option (B) is correct.**
Explanation: Anil, born on 01.09.1972, has obtained 70% marks in post-graduation and completed his CA. He can pay the required deposit, is fluent in Hindi and English, and is willing to give a 5-year undertaking. However, he is over 25 years old.

17. **Option (C) is correct.**
Explanation: Saurabh, a 24-year-old post-graduate in commerce with 64% marks, is fluent in Hindi and English. He can pay the required deposit and is willing to give a 5-year undertaking, meeting all criteria.

18. **Option (B) is correct.**
Explanation: Neelan Garg, born on 01.08.1963, has a CA degree, is fluent in Hindi and English, can pay the deposit, but is willing to give only a 4-year undertaking, not meeting criterion (e).

19. **Option (D) is correct.**
Explanation: Madan, who is, 24 years old has got 62% in graduation with Commerce. He has fluency in Hindi and English. He can pay the required deposit and is also to give 5 year' undertaking. Thus, he fulfills all the criteria, except (a). So, he should be referred to the Managing Director of the company.

20. **Option (C) is correct.**
Explanation: Sujan Ray, a 23-year-old post-graduate with 65% marks and a CA, is fluent in Hindi and English and is willing to give a 5-year undertaking, meeting all criteria.

21. **Option (E) is correct.**
Explanation: Partha Shah is 37 years old as of 01.01.1995, which makes him over 35 years of age on 01.06.1996. He is a graduate in music and has given music for several TV serials, fulfilling criteria I, II, and IV. Although he has given music in feature films, there is no information about a recorded cassette of his music, which is required by criterion III.

22. **Option (A) is correct.**
Explanation: Manju Mujumdar was born on 07.02.1960, making her over 35 years of age on 01.06.1996. She has given music in five TV serials and two feature films, and she has seven cassettes of her music, fulfilling all the criteria.

23. **Option (A) is correct.**
Explanation: Manu Srivastava has several cassettes of his music and has given music in four TV serials and three feature films. He is a graduate in music and older than Manju Mujumdar, who was born in 1960, fulfilling all the criteria.

24. **Option (C) is correct.**
Explanation: Shravan Mohapatra has a graduate degree in music and is 40 years old. He has recorded some cassettes of his music, fulfilling criteria I, II, and III. However, he has not given music for any TV serials or films, not meeting criterion IV.

25. **Option (C) is correct.**
Explanation: Mohit Saxena has given music in several TV serials and was born on 07.08.1969, making him over 35 years of age on 01.06.1996. He is a graduate in music and has recorded ten cassettes of his music. However, he has only given music in documentary films, not meeting criterion IV.

Level-2: INTERMEDIATE

1. **Option (E) is correct.**
Explanation: Sudhir Kashyap, born on 1st July 1969, is over 33 years of age as of 1st August 1995, violating criterion I. Nothing is known about his TOEFL score or criminal background clearance.

2. **Option (E) is correct.**
Explanation: Anju Kulshreshtha has not revealed her TOEFL score and her possession of requisite certificates. So, data is inadequate.

3. **Option (A) is correct.**
Explanation: Rakesh Yadav is 26 years old, has a

TOEFL score of 720, possesses a passport and a visa, and is sponsored by a company with sufficient equity, meeting all criteria including criterion IV through sponsorship.

4. Option (C) is correct.

Explanation: Pranav Das Gupta is 24 years old and has a TOEFL score of 570. He is ready to make the statutory deposit but lacks a visa, meeting all criteria except II.

5. Option (B) is correct.

Explanation: Shantanu Mukherjee is 27 years old and has a TOEFL score of 600. He possesses a passport and a visa but cannot make the deposit and is not sponsored, violating criterion IV.

6. Option (B) is correct.

Explanation: Rana Kumar Bhadra Singh is willing to make the deposit and has a TOEFL score of 600. He was born on 2nd August 1973 but lacks a visa and character certificate, violating criteria II and V.

7. Option (C) is correct.

Explanation: Umesh Unnikrishnan was born on 2nd September 1974, has a TOEFL score of 660, and is sponsored by a company with sufficient equity, meeting all criteria including criterion IV through sponsorship.

8. Option (B) is correct.

Explanation: Rakesh Mohapatra is 27 years old and sponsored by a company with sufficient equity. He possesses all relevant certificates but has a TOEFL score of 546, violating criterion III.

9. Option (B) is correct.

Explanation: Madan Varshneya was born on 2nd September 1963, making him over 33 years of age as of 1st August 1995, violating criterion I. He also lacks a health certificate, violating criterion V.

10. Option (E) is correct.

Explanation: Ranjan Madhusudan is 28 years old and has a TOEFL score of 620. He possesses a passport and a visa and has the required character certificate. However, the deposit amount is not specified in dollars, and there is no information about a health certificate, leading to inadequate data.

11. Option (B) is correct.

Explanation: Mr. Sanjeev Rana, an IAS Officer, earns a salary of ₹6,500 per month, which amounts to ₹78,000 annually, failing to meet condition 2. He also lives in government accommodation, not fulfilling condition 3.

12. Option (C) is correct.

Explanation: Ms. Sangeeta Seth earns ₹8,500 monthly, which is ₹1,02,000 annually, meeting condition 2. She owns a house and has a record in fine arts, fulfilling conditions 3 and 5. However, her age is not provided, leading to inadequate data.

13. Option (E) is correct.

Explanation: Mr. Ashoka Taneja, 25 years old, lives with his parents and grandparents, making a family of five, which violates condition 4. However, he draws a salary above ₹2 lakhs per annum.

14. Option (C) is correct.

Explanation: Mr. Radha Kapoor's age is not provided, which is necessary to determine eligibility based on condition 1.

15. Option (B) is correct.

Explanation: Mr. Kantians, with a family of five, violates condition 4. His salary is not clearly stated, but if it is ₹1,12,000 per month, he meets condition 2.

16. Option (D) is correct.

Explanation: Mr. Vipin Chandra, 35 years old, does not own a house as he lives as a tenant, which is a deviation from condition 3.

17. Option (A) is correct.

Explanation: Mr. Rajan Khanna, born in October 1958, is within the age limit, owns a house, has a family size within the limit, and has exhibited excellence in sports, meeting all conditions.

18. Option (C) is correct.

Explanation: Mr. Vivek Chandrawal's salary and record in arts or sports are not provided, which are necessary to determine eligibility based on conditions 2 and 5.

19. Option (E) is correct.

Explanation: Mr. Ajay Bhatnagar, born on 16th November 1968, is within the age limit, draws a salary above ₹2 lakhs per annum, owns a house, has a family size outside the limit, as it includes 5 members. So the case will be referred to the club President.

20. Option (B) is correct.

Explanation: Mr. Pankaj Mehta, 37 years old, does not meet the salary requirement of ₹1 lakh per annum as his monthly salary is ₹7,500, which amounts to ₹90,000 annually, failing to meet condition 2.

21. Option (E) is correct.

Explanation: Amit Sharma has a Master's Degree in Library Science with 70% marks and a one-year specialization in Information Technology, fulfilling conditions (1) and (2). He also has evidence of innovative library service, meeting condition (4). With over 15 years of experience as a College Librarian, his case should be referred to the Vice-Chancellor.

22. Option (A) is correct.

Explanation: Rahul Sehgal, with an M.Phil in Library Science, has been a Deputy Librarian for over ten years and has a Master's Degree in Archives and Manuscript-keeping. He also has evidence of innovative organization of published work, meeting conditions (2), (3), and (4). Condition (1) is waived due to his M.Phil degree.

23. Option (B) is correct.

Explanation: Sanjay Verma has been a Deputy Librarian for over ten years and has evidence of contributing to library service, fulfilling conditions (3) and (4). However, he has a Master's Degree in Library Science with 53% marks, which is below the required 55%, not meeting condition (1).

24. Option (A) is correct.

Explanation: Ramesh Singhani, with a Ph.D. in Library Science and a one-year specialization in

Archives and Manuscript-keeping, has been a Deputy Librarian for over ten years. He also has a certificate of innovative library service, meeting conditions (2), (3), and (4). Condition (1) is waived due to his Ph.D. degree.

25. **Option (D) is correct.**
Explanation: Mohit Saxena has given music in several T.V. serials. He was born on 07.08.1969. He does not meet the age factor. So he must be referred to the Director.

Level-3: EXPERT

1. **Option (A) is correct.**
Explanation:
Foreign Investment Proposals: Aiwa of S. Korea meets all criteria, including a global turnover above $100 million and an investment proposal above $1 million. It also agrees to employ only Indians.

2. **Option (B) is correct.**
Explanation: Sotiza of Japan meets the global turnover requirement and agrees to employ only Indians except for the chairman. However, the investment amount is not clear ($1000s is not specified). So, the case will be referred to the finance ministry.

3. **Option (D) is correct.**
Explanation: PHILIPSIC of Holland meets all criteria, including a global turnover above $100 million and an investment proposal above $1 million. But the data is inadequate to come to a definite conclusion.

4. **Option (D) is correct.**
Explanation: STERLING INC. of USA meets the global turnover and investment proposal criteria. However, the nature of the business (power generation) is not specified as privileged or not.

5. **Option (E) is correct.**
Explanation: HAZARAT-UL-SULEMAN proposes to invest in space-research equipment, which is a privileged category.

6. **Option (A) is correct.**
Explanation: PETERPAN of Holland meets all the parameters , so the proposal will be cleared.

7. **Option (E) is correct.**
Explanation: STANDARD ORGANIC of Australia does not agree to employ only Indians and the investment amount is less than $1 million.

8. **Option (D) is correct.**
Explanation: CIPLA of U.A.E. does not agree to employ only Indians but meets the other criteria.

9. **Option (A) is correct.**
Explanation: SOMU ELECTRONICS INC. of U.A.E. meets the global turnover criterion and is willing to export 80% of its production, compensating for not employing only Indians.

10. **Option (A) is correct.**
Explanation: SECADA INC. of U.K. is not willing to employ Indian workers but is willing to export 100% of its production. The global turnover is above $100 million.

11. **Option (D) is correct.**
Explanation: Ran Jana Sabhmaval does not meet the age criterion and there is no information about her passport.

12. **Option (A) is correct.**
Explanation: Shantan Chavarria meets all criteria including age, passport, eyesight, and work experience.

13. **Option (E) is correct.**
Explanation: Ranjan Srinivasan exceeds the age limit and does not possess a passport.

14. **Option (E) is correct.**
Explanation: Manu Srivastava does not have the required degree (B.E. or B.Tech) in Mechanical Engineering.

15. **Option (C) is correct.**
Explanation: Sunita Vadhawar meets all criteria except for the work experience, which is less than 3 years.

■ ■ ■

Chapter 12

Critical Reasoning

LEARNING OBJECTIVES:

- Identifying the logical fallacies.
- Strengthening and weakening of Arguments

Critical reasoning is a key skill in analytical reasoning, which involves the ability to analyse and evaluate information, arguments and evidence in a logical and objective manner. It is a systematic approach to thinking and problem-solving that requires you to assess the strength and weaknesses of various claims, arguments, and assumptions.

In the context of analytical reasoning, critical reasoning involves:

- **Identifying assumptions:** Critical reasoning requires you to identify the underlying assumptions made in an argument or piece of information. Assumptions are unstated beliefs or premises that support an argument, and critically evaluating them can help you determine the validity and reliability of the argument.
- **Evaluating evidence:** When analysing information or arguments, critical reasoning involves carefully assessing the quality and relevance of the evidence presented. It requires you to examine whether the evidence is based on reliable sources, whether it is sufficient to support the conclusion, and whether any biases or logical fallacies are present.
- **Recognising logical fallacies:** Critical reasoning involves being able to identify and avoid logical fallacies, which are errors in reasoning that can weaken an argument. Common fallacies include ad hominem attacks, false analogies, straw man arguments and appeals to emotion. Being able to spot fallacies helps you to separate valid reasoning from faulty or misleading arguments.
- **Considering counterarguments:** Critical reasoning requires you to consider alternative viewpoints and counter arguments. By actively engaging with opposing perspectives, you can strengthen your own arguments and identify any weaknesses or flaws in your reasoning. This approach promotes intellectual rigor and helps avoid biases and one-sided thinking.
- **Drawing logical conclusions:** Critical reasoning involves drawing logical conclusions based on the information and arguments presented. It requires you to apply deductive or inductive reasoning to make reasonable and well-supported judgements or decisions.

Developing critical reasoning skills in analytical reasoning is essential for making informed decisions, solving complex problems, and engaging in rational and evidence-based thinking. It helps you to avoid cognitive biases, evaluate information objectively and arrive at well-reasoned conclusions.

LOGICAL FALLACIES:

➤ It is commonly found in reasoning. Here, are some common logical fallacies:

- **Appeal to Authority:** Relying on the opinion of an authority figure as evidence, even if the authority is not an expert in the field being discussed. Example: "Dr. Smith says that climate change is a hoax, so it must be true."
- **Slippery Slope:** Asserting that a particular action will inevitably lead to a series of increasingly negative consequences without sufficient evidence. Example: "If we allow same-sex marriage, it will lead to people marrying animals."
- **False Dichotomy:** Presenting only two options when more exist, oversimplifying the situation. Example: "You're either with us or against us."
- **Appeal to Ignorance:** Arguing that a claim is true simply because it hasn't been proven false, or vice versa. Example: "Aliens must exist because there's no evidence that they don't."
- **Circular Reasoning:** Using the conclusion of an argument as a premise, thereby assuming what you are trying to prove. Example: "I know the Bible is true because it says so, and the Bible is the word of God."

These are just a few examples of logical fallacies. It's important to be aware of them when analysing arguments to ensure that reasoning is sound and valid.

Example 1:

Statement: Should there be a complete ban on celebration of various 'days' in colleges?

Arguments:

I. No, there is nothing wrong in celebrating the days and enjoying once in a while.

II. Yes, children are giving more importance to such celebrations than the studies.

III. No, this type of celebration gives opportunity for children to express their feelings.

(a) I and II are strong (b) II and III are strong
(c) Only III is strong (d) Only II is strong
(e) None of these

Sol. (b) Argument I is ambiguous because it lacks a solid justification. Strong arguments II and III offer a suitable response to the query. Argument II clarifies the proper justification for prohibiting such days. Additionally, the kids can express their emotions on these days, thus III is also true.

Example 2:

Statement: Should the consumption of aerated drinks be banned in India?

Arguments:

I. Yes, this is the only way to reduce the risk of exposing people to some diseases.

II. No, each individual should have right to choose what he wants.

III. No, there is no confirmed evidence that such products have adverse effects on human body.

IV. Yes, it is banned in many other countries also.

(a) Only I is strong (b) I and II are strong
(c) Only III is strong (d) I and IV are strong
(e) All are strong

Sol. (c) The term "only" undermines Argument I. Argument II is weak since it lacks support, and Argument III is powerful because there is no proof that these products have harmful impacts on the human body. We should not follow mindlessly what other nations are doing. Therefore, Argument IV is weak.

STRENGTHENING AND WEAKENING ARGUMENT:

➢ The strength or weakness of an argument depends on the soundness of its premises and the logical coherence of its structure. Here are some ways to strengthen or weaken an argument:

STRENGTHENING AN ARGUMENT:

➢ **Provide additional evidence:** Introduce new facts, statistics, expert opinions, or studies that support the premises of the argument. The more evidence you present, the stronger the argument becomes.

➢ **Improve the quality of evidence:** Replace weak or unreliable sources with more credible ones. Use primary sources, peer-reviewed studies, or expert testimonies to enhance the credibility of the argument.

➢ **Enhance logical coherence:** Ensure that the reasoning flows logically from the premises to the conclusion. Strengthen the logical connections by eliminating fallacies, inconsistencies, or gaps in the argument.

WEAKENING AN ARGUMENT:

➢ **Identify logical fallacies:** Point out any errors in reasoning, such as hasty generalisations, circular reasoning or ad hominem attacks. Expose these flaws to weaken the argument's credibility.

➢ **Highlight inconsistencies:** Identify any contradictions or inconsistencies within the argument. Show how these discrepancies undermine the overall coherence and reliability of the argument.

➢ **Challenge the evidence:** Examine the quality and relevance of the supporting evidence. If the evidence is outdated, biased, or based on unreliable sources, it weakens the argument.

Example 3:

Statement: Should parents in India in future be forced to opt for only one child as against two or many at present?

Arguments:

I. Yes, this is the only way to check the ever increasing population of India.

II. No, this type of pressure tactic is not adopted by any other country in the world. **[UCO Bank (PO) 2008]**

(a) If only Argument I is strong.
(b) If only Argument II is strong.
(c) If either I or II is strong.
(d) If neither I nor II is strong.
(e) If both I and II are strong.

Sol. (d) Argument I is insufficient since it is not necessary. The rationale for population control is not covered. Argument II is weak since it is an example-based argument.

Example 4:

Statement: Should all the slums in big cities be demolished and the people living in such slums be relocated outside the city limits?

Arguments:

I. No, all these people will lose their home and livelihood and hence, they should not be relocated.

II. Yes, the big cities need more and more spaces to carry out development activities and hence, these slums should be removed.

(a) If only Argument I is strong.
(b) If only Argument II is strong.
(c) If either I or II is strong.
(d) If neither I nor II is strong.
(e) If both I and II are strong.

Sol. (e) Humanitarian considerations make Argument I persuasive.

On a financial level, Argument II is compelling.

1 Beginner Level

Directions (Qs. 1–4): In making decisions about important questions, it is desirable to be able to distinguish between 'strong' arguments and 'weak' arguments. 'Strong' arguments are those which are both important and directly related to the question. 'Weak'arguments are those which are of minor importance and also may not be directly related to the question or may be related to a trivial aspect of the question. Each question below is followed by two arguments numbered I and II. You have to decide which of the argument is a 'strong' argument and which is a 'weak' argument? Give answer

(A) If only Argument I is strong.
(B) If only Argument II is strong.
(C) If both I and II are strong.
(D) If neither I nor II is strong.

1. Statement: Are 21st century teenagers under stress?

Arguments:

I. Yes, teenager's perception is that they are expected to be successful or good at everything. Failure has somehow gone from being viewed as a learning opportunity to being clearly unacceptable.

II. No, stress is a relative perception that can be managed by proper guidance.

[RRB Group D 2018]

2. Statement: Should only reputed NGO's be authorized to distribute the commodities to the public under the program of Public Distribution System (PDS)?

Arguments:

I. Yes, the move will be helpful to implement the program more effectively and will keep a tab on various problems like black marketing of the commodities supplied under PDS.

II. Yes, NGO's have helped government on many occasions. **[MPPSC 2018]**

3. Statement: Should the private companies be allowed to operate passenger train services in India?

Arguments:

I. Yes, this will improve the quality of service in Indian Railways as it will have to face severe competition.

II. No, the private companies may not agree to operate in the non-profitable sectors

[MPPSC 2018]

4. Statement: Should a cricket team have more than one captain during a match?

Arguments:

I. No, one needs to make decisions on the spot and there won't be time to resolve conflicting ideas between the captains on the field if such a scenario emerges.

II. Yes, it is always better to have more brains coming to an understanding before taking a decision.

[UP Police Constable 2018]

Directions (Qs. 5–8): In making decisions about important questions, it is desirable to be able to distinguish between 'strong' arguments and 'weak' arguments. 'Strong arguments must be both important and directly related to the question. 'Weak' arguments may not be directly related to the question and may be of minor importance or may be related to the trivial aspects of the question. Each question below is followed by three arguments numbered I, II and III. You have to decide which of the arguments is a 'strong' argument and which is a 'weak' argument?

5. Statement: Should there be a complete ban on setting up thermal power plants in India?

Arguments:

I. Yes, this is the only way to control further addition to environmental pollution.

II. No, there is a huge shortage of electricity in most parts of the country and hence, generation of electricity needs to be augmented.

III. No, many developed countries continue to set up thermal power plants in their countries.

[UCO Bank PO 2010]

(A) None is strong **(B)** Only I is strong
(C) Only II is strong **(D)** Only III is strong
(E) Either I or II is strong

6. Statement: Should there be only few banks in place of numerous smaller banks in India?

Arguments:

I. Yes, this will help secure the investor's money as these big banks will be able to withstand intermittent market related shocks.

II. No, a large number of people will lose their jobs as after the merger many employees will be redundant.

III. Yes, this will help consolidate the entire banking industry and will lead to healthy competition.

[SBI PO 2012]

(A) None is strong
(B) Only I and II are strong.
(C) Only II and III are strong.
(D) Only I and III are strong.
(E) All are strong

7. Statement: Should there be a common syllabus for all subjects in graduate courses in all the universities across the country?

Arguments:

I. Yes, this is the only way to bring in uniformity in the education system in the country.

II. Yes, it will help to standardise the quality of graduation certificates being given by different universities in the country.

III. No, each university should have the autonomy to decide its syllabus based on the specific requirement of the university.

[RBI Grade B 2009]

(A) None is strong (B) Only I is strong
(C) Only II is strong (D) I and II are strong
(E) II and III are strong

8. **Statement:** The Captain Amarinder Singh-led government in Punjab has announced free education for girls in government schools and colleges from Nursery to PhD.

Arguments:

I. Good social welfare law. It is initially for girls as they are comparatively disadvantaged. Hopefully it will soon be followed by free education for everyone.

II. It is gender biased as if a poor or average person wants to educate his son for higher education, he has to pay higher bills. If you are introducing a law/scheme/bills under no circumstance it should not favor any particular gender, if they are really concerned about education.

III. Do not differentiate a poor or average person on gender. A poor boy or man should also get free education as well.

Which of the following argument holds strong for the given statement?

[IBPS Clerk Mains 2019]

(A) Only II (B) Only III
(C) II and III (D) I and II
(E) All of these

Direction (Q. 9): Read the following information carefully and answer the given question. **[SBI PO 2013]**

Despite repeated announcements that mobile phones are not allowed in the examination hall, three students were caught with their mobile phones.

I. Mobile phones now-a-days have a lot of features and it is easy to cheat with their help.

II. The invigilator must immediately confiscate the mobile phones and ask the students to leave the exam hall immediately.

III. Mobile phones are very expensive and leaving them in bags outside the exam hall is not safe.

IV. There have been incidents where students who left the exam hall early stole the mobile phones kept in the bags of the students who were writing the exam.

9. Which of the following among A, B, C and D may be a strong argument in favor of the three students who were caught with the mobile phone?

(A) Only I (B) Both I and II
(C) Both III and IV (D) Only III
(E) Both II and IV

10. **Statement:** Is it necessary that education should be job oriented?

Arguments:

I. Yes, the aim of education is to prepare persons for earning.

II. Yes, educated person should stand on his feet after completion of education.

III. No, education should be for sake of knowledge only.

IV. No, one may take up agriculture where education is not necessary. **[SSC CGL 2011]**

(A) I and II arguments are strong
(B) III and IV arguments are strong
(C) Only I argument is strong
(D) I and III arguments are strong

Directions (Qs. 11–14): Each of these questions, given below consists of a statement followed by two assumptions numbered as I and II. Decide which of the assumption (s) is /are implicit from the statement and then decide which of the answer is correct.

Give answer

(A) If only Assumption I is implicit.
(B) If only Assumption II is implicit.
(C) If neither Assumption I nor II is implicit.
(D) If both Assumptions I and II are implicit.

11. **Statement:** Warning - Smoking is injurious to health.

Assumptions:

I. Non-smoking promotes health.

II. Really, this warning is not necessary.

[UP Police SI 2017]

12. **Statement:** If people are intelligent they should be creative.

Assumptions:

I. Creativity and intelligence are related.

II. Creative people are intelligent. **[SSC CGL 2013]**

13. **Statement:** The human body produces Vitamin D when exposed to sunlight.

Assumptions:

I. The human body have Vitamin D even if it is not consumed via food.

II. A large portion of the global population suffers from Vitamin D deficiency. **[RRB ALP 2018]**

14. Rich people are more prone to have heart attacks.

Assumptions:

I. Most of the deaths among rich people are due to heart attacks.

II. Poor people do not have heart attacks.

[SSP 10+2 2011]

Directions (Qs. 15–18): In each of the questions below, is given a statement followed by three assumptions numbered I, II and III. An assumption is something supposed or taken for granted, you have to consider the statement and the assumptions and decide which of the assumption(s) is/are implicit in the statement.

15. **Statement:** Read the instructions before playing the game.

Assumptions:

I. A game is being played.

II. No blind person is playing the game.

III. All the players are literate. **[RRB Group D 2018]**

(A) Only I follows (B) All follow
(C) None follows (D) I and III follow

16. **Statement:** The company has decided to increase the price of all their products to tackle the precarious financial position.

Assumptions:

I. The company may be able to wipe out the entire losses incurred earlier by this decision.

II. The buyer may continue to buy its products even after the increase.

III. The company has adequate resources to continue production for few more months. **[NIFT PG 2013]**

(A) None is implicit
(B) II and III are implicit
(C) I and III are implicit
(D) Only II is implicit

17. Statement: The municipal corporation has given permission for holding fun fairs in the local football ground during the holiday season.

Assumptions:

I. The local residents may protest against the corporation's decision.

II. Many people may not participate in the fun fair.

III. Only children are allowed to take part in the fun fair. **[RRB Group D 2018]**

(A) None is implicit **(B)** All are implicit
(C) Only III is implicit **(D)** I and II are implicit

18. Statement: In a recently held all-India conference, the session on Brand Management in India surprisingly attracted a large number of participants and also received excellent media coverage in the leading newspapers.

Assumptions:

I. Nobody expected such an encouraging response to Brand Management.

II. Brands are not managed properly in India.

III. The Media is always very positive towards Brands. **[JMET 2011]**

(A) Only I **(B)** Both I and II
(C) Both I and III **(D)** I, II and III

19. Statement: The police authority cordoned off the entire locality for the entire day and stopped all vehicular movement for the visit of a top functionary of the government in view of the threat perception and advised all the residents in the area to limit their movement outside their dwellings.

Which of the following assumption(s) is/are implicit in the above statement?

I. The police personnel may not be able to control the vehicular movement in the locality and may seek help from the armed forces.

II. People living in the locality may move out of their houses for the day to avoid inconvenience.

III. The Government functionary may request the police authority to lift the ban on the movement of residents of the locality outside their dwellings. **[SBI PO 2010]**

(A) None is implicit **(B)** Only I is implicit
(C) Only II is implicit **(D)** Only III is implicit
(E) II and III are implicit

Direction (Q. 20): Study the following information carefully and answer the question.

The principal of St. Mary School organised extra classes for week students of Class X and the concerned teachers are getting paid extra amount for the classes. But the average salary of teachers more or less remains the same.

20. Which of the following can be assumed from the given statement?

I. The students of Class X of school Y will score more marks than students of St. Mary School.

II. Students of Class X are not serious about exams.

III. Extra classes arranged by the principal for students of Class X will help the students to score high marks in exams. **[IBPS Clerk Main 2018]**

(A) Both I and II **(B)** Both II and III
(C) Only II **(D)** Only III
(E) None of these

Directions (Qs. 21–25): In each of the questions below is given a statement followed by two courses of action. Course of action is a step for administrative decision to be taken for improvement, follow-up or further action in regard to the problem, policy, etc. On the basis of the information given in the statement, you have to assume everything in the statement to be true, then decide which of the given suggested courses of action is/are logically worth pursuing. Give answer

(A) If only I follows
(B) If only II follows
(C) If either I or II follows
(D) If neither I nor II follows
(E) If both I and II follow

21. Statement: The younger people do not look after their elders.

Courses of Action:

I. Legal action should be taken.

II. Old age homes should be opened. **[CGPSC Pre 2017]**

22. Statement: People see tax as a burden and thus devise ways to underpay or avoid it altogether.

Courses of Action:

I. Government should educate and inform citizens about the ways in which taxes help in development of the nation.

II. Tax rates should be increased so that the under-recovery in collection is compensated. **[SBI Clerk Mains 2016]**

23. Statement: Exporters in the capital are alleging that commercial banks are violating a Reserve Bank of India directive to operate a post shipment export credit denominated in foreign currency at international rates from January this year.

Courses of Action:

I. The officers concerned in the commercial banks are to be suspended.

II. The RBI should be asked to stop giving such directives to commercial banks. **[IBPS Clerk Mains 2017]**

24. Statement: Two persons, while on their daily walks in the jogger's park were killed by unidentified miscreants early in the morning.

Courses of Action:

I. The police authority should deploy police

constable near the jogger's park to prevent such criminal acts in future.

II. The citizens of the locality should go for early morning walks in groups to avoid such attacks.

[BOI PO 2010]

25. Statement: Almost 90% of the flights of one of the private airline company were cancelled for the fourth consecutive day as the pilots refused to join their duties in protest against sacking of two of their colleagues by the airline management..

Courses of Action:

I. The management of the airline company should be ordered by the Government to immediately reinstate the sacked pilots to end the crisis.

II. The Government should immediately take steps to end the impasse between the management and the pilots to help the helpless passengers.

[SBI PO 2009]

Level 2 Intermediate

1. Read the given information and answer the question.

Company Z and Company F launched similar high end cars last year. However, six months later it was found that the popularity of the car manufactured by Company Z sky-rocketed while the sales of the one manufactured by Company F did not pick up at all. Manager X: "The only reason our car did not succeed was the price of the car. Had our car been priced at a little lower value, the sales of our cars would also have been as good as the one manufactured by company Z".

Which of the following weakens the statement of manager X? **[NABARD Asst. Manager 2016]**

(A) Experts have suggested that there is always a segment of population which reviews the car after it has been launched and purchases it only after a certain amount of time has passed after the launch

(B) A few potential buyers had a problem with the fact that the only two air bags while the one manufactured by Company F had six

(C) In the past two years, all cars launched by Company F were of mediocre quality and needed frequent repairs and maintenance thus tarnishing the name of the company to a great extent

(D) The car launched by Company F is available in limited colours, although the owners can request for the colour of their choice

(E) A few other cars launched by Company F several years ago had been priced lower than most other cars in the market and they worked very well.

2. Statement: Should all the school teachers be debarred from giving private tuitions?

Arguments:

I. No, the needy students will be deprived of the expertise of these teachers.

II. Yes, this is an injustice to the unemployed educated people who can earn their living by giving tuitions.

III. Yes, only then the quality of teaching in schools will improve.

IV. Yes, now salary of these teachers is reasonable.

[Syndicate Bank PO 2009]

(A) I and III are strong

(B) I, II and III are strong

(C) III and IV are strong

(D) II, III and IV are strong

(E) None of these

3. Statement: Should all the indirect taxes in India be combined into a single tax on all commodities?

Arguments:

I. Yes, this will considerably simplify the tax collection mechanism and the cost of collecting tax will also reduce.

II. Yes, the manufacturers and traders will be benefited by this which in turn will boost tax collections.

III. No, no other country has adopted such system.

(A) None is strong **(B)** I and III are strong

(C) Only II is strong **(D)** II and III are strong

(E) None of these

4. Statement: Should all the students graduating in any discipline desirous of pursuing post-graduation of the subjects of their choice be allowed to enroll in the post-graduate courses?

Arguments:

I. Yes, the students are the best judge of their capabilities and there should not be restriction for joining post-graduate courses.

II. No, the students need to study relevant subjects in graduate courses to enroll in post-graduate courses and the students must fulfill such conditions.

III. No, there are not enough institutes offering post-graduate courses which can accommodate all the graduates desirous of seeking post-graduate education of their own choice.

(A) All are strong **(B)** I and II are strong

(C) II and III are strong **(D)** I and III are strong

(E) None of these.

5. Statement: Should sale of vital human organs be made legal in India?

Arguments:

I. No, it goes against our culture.

II. No, this will lead to unhealthy practices.

III. Yes, this will bring an end to the illegal trading of human organs. **[Canara Bank PO 2008]**

(A) None is strong **(B)** I and II are strong

(C) Only III is strong (D) II and III are strong
(E) All are strong

6. **Statement:** Should the conscription of citizens for defense services be made compulsory in India?

Arguments:

I. Yes, this is the only way to tackle the serious shortage of manpower in defense services.

II. No, instead the compensation package be made comparable to other job sectors to attract people to join defense services.

III. Yes, many other countries have made this compulsory. **[Andhra Bank PO 2008]**

(A) Only I is strong
(B) Only II is strong
(C) I and II are strong
(D) Either I or II is strong
(E) None of the above

7. **Statement:** Should road repair work in big cities be carried out only late at night?

Arguments:

I. No, this way the work will never get completed.

II. No, there will be unnecessary use of electricity.

III. Yes, the commuters will face a lot of problems due to repair work during the day

[Canara Bank PO 2010]

(A) None is strong (B) Only I is strong
(C) Only III is strong (D) I and III are strong
(E) I and II are strong

Direction (Q. 8): In the following question, a statement is given followed by two statements numbered as I and II. You have to read both the statements and decide which of them strengthens or weakens the statements.

[IBPS Clerk Mains 2018]

8. The company A used to outsource its recruitment process for some years but this year the company has decided to conduct the recruitment process within the organization.

I. The employees who have been working in the organization are aware of that hard work is required to work in the company.

II. The company has decided to appoint three new persons in its senior level authority for the smooth recruitment process.

(A) Both I and II strengthens
(B) I strengthen while II weakens.
(C) II strengthens while I is neutral.
(D) Statement I and Statement II is neutral.
(E) Both I and II weakens

9. **Statement:** Should there be uniforms for students in the colleges in India like they are in the schools?

Arguments

I. Yes, this will improve the ambience of the colleges as all the students will be decently dressed.

II. No, college students should not be regimented and they should be free to choose their clothes while coming to college.

[Syndicate Bank PO 2008]

Give answer

(A) If only Argument I is strong.
(B) If only Argument II is strong.
(C) If either I or II is strong.
(D) If neither I nor II is strong.
(E) If both I and II are strong.

10. **Statement:** Should there be only a uniform rate of income tax irrespective of the level of income?

Arguments:

I. Yes, this will substantially reduce the work of the officials of the income tax department.

II. No, this will reduce government tax collection to a large extent. **[SBI PO 2009]**

Give answer

(A) If only Argument I is strong.
(B) If only Argument II is strong.
(C) If either I or II is strong.
(D) If neither I nor II is strong.
(E) If both I and II are strong.

11. **Statement:** The apex body controlling universities in the country has decided to revise the syllabus of all the technical courses to make them focused towards the present needs of the industry, thereby making the technical graduates more employable than they are at present.

Which of the following assumption(s) is/are implicit in the above statement?

I. Technical college affiliated to different universities may not welcome the apex body's decision and may continue with the same syllabus at present.

II. The industry may welcome the decision of the apex body and scale up their hiring from these colleges.

III. The Government may not allow the apex body to implement its decision in all the colleges as it may lead to chaos. **[SBI PO 2010]**

(A) None is implicit (B) Only I is implicit
(C) Only II is implicit (D) Only III is implicit
(E) II and III are implicit

12. Pets are not allowed in the park premises–A notice put up at the park entrance by the authority that is responsible for maintenance of the park.

Which of the following can be an assumption according to the given information? (An assumption is something that is supposed or taken for granted).

(A) At least some people who visit the park have pets.
(B) This is the only park which does not allow pets.
(C) People who ignored this notice were fined.
(D) There are more than one entrances to the park.
(E) Many people have now stopped visiting the park

13. Installing scrubbers in smokestacks and switching to cleaner-burning fuel are the two methods available to Northern Power for reducing harmful emissions from its plants. Scrubbers will reduce harmful emissions more than cleaner-burning fuels will. Therefore, by installing stall mg scrubbers, Northern power will be doing the most that can be done to reduce harmful emissions from its plants.

Which of the following is an assumption on which the argument depends? **[IBPS PO Mains 2019]**

(A) Switching to cleaner-burning fuel will not be more expensive than installing scrubbers

(B) Northern Power can choose from among various kinds of scrubbers, some of which are more effective than others

(C) Northern Power is not necessarily committed to reducing harmful emissions from its plants

(D) Harmful emissions from Northern Power's plants cannot be reduced more by using both methods together than by the installation of scrubbers alone

(E) Aside from harmful emissions from the smoke stacks of its plants, the activities of Northern Power do not cause significant air pollution.

14. Statement: The Government has decided to auction construction of highways to private entities in several blocks across the country on build-operate-transfer basis.

Which of the following assumption(s) is/are implicit in the above statement?

I. An adequate number of private entities may not respond to the Government's auction notification.

II. Many private entities in the country are capable of constructing highways within a reasonable time.

III. The Government's proposal of build- operate transfer may financially benefit the private entities.

(A) I and II are implicit
(B) II and III are implicit
(C) Only II is implicit
(D) I and III are implicit
(E) None of the above

15. Statement: "If you have obtained 75% or more marks in X standard, your admission to our coaching class for XII standard is guaranteed", an advertisement.

Assumptions:

I. Bright students generally do not opt for attending coaching classes.

II. The coaching class has adequate capacity to accommodate all such students.

III. The advertisement will be ignored.

[Andhra Bank PO 2007]

(A) Only II is implicit **(B)** Only III is implicit
(C) None is implicit **(D)** Only I is implicit
(E) All are implicit

16. Statement: The telephone company informed the subscribers through a notification that those who don't pay their bills by the due date will be charged penalty for every defaulting day.

Assumptions:

I. Majority of the people may pay their bills by the due date to avoid penalty.

II. The money collected as penalty may settle off the losses due to the delayed payments.

III. People generally pay heed to such notices.

(A) None is implicit
(B) I and III are implicit
(C) Only II is implicit
(D) II and III are implicit

17. Statement: 'Smoking is injurious to health', A warning printed on the cigarette packets.

Assumptions:

I. People read printed matter on a cigarette packet.

II. People take careful note of a warning.

III. Non-smoking promotes health. **[MAT 2005]**

(A) Only I is implicit **(B)** I and II are implicit
(C) Only II is implicit **(D)** All are implicit

Directions (Qs. 18–20): In each question below is given a statement followed by two assumptions numbered I and II. An assumption is something supposed or taken for granted. You have to consider the statement and the following assumptions and decide which of the assumption(s) is/are implicit in the statement.

Give answer

(A) If only Assumption I is implicit
(B) If only Assumption II is implicit
(C) If either Assumption I or II is implicit
(D) If neither Assumption I nor II is implicit
(E) If both Assumptions I and II are implicit

[Andhra Bank PO 2009]

18. Statement: Many people fell ill after consuming meal at a wedding reception and were rushed to the nearby Government and private hospitals.

Assumptions:

I. The relatives of the affected people may refuse to take them to the Government hospitals.

II. The nearby hospitals may be able to attend to all the affected people.

19. Statement: The Government has recently announced an incentive package for setting up new business ventures in the rural areas and promised uninterrupted power supply to all the units.

Assumptions:

I. The Government may be able to supply adequate power to all such units.

II. People living in the rural areas may welcome the Government decision.

20. Statement: The municipal authority blocked movement of traffic in and around the temple on the main festival day.

Assumptions:

I. Very large number of devotees may visit the temple on the main festival day.

II. People travelling to the areas near the temple may postpone their journey by a day unless they have very urgent work in that area.

Directions (Qs. 21–25): Each question contains one statement and two Courses of Action I and II. Assuming the statements to be true, decide which of the two courses of action most logically follows.

Give answer

(A) If only I follow
(B) If only II follows

(C) If either I or II follows

(D) If neither I nor II follows

21. **Statement:** Due to heavy rain in Bangalore, the normal lives of the citizens are paralysed.

Courses of Action:

I. Government should take measures to help people and avoid life and property destruction.

II. Government should provide free treatment in all the hospitals of Bangalore. **[RRB ALP 2018]**

22. **Statement:** Majority of the students have failed in one paper in the first semester examination.

Courses of Action:

I. All those students who failed should be asked to drop out of the course.

II. The faculty teaching the paper should be asked to resign. **[CMAT 2013]**

23. **Statement:** The manufacturing companies in Tamil Nadu are facing acute power shortage.

Courses of Action:

I. Government should take steps to solve the power crisis.

II. Government should shut down manufacturing companies to save power. **[RRB ALP 2018]**

24. **Statement:** A man wants to get admission in a certain unique elite club.

Courses of Action:

I. Find and complete the procedure to get entry into the club.

II. Get admission into another club. **[UPSSSC Mandi Perished 2018]**

25. **Statement:** The pollution and air quality in Delhi is beyond the acceptable level. This is due to industrial and automobile exhaustion.

Courses of Action:

I. Automobiles should be divided into groups to be run only on odd and even days, respectively.

II. The government should stop the registration of new factories and vehicles.

3 Level Expert

Read the following information carefully and answer the given question.

Despite repeated announcements that mobile phones were not allowed in the examination hall, three students were caught with their mobile phones. **[SBI PO 2013]**

(a) Mobile phones now-a-days have a lot of features and it is easy to cheat with their help.

(b) The invigilator must immediately confiscate the mobile phones and ask the students to leave the exam hall immediately.

(c) Mobile phones are very expensive and leaving them in bags outside the exam hall is not safe.

(d) There have been incidents where students who left the exam hall early stole the mobile phones kept in the bags of the students who were writing the exam.

(e) The school authorities must ask the students to leave their phones in the custody of the invigilator before the exam in order to avoid thefts of mobile phones.

(f) None of the other students were carrying their phones in the exam hall.

1. Which of the following among A, B, C, D, E and F can be immediate course of action for the invigilator?

(A) Only (b) (B) Both (a) and (d)

(C) only (a) (D) Both (d) and (e)

(E) Only (e)

2. **Read the following information carefully and answer the question which follows.** **[SBI Associate (PO) 2015]**

Most students from State X prefer to move base to other States for higher education. The government of the State is concerned about this problem as these students might not come back even after completing their education.

Which of the following statements may be a course of action to deal with this problem?

(A) The Government should set-up well equipped State of the Art universities which will provide quality education

(B) The Government should not give much importance to this problem as there is high density of population per square km in the State

(C) Scholarships should be declared for those students who perform well in tenth and twelfth standard examinations

(D) All the colleges and universities should be asked to emphasis e the importance of higher education and benefits of studying in their institute should also be highlighted

(E) The Government should make education free for all people of the State

3. **Statement:** The prices of vegetables and other food articles have decreased in the recent months raising hope among policy planners that the RBI's (Reserve Bank of India) tight grip on supply of liquid money in the market for controlling inflation may be eased.

Which of the following may be a possible action of the above situation? **[IBPS SO 2012]**

(A) The Reserve Bank of India may not reduce its key interest rates in near future.

(B) The government may step in and make certain concessions to the common people on various issues.

(C) The Reserve Bank of India may consider lowering certain rates to bring in more liquidity in the market.

(D) The RBI may wait for at least another year before taking any step.

(E) The RBI may collect more data from the market and wait for another four months to ensure that they take the correct step.

4. Statement: A severe cyclonic storm hit the Eastern coastline last month resulting in huge loss of life and property on the entire East coast and the government had to disburse a considerable amount to relief activities through the district administration machineries. **[IBPS SO 2012]**

Which of the following may possibly be a follow upmeasure to be taken up by the government?

(A) The government may setup a task force to review the post relief scenario in all districts and also to confirm proper and user receipt of the relief supplies.

(B) The government may setup a committee for proper disbursement of relief supplies in future.

(C) The government may empower the District Magistrates to make all future disbursements of relief.

(D) The government may send relief supplies to the affected people in future only after proper assessment of the damage caused by such calamities.

(E) The government may not need to activate any follow up measure.

5. Statement: Many people in the locality have fallen sick and admitted in the local hospital after consuming sweets served during a community meal. **[SBI PO 2010]**

Courses of Action:

I. The police should immediately arrest all the people responsible for making the sweets.

II. The people admitted in the local hospital should immediately be shifted to bigger hospitals.

III. The local food and drug authority should investigate to find out the cause of the sickness and take necessary action.

(A) Both I and III follow
(B) Both II and III follow
(C) Only III follows
(D) All of them follows
(E) None follows

6. Choose an option that is a valid assumption for the below statement.

[UPSSSC Combined Lower Subordinate 2019]

Statement: The ministry of railways introduces additional holiday special trains and also adds extra coaches to existing trains during vacations.

(A) During vacations, kids love to travel by trains instead of aero planes.

(B) Passenger traffic in trains significantly increases during vacations.

(C) People need change and like to see new trains during vacations.

(D) Engine drivers like to work for more hours during vacations.

7. Statement: The airlines have requested all their bonafide passengers to check the status of flight operations before leaving their homes as heavy fog is causing immense problems to normal flight operations.

Which of the following assumption(s) is/are implicit in the above statement?

I. Majority of the air passengers may check the flights status before starting their journey to the airport.

II. The Government may take serious objection to the notice issued by the airline company.

III. Majority of the passengers may cancel their tickets and postpone their journey till the situation become normal.

(A) None is implicit
(B) Only I is implicit
(C) Only II is implicit
(D) Only III is implicit
(E) I and III are implicit

8. Statement: The school authority decided to open a summer school this year in the school compound for the students in the age group of 7–14 yr.

Assumptions:

I. All the students will attend the summer school.

II. All the parents will prefer to remain in city than going out of town for enabling their children to attend the summer school.

III. Those who cannot afford to go out of the station, will send their children to summer school.

(A) Only II is implicit
(B) II and III are implicit
(C) None is implicit
(D) All are implicit
(E) Only III is implicit

9. Statement: The residents of the locality wrote a letter to the corporation requesting to restore normalcy in the supply of drinking water immediately as the supply at present is just not adequate.

Assumptions:

I. The corporation may not take any action on the letter.

II. The municipality has enough water to meet the demand.

III. The water supply to the area was adequate in the past.

(A) I and II are implicit
(B) II and III are implicit
(C) Only II is implicit
(D) Only III is implicit
(E) None of the above

10. Statement: Training must be given to all the employees for increasing productivity and profitability.

Assumptions:

I. Training is an essential component of productivity.

II. Employees cannot function effectively without proper training.

III. Profitability and productivity are supplementary to each other.

(A) None is implicit
(B) All are implicit
(C) Only III is implicit

(D) and II are implicit

(E) I and III are implicit

11. Read the following statements carefully and answer the given questions.

Cocoas and chocolate products have been used as medicine in many cultures for centuries. Chocolate is made from plants which means it contains many of the health benefits of leafy vegetables.

Which of the following statements weakens the above arguments? **[IBPS PO 2014]**

I. Dark chocolate contains a large number of antioxidants which slow downs the aging process.

II. A small study revealed that regular intake of chocolate increase insulin sensitivity thus, lowering the chances of diabetes.

III. Green leafy vegetables have flavonoids which protect skin from UV rays.

IV. Chocolates have 3 types of fats one out of which increase the cholesterol level.

V. Cocoas increases blood flow to the retina thus giving a boost to vision.

(A) Only IV

(B) A and V

(C) Only III

(D) None of the given statements

(E) Both III and IV

12. Statement: Should 'literacy' be the minimum criterion for becoming a voter in India?

Arguments:

I. No, mere literacy is no guarantee of political maturity of an individual.

II. Yes, illiterate people are less likely to make politically wiser decisions of voting for a right candidate or party.

III. No, voting is the constitutional right of every citizen.

(A) None is strong

(B) I and II are strong

(C) III is strong

(D) II and III are strong

(E) All are strong

13. Statement: Should all those students who failed in one or two subjects in HSC be allowed to take admission in degree courses and continue their study, subject to their successfully passing in the supplementary examination?

Arguments:

I. Yes, this will help the students to complete their education without a break of one year.

II. Yes, this is a forward looking strategy to help the students and motivate them for higher studies.

III. No, such students do not choose to continue their studies without having passed in all the subjects in HSC.

(A) Only I is strong

(B) Only II is strong

(C) Only III is strong

(D) Either II or III and I are strong

(E) None of the above

14. Statement: Should the Government impose restrictions on access to sensitive information to the journalists to avoid the media hype?

Arguments:

I. Yes, the media creates hype and publishes distorted information at times.

II. No, journalists should have an access to all the information as media is the best source to expose the malfunctions in the society.

III. Yes, at times it leads to harassment of those who are affected and alleged to be involved in the crisis.

(A) All I, II and III are strong

(B) I and II are strong

(C) II and III are strong

(D) Only II is strong

(E) None is strong

15. Statement: Should there be a complete ban on genetically modified imported seeds?

Arguments:

I. Yes, this will boost the demand of domestically developed seeds.

II. No, this is the only way to increase production substantially.

III. Yes, genetically modified products will adversely affect the health of those who consume these products.

(A) I and II are strong

(B) Only II is strong

(C) II and III are strong

(D) I and III are strong

(E) All are strong

ANSWER KEY

Level-1: Beginner

1.	(C)	2.	(A)	3.	(A)	4.	(A)	5.	(C)	6.	(A)	7.	(E)	8.	(C)	9.	(C)	10.	(D)
11.	(A)	12.	(A)	13.	(A)	14.	(C)	15.	(B)	16.	(C)	17.	(A)	18.	(A)	19.	(A)	20.	(D)
21.	(A)	22.	(A)	23.	(D)	24.	(E)	25.	(B)										

Level-2: Intermediate

1.	(B)	2.	(E)	3.	(E)	4.	(E)	5.	(A)	6.	(E)	7.	(C)	8.	(C)	9.	(B)	10.	(B)
11.	(C)	12.	(A)	13.	(D)	14.	(B)	15.	(A)	16.	(B)	17.	(C)	18.	(B)	19.	(E)	20.	(E)
21.	(A)	22.	(D)	23.	(A)	24.	(A)	25.	(D)										

Level-3: Expert

1.	(A)	2.	(D)	3.	(C)	4.	(B)	5.	(C)	6.	(B)	7.	(B)	8.	(C)	9.	(C)	10.	(D)
11.	(A)	12.	(E)	13.	(D)	14.	(A)	15.	(D)										

Solutions with Detailed Explanations

Level-1: BEGINNER

1. **Option (C) is correct.**
Explanation: Argument I is strong because it reflects the societal pressure on teenagers to excel in all areas, which can lead to significant stress. Argument II is also strong as it suggests that stress is subjective and manageable with appropriate guidance, acknowledging the role of support systems in mitigating stress.

2. **Option (A) is correct.**
Explanation: Argument I is strong because it addresses the effectiveness and oversight that reputed NGOs can bring to the PDS, potentially reducing issues like black marketing. Argument II, while recognizing the contributions of NGOs, does not directly relate to their role in PDS, making it a weaker argument in this context.

3. **Option (A) is correct.**
Explanation: Argument I is strong as it points out the potential benefits of competition in improving service quality within the railways. Argument II is weak because it assumes private companies' unwillingness to operate in non-profitable sectors without considering possible incentives or regulatory frameworks that could be established.

4. **Option (A) is correct.**
Explanation: Argument I is strong because one needs to take quick decision, and with only one captain the issue and conflict can be resolved in no time. Argument II is weak as it overestimates the benefits of collective decision-making without addressing the potential for conflict and delay in critical situations during a match.

5. **Option (C) is correct.**
Explanation: Argument I is weak because it oversimplifies the solution to environmental pollution. Argument II is strong as it addresses the practical need for electricity and the consequences of a complete ban. Argument III is weak because the practices of other countries do not necessarily justify actions within India.

6. **Option (A) is correct.**
Explanation: With few banks in place of many banks, the security of the investor will be at risk. Even the consolidation of banking industry is not attainable through this approach. So, all arguments are weak.

7. **Option (E) is correct.**
Explanation: Argument I is weak because uniformity is not the sole method to improve education. Argument II is strong as it points to the benefit of standardizing educational quality. Argument III is strong because it respects the autonomy of universities to cater to specific educational needs.

8. **Option (C) is correct.**
Explanation: **I. "All the students will attend..."** — Too strong. The decision to open a summer school doesn't require all eligible students to attend.
II. "All the parents will prefer to remain in the city..." — Unrealistic universal. The school's decision doesn't rest on every parent staying back.
III. "Those who cannot afford to go out... will send their children..." — Again too definite. The school's decision doesn't assume that every such family will enroll.

9. **Option (C) is correct.**
Explanation: **I. "The corporation may not take any action on the letter."**
Not required. Writing a letter presumes the authority can act and is being asked to do so; it doesn't rely on the belief that they may not act. This is a mere possibility, not a necessary assumption.
→ Not implicit.
II. "The municipality has enough water to meet the demand."
For residents to sensibly request restoration of normal (adequate) supply now, they must assume the authority has (or can arrange) sufficient water/resources to meet normal demand. Otherwise, the request would be pointless.
→ Implicit.
III. "The water supply to the area was adequate in the past."
"Restore normalcy" can refer to returning to the standard/official norm (e.g., the usual citywide schedule/level), not necessarily this locality's own past level. Even if their area had never received adequate supply before, asking for "normal" civic supply still makes sense. Thus, the action doesn't require the belief that it was adequate earlier.
→ Not implicit.

Assumption II is not implied because it is nowhere implied that creative people should be intelligent. It is stated otherwise.

13. Option (A) is correct.

Explanation: Assumption I is implicit because the statement indicates that the body can produce Vitamin D without dietary intake. Assumption II is not mentioned in the statement and thus is not implicit.

14. Option (C) is correct.

Explanation: Neither assumption is implicit. The statement does not provide enough information to conclude that most deaths among rich people are due to heart attacks (I), nor does it imply that poor people are immune to heart attacks (II).

15. Option (D) is correct.

Explanation: Assumption I is implicit because the instruction to read before playing implies a game will be played. Assumption III is implicit as reading instructions assumes literacy. Assumption II is not necessarily implicit; the statement does not indicate whether visually impaired individuals are playing or not.

16. Option (C) is correct.

Explanation: Since the company has taken the decision to make up for the financial deficit, so, with the increase in the price of all its products, the company may be able to wipe out the entire losses So, I is implicit. The response of the buyers to the increased prices cannot be deduced from the statement. So, II is not implicit. Assumption III is implicit as the company plans to tackle financial issues, implying it has resources to continue production. Assumption I is not implicit as the statement does not guarantee the recovery of all losses.

17. Option (A) is correct.

Explanation: None of the assumptions are implicit. The statement does not suggest local residents will protest (I), that many people will not participate (II), or that only children are allowed (III).

18. Option (A) is correct.

Explanation: Assumption I is implicit because the response was unexpected, indicating that no one anticipated such a positive reaction. Assumptions II and III are not implicit as the statement does not comment on the current state of brand management in India or the media's consistent attitude towards brands.

19. Option (A) is correct.

Explanation: None of the assumptions are implicit. The statement does not suggest the police may seek help from armed forces (I), that residents will move out to avoid inconvenience (II), or that the government functionary will request lifting the ban (III).

20. Option (D) is correct.

Explanation: The statement suggests that the principal's initiative for extra classes is aimed at improving the performance of weak students. Therefore, it can be assumed that these classes are intended to help students score higher marks in exams, making Statement III an assumption that can be drawn from the given information.

21. Option (A) is correct.

Explanation: If younger people are not looking after their elders, taking legal action could be a way to enforce responsibility. Opening old age homes may provide care for the elderly but does not address the issue of neglect by younger family members.

22. Option (A) is correct.

Explanation: Educating citizens about the benefits of tax contributions to national development is a proactive approach in changing the perception of taxes. Increasing tax rates could exacerbate the problem of avoidance and is not a solution to the underlying issue of perception.

23. Option (D) is correct.

Explanation: Neither course of action addresses the root cause of the issue. Suspending officers does not resolve the alleged violation, and asking the RBI to stop issuing directives is not a practical solution. A better course of action would be to investigate the allegations and ensure compliance with directives.

24. Option (E) is correct.

Explanation: Both courses of action are practical steps to enhance safety. Deploying police near the jogger's park can deter criminal activity, and citizens walking in groups can reduce the risk of attacks.

25. Option (B) is correct.

Explanation: The government intervening to reinstate the sacked pilots may not address the underlying issues and could set a precedent for future conflicts. Taking steps to mediate and resolve the impasse is a more balanced approach that considers the interests of both the management and the pilots, as well as the passengers affected by the cancellations.

Level-2: INTERMEDIATE

1. Option (C) is correct.

Explanation: The statement by Manager X is weakened by the fact that Company F's cars had a history of mediocre quality requiring frequent repairs (Option C), which could have significantly affected consumer trust and sales, regardless of the price.

2. Option (E) is correct.

Explanation: None of the arguments are compelling enough to justify a complete ban on private tuitions by school teachers. The need for additional support for students (Argument I) and the potential improvement in school teaching quality (Argument III) do not necessarily correlate with a ban on tuitions.

3. Option (E) is correct.

Explanation: Arguments I and II are strong as they highlight the benefits of a simplified tax system for both the government and the business community. Argument III is not a strong counterargument as the adoption of a system by other countries does not determine its efficacy.

4. Option (E) is correct.

Explanation: None of the arguments are strong enough to justify allowing all students to enroll in any post-graduate courses without restrictions. The need for relevant undergraduate education (Argument II) and the limited capacity of post-graduate institutions (Argument III) are significant considerations.

5. **Option (A) is correct.**
Explanation: None of the arguments strongly justify the legalization of the sale of vital human organs. Cultural considerations (Argument I) and the potential for unhealthy practices (Argument II) are not sufficiently compelling, and the assumption that legalization would end illegal trading (Argument III) is not substantiated.

6. **Option (E) is correct.**
Explanation: None of the arguments are strong enough to justify compulsory conscription. The assertion that it is the only way to address manpower shortages (Argument I) is not substantiated, and the suggestion to increase compensation (Argument II) does not address the broader implications of conscription.

7. **Option (C) is correct.**
Explanation: Argument III is strong as it considers the practical difficulties commuters face due to daytime road repairs. Arguments I and II are not strong as they do not adequately address the complexities of road repair scheduling and the use of electricity.

8. **Option (C) is correct.**
Explanation: Statement I is neutral because it does not directly impact the decision to conduct recruitment internally. Statement II strengthens the decision as appointing new senior personnel indicates a commitment to managing the recruitment process effectively.

9. **Option (B) is correct.**
Explanation: After following a formal dress code of the school for so many years, the students must be granted some liberty in college life. Moreover, schools adopt uniforms to take care of the security of the child an aspect which doesn't matter much in the colleges. So, argument II holds strong. Also, the environment of the college depends on the students dedication and etiquettes and not on their uniforms. So, argument I is vague.

10. **Option (B) is correct.**
Explanation: Argument II is strong because a uniform tax rate could lead to a significant reduction in government revenue, especially from higher earners. Argument I is weak because simplifying tax officials' work is not a strong enough reason to justify a uniform tax rate.

11. **Option (C) is correct.**
Explanation: Assumption II is implicit because the revision of the syllabus aims to make graduates more employable, which suggests industry acceptance. Assumptions I and III are not implicit as they suggest resistance to change, which is not indicated in the statement.

12. **Option (A) is correct.**
Explanation: The assumption that some park visitors have pets is implicit because the notice would be unnecessary otherwise. The other options are not supported by the information provided.

13. **Option (D) is correct.**
Explanation: The argument depends on the assumption that using both methods together would not reduce emissions more than scrubbers alone, which is not necessarily true.

14. **Option (B) is correct.**
Explanation: Assumptions II and III are implicit because the government's decision to auction highway construction suggests confidence in private entities' capabilities and the financial attractiveness of the proposal.

15. **Option (A) is correct.**
Explanation: Assumption II is implicit because the advertisement guarantees admission, suggesting the coaching class can accommodate all qualifying students. Assumptions I and III are not implicit as they contradict the purpose of the advertisement.

16. **Option (B) is correct.**
Explanation: Assumptions I and III are implicit because the notification's intent is to encourage timely payment and it assumes people will heed the notice. Assumption II is not necessarily implicit as it does not directly relate to the intent of the notification.

17. **Option (B) is correct.**
Explanation: Assumption I is implicit because the warning is printed with the expectation that it will be read. Assumption II is implicit because warnings are meant to be heeded.

18. **Option (B) is correct.**
Explanation: Assumption II is implicit because the statement implies that the hospitals are expected to be able to attend to all the affected people. Assumption I is not implicit as there is no indication that relatives would refuse government hospitals.

19. **Option (E) is correct.**
Explanation: Both assumptions are implicit. Assumption I is implicit because the government promises uninterrupted power, suggesting it can deliver. Assumption II is implicit because the incentive package is likely to be welcomed in rural areas.

20. **Option (E) is correct.**
Explanation: Both assumptions are implicit. Assumption I is implicit because blocking traffic suggests a large number of devotees are expected. Assumption II is implicit because it is reasonable to assume people will adjust their plans due to the traffic block.

21. **Option (A) is correct.**
Explanation: Course of Action I follows because it directly addresses the issue of life and property protection during heavy rains. Course of Action II, while beneficial, is not a direct response to the issue of paralyzed city life.

22. **Option (D) is correct.**
Explanation: Neither course of action logically follows. Dropping out students or asking faculty to resign does not address the root cause of the failure and is not a constructive approach.

23. **Option (A) is correct.**
Explanation: Course of Action I follows because it addresses the issue of power shortage. Course of Action II does not follow as shutting down manufacturing companies is not a sustainable solution.

to assume people will adjust their plans due to the traffic block.

21. **Option (A) is correct.**
Explanation: Course of Action I follows because it directly addresses the issue of life and property protection during heavy rains. Course of Action II, while beneficial, is not a direct response to the issue of paralyzed city life.

22. **Option (D) is correct.**
Explanation: Neither course of action logically follows. Dropping out students or asking faculty to resign does not address the root cause of the failure and is not a constructive approach.

23. **Option (A) is correct.**
Explanation: Course of Action I follows because it addresses the issue of power shortage. Course of Action II does not follow as shutting down manufacturing companies is not a sustainable solution.

24. **Option (A) is correct.**
Explanation: Course of Action I follows because it is a logical step for someone wanting to join a club. Course of Action II does not follow as it does not address the desire to join the specific elite club.

25. **Option (D) is correct.**
Explanation: Neither course of action follows as a long-term solution. They are temporary measures and do not address the root causes of pollution in Delhi.

Level-3: EXPERT

1. **Option (A) is correct.**
Explanation: The immediate course of action for the invigilator should be to confiscate the mobile phones and ask the students to leave the exam hall immediately, as per the rules stated in option (b).

2. **Option (D) is correct.**
Explanation: To address the issue of students moving to other states for higher education, all colleges and universities should emphasize on the importance of higher and highlight the benefits of studying in their institute.

3. **Option (C) is correct.**
Explanation: Given the decrease in food article prices, the RBI may consider lowering certain rates to increase market liquidity, as indicated in option (C), to stimulate economic activity.

4. **Option (B) is correct.**
Explanation: Following the cyclonic storm, the government may setup a committee for proper disbursement of relief supplies in future.

5. **Option (C) is correct.**
Explanation: The most logical course of action for the local food and drug authority is to investigate the cause of the sickness and take necessary action, as stated in option (III), to prevent further incidents.

6. **Option (B) is correct.**
Explanation: The valid assumption for the introduction of additional holiday special trains and extra coaches is that passenger traffic significantly increases during vacations, as stated in option (B).

7. **Option (B) is correct.**
Explanation: The implicit assumption in the airline's request is that the majority of air passengers may check the flight status before starting their journey to the airport, as indicated in option (I). This is a reasonable expectation given the circumstances described.

8. **Option (C) is correct.**
Explanation: None of the assumptions are necessarily implicit. Assumption I is too absolute, and Assumption II does not consider various factors that influence parents' decisions. Assumption III is also not necessarily true as it assumes financial constraints as the only reason parents would send their children to summer school.

9. **Option (D) is correct.**
Explanation: Only Assumption III is implicit because the request for restoration implies that the supply was adequate in the past. Assumption I is not necessarily implicit as it assumes inaction without basis, and Assumption II is not supported by the statement.

10. **Option (D) is correct.**
Explanation: Assumptions I and II are implicit as they are foundational to the statement's claim that training increases productivity and profitability. Assumption III, while related, is not directly supported by the statement.

11. **Option (A) is correct.**
Explanation: Only Statement IV weakens the argument as it points out a negative health impact of chocolate, which contradicts the claim of health benefits.

12. **Option (E) is correct.**
Explanation: Arguments I is strong as any literate person does not guarantee to have a sound background of politics. An Illiterate person can easily be misled on various factors but voting is also a constitutional right of every citizen. So, Arguments II and III are also strong.

13. **Option (D) is correct.**
Explanation: Arguments I and either II or III are strong. Allowing students to continue their education without a break (I) is a valid point, and either a forward-looking strategy (II) or the tendency of students to not continue studies without passing all subjects (III) could be true, but not both simultaneously.

14. **Option (A) is correct.**
Explanation: All arguments I, II, and III are strong as they present valid concerns about media hype, the role of journalists, and the potential harassment caused by sensitive information leaks.

15. **Option (D) is correct.**
Explanation: Arguments I and III are strong as they address the potential benefits of banning genetically modified seeds for domestic seed demand and health concerns, respectively. Argument II is weaker as it assumes that genetically modified seeds are the only way to increase production substantially.

■ ■ ■